I0603805

Disputing the Deluge

Disputing the Deluge

Collected 21st-Century Writings on Utopia, Narration, and Survival

Darko Suvin

Edited by
Hugh C. O'Connell

BLOOMSBURY ACADEMIC
NEW YORK • LONDON • OXFORD • NEW DELHI • SYDNEY

BLOOMSBURY ACADEMIC
Bloomsbury Publishing Inc
1385 Broadway, New York, NY 10018, USA
50 Bedford Square, London, WC1B 3DP, UK
29 Earlsfort Terrace, Dublin 2, Ireland

BLOOMSBURY, BLOOMSBURY ACADEMIC and the Diana logo are trademarks of Bloomsbury Publishing Plc

First published in the United States of America 2022

Copyright © Darko Suvin, 2022

Editor's Preface © Hugh C. O'Connell, 2022

For legal purposes the Acknowledgments on p. vii constitute an extension of this copyright page.

Cover design by Eleanor Rose
Cover image: Utagawa Hiroshige, "Sudden Shower over Ōhashi Bridge and Atake," 1857, Japanese ukiyo-e woodblock print. Photograph © Alan King / Alamy Stock Photo

All rights reserved. No part of this publication may be reproduced or transmitted in any form or by any means, electronic or mechanical, including photocopying, recording, or any information storage or retrieval system, without prior permission in writing from the publishers.

Bloomsbury Publishing Inc does not have any control over, or responsibility for, any third-party websites referred to or in this book. All internet addresses given in this book were correct at the time of going to press. The author and publisher regret any inconvenience caused if addresses have changed or sites have ceased to exist, but can accept no responsibility for any such changes.

Library of Congress Cataloging-in-Publication Data
Names: Suvin, Darko, 1930- author. | O'Connell, Hugh C., editor.
Title: Disputing the deluge : collected 21st-century writings on utopia, narration, and survival / Darko Suvin; edited by Hugh C. O'Connell.
Description: New York: Bloomsbury Academic, 2022. | Includes bibliographical references and index.
Identifiers: LCCN 2021022802 (print) | LCCN 2021022803 (ebook) | ISBN 9781501384776 (paperback) | ISBN 9781501384813 (hardback) | ISBN 9781501384783 (epub) | ISBN 9781501384790 (pdf) | ISBN 9781501384806
Subjects: LCSH: Science fiction–History and criticism. | Utopias in literature. | Literary form. | LCGFT: Essays.
Classification: LCC PN3433.5 .S94 2022 (print) | LCC PN3433.5 (ebook) | DDC 809.3/8762–dc23
LC record available at https://lccn.loc.gov/2021022802
LC ebook record available at https://lccn.loc.gov/2021022803

ISBN: HB: 978-1-5013-8481-3
PB: 978-1-5013-8477-6
ePDF: 978-1-5013-8479-0
eBook: 978-1-5013-8478-3

Typeset by Deanta Global Publishing Services, Chennai, India

To find out more about our authors and books visit www.bloomsbury.com and sign up for our newsletters.

This book is dedicated to my friendly guides, in more hopeful times; all of us, both human collectives and single people, were imperfect, but the former could turn into their own contraries more easily:

> *–to Yugoslavia: my parents, Truda & Miro; my teachers, thanked elsewhere; Savez Komunističke Omladine Jugoslavije, Komunistička Partija Jugoslavije, Marijan Matković, Dejan Đurković, Miša Stambolić*
> *–to England: Alice and Otto Glas, Valery Owen, Patrick Parrinder, John and Judy Clute*
> *–to the US: Marcelline Krafchick, Jules and Anne Chametzky, Sally Cornell, Fred Pohl, Jim Blish, Lee Baxandall, Mike Holquist, Fred Jameson, Dick Ohmann*

and to Walter Benjamin, the best politico-economical critic of his times and the deep currents reaching into ours

Afístamai: I part company with, I dissent from

Pindar, *Olympica 1* (ca. 475 BC)

I met a traveller from an antique land,
Who said – "Two vast and trunkless legs of stone
Stand in the desert [. . .].
And on the pedestal, these words appear:
My name is Ozymandias, King of Kings;
Look on my Works, ye Mighty, and despair!
Nothing beside remains. Round the decay
Of that colossal Wreck, boundless and bare
The lone and level sands stretch far away.

Percy B. Shelley, *Ozymandias* (1818)

Don't agonize – organize!

Ursula K. Le Guin, "The Death of the Book" (2012)

I am a playwright. I show
What I have seen. On the markets
I have seen how human beings are traded.
[. . .]
I see snowstorms come to pass.
I see earthquakes come to the fore
I see mountains barring the way
And rivers I see overspilling their banks
But the snowstorms *wear top hats*
The *earthquakes* have money in their pockets
The mountains step out of limousines
And the tearing rivers command police.

Bertolt Brecht, *Song of the Playwright* (1935, transl. DS)

There is no alternative to utopia.

Fredric Jameson, *Archaeologies of the Future* (2005)

Contents

Acknowledgments

Darko Suvin wishes to thank all the periodical editors where many of these chapters appeared in various versions, too numerous to list. The original publication information can be found in the Appendix. Other help is acknowledged in various chapters.

Every effort was made to locate the copyright for the illustration accompanying "Utopia or Bust." We failed to find the author and hereby solicit information, and the the copyright holder will be pleased, if notified, to make the necessary arrangement at the first opportunity.

Editor's Preface

There Is No Alternative: Non-Reading Suvin, Anti-Antiutopianism, Science Fiction, and Communism

"There Is No Alternative!" These are the final resounding words of this collection by Darko Suvin. For many readers, this phrase and its shortened acronym TINA are most readily identifiable with the architect of British neoliberalism, Margaret Thatcher, and her dictate that the free-market economy is the only way forward. Yet Suvin seeks an older sense, one more aligned with the spirit of Lenin whose analysis of the intrinsic deprivations of capitalism made communism necessary for a human society free of the tyrannies of exchange, exploitation, and imperialism. If there is a red thread that stitches together the various essays, interviews, remembrances, and poems collected between these covers, it is that, if we are to go on, then there is no alternative to communism/utopia. Indeed, Suvin's emphatic phrasing presents this as a prospect *and* warning now made even more dire among the rising waters of antiutopia that threaten to submerge this call before it can be answered.

Disputing the Deluge represents the culmination of Suvin's decades-long career as a preeminent SF and utopian scholar. As Gerry Canavan writes in the introduction to the expanded edition of *MOSF*, as the founder of a discourse, Suvin is practically synonymous with the development and growth of the academic disciplines of SF and utopian studies. Yet, as much as scholars turn to Suvin in order to align or disalign their work with the existing traditions of these fields, this orienting is not always as accurate as one might hope. Consequently, Suvin's name is frequently invoked in a ready-made fashion, filtered down through many layers of commentary and hardened into an increasingly narrow set of claims. However, as this volume of his latest work attests, such critical pigeonholing can produce a warped reflection. The sketch of the Suvinian position given in many contemporary SF articles and monographs habitually relies on a series of positions developed in the 1960s and codified in the late 1970s, often failing to capture the nuance of these positions or to engage with their development in subsequent decades. As readers, then, we are often provided an incomplete and occasionally deeply misleading picture.

This volume seeks to disabuse the reader of this received Suvin and reacquaint them with the living Suvin. The texts gathered here extend Suvin's earlier positions, refine them, and stake new critical ground to grapple with the twenty-first-century transition from anti-utopianism as a burgeoning tendency to antiutopianism as the hegemonic ideology of contemporary reality. In so doing, they reveal how Suvin's much-discussed foundational formal concepts of cognitive estrangement and the novum take center stage as properly heuristic tools for the task of engaging with the structural limits of neoliberal globalization, environmental degradation, increased immiseration, and the escalating surveillance state.

Consequently, while these works cover a vast range of styles and topics, they all converge on a common set of concerns: the antiutopian conditions of our global capitalist present and the seeming foreclosure of political possibility under such hegemony. They intersect with the pressing concern for new knowledge about our present that Suvin investigates under the banner of "political epistemology." As such, they probe the circuits of resistance and seek new pathways through the present impasse. As late works grappling with the exigencies of late-stage capitalism, they provoke the necessity of fresh critical engagements with Suvin's work that Philip E. Wegner develops under the term "non-readings." In this spirit, I offer my own reflections as a set of non-readings spurred by my engagement with Suvin and this important volume.

TINA I: Non-Reading (with) Suvin

Writing an introductory preface to another author's work produces a strange critical genre. One finds oneself staking many claims, but whose claims? Sometimes they are the claims of the principal author (which are not necessarily shared by the introducer). Other times it is the introducer's own standpoint (which might not be shared by the principal author). Still others are an indecipherable blend of the two (risking chimeras as well as synthesis). Throughout this preface, I find myself "speaking" in all the above possible permutations, and both slippages and fissures abound. In other words, this is to invite what Wegner describes as the sine qua non of all criticism worthy of its name: non-reading.

Drawing on Pierre Bayard's work, Wegner develops a utopian model of critical textual engagement as the ongoing practice and dialog that constitutes non-reading:

> Non-reading stresses the deep, active creativity involved in all reading of, as well as all talking and writing about, books. This notion thus shifts our attention away from the impossible goal of giving an accurate account of the singular truth of a book – that is, the fantasy of an objective, disinterested reading – and toward a heightened awareness of the specific and local aims and interests we always have in mind consciously or not. (*Invoking* 75)

Rather than providing the positivist description – a quantitative gesture that risks little in its effort to balance the account – critical readings take the form of interpretation. They therefore arise from within fields of interest that necessarily entail presuppositions and standpoints, and as such, they risk the opening of difference in the name of qualitative transformation. All non-readings are thus deeply situated and historical:

> This is by no means to suggest that all non-readings are equal: people make their own readings, but they do not make them in circumstances of their own choosing. This recognition shifts the criteria for evaluating any particular non-reading from its truthfulness in re-presenting the book in question to the success, or limitations, encountered in enacting the specific aims of its reading in its particular situation. (*Invoking* 75)

In this way, every non-reading is a dialog *with*, is ongoing as opposed to static or finished, and produces an opening outward rather than a closing inward (84–5). Rather than the series of "not readings" that reduce Suvin to a reified set of received closed positions – ahistorical formalist, scourge of fantasy, uncritical apologist for rationality and techno-science – non-readings require us to reengage with Suvin through deep listening.

In an interview with Zorica Đergović-Joksimović, Suvin openly invites such non-readings:

ZĐJ: You are a cult figure among Serbian researchers and fans of SF. Do you have something to say to them?

DS: First, I hope you're wrong because I don't like cults of anything and anybody. Reverence for teachers is another and a necessary matter, but always with a critical affection, I hope. I'm certainly glad if they read my works and even more if this turns out to be useful for their own thinking, which, what's more, makes agreeing in particulars of quite secondary importance: the readers should think and act further and better than me. (243)

Throughout *Disputing*, Suvin's own encounters – be they with Marx, Le Guin, or Orwell – serve as models of such critical, utopian non-readings of each texts' "Possible World." Those expecting Suvin to mechanically apply some formulaic notion of cognitive estrangement based around the introduction of a totalizing novum in order to separate the SF wheat from the (science) fantasy chaff will be happy – or perhaps disappointed, depending upon one's presuppositions – to see that this is absolutely not the case.

Eric D. Smith reminds us that Suvin's formal methodology was always more concerned with offering a heuristic than a canon, even if it does epiphenomenally produce a canon of privileged texts:

> The germinal provocation that Suvin derives from this cognitive nucleus is thus two-fold: on the one hand, a ruthless (for some readers, intolerable) evaluative discrimination between "good" and "bad" SF and, on the other, a rigorous analytical distinction between cognitively estranging and non-cognitively estranging texts. In either case, Suvin's categories are not simple reductions but

> function in concrete practice as heuristics that both actively frame and are subsumed within the practice of textual analysis and literary criticism hinging on a discernment between the freedom of utopian intervention (truth, cognition) and the nonfreedom or false freedom of anti-utopian reiteration (expressed in "subliterature[s] of mystification"). ("Preface" xxviii)

What we find in Suvin's own non-readings, then, are intensive, "depth" investigations of key texts, some that have haunted Suvin since his earliest forays into SF criticism (notably *Nineteen Eighty-Four*, which he wrote about as far back as the 1950s in the context that the book needed to be published, studied, and debated in his home country of Yugoslavia) and still others that are new to his scrupulous eye (most notably Ursula Le Guin's *Earthsea* series).

Although, as critics ourselves, we may disagree with this or that point raised by Suvin, we must engage these non-readings generously and generatively. For unlike mere mechanical essays, they ask us to critically encounter these texts again, awash in new lights and new contexts. We are thus charged with considering the text's historical contexts as well as the new contexts in which Suvin non-reads them again (and this is, of course, compounded by the contexts within which we subsequently encounter them in our own non-reading with and of Suvin).

This is all to remember, then, that for Suvin, SF is an artform, and thus it deserves to be read in line with the highest vocation of art: the ability to transform our limited perspectives on our occluded and occulted present condition of capitalist realism. This is not to suggest that art can't or doesn't do other things, but that a critical judgment must begin with some criterion, some standpoint, and as a marxist critic, it would be churlish to expect a different criterion from Suvin. As Wegner in his foreword to *Darko Suvin: A Life in Letters* suggests, it seems it is these overt political convictions more than the formal method that Suvin's critics so often object to. What Wegner reminds us of, and which is borne out by this volume's "unmasking of the ideological steamrolling" of antiutopianism (Suvin "Afterword" 255), is that for Suvin, SF, utopianism, and form can only be disentangled to the extreme peril of both SF *and* criticism:

> Anyway, "ideas" are in such taboo debates always a codeword for "political ideas," and more precisely for "explicit political ideas this critic disagrees with" (for if politics is the way people can live together, say without mass hunger or mass repressive weapons against the hungry, surely this is what SF, as all art, is about, and even more surely SF criticism cannot but be imbued with value notions about what its object does). ("Afterword" 242)

As Wegner makes clear, "the ideological trap" of privileging historicism at the ultimate expense of form results in criticism of "no particular material consequences, and [that] foster[s] no particular change" ("Foreword" 15). I would simply add to this that it also undoes the dialectical force of Suvin's critique in which history, politics, and form cannot be sundered. Wedding the utopian to SF and the cognitive to political epistemology in a critically dialectical feedback loop, there was always more at stake in

Suvin's protestations couched in terms of narrative formalism than what simply counts as "science fiction" proper.

Throughout this volume, then, Suvin remains an intensely dialectical critic, where each local intervention into a particular SF text or subgenre is an intervention into SF itself. SF form, in this non-reading of Suvin, becomes something more like the notion of the marxist problematic: "not a set of propositions about reality, but a set of categories in terms of which reality is analyzed and interrogated, and a set of 'contested' categories at that" (Jameson, "Science" 283). Thus, the form of SF, rather than a static, idealist concept, is reconceived as a shifting historical problematic that mediates the transformations from an older welfare state-oriented Fordist capitalism to what Suvin refers to as contemporary "Global Capitalism without a Human Face" (101).

TINA II: Anti-Antiutopianism

Disputing consolidates Suvin's late phase in which antiutopia as "world-historical novum" (302) takes the center stage not simply as a stance (anti-utopia) but as a presupposition. As Suvin attests, "*Antiutopia is a targeted ideologico-political use of a closed horizon not simply to refute or ridicule, but to* render unthinkable *both the eutopia of a better possible world and the dystopia as awful warning about the writer's and readers' present tendencies*, thus to stifle the right to dissent and to strive for radical novelty, to dismantle any possibility of plebeian democracy" (301). In this light, antiutopianism is an intrinsic, substantive, aspect of a late-stage capitalism that subsumes the human body under what Melinda Cooper refers to as "life as surplus" and colonizes the future through indebtedness and the financial turn in what Sherryl Vint terms capitalism's "promissory futures."

At its most basic, we might think of antiutopianism today as the blurring of the boundaries between a stalwart negation of all utopian thought – now marked under the banner of naivety, at best, and totalitarianism, at worst – and the hallucinatory proclamations of the End of History accompanying the triumph of the global capitalist world system. Indeed, as Tom Moylan argues, one of the greatest tricks that global late capitalism ever pulled was to cloak its own exploitative practices in the guise of utopia: "Under the pseudo-utopian flag of rational choice and the free market, a renewed capitalism reached toward its own dream of total exploitation and administration of workers and consumers through a worldwide division of labor in a world market of goods and services" (184). In an epistemological bait and switch, the end of history thesis with its valorization of the market – "the central exhibit in the anti-Utopian arsenal" (Jameson, *Seeds* 60) – as the arbiter of freedom and liberty subsumes the place of oppositional utopianism proper. Through this paradoxical operation, the utopian impulse is rendered mute, resulting in the "political fatigue and demoralization of people today around the world" (Jameson, *Seeds* 62).

Antiutopianism has long roots, from the eighteenth-century counterrevolutionary thought of Edmond Burke (Jameson, *Seeds* 31–2, 53) and nineteenth-century writings like Dostoevsky's *Notes from Underground* to the twentieth- and twenty-first-century political philosophies of Karl Popper and John Gray (Sargisson 24–31). Yet what could once be thought of as an intellectual countertendency has hardened into a dominant feature of concrete life. As Moylan painfully reminds us, the neoliberal project inaugurated by the right was ultimately fully realized by the rearguard transformation of the Global North's (often nominally) center-left parties in the 1990s. What the Reagan Republicans could only dream of was instead accomplished by the ascendency of the post-Reagan New Democrats. It is this transformation from tendency to neoliberal dominant that Suvin's insistence on antiutopianism elucidates throughout *Disputing*.

Neoliberalism's hegemony, as Wendy Brown attests, had the effect of not only placing the market at the center of politics but also of removing democracy and radical possibility altogether:

> Within thirty years, Western democracy would grow gaunt, its future increasingly hedged and improbable. [. . .] And more than merely cutting away the flesh of liberal democracy, neoliberalism also cauterized democracy's more radical expressions, those erupting episodically across Euro-Atlantic modernity and contending for its future with more robust versions of freedom, equality, and popular rule than democracy's liberal iteration is capable of featuring. (9)

In many ways, tracking this withering of utopian possibility has been the story of the second half of Suvin's career and subtends this volume. If "Orwell and *1984* Today" sketches and forewarns the latent antiutopian impossibility of plebeian democracy that resides within capitalism's potentiality, then "Antiutopia in Coronisation Times" supplants such latency with actuality.

In response to the full imbrication of antiutopianism within reigning political orthodoxy both right and left, Suvin moves from the hyphenation for anti-utopia to its nonhyphenated form: antiutopianism. The change indicates the shift from a conservative (and liberal) structure of feeling of anti-utopia to a concrete condition of antiutopia, noting a qualitative distinction under the hegemony of neoliberalism to something approaching a post-neoliberalism, which of course brings with it a further turn of the antiutopian screw. As Suvin traces in the later chapters in this volume, this period of post-neoliberalism is at once the disastrous fulfilment of neoliberalism's austerity programs, environmental devastation, and upward redistribution of wealth, and the state's transmogrification into a financial hub and military apparatus. Indeed, if the end of history thesis popularized by Francis Fukuyama has not aged well on the intellectual plain, the belief in any rigorous opposition to or replacement for capitalism has not particularly benefited from this. If anything, antiutopianism has promulgated a growing cynicism far more effective than any cunning of history, as (post-)neoliberalism slowly lurches on as a faithless ideology that outstrips any necessary conviction.

In this volume, we can turn to Suvin's essay on right-wing militarism in SF as an early harbinger of the hegemonic return of ethnonationalism that compensates for the gutting of the welfare state and increasing immiseration. Such tendencies glimpsed in late twentieth-century SF become manifest in our current political reality. As Suvin notes in the final chapter of this volume, "The antiutopia and its 'common sense of capitalist biopolitics' can therefore reach for a more oppressive dispensation. We are seeing strong signs of system mutation into a more maleficent sociopolitical formation that would employ both the State and intolerant nationalism up to racism to again save the profits and bamboozle the outraged people" (319). The outline of this post-neoliberal landscape has become particularly visible in the United States during the period of covidization with the growth of billionaires pitted against the impoverishment of the lower classes, the over 600,000 deaths disproportionately affecting BIPOC populations, and the rising insurgency of nativist, white ethnonationalism. Indeed, perhaps the surest sign that we're running out of options is the troubling rise of neoliberal nostalgia (the rehabilitation of the dynasty of war criminals of the Bush and Obama administrations, the unbelievable triumph of the Biden campaign, the desire for a return to our inimical past normalcy as the close of the Covid era): first tragedy, then farce, and finally cynicism.

Against this dark background, then, there is no alternative to anti-antiutopianism. As Suvin reminds us, we too as intellectuals must not be complicit. It is our job to reveal as well as make choices. This, then, ultimately seems to be at the heart of his critical practice with its focus on "the best works" and the anchoring of his formal criticism within a politically prescriptive stance. The choice is starkly clear: anti-antiutopianism or, as Suvin's non-reading of Orwell reveals, "a boot stamping on a human face–for ever." What better image for our "capitalism without a human face?"

There is no alternative: it is the deepest truth of anti-antiutopianism.

TINA III: SF

SF may be our most necessary and most compromised form for combating antiutopianism. SF has often walked lockstep with the deep structural ambivalences that undergird modernity, mapping the incongruities of rationality that have given us penicillin and the gas chambers, the realities of imperialism but only the dream of communism. It is this deep affinity with the ambivalence of modernity that makes SF so powerful to think with and through. We can glimpse the potential for SF in Suvin's reflections on Stanislaw Lem's *Solaris* as "an optimal example of what great SF can give us: it shows us our age (for in SF, more clearly than in most other genres, *de nobis fabula narrator* – the story tells of us) as 'the time of cruel miracles,' an age which bears at least the chance of a skeptical belief" (184). However, drawing outward from Suvin's ruminations on militaristic SF, SF's dalliance with the dark side of the Enlightenment can be seen in its overlap with the fascist futurists and their love of the technology of slaughter as well as in the relationship between techno-scientific development and imperialism.

In his work on Afrofuturism, Kodwo Eshun explores this intensifying techno-fetishistic relationship between SF and neoimperial capital. Drawing on Mark Fisher's notion of "SF capital" to develop his own concept of the "Futures Industry," Eshun argues that if imperialism functioned through the control of the past and the archive – casting Africans and so many others outside of the narratives of World History and progress – then today neoimperialism operates via the power of prediction and the control of the future "through the envisioning, management, and delivery of reliable futures" (289). Such envisioned futures draw on the SF imaginary to produce self-fulfilling prophecies through "the positive feedback between future-oriented media and capital" (290). Consequently, they arrest the potentially radical utopian future before it has the chance to take shape.

The problem then is not SF itself but the imbrication of SF with capital. "Science fiction," Eshun argues, "operates through the power of falsification, the drive to rewrite reality, and the will to deny plausibility, while the [market-oriented, futures industry] scenario operates through the control and prediction of plausible alternative tomorrows" (291). Yet even here, we can hear whispers of estrangement and negation ("the power of falsification"; "the drive to rewrite reality") even as they are recuperated by the affirmative powers that seek to delimit futurity and cognition. For Eshun, one needs to strike at this join: "Afrofuturism, then, is concerned with the possibilities for intervention within the dimension of the predictive, the projected, the proleptic, the envisioned, the virtual, the anticipatory and the future conditioned" (293). It's a powerful reminder from one of the most non-Suvinian corners of SF studies of the continuing necessity of SF's utopian potential, especially since that potential can no longer be theorized as singularly aligned with anti-hegemonic forces. As this conjoined non-reading of Eshun and Suvin suggests, rather than a singularly decisive utopian – or conversely fascist – orientation, SF limns the contradictions and ambivalences of modernity: the systemic conditions and employment of novums that could bring us to an epoch of utopian rest (e.g., Iain M. Banks' Culture series) or conversely to an epoch of dystopian rest (e.g., Theodore Sturgeon's "Thunder and Roses" or Ray Bradbury's "There Will Come Soft Rains").

This brings us, then, into the ambit of that often-occluded term when Suvin's definition of SF is broached, the orientation of the novum: "Antiutopia effects as it were a counterrevolution within the utopian revolution by flattening all possibilities of radical alterity or Novum into the dominant 'one-eyed' capitalocene hegemony that absolutely takes what is as the ultimate limit" (303–304). As Suvin develops through much of his later writings, beginning with "Novum Is as Novum Does" in the 1990s and continued through many of the essays here such as "On Splitting Notions," the relationship between the novum and capitalist science undergoes an antiutopian operation. As he argues in the latter essay, "To base novums on formal innovation as hegemonised by modern science grew quite untenable after its overarching novum became the transformation of [knowledge] into capital: and clearly so when it was force-fed by much Rightwing money into 'hard' SF, the 'space cadets' of imperialist warfare" (250).

If Suvin remains dismayed at the triumph, in market share, of the pseudo-utopian or right-wing over the substantial in SF, this is in part related to the subsumption of the novum, its epistemological alignment with a comprador liberalism-*cum*-neoliberalism that tamps down the revolutionary in the name of the elongation and prolongation of the antiutopian capitalist present. Estrangement remains in such works, but it is the estranging alienation of the market that dissects and alienates humanity, reconstituting us not only as consumers but also as so many reified bespoke brands, as ambassadors of ourselves as products. Cognition, likewise, becomes trivialized as efficiency, as the irrational (i.e., life and world destroying) rationality of *homo economicus*. No longer in a dialectical relationship with estrangement, such cognition as instrumental rationality simply amplifies the market-driven logic of neoliberalism's disruption as estrangement. Thus, when the novum's efficacy is replaced by the pseudo-novum's ability, in our neoliberal parlance, to disrupt and reshape the market in favor of strengthening it and when SF at worst simply reflects this (as in Suvin's critique of market cyberpunk), how do we begin to imagine our way out?

Yet Suvin's analysis doesn't rest at identifying this question. Elucidating the anti-antiutopian position that our age demands, Suvin calls for a renewed utopian novum:

> a new reasonableness: a rationality that incorporates much refurbished science but also permanent self-estrangement and self-criticism under the eyes of plebeian salvation, including practices not reducible to clear-cut concepts yet articulated in topological propositions – for example, those usually called emotions and approached in pioneering ways by some Feminist theoreticians. (252)

Ultimately, as this non-reading of Suvin suggests, we must critically live with the ambivalence of SF: to dwell only in the utopian ignores the fascist rearguard of SF that may be outstripping it, while to dwell too much in the fascist, (neo)imperial, antiutopian "planning scenarios" (often accompanied by a full-bodied rejection of Suvin's position, and thus throwing the utopian baby out with the bathwater) is to limit and blinker ourselves and to forego the radical possibility and mutability of the future in a reifying presentism (whether naively or uncritically optimistic or cynically pessimistic).

If SF in Suvin's early "discourse founding" works was necessarily aligned with the subversive, throughout his later works we find a more complicated approach. Even Suvin has come to see how his position on the inherent subversiveness of SF was shaped by the context of the radicality of the 1960s ("Postscript"), and one that missed the rearguard ascendency of conservativism that we now know as neoliberalism (and of course, in this, Suvin was hardly alone). While the notion that the "truth" of 1968 was neoliberalism or perhaps more alarmingly the Alt Right has become fashionable, it risks the kind of historical determinism that Walter Benjamin warns against, forgetting those utopian monads waiting to blast open – that because those novums were captured by capitalism doesn't mean that they had to be. Therefore, rather than stepping too far into the role of the future interlocutor that blames the past cadre for what they could not see coming (like so many critics who take joy in poking at what SF "got wrong" about the future), I want to stress here, in my non-reading of Suvin, that the point is the need for better novums and to engage with the best of what SF can be and do while remaining fully cognizant of the worst: we must tarry with the ambivalence or risk being blind to it. There is no alternative.

TINA IV: Utopia/Communism

As Suvin argues elsewhere, our need for communism stems from our lack of it: "We need communism for many reasons, but the most pressing one is to stop warfare and other sources of mass killings as well as eco-destruction. Our dire need is for 'survival studies' or salvational politics. An indispensable foundation stone for it is enlightening ourselves and others" (Suvin, "Shadows" 217). Each essay, each poem, each remembrance contained within this volume represents a moment, a step, an aspect of or plea for this "salvational politics."

If these names – utopia, communism – seem insufficient it is less due to any supposed or actual past failures they entail but instead due to the problem of the antiutopian that inures and inveighs against utopian thinking. The cynicism that chides us for the names communism or utopia reveals the relative paucity of our currently situated imagination to grasp the radical structure of feeling of the utopian horizon, mired as it is not only in our lack of this Not-Yet but also due to the baleful, dolorous stranglehold of antiutopian capitalist realism that demands the exclusive fidelity and fealty of our desires to its infinitely commodifying and atomizing machinations.

Therefore, in my non-reading of Suvin, I name utopia "communism":

> In between ["hi-tech Leviathan" and "competing monoalethists"] there is the straight gate of a stance, belief, and practice that would be both unshakeably liberatory, opposed to all forms of repressing humanity, and yet a severe way to our only possible salvation – ending class society. In my latest book *Communism, Poetry*, I call this force <u>*communism*</u>, in a generous historical sense that rejects social democracy, Bakunin, and Stalin but runs from Marx and Morris through Lenin and Gramsci to Brecht and much great poetry. (17)

It is, therefore, not in the name of some absolutist or stagist counter-end-of-history (need it be stated yet again that Marx conceived communism as the beginning of history?). Instead, it is in fidelity with Suvin and his dictum that we "begin with" categories in order to align our thinking even if such "categories are not sufficient to dispose of any matter" (58). As Adorno long ago counseled, the "Utopia of cognition" would be "to open up the non-conceptual with the aid of the concept, without reducing it to the concept" (Adorno, *Lectures* 66). Such an epistemological utopianism in the name of communism or utopia reminds us that these concepts are only ever preconceptual and indeed cannot capture the excess of that which will by necessity of history outstrip them in their limits.

To that end, as Suvin argues, "utopia is an epistemological and not ontological beast," yet one that dialectically "spills over from epistemology to ontology" through its "political embodiment" and opposition to antiutopia (302). Communism, utopia, anti-antiutopia, "or whatever better name we'll find for it in the future" (101) is necessary to orient the pessimism of the intellect toward freedom, which as Adorno, perhaps the most pessimistic of philosophers of freedom, reminds us:

> is not a mere abstraction suspended somewhere above the heads of human beings who snatch at it without being able to jump high enough to reach it. Instead, we can only speak meaningfully of freedom because there are concrete possibilities of freedom, because freedom can be achieved in reality. And in contrast to the entire dialectical tradition of Hegel and Marx, I would almost go so far as to say that actually this has always been possible, that it has been possible at every moment. (Adorno, *History* 181)

Every one of Suvin's non-readings in this collection is premised on this end – even when detailing the overburdening weight of the antiutopian. The alternative, as Suvin examines in the final three essays – on Orwell's *Nineteen Eighty Four*, the state of utopian studies in relation to antiutopianism, and the political uses of the devastating Covid-19 pandemic – is to surrender to what Gerry Canavan refers to as necrofutures, "those capitalist-realist anticipations of the coming decades that anticipate the future as a devastated world of death, and yet simultaneously insist that this world of death is the only possible future" (48). There is no alternative: communism/utopia.

TINA: Concluding, or Utopia Always

As Wegner suggests, just as utopia itself permanently retreats into the horizon, necessitating our continual striving toward it, there is no conclusion to non-reading. There is only non-reading again. Yet one must conclude, for now, to make way for such new non-readings. As all non-readings are historically situated, it is worth reflecting on this moment. This project began among the renewal of Black Lives Matter and carried on through the Covid-19 pandemic, situations that revealed, in deep, systemic ways, the intrinsic and inimical forces of our antiutopian present.

Yet as I've worked on this project with Suvin over the last year and a half, reflecting on the deep reality of pervasive antiutopia that this volume takes as its principal object of study, I've also watched my students take to the streets to demand not reform but instead wholly new ways of organizing our society from the ground up – ways that both their liberal and conservative critics deem impossible. I'm reminded, then, of the most important lessons this non-reading with Suvin has provided. It is not enough to lament the waning of utopia in neoliberalism with the commercialization of the novum, the commodification of desire, and the colonization of authentic freedom by the market. To simply surrender the utopian to neoliberalism is antiutopianism at its most virulent (all the more so for the very reason that it so often comes from the left). While one is correct to note the ways that utopianism has been co-opted (and this is centrally important work), one cannot at the same time give up on utopianism, the heuristics of cognitive estrangement, and the need for new novums. To do so is to admit that we always already lost, and it is to risk therefore giving up on moments of real radical possibility when and where they present themselves, even if they must be grasped from the jaws of degradation, repression, and dehumanization. As Wegner reminds us, "what all utopias [. . .] teach us is that the throw of the dice – the gamble, effort involved, and likelihood of failure – are well worth it. For we always fail; that is, until we succeed" (*Invoking* 96). Yes, the present *seems* indelibly compromised, but anti-antiutopianism reminds us that it need not be. To anti-antiutopianism, we must insist, once more with Suvin: There Is No Alternative!

Hugh C. O'Connell
Salem, MA
April 2021

Works Cited

Adorno, Theodor W. *History and Freedom*. Ed. Rolf Tiedemann, trans. Rodney Livingstone. Polity, 2006.

Adorno, Theodor W. *Lectures on Negative Dialectics*. Ed. Rolf Tiedemann, trans. Rodney Livingstone. Polity, 2008.

Brown, Wendy. *Undoing the Demos: Neoliberalism's Stealth Revolution*. Zone Books, 2015.

Canavan, Gerry. "'If the Engine Ever Stops, We'd All Die': *Snowpiercer* and Necrofuturism." *SF Now*, special issue of *Paradoxa*, 26 (2014): 41–66.

Cooper, Melinda. *Life as Surplus: Biotechnology and Capitalism in the Neoliberal Era*. U of Washington P, 2008.

Eshun, Kodwo. "Further Considerations on Afrofuturism." *CR: The New Centennial Review* 3.2 (2003): 287–302.

Jameson, Fredric. "Science versus Ideology." *Humanities in Society* 6 (1983): 283–302.

Jameson, Fredric. *The Seeds of Time*. Columbia UP, 1994.

Moylan, Tom. *Scraps of the Untainted Sky: Science Fiction, Utopia, Dystopia*. Westview Press, 2000.

Sargisson, Lucy. *Fool's Gold: Utopianism in the Twenty-First Century*. Palgrave, 2012.

Smith, Eric D. "Cognition and Event: A Purveyor of Truth's Possible Worlds," in Darko Suvin, *Parables of Freedom, Narrative Logics: Positions and Presuppositions in Science Fiction and Utopianism*, by Darko Suvin, edited by Eric D. Smith. P. Lang, 2021.

Suvin, Darko. "Afterword: With Sober, Estranged Eyes." *Learning from Other Worlds: Estrangement, Cognition and the Politics of Science Fiction and Utopia*, edited by Patrick Parrinder, Liverpool University Press, 2000, pp. 233–271.

Suvin, Darko. Postscript. "Estrangement and Cognition." *Strange Horizons* Nov. 24, 2014, strangehorizons.com/non-fiction/articles/estrangement-and-cognition/.

Suvin, Darko. "In the Shadows of Never-Ending Warfare: Use-Values of Lenin Today." *Communism, Poetry: Communicating Vessels*. Political Animal Press, 2020.

Vint, Sherryl. "Promissory Futures: Reality and Imagination in Finance and Fiction." *Speculative Fiction/Speculative Finance*, special issue of *CR: The New Centennial Review*, 19.1 (2019): 11–36.

Wegner, Philip E. "Foreword: Crossing the Border with Darko Suvin." *Darko Suvin: A Life in Letters. Paradoxa* 23 (2011): 9–20.

Wegner, Philip E. *Invoking Hope: Theory and Utopia in Dark Times*. Minnesota UP, 2020.

Author's Introduction

Words, Shapes, and Our Common World

Le peintre ne doit pas faire ce qui'il voit, mais ce qui sera vu

[The painter shouldn't render what he sees but what shall be seen]

Paul Valéry

0. An introduction should provide the reader with an overview of what the author believes are the salient points in the book and other matters helpful for approaching its text. Since this one is organised chronologically, I shall begin by grouping the chapters for our present interests. I shall proceed with second thoughts and special stresses arising from them.

The chapters may be assembled into four main groups, here summarily identified by their number: narratology enmeshed with epistemology and values: 1 + 10, 11, 22; the political context and prospects or potentialities of SF, Utopia/nism, and Fantasy: 3, 5, 18, then 2, 4, then 9, 14; and a culmination and revaluing of stance at length in extensive probes in and for these two last years: 22, 23, 24. Finally there are the more occasional (though in a nobler sense all the texts here are occasional) short incidentals or paralipomena: 6–8, 12–13, 15–17, 21. Though their importance may be gauged by a good part of them being my poems and my lone try at an apologue (16), I shall leave them to speak by themselves for their necessity in this book.

1. Words Shaping the World

I much regret there was no possibility in this book to systematise my narratological horizons and their reliance on a specific political epistemology and will therefore attempt to fill a major gap or two here. This book is focussed – as most of my previous ones but perhaps more consciously so, forced by "the bitter disposition of the time" (Shakespeare) rubbing all our noses into further horrors and necessities – on the traffic and feedback between our common world and various authors (including myself) intervening into it by means of narrative positions and presuppositions, stories, and comments. The only piece in the book exclusively devoted to narratology is "Kick-Off: An Introduction to Literary Genres with a View to SF," which I have exceptionally lifted out of its chronological place in the middle and put as chapter 1 in order to clear up for myself what I was doing in my text analyses here, and not so incidentally to help the reader see on what presuppositions I was doing that. Any coherent book obeys a group of compatible presuppositions, most often implicitly – but it seemed after half a century of writing that I should briefly indicate this set that goes much beyond literary genres (though it continues to squint at them).

1.1. Art as Freedom and Knowledge

My first frame of determining sense and meaning here is the *epistemic regime*, always consubstantial with an institutional framework, reigning or dreamed of. My general approach to epistemology, listed at the end, commits to a "soft" skepticism: right and wrong persist, but the rightness must be created by human communities, with skill and responsibility, within contingent historical situations and durations (see Elgin, Goodman-Elgin, Prieto). It follows that rightness or wrongness is inescapably situated between the poles of knowledge used for wisdom furthering human *freedom* – as in the best of Greek, Hebrew, and some Asian traditions – and *Herrschaftswissen*, knowledge used for *domination*. Most significant concepts undergo therefore a polar splitting: this seems to me a central procedure of critical reason, dissatisfied with the present nominations and trying to insinuate opposed meanings under the same term (I applied it in chapter 20 to two notions of highest importance to me). It is accompanied by the rare invention of new concepts, for example, Marx's "labour force" or Brecht's "estrangement."

All modes of cognition – science, art, and others – are thus human constructions elucidating the human species' traffic with aspects of the universe or nature. Up to *c.* 1945 on (when one should date the advent of the capitalocene, see chapters 23 and 24), this traffic primarily pivoted on and was constricted by the available forces of production; after it the weight of relationships of production between various human classes grew decisive. All modes of cognition share some aspects, such as (a) a striving for understanding: literary knowledge, say, was posited by Auerbach as an attempt "to designate man's place in the universe" (17); (b) fundamental assessments that are epistemologically indispensable but not specifiable as a proposition or argument (and thus often, faute de mieux, called beautiful or esthetic); (c) a sense of relevance that includes awareness of topological *Gestalt* – say Kekulé's dream of the benzene ring – and intuitive perception of form (cf. both Gendlin titles) within the fates of human communities, and today of the human species.

The arts occupy a special place in cognitive endeavours – though I can theorise with some confidence only about the language arts (poetry and narrative). Their understandings do not essentially refer back to general theories or principles but rely much more strongly on the specific epistemic regime and cognitive paradigm used. In other words, the indispensable role of ideological interests and practical human relationships, their weight and constriction, always in the fundaments of all cognition in class society, is nearer to the foreground in arts; however, they are subjected to feedback with metaphorical systems, rooted in an imaginary sensual topology (see Suvin "On Metaphoricity"). In particular, poetry and fiction always imply a reader standing for a collective audience, ideally his/her whole community – this is foregrounded in plays – or at least for one value horizon out of a very few, usually two or three, available in a given sociopolitical spacetime. It was the accepted norm not only for ancient Greece but also for Leibniz or Kant that such creations in words reach some transmittable understanding of human relationships so that Baumgarten called his foundational *Aesthetica* of 1750 the "science of sensual cognition."

Poetry and storytelling have often filled in the voids left by institutionalised science and institutionalised philosophy, and of course by most institutionalised politics, inimical to humanity because enmeshed in oppressive and exploitative class rule. All of them, including ruling politics as a most miserly example, use generalisation irremediably wedded to concepts, which cannot fully account for the relationship between people and nature, the finite and the infinite. Poetic creativity sutures conceptual thought to justification from recalled immediate sensual, bodily experience. As important is its ranging through richer time horizons, recalled in Williams's categories of the dominant, emergent, and residual in culture (121–27): remembering supposed qualities within human relationships, absent today, in the past and expecting them in the future. The central meta-message of all significant poetry and storytelling is freedom as the possibility of things being otherwise. They carry a historically situated and political experience of the sensual, which is necessarily also a polemical swerve from and against the *doxa*, in favour of fresh cognition. This freedom is intimately melded with knowledge or cognition. The story or the poem gives shape and voice to a previously uncognised, mute, and nonarticulated category of being.

1.2. On Narrative Agents

As I instantiate in the essay on Orwell and *1984* (but see also chapter 9, "Starship"), narratological analysis classically consists of melding the accounts of the story's flow (syntagmatics) and its underlying structure or model (paradigmatics). In a way, *narrative agents* are a privileged mediator between them, and I wish to present here a hypothesis about them I have held since the early 1980s but never developed at monograph length. It arose out of my work on dramaturgy where it is easier to detect – hence the stress on visualising – but I would defend its extension to all narration. To cut a long story short, I have condensed my findings in table form and asked the interested reader to look up the justifications and details in Suvin "Levels," "Can," and "Chronotope" (see much more also in the chapter 9, Sections 4.1 and 4.2). The table is organised with the depth agents downmost and rising toward the textual surface from 1 to 3.

Table of Narrative Agents

Agential Level	**Predicative Articulation**	**Narratological locus**	**Verbal Status; Deep Structure**	**Visualizing Status**	**Definition**	**Historical Duration**
3. CHARACTER *personnage* or *personnage-personne*; "round"; presence not obligatory	A great (though not unlimited) number of predicates/ traits, at least two of them conflict	Always textual and a dramatis persona (when it exists)	*Proper name*; deep str. = illusion of large number of not fully fixed attributes, only imperfectly retrievable from text + all contexts	Necessarily figurative (depictable); necessarily individual	Individuality as presupposed by bourgeois practice (e.g., economics) and ideology (e.g., psychology)	Almost point-like, changeable for each different ensemble (interest group) of spectators or readers

2. TYPE *type* or *personnage-type*; "flat," e.g., Vice, Pantalone, Miser, Father, Soubrette; presence obligatory	A small number, usually 2 to 6, of compatible predicates/traits	Metatextual or textual, according to whether level 3 exists or not	*Common or generic noun*, incl. proper name raised to that status; deep str. = noun + one or a few attributes, or nominal syntagm	Necessarily figurative; not necessarily individual	Societal type, by age + sex + profession, and/or social group, and/or temperament...	Middle historical duration: generations or centuries
1. ACTANT Protagonist, Antagonist, Value, Mandator or Arbiter, Beneficiary, and Satellite; presence obligatory	One predicate as common denominator of a bundle of semic predicates	Always metatextual; no discrete appearance as *dramatis persona*	*Common noun*; deep str. = "force which does what is indicated by the noun"	Not necessarily figurative; necessarily not individual	Function in narrative action	Long duration: epochs or millennia

2. The World Constricting Words and Shapes

2.1. The Sickness unto Death, and the Only Remedy

I speak of freedom in an unhappy epoch where millennial class society is breaking down yet redoubles its tenacious hold in its death throes (by repressive *in*tolerance), while the truly free society of the associated producers cannot yet be born. Here, freedom can only come about as a suppression of nonfreedom and anti-freedom. Every reading and interpretation is a denial and suppression of other readings, meanings, and values. Any positive act is also the negation of a negation; any truth a denial of opposed "untruths." So what is today the active antagonist of collective human freedom, our supreme truth and Supreme Good? If every major epistemic act and regime are political in Aristotle's sense of "affairs of the human community," when does this spill over into politics in the miserable sense of daily newspapers and TV? When does history call into the foreground matters of political power and violence? Obviously, in times when human affairs are unable to go on as heretofore because of major breakdowns, which then lead either to revolution or preemptive counterrevolution (fascism).

Such a historical moment for me began with 2001, in the twin outrages of Al Qaeda's killing thousands of civilians in the United States and the US government's adoption of an offensive defence posture by all means licit or illicit, eventually killing and torturing many more thousands. In this age, I see first of all the rise of a hi-tech Leviathan, more threatening to people's freedom and survival than any other ruling class of history. Second, I see the response of a clash of competing monoalethists (from *alethé*, truth) – from monotheists to lay dogmatists (fascists, Stalinists, and capitalist believers in the Invisible Hand of the Market) – who hold they have the Absolute Truth. A historically pernicious variant was the "weak thought" of postmodernism, proclaiming that relativism is absolute; but for mass consumption, the mask efficiently donned by the new family of our half or three-quarter fascisms is, as a rule, nationalism. However, the latest depth form of this absolutism is the oppressive antiutopia to which I speak in the last two essays of this book, putting the state into the immediate service of the 1% of plutocrats. In between there is the straight gate of a stance, belief, and practice that would be both unshakeably liberatory, opposed to all forms of repressing humanity, and yet a severe way to our only possible salvation – ending class society. In my latest book *Communism, Poetry*, I call this force *communism*, in a generous historical sense that rejects social democracy, Bakunin, and Stalin but runs from Marx and Morris through Lenin and Gramsci to Brecht and much great poetry (see more in chapter 20, "Splitting").

In this most dangerous interregnum of ours, the arts, and imagination in general, register deeply and durably both the disalienated horizons and the fullness of human alienations. As an extraordinary passage by Simmel has it, "the intellect is egalitarian and as it were communist," for its contents are both generally communicable and, if correct, generally shareable "by every sufficiently educated mind (*Geist*) . . . and the potential infinity of disseminating theoretical imaginations has no influence on their meaning, [so that] they exclude private property" (603); he is probably echoing, with more prudence in more complexly alienated times, Plato's equally astounding proposition in *Meno* that any slave boy is capable of understanding geometry. Centrally, disseminated fiction's contract with the reader is "not just egalitarian . . . [but constitutive of] the story-teller's art itself. The moral of the very act of fabulation was the equality of the intelligence" (Rancière 82). Such a striving for *freedom through understanding*, assumed from Aristotle to Rousseau as a natural human right though often unnaturally suppressed, is here discussed within the "word art," literature in the widest sense of all oral and written instances.

Franco Fortini, one of the 20th Century's best Italian poets and critics – and an intimately epistemological and political one to boot – defined "the literary use of language" as a homology to "a formalised [that is, conscious and conscientious] use of life that is the end and goal of communism" (*Saggi* 184). This homology, which I take to be part annunciation-cum-denunciation and part prefiguration, necessarily transgresses the hegemonic discourse, in our times sadly clichétised; I would call it cognition constituted by memorable pleasure. It remembers the past, disputes the present "use of life into which we are forced by alienation of labour" (Fortini, *I confini* 35), and carries their lessons into projects of possible lives reaching for the future. What he means by form can be briefly characterised as an interpretation of the world by means of what word constellations both say and leave unsaid but suggest and give clues to, always suffused by firm if dynamic values shared by a societal class standing at that point in the vanguard of humanity.

2.2. Antiutopia: A Fake Political Ontology

As I just suggested, the final chapters of this book culminate in the discussion of a new beast trudging toward Bethlehem, as Yeats put it: the Antiutopia. The latter is what I saw ensuring "bust" in the title of chapter 23 by blockading utopia/nism, for it is an active and far-reaching blockading of all SF and other utopianism in the most efficient guise of making it unthinkable, a perpetual taboo.

An earlier counterblast to the potentially liberating and therefore subversive horizon of SF and other utopianism were two genological novelties. The first was a well-orchestrated irruption of virulent militarist and war-mongering SF to which I shall return, but I speculate this reaches mainly youngsters of the White racist belt (there are no publicly available data on the sales of various subgroups I deal with in this book). The second is a turn to the much more ancient Fantasy genre, which I discuss in chapters 2 and 4, my earlier brusque attempt to brush it off in *MOSF* having historically proved insufficient. This turn had the advantage of potentially appealing to the whole "precariate" generation under the boot of "austerity for the people" capitalism, but also a statistically small but important disadvantage: it had rich roots from the Gothic literature and the Romantics on (attempts to project this reaction to the bourgeois Enlightenment and revolutions into the past of Rabelais if not tribal tales or the depths of the human brain, as in a special 2002 issue of *Historical Materialism* devoted to the protean term "fantasy," are obviously unhistorical and self-serving). These European roots, renewed by major US writers from Poe and Hawthorne down to Mark Twain, had a strong grounding in the impulse to escape the impasses and indignities of class history that kept growing and hurting. In the high-minded racists Lovecraft and Tolkien, who had overtly posited the Black Gods, they created veritable quasi-religious sects of fandom. These were small but the total collapse of the welfare state by the mid-1970s provided the ideal ground for proto-fascist massification, as proved by the US-centered Tolkien boom in books and finally movies. The problem was that the ever unreliable literary fiction and poetic imagination left open the possibility of not only Marx's capitalists as vampires but even of feminist anarchism (as in Le Guin's *Earthsea* series, discussed in chapter 11) and of overtly rebellious movements (as in Miéville's *Iron Council* and some other works). Thus even the welcome rise of Fantasy did not quite preclude liberatory utopianism. Enter antiutopianism, raised from the feeble superman fantasies à la Ayn Rand to an extraliterary, culturally dominant, and existentially widespread stance and horizon that became the iron norm for all the *gleichgeschaltet* capitalist medias in much more efficient ways than Goebbels and the Gestapo. Itself a supreme ideologised fiction of Social Darwinist human nature reduced to nature red in tooth and claw (discussed in chapter 14, "Darwinism"), it no longer needed literary fiction.

I discuss such matters at length in the last two chapters of this book, which should ideally be factored in for what follows, but the subject is so new and so important that it will bear having a momentarily final capping. My thesis is that antiutopia as horizon and form is a major novelty, correlative to its original bearers being not only and not primarily professional intellectuals but professional politicians, the state apparatus of violence, and its embedded think tanks. Antiutopia is the latest crown of the ruling classes' repressive tradition, evolving in my generation from the welfare state pseudo-tolerance into intolerance. Intolerant repression was always the material truth of violent power. Lately, it ranges from refusal of money and careers for deviant thinkers, proclaimed unthinkably confused and/or dogmatic (!), to incarceration (probably the case for a great majority of officially assumed "terrorists," if we are to judge from the US criminal justice as applied to the poor, beginning with the visible "others" of women, Blacks, and immigrants). It ends with assassinations, so frequently instanced in US politics by the Kennedys, the Black Panthers' leadership, M. L. King, Malcolm X, and many humbler people under media radar. Antiutopia is the horizon of holding that all the central power and ideological pillars are untouchable, like Yahweh: I am that I am; but it is also the vector of intolerant repression in order to eternalise the ruling system as the best possible locus (see more in chapter 23). The ruthless saturation of imaginary space in an eternal present makes antiutopia's grip powerful.

A very revealing light is thrown on the genesis and form of antiutopia, and on its rise to the age's ruling common sense or indeed sense of destiny, by the new political ontology of the US ruling class – and to a degree all rulers of its allied and even enemy states – after September 11, 2001, as suggested above. In this oligarchic ontology imagination directly issues into factual states. Whether the US federal government really feared a worldwide "Islamist" insurrection or simply used this as a godsent opportunity to invoke "Homeland security," creating in 2002 the titanic eponymous department, what it also excogitated and engaged upon was the evil novum of "a parallel . . . extra-legal universe" (Scarry xviii–xix). This is an alternative, largely secret and hidden world obeying new procedures of violent power and creating new spaces for it: on the one hand "extraterritorial rendition networks, prison archipelagos, and secret >black site< facilities," on the other, "indefinite detentions, military tribunals, and executive circumventions of national and international law," permitting planned kidnappings and killings of anybody the central security agencies deemed important enough (Saint-Amour). This parallel world in the interstices of our daily one ruthlessly jettisoned not only basic principles of international law but the whole of lay theory and practice of humanist-cum-liberal history and culture; that is, it jettisoned the revolutionary *citoyen* values in favour of a blend of slave-owning empires, colonial subjugation, the Holy Inquisition, and strictest World War-type secrecy and disinformation. Its current culmination is Trumpism. It is the best empirical approximation to Lovecraft's vague but malignantly powerful Dark Gods.

Two factors seem to me central here: first, the establishment of what Elaine Scarry calls an alternative universe with different permissibilities – "different bases for fact, standards of proof, evidentiary parameters, rights, procedures, penalties, guarantees, and expectations" (Saint-Amour). It fits well the passion of rulers in late capitalism for the state of exception or a *de facto* martial law, piecemeal applicable at will. This was theorised most clearly by the Nazi theoretician Carl Schmitt, undergoing a revival at those times, and observed also by Judith Butler within a critical Agambenian frame. However, Butler goes one important step further, noting that it is "a paralegal universe that goes by the name of law" (61). For the second defining factor of the existential antiutopia systematically developed from within the nuclei of our ruling classes – and zealously followed by (sad to say) very many intellectuals right down to a tacitly new understanding of dystopia à la *A Game of Thrones* series – is that this new universe is not openly affirmed, as in its four historical predecessors identified above and their culmination in Nazis. On the contrary, it is occulted: it propositionally and axiologically splits off from the official universe, still ruled by publicly accessible contracts and remaining in force for the docile masses of the ruled (in the more affluent North, at least) insofar as they remain exploitable or otherwise usable. The secret world works by covertly yet systematically *infiltrating* the overt one, in which it is revealed first by macro-events that cannot be denied (but can be misnamed), such as the mass bombings from Afghanistan and Serbia to Syria or Libya, and then by the occasional courageous whistleblower, who is made to pay dearly: from Frank Snepp, relating to CIA 1977, and Mordechai Vanunu, Israeli nuclear weapons 1986, to John Kiriakou, CIA 2007, Chelsea Manning, US Army 2010, Edward Snowden, NSA and so on 2013 (see the rich "List," which strangely does not include the most famous one, Julian Assange of WikiLeaks).

Were there space, I would undertake to show that existential antiutopia is the left hand of darkness, whose right hand is the incessant murderous warfare of late capitalism that has never stopped from 1914 on. It is indeed warfare that in our capitalocene first clearly grew into the substitute for liberatory politics and unacknowledged economical pillar of the system (see more in my chapter 9 and 23). And the first offensive of the US Right within SF, detailed in chapter 9, was precisely one of "private-enterprise-riding-new-military-technology" SF (I'm adapting John Clute on "hard" SF 362–4, by adding "military").

I concluded that antiutopia was a targeted and embattled ideologico-political use of a closed horizon to render unthinkable both the eutopia of a better possible world and the dystopia as awful warning about the writer's and readers' present tendencies. It stifles not only the right to dissent but primarily the imaginability of (and therefore the desire for) radical novelty – in brief, it dismantles any possibility of plebeian democracy. This was a world-historical novum by which the ideologico-political development of capitalism, which had all along produced fake novums galore, morphed by the beginning of 21st Century into this encompassing monster – the existential antiutopia as a super weapon. One of its pillars was the Cold War misuse of *1984*, whose ambiguities, weaknesses, and plain errors (see chapter 22) allowed its use for proving that any alternative to capitalism would be even worse. I think Orwell himself would be horrified by the horizon of a world where all people and human possibilities existed only as adjunct exploitable labour for profit – unless also as mercenary servants.

In the style of the *Communist Manifesto* and Brecht's question "What is the robbing of a bank compared to founding a bank?" we could ask: within the production of human suffering, what are Attila, Gengis Khan, Stalin, and even the most horrible but short-lived Hitler state compared to agribusiness, Big Pharma, the Seven Sisters of oil, and the capillary grip of financial capital? And especially, adding insult to injury, when their values are blandly infiltrated as the new existential norm: antiutopia.

2.3. *Ausklang*: The World, the Story, and the Devil

Since this book may well be my final one on SF and utopia, it might be just as well to risk a brief comment to the ancient Chinese story, beloved by Walter Benjamin, whose shade I invoke in this *Ausklang*, where the painter disappears finally into his painting. This is unavoidable after the author's death – when Mallarmé's Edgar Poe is "changed into himself" (i.e., into the image given by his *Nachlass*, meaning both inheritance and reduction) "by eternity" – but it is always somehow properly anti-privatising. "Trust the tale not the teller," admonished D. H. Lawrence: though dialectically, we would know that without the teller the tale may not only have remained unactualised for new situations as a new variant but may have simply been inaccessible, nonexistent for us.

However, I feel that today the painter can only decently reappear behind or in front of the painting in order to explain better what situation, personal but superindividual, led to just this painting, as a trace, testimony, and above all warning. The mega-situation is that we have to "once again begin to distinguish the forces of communism and fascism at work beneath the surface of [capitalist] world politics" (Jameson, *Benjamin* 207); the simple reason is that the hugely powerful ruling classes of our world have already jettisoned *citoyen* democracy and are reaching for the only remaining fix, some form of Fascism 2.0 (cf. an approach in my "To Explain"). The limited, though precious, "rule of people" looks now increasingly as a concession *ad evitanda mala maiora*, that is, to forestall by homeopathic doses the spectre of Leninist revolution, until the time when such concessions can be voided. The time arrived after seventy years, and what remains since is sterile shadowboxing on the surface, eyewash, and fossile façade. Therefore, as I have also argued elsewhere (say in "Prescience," *Lessons*, and *Communism*), the only antagonist to centennial Iron Heel and repristinator of true plebeian democracy for the associated producers can be a libertarian communism. Given the high level of our production forces, all that prevents social justice or even survival for uncounted millions of people are the <u>*relations of production*</u>, pivoting on labour and knowledge but reaching into all spheres of life. A remarkably stark example of this is the capitalocene and then the "covidisation" I address in the last two chapters of this book.

Narratologically this means for me that, in the stories by which we explain the world and ourselves, the primacy of linear plot is to be spurned – as most High Modernism already did and Brecht best explained. This primacy, the second superweapon of Hollywood and mass-media kitsch alongside the character as three-dimensional interiority, should suffer the invasion of Sartrean and Benjaminian (and Harawayan) <u>*situations*</u>, and wherever possible get submerged by them. There is no need to deny a red thread can come about somewhere, but it is not only more like a ball of yarn or amoeba rhizomatically reaching here and there, it is uncertain and open – after every situation a new one opens, for the collective if not for the individual (who ends in death). A "well-made" story on the contrary leads the reader-victim to believe there are only two plots, both Social Darwinist and mimetically transposable into empirical life: either the Great American Success Story (Horatio Alger) or its equally monochromatic obverse, gloom and murder (*The Game of Thrones*). Before our eyes, this has turned into a mega-lie and door opener to fascism in President Trump. Again it is Jameson, our Virgil among the gloomy shades, who has found the strategic formulation: instead of linear progressing, a train ride or air flight to known destinations, the truly new (the Novum) is by definition yet unknown, strange, and risky, while the prospects it opens may be uncertain or dangerous – like a love affair, a scientific investigation, or a new poem, all fallible probes into potentiality. As against fake bourgeois progress, "the 'new,' on the contrary, is an experience of the present" (Jameson 216), a rearranging of the complex Darwinian embankment rather than the exemplary self-willed arrow already arrested by Zeno. The new embankment or biome may produce new flowers, predators, or simply midden for coming generations, and for given interests it can be evaluated as progress or regress. But it is existentially itself – for the equanimous Ranke, every historical age was at the same distance from God.

True, there are momentous salvational exceptions, in which an age is nearer to the Benjaminian "divine" power because it harrows Hell. These are ages of *revolutions* that give, as Brecht said, the coolie several handfuls of rice per day instead of one and perhaps even a decent roof over his head and his family: but to do this, the wry Leninian added, he must destroy three empires. I had the historical privilege at the age of thirteen to briefly witness the fringes of one – the Titoist People's Liberation Struggle – on a sunny Dalmatian island. In my memoirs on that time, I cited the young Wordsworth's poem *French Revolution*:

> Oh! pleasant exercise of hope and joy!
> For mighty were the Auxiliars, which then stood
> Upon our side, we who were strong in love!
> Bliss was it in that dawn to be alive,
> But to be young was very heaven! . . .
> - - - - - - - - - - - - - -
> Not in Utopia, subterraneous Fields,
> Or some secreted Island, heaven knows where!
> But in the very world, which is the world
> Of all of us, – the place where in the end
> We find our happiness, or not at all!

He was right.

P.S. Some Unavoidable Info, Acknowledgements, and Thanks

The title of this book arose from discussions with my late friend Dale Mullen, long ago, but alas not out of date. The major thanks for the whole of the text growing coherent go to the work and patience of Hugh O'Connell, without whom there would have been no book amid this coronisation, and any later one would have been much poorer. For the Introduction and a number of chapters I am very grateful for discussion with Fredric Jameson and much good counsel by Tom Moylan – also to Kasia Baran. I attempt to name people I'm thankful to for help and illumination in various chapters, as I also did in the original publications. They were many and I apologise if I've missed or slighted anybody. Of course opinions and mistakes are mine.

I have been worrying about epistemology – what is cognition/knowledge/understanding (*Erkenntnis*) or not, how can we know that, and what, we know – and its major importance, conscious or not, for any political stance ever since the later 1990s. Thus much more can be seen in the essays in my *DBH* (such as chapters 10, 12, 15, and especially 16), and also in "Horizons," "Approach," and some further ones; in this book it is acknowledged at the beginning of chapter 1, and often thereafter. As a part of this central worry, I return often to what may be knowledge or cognition or understanding. I regret not to have had time, energy, and money for a larger treatment, perhaps a book, on this.

On Semantic Hygiene Utopia is in this book used without a capital letter unless it refers to More's country and title. Antiutopia, a potent new beast intruding into all our brains, deserves to be treated most seriously, and thus loses its hyphen. Notably, instead of America, "USA" is used whenever that country and not the whole double continent is meant; furthermore – following complaints from Mexico through Grenada, Panama, and Nicaragua to Colombia, Bolivia, and Chile about the semantics of the Monroe Doctrine – "US," or a form like "US-based," is used as adjective instead of American wherever possible, since I did not have the courage to adopt the universal German usage of "US-American." Citations are, of course, left as found. All unattributed translations in this book are mine. I am apologetic about the number of self-references, a ploy to prevent many long essays from being much longer.

My editor suggested, and I agreed, that throughout this volume, references to Suvin's major works on SF and utopianism shall be abbreviated as the following:

MOSF = *Metamorphoses of Science Fiction: On the Poetics and History of a Literary Genre*
VSF = *Victorian Science Fiction in the UK: The Discourses of Knowledge and of Power*
Positions = *Positions and Presuppositions in Science Fiction*
DBH = *Defined by a Hollow: Essays on Utopia, Science Fiction, and Political Epistemology*

Works Referred To

Auerbach, Erich. "Philology and Weltliteratur." *Centennial R.* 13.1 (1969): 1–17.
Butler, Judith. *Precarious Life: The Powers of Mourning and Violence.* Verso, 2004.
Elgin, Catherine Z. *With Reference to Reference.* Hackett, 1982.
Fortini, Franco. *I confini della poesia.* Castelvecchi, 2015.
Fortini, Franco. *Saggi ed epigrammi.* Ed. L. Lenzini. Mondadori, 2003.
Gendlin, Eugene T. *A Changed Ground for Precise Cognition.* 2009, www.focusing.org/gendlin/pdf /gendlin_a_changed_ground_for_precise_cognition.pdf
Gendlin, Eugene T. "Thinking beyond Patterns: Body, Language, and Situations," in B. denOuden and M. Moen eds., *The Presence of Feeling in Thought.* P. Lang, 1991, 27–189, www.focusing.org/gendlin/docs/gol_ 2159.html.

Goodman, Nelson, and Catherine Z. Elgin. *Reconceptions in Philosophy and Other Arts and Sciences*. Hackett, 1988.

Jameson, Fredric. *The Benjamin Files*. Verso, 2020.

Prieto, L. J. *Pertinence et pratique*. Minuit, 1975.

Rancière, Jacques. *On the Shores of Politics*. Trans L. Heron. Verso, 1995.

Saint-Amour, Paul K. "Counterfactual States of America: On Parallel Worlds and Longing for the Law." Sept. 20, 2011, http://post45.org/2011/09/counterfactual-states-of-america-on-parallel-worlds-and-longing-for-the-law/#identifier_4_1063.

Scarry, Elaine. *Rule of Law, Misrule of Men*. MIT P, 2010.

Simmel, Georg. *Die Philosophie des Geldes*, 2nd ed. Suhrkamp, 1989.

Suvin, Darko. "An Approach to Epistemology, Literature, and the Poet's Politics." *Annual Review of the Faculty of Philosophy, University of Novi Sad* (2016): 421–40.

Suvin, Darko. "Can People Be (Re)Presented in Fiction?" (1988), rpt. in *Darko Suvin: A Life in Letters*. Ed. Ph. E. Wegner. Paradoxa, 2011, 53–72.

Suvin, Darko. *Communism, Poetry: Communicating Vessels*. Political Animal, 2020.

Suvin, Darko. "The Chronotope, Possible Worlds, and Narrativity," in J. Bessière ed., *Fiction—Narratologie—Texte—Genre: Proceedings of the International Comparative Literature Assn. XI Congress*. Lang, 1989, 2: 33–41.

Suvin, Darko. "To Explain Fascism Today." *Critique* [Glasgow] 45.3 (2017): 259–302.

Suvin, Darko. *Lessons from the Russian Revolution and Its Fallout*. Rosa Luxemburg Foundation Southeast Europe, 2017.

Suvin, Darko. "Levels of Narrative Agents," in C. Guillén ed., *Theory of Poetic Form: Proceedings of the International Comparative Literature Assn. X Congress*. Garland, 1985, 2: 227–32.

Suvin, Darko. "On the Horizons of Epistemology and Science (2008–09)," in his *In Leviathan's Belly*. Wildside P for Borgo P, 2011, 261–307.

Suvin, Darko. "On Metaphoricity and Narrativity in Fiction." *SubStance* no. 48 (1986): 51–67.

Suvin, Darko. "The Prescience of Lucio Magri." *Socialism and Democracy* 29.2 (2015): 91–8.

Williams, Raymond. *Marxism and Literature*. Oxford UP, 1977.

1

Kick-Off: An Introduction to Narrative Genres, with a View to SF (2007, 2020)

In memory of the writer and critic Stanisław Lem

Note 2020: This text was prepared as an Italian lecture for the doctoral studies at University of Roma II – Tor Vergata in early 2007, for which my thanks go to Andrea Gareffi and my long-time friend Daniela Guardamagna. Its function was to introduce the approach to SF as a literary genre taken from MOSF, which had arisen within a rich discussion on the status and importance of literary genres in the five main European languages, beginning with Lukács, Russian Formalism, and Propp. To my mind this culminated in works by Fredric Jameson, particularly in his Political Unconscious, but I was also very aware of the work and national context of, say, Eco and Vosskamp, and had oral discussions with all three colleagues; and I followed the raging French debates around Barthes and a plethora of other names at the time. Without this context, my position on SF lacks the necessary presuppositions for today's readers unfamiliar with my earlier work, even if I reuse in this book the opposition between the lay and mythical narration. I have now freely retranslated this back from the Italian, expanding the beginning.

1.0. On Epistemic Regimes

1.01. An epistemic regime within an artistic and/or scholarly discipline indicates the preconditions and framework of what understanding (knowledge, cognition) that discipline conveys how, and at least implicitly also what for and to whom; it always comes about within a more or less strict *institutional* framework. The epistemic practices in such disciplines follow norms for methods and procedures that are to be recognised as valid both for the practitioners and the users of the discipline.

To choose our path here, it is indispensable to reject the *monoalethists* (see my Introduction) who hold they have the Absolute Truth, even when it is the belief that relativism is absolute. A useful horizon and way beyond this bind would be an operative epistemological realism recognizing there are still some logical ways at least of defining untruth (Goodman & Elgin 136). All opinions are constructed and up to a point wrong or limited, but even so some are valid within given limits: this needs a sense of relevance or pertinence, impossible to detach from the situation and interests of the knowing collective subject (cf. Prieto). Some beliefs and orientations are much more wrong than others, and a belief in the absolute right is absolutely wrong.[1/]

I cannot survey here the shoreless ocean of narratology as a means of organising human time and meaning/s, on a par with metaphor (trope). Fredric Jameson, who has wrestled with narrative and brilliantly illuminated it throughout his opus, remarked discussing Ricoeur's *Time and Narrative*, that narrative is "a primary instance of the human mind," and that it powerfully intervenes into the human understanding of temporality (Jameson, *Valences* 486). I agree, even though we should beware of overweening linguistic imperialism – the embodied human imagination has a variety of means to apprehend meaning and time. Furthermore, narrative is inextricably bound up with the constitution of any kind of subject: an excellent proof by contraries being Althusser's definition of scientific discourse as obviously bereft of any explicit signifier designating subject (*Humanist* 49, cf. Jameson, *Allegory* XII, and Suvin "Horizons"). In the study of narrative and performance such methods and procedures are called *poetics*, with a nod to its first Euro-Mediterranean practitioner to exert an immense influence, Aristotle (for whom the term seems to have meant both how to create and how to understand a verbal work). Much expanding on the old Hellenic source, all matters of narration, visualisation, and theatricalisation can by now be taken to fall under poetics: and it is difficult to say what does not at least partly fall under it, since human lives are shot through and imaginatively oriented by narratives through which all of us, and especially those with power over mass communication, account for our and others' everyday lives (cf. Bowlby). As Kenneth Burke phrased it, "Literature [is] equipment for living" (293).

1.02. One ought philosophically to start with a general inquiry into *forms*, probably omnipresent in our lives but foregrounded and clearly analysable in the arts. The useful book by Caroline Levine focusses on the subdivisions of "Whole, Rhythm, Hierarchy, Network," but I would say that a first ineluctable articulation of *value-bearing shapes* would be into the syntagmatics and the paradigmatics, as pioneered in post-Saussurean linguistics. Paradigmatics is a synoptic view of the whole as based on articulating co-occurring entities, its model is "X and Y and Z"; while syntagmatics is about how the paradigm is gradually built up and manifested in a temporal flow actualising mutually exclusive choices, its model is "X or Y or Z". The relationship of paradigmatics to syntagmatics is spiral and passes through the narration's plot, itself reposing on the interaction of chronotopes (spacetimes) and agential systems changing in time. The central device of form seems to me a *boundary*, exemplified by the "empty" spaces that constitute words or by analogous beginnings and ends of, say, a line of poetry or a narrative text. A boundary determines what can be considered in its discussion or not, with the attendant train of borders, liminality, cross-overs, purity, and contamination. My identification of any form as bearing a (positive or negative) value, meaning or quality is axiomatic: humans organise their horizons and orientations around values of physical and psychic survival and enrichment. Since in any society more complex than a tribe there will be a number of competing values for different pursuits of different groups of people, a hierarchical organisation of values (as to which is more or less basic, central or supreme) is also unavoidable.

Within a formal boundary, there is always a reproducible arrangement of elements (existents and relationships), an organised – often institutionalised – ordering or patterning in paradigmatic ideal space and syntagmatic flowing time (cf. Levine 3 and passim). Chaos may sometimes be a bitter herb necessary to counteract ossification, but only if it issues in a new and more useful pattern, as a star is born from coalescing lumps of matter. Since all that we call politics is an ordering of power in human communities to achieve certain values as ends, no hierarchical inclusion/exclusion is bereft of politics. As I put it in a paper: form is always involved in epistemological politics; or, more or less but always, "forms constrain" (Levine 4). Last not least, form in literature (including its genres) is the only way allowing you to get at the meaning.

What is then *not* form? I would point to most situations in empirical life and very many in the lower reaches of arts that are chaotic, not fully fleshed out, in contention between dimly understood forces. Our lives are often poorly articulate, from hand to mouth, rife with Baconian idols.

Here I wish to approach a poetics of literary – or in fact of all narrative – genres.

1.1. Narrative Genres as Superindividual Entities

Traditionally, literary studies that want to liberate themselves from the initially necessary but insufficient fixation on The Text opt for the communicational trinity of Writer (or Author) -> Text (or Work) -> Reader (or User). Even if one is interested mainly or quite centrally in The Text, as a student of literature should be, Writer and – less clearly but powerfully – Reader contribute not only to its existence but also to its most intimate forms.

My *first axiom* is therefore that *cultural texts are* sometimes individual but *always also superindividual*. The concept of originality in the sense of being novel or newfound, even unique, arose as a critical term in Romanticism: it did not exist between Homer and Victor Hugo. It has been degenerating from the 20th Century on – on the one hand the age of massification, of world wars, and of movies, all hostile to individualism and autonomy, and on the other hand wedded to copyright and especially patent law, which is intimately bound up with the pulsating heart of capital, and slops over into art with the claim that only what is original can be interesting. Originality did not exist, for example, for Boccaccio, Chaucer, Shakespeare or Milton, all of whom worked recombining the existing literary *topoi* and forms (such as genres). All of them followed the general maxim *non nova sed nove* (not new matter but in new ways). Historically clearest is perhaps the tradition of the epic poem in verse, from Homer through Virgil by way of Dante and Milton, and then on to Fielding – who transformed it, as he wrote semi-ironically in his preface to *Joseph Andrews*, into "a comic epic in prose" and to Byron's *Childe Harold*.

The most fertile way to talk about the superindividual or collective (group) aspects of texts seems to me to approach them inside genres – though when we talk of an individual text or smaller grouping of texts, it is indispensable to consider also its particular characteristics. I adopt here Jameson's approach to genres as mediations between the formal analysis of texts and their history in social life: "Genres are essentially literary institutions, or social contracts between a writer and a specific public, whose function is to specify the proper use of a particular cultural artifact." (*Political* 106). Therefore, before being explicated as classificatory devices used by literary critics to orient themselves, literary genres are spontaneously and necessarily generated inside fiction as an implied contract with the reader. Ursula Le Guin put it with luminous precision: "If fiction is how it says what it says, then useful criticism is what shows you how fiction says what it says" (23).

I am forced to swat a noxious Summer fly here: the Post-Modern *a priori* refusal of genre, very fashionable in the 1970s–90s (cf. the able critique of Derrida and early Culler by Bolongaro 302–03). If genres are institutionalized and convention-bound vehicles of communication so that the necessary process of cognition could take place (ibidem 304–05), then literature is, as Guillén named it, a "system of genres," changing with and within the concrete historical hegemony of the period. This leads to two clarifications: first, to a welcome relativising of what I shall continue to develop here in view of the overriding usefulness of genre in many (not all) cases. Genre "is not a law, a rigid taxonomic landscape"; as Dimock concludes, genre is "a provisional set, that will always be bent and pulled and stretched by its many subsets," in brief a more or less quickly changing "family" (73–74) – with Wittgensteinian family resemblances, eccentrics, black sheep, and pillars of righteousness (I discussed a case at length in an essay unwillingly split into "Against" and "Synchrony").

Second, it leads to the motor and evidence of both stability and change, societal history. Genre was first discussed in the European tradition by Plato and Aristotle, revived in the Renaissance. At times of political absolutism subject to rigid laws, as in Baroque, the official genre system could and did degenerate to "a clearly delineated model in which not only an obligatory complex of subject-matters, motifs, and agents, not only an obligatory diction and technique, but also a prescribed world-image and a prescribed thought-content fit together so that none of these components was displaceable or replaceable" (Alewyn 22). Predictably, oppression and monotony were rife, finally leading to a breakdown and to the equally stultifying theoretical reaction in the notion of individual "genius." However, this process also gave rise to a technical critical problem: in much more complex societies that ensued with the rise of the bourgeoisie and capitalism, describing such a system proved very onerous for a single critic because it could only be based on a large range of texts subjected to induction. Thus despite very valiant critical pioneers, say Lukács for the novel in general and the historical novel in particular (maybe also for the 19th-Century realistic novel), and then Propp and the Russian Formalists on various generic morphologies and aspects beginning with the folktale, arguing about all-encompassing systems became practically prohibitive. Most 20th-Century attempts were either programmatically ahistorical, such as much French work, or confined themselves to either a useful but vague general sketch and/or (more often) a focus on one or a small group of cognate genres – certainly mine too have done so, with the dichotomy between estranged and naturalistic genres plus focus on a few estranged ones around the center of Science Fiction. What the current I learned most from concluded was that a genre had no transhistorical essence, much less a template in some (human) organic body of which it would be a constitutive member; it is more akin to a biotope, or even an ecological niche that is constituted by all interactions with other entities, than to a biological genre of animals or plants. Biotope or family is a cognitive metaphor implying that genre is a living – that is, changeable – entity.

1.2. What Is a Genre: Horizons of Epistemological Expectation

The term comes from the Latin *genus*, meaning a kind or a sort: it is a classifying term that subsumes an entity under a higher universal notion, of which it becomes a species, and implies there are further such subsumable species. In terms of a psychology of cultural production and usage, it is an implicit contract between authors, readers, and their mediators (publishers, media, commentators, etc.) as to which expectations of a text may be permissible – sometimes indeed prescribed – or impermissible. In theory this is often called *vraisemblance* or verisimilarity, in other words which events and existents are believable or not. The famous SF example "The door irised open" (Robert Heinlein, 1942) meant for the original reader and author that we are in another spacetime, for no door known at that time opened as the iris diaphragm of the eye or of the camera, that is, by widening a central opening toward the periphery. Thus after such a positioning phrase, it is licit to expect that we could be in an SF text and that other deviations from the reader's Zero World or accepted normality would follow, while it is illicit to say that no such doors exist and the text is therefore simple nonsense (though if it were verse, it could be part of the "nonsense" poetry of Edward Lear). Or: an angel is normal in Milton but in Wells's "The Wonderful Visit" it must permit the suspicion that it is an alien species. In the two writers, different epistemological norms obtain: theological or religious in the first, biological or scientific in the second one. To generalize, narratives are strategies based on an attitude – Brecht's "bearing" (cf. Suvin "*Haltung*") – for dealing with interhuman situations by strategic naming and other devices (Burke 296–97 and 300); a foremost form for and in such strategies is *genre, a situational entity*. Within it, transplants from empirical ideology onto poetics and vice versa are rife, beginning with power and value hierarchies of race, gender, and class.

As already argued, a cultural contract is not an "iron" or natural law, rather it is similar to a dress code, which may be easily varied but as a rule only within clear limits of expectation. Such *horizons of expectation* (Jauss), inly interfusing textual and extratextual – for example moral – norms, delimit and make intelligible both the compliance and the deviance from the implied system of norms – say, Shakespeare's Dark Lady as compared to the Petrarchist Laura ("If snow be white, why then her breasts are dun"). In precapitalist societies, the dressing code was rigidly tied to class, gender, and age, and legally enforced; today it is less strict, but try to come naked to your university class and you'll learn it is not non-existent. Then try to shave your head if a female or to put on a skirt if you are a non-Scottish male, and you'll see that extra-legal sanctions may ensue. Literature is milder, yet unforgiving: your sanction for mistaking the coding or genre will be that the text you wanted to read has become unintelligible, impossible to understand. No doubt, texts may, and in SF often do, work with multiple codes, taken not only from different sub-genres but also from different genres, such as the noir and/or heist thriller ones in Gibson's *Neuromancer*, often switching to a collage of "generic discontinuities" in Aldiss's *Nonstop/Starship*, modulating from the exotic adventure story through "collective catastrophe" and finally "political fable" type of story (Jameson, *Archeologies* 258–63).

A classification presupposes a system with vertical and horizontal elements. Vertical or *subordinate* elements are either historically narrower cultural forms called sub-genres (for example the epithalamium – a poem celebrating a marriage, the drawing-room comedy, the horror fantasy) or single texts; horizontal or *coordinate* elements are other genres, or single texts and sub-groups within a genre when looked at in their differences. There exist also *superordinate* elements, usually called modes, which are in the Mediterranean-cum-European tradition classically the epic, the lyric, and the theatre play. As codified by this tradition, the modes are differentiated by focusing on who is talking (the narrating pronoun, so to speak) and who is being talked to: the *epos* should be narrated in the third person and the lyrical poem in the first person and they both talk to absent users (readers), while the theatre play or drama – divided in Athens into clear genres of comedy, tragedy, and satyr-plays – talks to present users. To these parameters of slower times, Goethe and Schiller began to add a new and most significant one, *time*: the epic talks of matters past, the drama of those present; rather puzzling for two major poets, the lyric's relation to time is left out (an eternal present?). In China meanwhile, the classification was wider, not divided into factual and imaginary, and of an overtly moral-cum-political kind: it stressed how much a genre can teach us about people living together. On the scale of this value, the highest genre is philosophical writings (by Kong Fu or Lao Tse), then historiography, then verse poetry: while prose, first stories and then novels, was derisively called "small talk" (*xiao shuo*). Similarly, in all theocratic societies, as in the Euro-mediterranean Middle Ages, THE one sacred Text was the Tanakh or the Bible or the Qur'an, with a huge comet trail of comments of various statuses, and all the rest are either small talk or even noxious – the theocrats rightly see in non-canonical "fictions" potential perils for their doctrine. All these generic norms, as well as their superordinated level, are determined by ideologico-political history: the European theatre was played during at least eight centuries without a fixed script, while in post-Renaissance Europe the rising complexity, diversity, and thisworldly orientation brought about written "epic" prose such as the *novella* (short story), drama, and the novel. Here should follow two long and intertwining discourses about the axes of "written vs. oral genres" and "socio-politically high or noble *vs.* low or vulgar genres," which I must omit.

My *second axiom* is that genres – also modes and other classifications – are literary institutions modelled by social history (cf. Vosskamp): regulatory but competitive and flexible possibilities for using generic types, which then in practice commingle and allow for all kinds of "impurities." Genres are obviously manifested or happen within human societal history, produced and received in it, but my point is stronger: it poses that there do not exist ahistorical essences of genre/s, descending from the heights of Plato's hyperuranian ideas or ascending from an ahistorical biopsychic subconscious. Genres are born, developed, and die not only *within* history but also *because of* history, or perhaps better: as an *intimate component part of history*, in feedback with all other components.

The aims and therefore the forms of a genre are historical models. It follows that genres – and any text belongs in a genre, even if one may be so dominant that it is not felt as a genre any more – exist in a tension between two types of fidelity or *pietas*: to masterpieces and models of the past, and to the needs, values, and so on, of the contemporary world that the Author wishes to share with the Reader (cf. Suvin "Synchrony").

1.3. Genre Criticism Is Sociohistorical

There is a difficulty, almost an *aporia*, in defining literary genres. One begins with prototypes, undoubted or typical examples, such as Homer and Virgil for the *epos*. Norms are induced from these exemplary works: heroic plot dealing with violent aristocratic politics, intervention of gods, division into cantos, and so on. Then one investigates Ariosto and says: but he introduces comicality, he stresses elements from the pastoral (love) instead of politics, etc.; this is popular with readers and admired by critics, therefore we must allow for a new such-and-such sub-genre of epic poem. Yet if we had right from the beginning started with norms that dispense with heroes, that is from the *Batrachomyomachia* (the Hellenic comic epic on the Battle of Frogs and Mice) and established that *epos* is comical and possibly anti-aristocratic – as quite probably much of the lost oral literature of the ruled classes was – then we should have said instead that Homer and Virgil are the serious sub-genre of the epic poem that is largely comical (and we could then cite Ariosto, Fielding, and Byron in support). We do not say so mainly because Homer and Virgil are much more famous, known, and esteemed within the agenda of a bellicose patriarchal upper-class. Not only are, as Marx precisely remarked in *The German Ideology*, the ideas of the ruling class the ruling ideas (on the whole); furthermore, successive ruling classes have as a rule admired their predecessors' glory in a kind of transhistorical solidarity of rulers. Formally, the two opposed classificatory norms are equivalent; therefore our reason for accepting Homer and Virgil as norm is mainly "doxic," that is, what is taken for self-evident in the ruling opinion and consensus (cf. Bourdieu, both titles). We might wish to use the criterium of historical priority, for after some doubt it is today accepted that the *Batrachomyomachia* is a very late parody of Homer, but before the 19th Century historical criteria were not considered weighty and were not used in the *doxa* – and I think ancestry remains insufficient for a full value judgment.

1.4. Genre Criticism Develops within Ideologico-Political Horizons

This subtitle does not mean that all of genre criticism is simply ideologico-political, far from it (especially if "ideology" is taken as a swearword). I cannot enter into theoretical refinements here, either dealt with or implied in the rest of the book, but shall try to clarify what I mean by means of SF examples.

Here too one begins with undoubted exemplars such as H.G. Wells, and maybe some E.A. Poe and some Jules Verne. Then a critic says: but the exemplary ancestor of SF is for me Mary Shelley's *Frankenstein*, therefore SF is a "black Gothic" or awful warning genre about incarnated horrible possibilities. Since he (Brian Aldiss) can not only point to many SF texts that are undoubtedly such but also centrally draws this axiomatic conviction from the fact that he writes SF of a Gothic or dark kind, we are in a vicious circle. Instead, I prefer to say that the exemplary ancestors of SF are, together with Wells's *Time Machine*, Thomas More's *Utopia* and parts of Swift's *Gulliver's Travels*, joined by the great dystopian warning of Evgeniy Zamyatin's *We*. Thus I see SF as situated between the utopic and dystopic, rosy and black, horizons, and dealing with forms of human (or psychozoic) living together that are radically better or worse than those in the author's spacetime or Zero World. For me, SF is a genre that is directly or indirectly about political cognitions or understanding in the Aristotelian sense of politics as affairs of human community or social organization of life. I take such axiomatic conviction from my general, extra-literary horizons. Are we in this case too in a vicious circle?

Two matters seem to me here of importance. *First*, Aldiss and I agree in many matters, such as which texts should be used in a history of the genre: at least 80% of such a set would be identical for both of us. We would both exclude on the one hand Tolkienian or "Conanian" hero-fantasy writings and movies, the horror stories from E.T.A. Hoffmann, Poe, and Lovecraft up to zombies, and classical folktales and fairy tales; and on the other hand the "mainstream" naturalistic prose from *Don Quixote* through Stendhal and Tolstoy to detective and love stories. Both of us say – perhaps I do so more openly – that underneath the SF surface, dear reader, *mutato nomine de te fabula narrator* (change such naming and the story is about thee). We both agree that the plot can very well be taken from adventure stories, but that restricting it only to Western-type fights with laser guns and aliens substituting for six-shooters and American Indians leads to inferior SF, even if perhaps usable when you're twelve or desperately trying to kill time in an airport waiting for cancelled flights. Aldiss and I can thus have a potentially fertile disagreement about which sub-set of our set is privileged. Furthermore, both of us would use the same methods of arguing: delve into the structure of our models, Mary Shelley or More-Wells-Zamyatin, trace its effect for latter SF, and so forth.

But then, *second*, no decision can be arrived at without a value judgment which aspect to prefer, the thrill of estranging horror in Aldiss, or the hope, despair, and wrath founded on new horizons (better or worse) for our common life in Suvin. This partakes of a double and complex *evaluation*, empirical and cognitive. Sociometrically, which aspect pleases more strongly and pleases a greater number of people in space and time? Axiologically, which aspect furthers more profoundly and quickly the hominisation of humans or if you prefer the disalienation – that cannot but be anti-capitalist? Both evaluations are relevant but to my mind the second one is decisive: for, as Kant told us, 1000 years of something being so (for example, the taste for heroic killing) doesn't make it right. And any value-judgment reposes also upon desires and fears of the evaluator. Alas, there is no evaluation outside of huge ideologico-political flows that make the evaluator what s/he is. The only thing the evaluator can do to mitigate distortion is to be self-critically aware of this very fact, and be ready to be in turn judged for her/his judgments.

1.5. What Genre Does Not Do

Within any genre we shall always find more or less famous texts, whose reception career has lasted from immediate oblivion (a "dud") to centuries: in the "psychological novel," for example, the spectrum goes from nurse romances to works by Dickens, Balzac, Dostoevsky, Proust or Joyce. Genre criticism can, I strongly believe, take its criteria only by induction from the best texts, in order to explain why a majority of other texts are inferior and should not be bothered with either in histories or in poetics; this is as necessary in cognition, that heavenly food, as digestion and excretion is in earthly food: "Let us then be severe in our judgments; let us compare each book with the greatest of its kind" (Woolf 204). Such criteria – inherent to most narration – are technical such as coherence and clarity, or thematic such as richness, or "mimetic," translated from the common Zero World, or ideally all three in interaction (as in my negative example of SF modelled upon the Western). But I have found no convincing esthetic or moral-cum-political grading of genres: that is, why should the psychological novel be in itself a genre superior from the adventure story or SF? This "distinction" (Bourdieu) no doubt exists but it is based on social prestige and pedagogic usefulness, about which differing critical schools will have differing opinions in time and space. It is of course possible to say, as I would for the parallel between SF and Fantasy, that the *maximum potentials* of SF are much higher, as I argue in the essay on Le Guin's *Earthsea*, but it is not possible to foresee whether a particular SF text will be "better" than that trilogy or than Tolkien.

2. Genres in Relation to Classes or Other Power Groupings

Before the sway of capitalism, it was clear to everybody that literary genres are connected to social classes, as a rule also in different idioms, dialects or languages. The nobles read or listened to stories of King Arthur and his knights, the peasants sang traditional work or faith chants, the clerics read and wrote in Latin. The English and French novels were written by, about, and for the rising bourgeois or burgher class, as was the Boccaccian *novella*, which however already exhibited a yearning for superior-class nobility. Satire has always been a favourite of oppositional classes or fractions, as in the "Red Tory" Swift's opposition to the Whigs. There have been few examples of multivalent genres addressing themselves to several social classes, of which the best known one may be Elizabethan theatre performances whose spectators comprised most London classes from the apprentices and similar groundlings to the queen, or Italian Neo-realist cinema addressed to the antifascist block. As a rule, such breadth made for great strengths and interest, but also for strict confinement to the moment of the historical block that was the genre's addressee.

Within capitalist mass society matters get more complex, since a commodity ought to be sold to the maximum number of customers, those financial atoms of the market mega-colloid. Yet since not all commodities are for all tastes (even if all tastes are to be admitted to the market except those that want to abolish the market), niches of ideological sub-sets arose. As I discuss in "For a Social," SF is being read, in those Northern countries of the globe where bourgeois legality geared to consumption and bourgeois technology went hand in hand, mostly by the younger members of the so-called middle class aged ca. 12 to 30, that is, until their full entry in the world of paid work; they were traditionally male, but with the rise of first-class feminist readers and writers they were by the 1980s already one-third female. To clarify their status, it is important that in 1961–74 a majority had an educational level and an income superior, even two or three times, to that of the average US citizen, and furthermore that they considered themselves, rightly or wrongly, to be a rising group and had confidence in their path to success. Obversely, manual workers, "racial" and ethnic minorities, and the rural population were (together with women) highly underrepresented among US SF readers. After the torpedoing of the Welfare State by the rulers in favour of a smaller and "flexible" workforce, Heroic and Horror Fantasy came to predominate, reflecting the new Social-Darwinist ideological hegemony; by the end of the 20th Century Fantasy literature had overtaken SF in a 2:1 ratio that went constantly rising, especially in movies and TV. Interestingly enough, Fantasy was always strongly characteristic of the comics, which to my mind indicates a huge infantilisation of the adult readers in the last half century.

The classical SF fans thus belonged in this golden ca. 1935–75 period to the upwardly mobile layer of the US socioeconomical pyramid middle, best defined as the professional-managerial class, and were a congeries of class fractions within that layer. They were as a rule in the tertiary or "service" sector of production that includes the media, education (teachers and students), and working women. This intermediary position opened the door in US SF both to a coexistence of ideological extremes, the clearest example being permanent militarism vs. antimilitarism, and to rapid ideological shifts. After the mid-70s, it led to an abrupt change of dominant orientation from the strongly oppositional tendency of most top writers in 1961–74 to conformism and privatisation, and for about one-third of SF to an exaltation of militarism (cf. "Starship," chapter 9 in this book). At the same time, the acceptance of SF in mainstream discourse encouraged some leading writers (as Heinlein) to angle for the best-seller audience or movie rights at the expense of the more sophisticated readers. Quality SF is in Post-Modernism in a pincer grip between militarism, favoured by Right-wing funding, and the rise of Fantasy – in brief, between a savage crypto-rationalism and irrationalism, between a corrupt historical cognition and the refusal of any historical cognition.

The fans of Fantasy's *ahistorical worlds* (as best as one can understand them in the absence of further studies – see "Considering" in this book) may be mainly young people from the above sketched "middle" classes, usually below the age of 30–40 and again mainly male, who do not have full and permanent employment any more in savage capitalism and realistically don't see that changing in their lifetime. As in the earlier phases, many of them have frequented the university, but this no longer guarantees an entry into the professional-managerial class; many seem to be, whatever their diplomas or lack of them, already part of the "de-scholarised" generation – at any rate the quality of their education is obviously inferior, both as concerns the scientific method and the civic knowledge of humanities, to the Fordist or Modernist period. As suggested above, SF was in feedback with social groups that believed a collective historical future could be worked for – if largely but not only (see my essays on SF in *DBH*, especially the one on Le Guin's *The Dispossessed*) in the guise of terrible warnings by contraries. This often implied a comfortable relationship to technoscience, reaching sometimes for a real alliance with or even a commitment to it. To the contrary, Fantasy attracts uncertain and drifting social fractions that face their own present with horror or with the resolve to make hay while the sun still shines and the Deluge is only knocking on the door – or by fusing both these attitudes; as to the future, it has been abolished. Therefore the epistemology of SF can reach for the cognitive universalism of natural and/or societal laws, however renovated, while the individualist and pluralist epistemology of Fantasy recurs to occultism, whimsy or magic to oppose the SF model while leaning on it.

3. A Door Opening

To conclude: the conceptual universe of this book (and of my previous work) takes it as a key strategic given, as I formulated it in 1973, "that there exist literary genres … as socioesthetic entities; that they have an inner life and logic of their own, which do not exclude but on the contrary presuppose a dialectical permeability to themes, attitudes, and paradigms from other literary genres, science, philosophy, and everyday socioeconomic life…" (*MOSF* 29). Thus I was proposing a heuristic model for SF, namely a theoretical entity reposing on analogy, "whose use is … permissible, desirable, and necessary because of its practical results" (ibidem 30).

Form is then the strategic royal road to both understand and explain a text. Within emplotted narrative fiction, I concluded further in that book, SF is a genre whose necessary and sufficient conditions are *the presence and interaction of estrangement and cognition*, and whose main formal procedure is *an imaginary frame or Possible World alternative to the author's empirical world*.

To this I wish to add here two suggestions as signposts:

First: in 2014 for an electronic reprint of my "Estrangement and Cognition" (see "Postscript"), I added a longish explanation sharpening the focus. Namely: in the present class-war tsunami from above, it ought to be foregrounded that *what is* cognition (and in particular the defining factor of SF, the novum) cannot be answered in a vacuum but only within an explicated value system wedded to the labouring, exploited, and dominated classes – that is: *from their standpoint*, as guessed at by the critic. The values of humanity as a whole are by now represented only by them.

Second: a Possible World is a provisional notional totality with a defined spacetime or chronotope entailing existents and agents as well as relationships between all of these – all else is open. Rather than pertaining to logic à la Kripke or the rigid semiotics that follow logics à la Eco, a useful Possible World is epistemological: modelled on our historical world (that is, on dominant conceptions thereof, on its imaginary encyclopedia) yet significantly different from it. The possible cognitive increment lies in the difference and its applicability, direct or very indirect, to our common world. All art and all planning deals implicitly with Possible Worlds. This is foregrounded for example in Science Fiction or Five-Year Plans. It is the *raison d'être* for utopias of all kinds. It also hinges on differentiating within the concept of the novum (see further in chapter 6 and at length in chapter 20).

A Possible World must explain to the reader any significant deviation from his/her/our current encyclopedia as coherent; it is believable and esthetically successful in precise relation to how clearly and fully it manages this explanation. However, it contains in principle no guarantees of success – or failure – for the agents and actions in it: you commit yourself and then see, said Napoleon (*on s'engage et puis on voit*). Some variants may have inbuilt felicific rules (for example fairy-tales or Sun-hero myths à la St. George, or official optimism about a plan); some may have inbuilt horrific rules (for example Horror Fantasy after Poe and Lovecraft, much Kafka, apocalyptic pessimism, Orwell's *1984*), but these are protocols superadded to its fundamental neutrality. These protocols are therefore special cases, very limited in epistemic relevance and spacetime applicability. The wholly rosy and wholly bleak horizons can still be used as suggestive hyperbolae, first, for extreme situations (when they may be extremely relevant), and second, for propedeutic exaggeration in various other limited situations.

Third: once we agree on something like the above baseline, we would have to use further tools when talking about any particular text, to begin with the narratives, forms or sub-genres brilliantly opened for discussion by Jameson in *Archaeologies* (256–57 and 259–61).

From this grounding in literary genres and Possible Worlds, I hope the reader can understand better how and why I am approaching the matters in other essays, at a level usually nearer to empirical history.

Works Cited

Aldiss, Brian. *Billion Year Spree*. Weidenfeld & Nicolson, 1973.

Alewyn, Richard. "Der Roman des Barock," in H. Steffen ed., *Formkräfte der deutschen Dichtung vom Barock bis zur Gegenwart*. Vandenhoeck & Ruprecht, 1963, 21–34.

Althusser, Louis. *The Humanist Controversy and Other Texts*. Ed. F. Matheron, trans. G.M. Goshgarian. Verso, 2003.

Bolongaro, Eugenio. "From Literariness to Genre." *Genre* Summer/Fall (1992): 277–311.

Bourdieu, Pierre. *La Distinction*. Minuit, 1979.

Bourdieu, Pierre. *Outline of a Theory of Practice*. Trans. R. Nice. Cambridge UP, 1977.

Bowlby, Rachel. *Everyday Stories*. Oxford UP, 2016.

Burke, Kenneth. *The Philosophy of Literary Form*, 3d edn. U of California P, 1973.

Culler, Jonathan. "Toward a Theory of Non-Genre Literature," in R. Federman ed., *Surfiction*. Swallow, 1974, 255–62.

Derrida, Jacques. "The Law of Genre," in his *Acts of Literature*. Ed. D. Attridge, trans. A. Ronell. Routledge, 1992, 221–52 [original 1979].

Dimock, Wai Chee. *Through Other Continents*. Princeton UP, 2015.

Eco, Umberto. *Lector in fabula*. Bompiani, 1979 [*The Role of the Reader*. Indiana UP, 1979].

Goodman, Nelson, and Catherine Z. Elgin. *Reconceptions in Philosophy and Other Arts and Sciences*. Hackett, 1988.

Jameson, Fredric. *Allegory and Ideology*. Verso, 2019.

Jameson, Fredric. *Archaeologies of the Future*. Verso, 2005.

Jameson, Fredric. *The Political Unconscious*. Cornell UP, 1981.

Jameson, Fredric. *Valences of the Dialectic*. Verso, 2009.

Guillén, Claudio. *Literature as a System*. Princeton UP, 1971.

Le Guin, Ursula K. *Words Are My Matter*. Small Beer P, 2016.

Levine, Caroline. *Forms: Whole, Rhythm, Hierarchy, Network*. Princeton UP, 2015.

Marx, Karl. *The German Ideology*. www.marxists.org/archive/marx/works/1845/german-ideology/ch01b.htm

Prieto, L.J. *Pertinence et pratique*. Minuit, 1975.

Suvin, Darko. "Against Originals: *honkadori* and the Horizons of Pastiche," in P. Mildonian ed., *Parodia, pastiche, mimetismo*. Bulzoni, 1997, 65–80.

Suvin, Darko. *Defined by a Hollow: Essays on Utopia, Science Fiction, and Political Epistemology*. P. Lang, 2010.

Suvin, Darko. "*Haltung* (Bearing) and Emotions: Brecht's Refunctioning of Conservative Metaphors for Agency," in T. Jung ed., *Zweifel - Fragen - Vorschläge*. Lang V, 1999, 43–58.

Suvin, Darko. *Metamorphoses of Science Fiction*, 2nd enlarged edn. Ed. G. Canavan. P. Lang, 2016.

Suvin, Darko. *Positions and Presuppositions in Science Fiction*. Macmillan and Kent State UP, 1988.

Suvin, Darko. "Postscript (2014)" [to rpt. of "Estrangement and Cognition"]. http://strangehorizons.com/non-fiction/articles/estrangement-and-cognition/

Suvin, Darko. "For a Social Theory of Science Fiction: Programmatic Reflections" (forthcoming in my *Parables of Freedom and Narrative Logics*, ed. E.D. Smith, P. Lang).

Suvin, Darko. "Synchrony as Aim and Reference: A Thesis on Parody's Horizons." *Canadian R of Comparative Lit.* 23.2 (1996): 475–83.

Vosskamp, Wilhelm. "Gattungen als literarisch-soziale Institutionen," in W. Hinck ed., *Textsortenlehre - Gattungsgeschichte*. Winter, 1977, 27–44.

Woolf, Virginia *The Second Common Reader*. Penguin, 1944.

2

Fantasy as Critique and Cognition: Marx's Black Metamorphoses of Living Labour (1999–2003)

Note 2020: *This piece has been slightly added to, and the works cited updated.*

1. Introductory

1.1. The following leans on previous writings of mine that explore two axioms: a/ that the insight of Karl Marx is indispensable to avoid catastrophe for humanity; b/ that this insight is best understood as being constituted by a fusion of three domains and horizons: *cognition*, *freedom*, *and pleasure*, with a set of regulative principles and a focus applying them to the determining factor of capitalist and any post-capitalist life: work, or better *living labour*. I shall in this excerpt talk only about one aspect of this focus: that the mortification of living labour, effected by trading creativity for alienation, leads with accelerating speed to personal and collective death. This is why both Marx and his predecessor Fourier feel it as a monstrous world of upside-down relationships and end up in a radical refusal; but it is also why they largely must talk about it, intertwining precise analysis of their contemporary life and labour with fantastic imagery: Fourier within the horizon of utopian projections, Marx within the horizon of horror fantasy.

1.2. Before getting into my analysis proper, I wish to discuss some of its methodological presuppositions relating to *cognition or understanding*, a quite central domain in Marx. This is for him on the one hand science but on the other hand integral human practice. I've argued in three earlier essays ("Transubstantiation," "Utopian," and "What") how *Wissenschaft* or knowledge was in German subsumed by Kant to mean a systematic body of cognition with a proper correlation of principles and consequences. Now, on pain of having no transmittable knowledge, scientific or other, we cannot do without systems in the sense of articulated wholes or provisional totalities organised according to an overarching method; yet only dynamically equilibrated systems, with a deniable and thus changeable rather than closed history can today be defended. Therefore, we may still wish (I would) to retain the methods and name of science for strictly articulated and formalised cognition, as opposed to what Aristotle called "opinion" (*doxa*). But this can be rescued from the present dominant use of science as a death-dealing variant of absolutist belief, enslaved to capitalist profit, only if it gets into continual feedback with values and interests from human practice. Science is nothing without humanity: as Gramsci remarked, whether the universe would exist in the absence of humanity is for us (today) an empty question.

It is possible to find in Marx an oscillation between, on the one hand, the constantly changing inductions from *praxis*, which then necessarily and prominently employ metaphoric clusters as an indispensable cognitive tool, and on the other hand the institutionalised science of his time which proceeds through fixed ("iron") laws. But usually, and especially in all of his depth analyses such as those in the *Grundrisse* which I shall be using here (further as G with page number), his dialectic does not use the pain of the antithesis – the blood, sweat, and tears of what he called "the wrong side of history" – as a rhetorical ploy on the order of a double negation necessarily ending in the victory of the good synthesis, that is, in a Hegelian *theodicea* (justification of Providence). Contrary to an illustration of pre-existing speculative schemes, Marx envisages an open-ended process and stresses the unforeseen ruses of history. If history is necessarily a dialectic of free vs. unfree self-creation through struggles of societal classes and fractions, which is since the rise of capital centered on the existential tug-of-war of living labour versus commodification and fetishism, then it has no end – but untold catastrophes and triumphs: Rosa Luxemburg's "socialism or barbarism."

2. Fourier

2.1. The Absolute Swerve

Marx's argument oscillates between his 19th-Century urge toward Newtonian scientificity and a cognition in no way bound by those "positive" parameters, but instead inextricably fused with visionary or poetic elements (which are not irrational but supply what conceptual reason has yet no instruments for). He thereby recognizes that both philosophy and science begin by transforming practice into allegorical personifications and then micro-metaphors, and end in one vast macro-metaphor (which is, for example, Wiener's definition of mathematics). Neither can reflect upon itself unless each recognises how deeply consubstantial it is to poetry: Eros turns into Newton's attraction, geometry into gravitational fields, the wayfarers' horizon into Einstein's relativities. Thus, in order to understand Marx properly, the strengths of his greatest precursor and complement, Charles Fourier, have to be factored in.

Fourier's major strength is to have responded to the system of bourgeois "industry" (which for him means artisanal work and commerce) by an "absolute swerve" (*écart absolu*) based on the pleasure principle as a totalising horizon that is both personally sensual and socially combinatory. His major weakness is that he did not understand revolutions, industrial or political; but he grasped supremely well their consequences.

Fourier judged "civilization" (class society, in particular bourgeois commercialism) to be, in a popular image, a "world upside down."[1] In it, the lawyer has to wish for "good lawsuits," the physician for a "good fever," the officer for "good wars, that killed half of his colleagues," the priest for the "good dead, that is, funerals at one thousand francs apiece," the monopolist for a "good famine, which doubled or tripled the price of bread," the wine merchant for "good frosts," and the builders for "a good conflagration to consume a hundred houses and further their trade" (*Théorie* I: xxxvi); family means adultery, riches mean bankruptcy, work is constraint, property ruins the proprietor, abundance leads to unemployment, and the machine to hunger. There is no reforming this ridiculous and pernicious set-up except by a new set-up, the harmonious association based on passionate attractions among people. The absolute deviation or swerve is the necessity to turn once more upside down the deadly social world in order to make it livable.

2.2. Passionate Attraction and Groups

People are by ineradicable nature bundles of passions for Fourier, which can only be steered and organised. The central problem of bourgeois individualism was how to shape a community which would, as Rousseau put it, protect the person and goods of each without making him obey anybody but himself. Fourier's politics are a radical quest for sensual happiness for one and all. He starts from enlightened egotism and aims for a society where the individual can only find his benefit through operations profitable to the whole collectivity; he calls this new regime of free association the Phalanstery. As in the 18th-Century sensual materialism, passionate attraction or appetite is a universal principle, and Fourier extends it from Newton's matter to the other three worlds of plant, animal, and social life. People and their passions are not equal but varied yet complementary. Therefore, their appetites, primarily sexual and gustatory, are in Phalanstery fully developed and harmonised by composing them into series where *groupings* of people (by sex and age) are, by an intricate and even maniacal system of idiosyncratic analogies, composed into a "calculus of Destinies."

The mainstream of Medieval European thought reposed on a dumbbell duality of individual vs. collective, called "soul" and "Church." The nascent competitive bourgeoisie lopped off the repressive and stifling representative of the collective human interests and was left with systematic individualism, communicating through gains or losses in the market, which Fourier tellingly stigmatised as an unending series of crises. This huge impoverishment was countered by Fourier's insistence on the group where various interests can be dynamically harmonised – as prior and opposed to the nuclear family and (later) to mega-groups stifling individuality as lay churches: the rising classes as enemy armies, and their eventual spearheads in parties, foregrounded in Fascism and Stalinism (cf. Jameson, *Allegory* 196 and *Archaeologies* 242–43 and 245–53). "Human individuals are biologically incomplete [so that] the intelligible human unit … [is] the larger group … assur[ing] their survival, and indeed their reproduction" (*Allegory* 213). Utter diversity of passions, emblematised in the supreme "butterfly" one, is thus in Fourier not only accepted but joyously identified as indispensable for their gratification.

This extends to the future and the universe: from the 18 different creations on Earth, ours is the first and worst, having to go through five horrible stages from Savagery down to

Civilization, before ascending through Guarantism (the economico-sexual welfare state of the federated *phalanstères*) to Harmony. At that point there will be no more sexual or economic repression, hunger, war, States, nations, illnesses or struggle for existence. Most important for Marx, there will also be no split between intellectual and manual labour, or labour and "leisure" (see *Critique of the Gotha Programme*, and Debout). The blessed life of Harmony, innocent of private property and salaried work, of nuclear family and the split between city and country, will right the proceedings of class Power: courts and priests will be courts of love and priesthoods of sex, wars will turn into competitions of (for example) pastry-making, armies will clean, plant, and reconstruct, work will become attractive as play and art, and swerving abnormality the norm of society.

Fourier's shattering interplay of maniacal poetry and ironical dialectic, rooted in the deep longings and genuine folk imagination of ancient working classes just being crushed by commerce and industry, was the first to take into account the necessities of huge demographic agglomerations. It will reappear in garden cities and kibbutzim, in Marx (see G 712) and the hippies. What it lacked was a reckoning with industrial labour under the rule of capital, and with the deep-seated, internalised and normalised, violence that its reign and its leaping technoscience bring.

3. Marx: Value Creation and Fantastic Metamorphoses

3.0. Two presuppositions are quite central to Marx's analysis of the "material mode of production" constituting capital and capitalism. The first one is living labour (*lebendige Arbeit*), "the living source of value" (G 296–97)[2]; Preve perspicaciously notes that this "absolute starting point ... functions for him as a true Being" (144). Marx's definition of humans is one of beings who "*produce* ... their material life" (*German* 37). The second presupposition, which is not dealt with here, is that labour in production is measured as time.

3.1. Alienation of Value-Creation

Creative power is appropriated by capital:

> The worker ... sells labour only in so far ... as its equivalent is already measured, given; capital buys it as living labour, as the general productive force of wealth. ... [I]n exchange for his labour capacity as a fixed, available magnitude, [the worker] surrenders its *creative power*, like Esau his birthright for a mess of pottage. ... The creative power of his labour establishes itself as the power of capital, as an *alien power* confronting him. He divests himself of [externalises, alienates – *entäussert sich*] labour as the force productive of wealth; capital appropriates it, as such. (G 307)

> The productivity of labour becomes the productive force of capital. ... Capital itself is essentially this *displacement, this transposition [of the productive force of*

> *labour]*, and ... *this transubstantiation*; the necessary process of positing its own powers as *alien* to the worker. (G 308)

The worker is impoverished by the process of production, during which he must enter into and be transformed by an "absolute separation between property and labour, between living labour capacity and the conditions of its realisation, between objectified and living labour, between value and value-creating activity." His "value-creating possibility" is transformed into capital as master over living labour capacity, as

> value endowed with its own might and will, confronting him in his ... poverty. He has produced not only the alien wealth and his own poverty, but also the relation of this wealth as independent, self-sufficient wealth, relative to himself as the poverty which this wealth consumes, and from which wealth thereby draws new vital spirits into itself, and realises itself anew. ... The product of labour appears as ... a mode of existence confronting living labour as independent ...; the product of labour, objectified labour, has been endowed by living labour with a soul of its own, and establishes itself opposite living labour as an *alien power*.... As a consequence of the production process, the possibilities resting in living labour's own womb exist outside it ... as *realities alien* to it. ... (G 452–54)

3.2. Fantastic Metamorphoses and Anamorphoses

The product of a subject (labour) is unnaturally born out of it as not simply an objectified reality – like a baby or an artefact – but as a malevolent usurper, taking from the subject its "vital spirits," vitality or indeed soul. This is not too bad an approximation to a Gothic tale, in two variants with a male or female protagonist: the first, in which the unclean capitalist Power seeds the womb of labour (here a *succuba*) with a demon birth; the second, in which the unsuspecting hero is beset by a power he unwittingly let loose out of his soul-substance or vitality and which turns upon him to suck the rest of such "vital spirits." Such figurations abound in Marx, from the Sorcerer's Apprentice tale (already used in *The Communist Manifesto*) to the popular image (though not the original novel) of Dr. Frankenstein and his monster.

Or, "[t]he accumulation of knowledge and of skill, of the general productive forces of the social brain is thus absorbed into capital ..." (G 694). As in horror-fantasy, brain-forces are absorbed into the villain, the "*animated monster*" of capital (ibidem 470). In older language, it/he practices soul-extraction, soul-transferral or soul-eating. For when value becomes capital, living labour confronts it "as a mere means to realise objectified, dead labour, to penetrate it with an animating soul while losing its own soul to it" (ibidem 461). The underlying image of vampirism and vampiric reincarnation, the evil incarnation process, is reproduced in Marx's very syntax:

> Capital posits the permanence of value (to a certain degree) by incarnating itself in fleeting commodities and taking on their form, but at the same time changing them just as constantly; alternates between its eternal form in money and its passing form in commodities; permanence is posited as the only thing it can be,

> a passing passage-process-life. But capital obtains this ability only by constantly sucking in living labour as its soul, vampire-like. (ibidem 646)

3.3. Labour as Living Fire

The most incisive formulation of "living labour" may be:

> Labour is the living, form-giving fire; it is the transitoriness of things, their temporality, as their formation by living time. In the simple production process ... the transitoriness of the forms of things is used to posit their usefulness. When cotton becomes yarn, yarn becomes fabric, fabric becomes printed etc. or dyed etc. fabric, and this becomes, say, a garment, then (1) the substance of cotton has preserved itself in all these forms ...; (2) in each of these subsequent processes, the material has obtained a more useful form, a form making it more appropriate to consumption; until it has obtained at the end the form in which it ... satisfies a human need, and its transformation is the same as its use. (G 361)

Labour power is a *vis viva*, the human incarnation of the "natural property of matter [being] movement ... as *impulse, vital spirits, tension*." The term *vis viva* (living force) seems derived from Leibniz and his polemic against Descartes' reduction of motion to pure quantity, pleading for a self-developing finality from inside any monadic form.[3] Perhaps it is by now not startling that "the advance of population ... too belongs with production" (G 486). It is confirmed by Engels's famous preface to *The Origin of the Family*: "... the production and reproduction of immediate life ... is of a twofold character. On the one hand, the production of the means of subsistence ...; on the other, the production of human beings themselves" (ibidem 455).

As opposed to production of exchange-values for profit, the production of use-values for consumption is a beneficent metamorphosis of life into more life, human quality into another human quality: "*living labour makes instrument and material in the production process* into the body of its soul and thereby resurrects them from the dead . . ." (G 364). The classless society or realm of freedom necessitated by the qualitative logic of human vitality, which sublates the quantitative logic of political economy, is one which has turned the vampiric dispossession of labour and its vitality into a Heraclitean but even more a Promethean "form-giving fire," that is, into a means of renewed life. *Humanised production or creativity replaces death with life*: the essential Marxian argument is as "simple" as this.

3.4. Marx as a Copernican Revolution in Metamorphic Imagery

Thus the *Grundrisse*, and then *Capital*, are the high point and crown of a whole millennia-old (if not millenary) plebeian tradition of metamorphic imagery, in which the immortal labouring people constitute the world's body in metamorphic feedback with the world's goods, refashioned by, in, and as their bodies – a tradition best set forth in Bakhtin's *Rabelais and His World*. This tradition runs on the affirmative side from early metamorphic myths – such as the central one here, Prometheus as both fire-bringer and shape-giver (*pyrphoros* and *plasticator*) – and from folktales, through what Bakhtin calls "prandial libertinism," such as the Cockayne stories and Rabelais that posit a magically unimpeded direct appropriation of nature without war, scarcity or work – to Fourier's future of passionate attractions. On the negative side, Carnival is accompanied by Lent: all that falls short of such full contentment is treated as a demonically unnatural state of affairs, a misappropriation of the people's living forces or vital spirits by vampiric villains. To mention only Marx's most likely sources, such a filiation runs again from the horrific elements in myths and folktales, culminating in those of the Grimm brothers, through classical antiquity (Homer's Circe and Lucretius rather than Ovid's codification of metamorphoses), to the Romantic elaborations on these motifs.[4] The twin subversive subaltern genres of horror fantasy and utopian alternative, radically alienated from the seemingly solid and unchangeable status quo and therefore committed to seemingly fantastic processual and metamorphic imagery, supplied Marx in the *Grundrisse* with the popular, spontaneously materialist imaginative tradition formulating the lot of exploited people as a struggle between living renewal of their forces and a zombie-like death-in-life.

Marx changed and fulfilled this tradition by fusing it with the materialist and dialectical intellectual traditions which stem from similar roots but developed somewhat independently from Heraclitus and Epicure to Hegel and Feuerbach, briefly fusing with the plebeian tradition also at such earlier high points as Lucretius, Rabelais, and Cyrano. Marx's main innovation was to alter *the people's body* into *labour's living body*, which makes out of the cosmic presupposition of ever-living fire a concrete, everyday matter of *living labour's formative fire*. This radically transcended the Greek vision of activity split between the *praxis* of free and wealthy citizens and the *poiesis* of the "mechanics," slaves, and women, substituting for it the deeper binary relationship of living labour and vampiric capital. It added to the plebeian defence of the consuming and hedonist body the crucially new cognition of the *producing body*, which both incorporated and criticised (that is, dialectically sublated) bourgeois political economy. It will last as long as that economy and the need to imagine a radical alternative to it does.

4. Prospect

If, as all creation, love as well as child-bearing and child-rearing belong to production in the non-bourgeois and anti-capitalist sense, then Marx takes this sense for his yardstick with which to measure the wrong character of capitalist production; however, he does not focus on this production as creation, nor did the whole Marxist tradition. Though many women and children worked in Marx's time on turning labour into reproduction of capital, this was eventually found less profitable than using them for the hidden costs of reproducing the labour force, and industrial labourers became as a rule male. There was much reason in his focussing on the problem as it concerned these male labourers, on labour as abstractly genderless, but that does not excuse the neglect after him.

A crucial and vital updating of Marx's insights for the 21st Century must use, beyond the insights from the new ways in which the Fordist and Post-Fordist epochs have inflected our inmost experiences, also those of materialist feminism. Besides adding new foci, such as the intertwining of the producing and the gendered body, they add new methods. There should be no deep obstacles for such an alliance (though many contingent ones, arising mainly out of opposed interests of male and female elites competing at the capitalist poker table). One would simply have to add holy birth – all creation that consecrates life – to the demonic birth.

Notes

1 *Nouveau* 14; see more on Fourier in my *MOSF* and in *DBH* 433–36, where 11 titles of secondary literature up to 1975 may be found.
2 A long list of secondary literature to Marx and the *Grundrisse* is given in Suvin "Transubstantiation" and Suvin-Angenot, to which today at least Negri should be added.
3 The quote is from Marx-Engels, *The Holy Family* 152. Marx's readings in (and then Engels's full impregnation by) Leibniz are discussed at length in Bellinazzi 116–17, 136–37, 257–49, and passim, and see Marx's "Auszüge zu Leibniz," *MEGA* Abt. 4, Bd. 1: 186–208.
4 It would be an interesting work of literary detection, which is approached in Suvin and Angenot, to find precisely from where Marx took his fantastic imagery; this would include Goethe's *Faust* (see also G 704) and Shakespeare. As far as vampires go, there are both French Enlightenment and German Romantic sources: Voltaire somewhere speaks about stockmarket speculators, tax gatherers, and businessmen in Paris and London who suck the people's blood in full daylight and do not live in graves but in beautiful palaces (cf. Caillois), and this was a commonplace of the Parisian plebeian melodrama and vaudeville in Marx's youth – for example in the vaudeville *Les trois vampirs* of 1820 identified as a judiciary official, a cashier, and a customs official (Milner 177). Marx no doubt knew Heine's famous critique in *Die romantische Schule* of German vampires, who include a field-marshal and a dead fatty who leaves his grave to earn ducats.

Works Cited

Bellinazzi, Paolo. *Forza e materia nel pensiero di Marx ed Engels*. Angeli, 1984.
Caillois, Roger. *Images, Images....* Corti, 1966.
Debout, Simone. *L'Utopie de Charles Fourier*. Payot, 1978.
Engels, Frederick. *The Origin of the Family, Private Property and the State*, in K. Marx and F. Engels, *Selected Works in One Volume*. Lawrence & Wishart, 1968, 455–593.
Fourier, Charles. *Le Nouveau Monde industriel et sociétaire. Oeuvres complètes*, Vol. 6. Librairie sociétaire, 1841–48.
Fourier, Charles. *Théorie de l'unité universelle.* Ibidem, Vols. 2–5.

Jameson, Fredric. *Allegory and Ideology*. Verso, 2019.
Jameson, Fredric. *Archaeologies of the Future*. Verso, 2005.
Marx, Karl. "Auszüge zu Leibniz." *MEGA* Abt. 4, Bd. 1, 186–208.
Marx, Karl. *Critique of the Gotha Programme,* in *The Marx-Engels Reader*. Ed. R.C. Tucker. Norton, 1972, 383–9.
Marx, Karl. *Grundrisse*. Trans. M. Nicolaus. Penguin-Vintage, 1974.
Marx, Karl. *The Holy Family*, in Karl Marx, *Selected Writings*. Ed. D. McLellan. Oxford UP, 1978, 131–55.
Marx, Karl, and Friedrich Engels. *The German Ideology*. Progress, 1976.
Milner, Max. "Il vampiro dal romanzo al melodramma di Nodier," in C. Bordoni ed., *Linee d'ombra: letture del fantastico in onore di Romolo Runcini*. Pellegrini, 2004, 169–78.
Negri, Antonio. *Marx beyond Marx*. Autonomedia & Pluto P, 1991.
Preve, Costanzo. *Il filo di Arianna*. Vangelista, 1990.
Suvin, Darko. *Metamorphoses of Science Fiction*. enlarged ed. Ed. G. Canavan. P. Lang, 2016.
Suvin, Darko. "Transubstantiation of Production and Creation." *The Minnesota R* no. 18 (1982): 102–15
Suvin, Darko. "'Utopian' and 'Scientific': Two Attributes for Socialism from Engels." *The Minnesota R* no. 6 (1976): 59–70.
Suvin, Darko. "What May the Twentieth Century Amount To: Initial Theses." *Critical Q* 44.2 (2002): 84–104.
Suvin, Darko, with Marc Angenot. "Uses of Marx: The Implicit of the Manifested (or, Demystification and Critique)." *Rab-Rab* [Helsinki] no. 3 (2016): 35–72.
Williams, Raymond. *Marxism and Literature*. Oxford UP, 1977.

3

A Note on Fascism as Well-Meaning Utopia (2000)

I've read with great interest the *Science Fiction Studies* issue #78 surveying the history of SF criticism. I don't enjoy backseat drivers and as a rule conduct my answers or polemics by developing further essays. But there is one matter in the lively survey by Donald M. Hassler that I think calls for brief dissent, both personal and general: his metaphoric use of "fascism" as a kind of escapist idealism yearning for "a fresh, universalized, purer narrative of heroes ... and of utopian possibilities for the future" (213). This defines not only SF but also all other products of the human mind – except for most Philistine babbitry lauding the present as the best of all possible worlds – as fascism, so none of us should be surprised if we are tarred with that brush. But if one wants to collapse into the same category a utopian liberal such as Asimov, a Puritan revolutionary such as Milton's Satan (one of the saints in my calendar), and more or less socialist left-wingers, from pink to deep red, by seeing them as "identified and defined by [an idealism] in contrast to stifling system" (222), then strange ambiguities (to say the least) will ensue.

As a well-meaning scholar, Hassler notes the commitment of all Marxians to the master's "demystification" (224–25), and he kindly and rightly includes me in that explicitly anti-fascist trend (228 and 229 passim). But in the same breath he also suggests, in spite of that, that my thinking "provides the logical support" for his interpretation of much SF and/or SF criticism as "fascist." This horrifying conclusion, a total novelty to me, calls for support beyond hints and metaphors.

For the grossly de-historicized context of present day postmodernism, I may appear too finicky. But as a pre-teenager, I've had my life seriously threatened by one real fascist state (Germany), I've been interned by another (Italy), and almost killed by a third (Croatia). I have had two grandparents, two uncles, and so on, killed by fascists (German and Croatian), and so cannot swallow the illicit metaphoric extension of the meaning of "fascism" – in Professor Hassler's account, by the way, bereft of its main economic, political, and indeed ideological connotations (racist, sexist, etc.) – even to liberals (the real ones, of the Jefferson-to-Mazzini kind), much less to socialists or communists like me. As developments all over the world show, fascism is resurgent underneath our fake globalization: in the US it calls itself "libertarian militias."

I do not impugn Mack Hassler's well-meaning aims, and I'm in favor of academic and other mischievousness. But I cannot risk falling under the adage "whoever remains silent, consents."

Dixi et salvavi animam meam [I have spoken and saved my soul]!

4

Considering the Sense of "Fantasy" or "Fantastic Fiction": On Ahistorical Alternate Worlds* (1999–2001)

[Le tourist naïf] frissonne au passage des chasses et des hordes. La comédie goutte sur les tréteaux de gazon. Et l'embarras des pauvres et des faibles sur ces plans stupides!... La même magie bourgeoise à tous les points où la malle nous déposera! Le plus élémentaire physicien sent qu'il n'est plus possible de se soumettre à cette atmosphère personelle....

[The naive tourist shudders at the passing of hunts and hordes. Drama drips onto these stages of turf. And the embarrassment of poor and weak people on those stupid levels!... The same bourgeois magic wherever our suitcase sets us down! Even the most rudimentary physicist knows it's no longer possible to submit to this individualist atmosphere.]

Arthur Rimbaud, "Soir historique," 1875

Der Kapitalismus war eine Naturerscheinung, mit der ein neuer Traumschlaf über Europa kam und in ihm eine Reaktivierung der mythischen Kräfte.

[Capitalism was a natural phenomenon with which a new dream-sleep overwhelmed Europe, and with it a reactivation of mythical powers.]

Walter Benjamin, 1930s

Managed affluence has slid into an anxiously managed but perhaps unmanageable depression.... It is then not surprising that the dominant messages are of danger and conflict, and that the dominant forms are of shock and loss.

Raymond Williams, 1979

0. Fantasy: Why Bother?

Si scopron le tombe, si alzan i morti
I martiri nostri son tutti risorti....

[The graves do ope, our dead rise up/ Our martyrs have all revived – Mameli's "Military Anthem"]

Goffredo Mameli, 1848

Criticism has plucked the imaginary flowers off the chain not in order that people continue to bear that chain without fantasy or consolation but in order that they throw off the chain and pluck the living flower.

Karl Marx, 1843

Fantasy with a capital F is in the 20th Century a literary genre or group of genres[1] whose audience and characteristics are in a close though confusing (multiple, unclear, love-hate, complementary, contradictory) relation with SF. Though fantastic fiction has a long pedigree in most European countries and the USA, for the first half of this century in the USA it "flourished only as a parasite on its more popular cousin, science fiction" (Scholes 12–13). In the 1960s, the Tolkien craze – and the *Conan* resurgence – began to change this relation by infiltrating and inflecting the US SF subculture. At the centre of publishing in the field, David Hartwell encapsulated this precisely: "In the latter half of the twentieth century, with certain best-selling exceptions, fantasy is produced by writers of science fiction and fantasy, edited by editors of science fiction, illustrated by SF and fantasy artists, read by omnivore fantasy and SF addicts who support the market. Fantasy is not SF but part of the phenomenon that confronts us" (20). He also noted that Arthurian romance and the occult horror best-seller à la Stephen King, whose mass success starts after the 1973 *Exorcist* movie, are for commercial reasons exempted from this symbiosis. This unhealthy confusion – grounded in the fact that "[t]he fantasy audience seems to be a whole lot less critical and demanding than the inner SF community, satisfied with whatever magical images are given it..." (Hartwell 156) – prompted me to a delimitation in *MOSF* which identified the "fantasy tale" as "ghost, horror, Gothic, Weird [tale]" and "a genre committed to the interposition of anti-cognitive laws into the empirical environment." While noting that it is qualitatively significant when it keeps the "tension between ... supernatural phenomena and the empirical norms they infiltrate," I concluded that the frequent absence of such tensions reduces the fantasy tale's horizon to indisputable Death, and that its commercial lumping into the same category as the disputable horizons of SF is a "rampantly socio-pathological phenomenon" (8–9).

This as it were drawing of borders for SF – not in order to preserve any illusory purity but in order to be able to speak about it – now has to be revised in the light of a change in epochal experience. That change condenses for me around two foci. First, the huge quantitative burgeoning of Fantasy from the late 1960s on, when Tolkien's term of "Fantasy" also came to the fore, constitutes a new lay of the land whose sense a materialist critic may to a large extent rightly dislike but cannot treat as not very pertinent to her/his concerns: it has to be mapped. Significantly, this burgeoning accompanies a quantitative stagnation of SF (see Hartwell 185–92) and certainly also a qualitative stagnation of its bulk. In 1987, the most knowledgeable John Clute estimated that, if one eliminates reprints and anthologies, out of 650 novels published in USA as "fantastic literature" 298 are SF and 352 "fantasy and horror novels."[2] The data we all use stem from the year-end breakdown of publications in the *Locus* magazine, which I find not wholly reliable as they put into SF a number of titles that are to my mind partly or wholly Fantasy. Even so, Clute estimates that in their 1992 data, the total of new novels is: 308 SF, 275 Heroic Fantasy, 165 Horror (e-mail communication to me of 30/1/2000), or a proportion of 440 titles of what I'd call Fantasy vs. 308 SF. And the equally knowledgeable Brian Stableford concluded from the sharp drop of SF titles in the 1990s (down 1/3 from 1991 to 1994) and the fact that by 1994 the ratio in new novels was 204 SF vs. 234 Heroic Fantasy plus 178 /!/ Horror that SF – which I believe has a better chance of cognitive approaches to history – "will soon be the least produc[ed] of the three genres..." (49). A glance into any bookstore teaches that this 2:1 preponderance is continuing and solidifying. Furthermore, the economically and consumer-psychologically important bestsellers were disproportionately tilted toward Fantasy. Indeed, Stableford went on to gloomy speculations that perhaps habitual SF readers have always had much in common with Fantasy readers, since the two genres as it were have a common denominator in "futuristic adventure stories which were essentially exercises in costume drama" and which always constituted a solid majority of SF (51–52). These facts delineate a whole different lay of the land for SF too, so even those much less interested in Fantasy (like me) have to take the new lay in.

The second focus, which stems from the evolution of my horizons about SF, genre theory, and semiotic meaning in general, is the conviction I reached somewhere before 1980 that the parable is a key form for understanding SF and other "metaphysical" genres, which entails a re-evaluation of the significance to be allotted to the textual foreground (whose characteristic elements and figures are the main obvious feature singling out fantastic fiction). For, the parable consists of a narrative body as "vehicle" and an intended meaning as "tenor," as a way of intimately relating art to truth or narrative and metaphoric imagination to conceptualised, normative doctrine – and vice versa (in my "SF as Chronotope…"). If all estranged genres aspire to be read as parables, then each Fantasy text also has a tenor and cannot be simply dismissed because of its vehicle. Yet obversely, the vehicle is not simply a ladder or raft to be jettisoned and forgotten after reaching a restful goal. The goal itself is not entirely (or at all) available before the reader has worked through the story; the story's shape and values – what it is seen to be – are constituted in a feedback with the narrative world. The cognitive import of even such idiosyncratic and watered down allegories as Fantasy, which approximate meaningful parable only in the clearest cases, consists in the experimental feedback between vehicle and tenor. One has to negotiate a text, or a class of texts, in each particular case. Most of them may (or may not) turn out to be socio-pathological: but they cannot be ascribed such a quality simply by virtue of dealing with necromancers, magic or horror. In what I suspect is a precious fraction, they may be vehicles of beneficence, critiques of alienating powers.

I should add that my work on some texts by Marx, whose favourite tropes include the fantastic creatures – spectres, vampires, zombies, idolatrous fetishes, sorcerer's apprentices – that pullulate in his writings (see my "Transubstantiation," "Fantasy as Critique" in this volume, and Suvin-Angenot), and more recently much reading and a little lecturing on Kafka, has confronted me with the fact that they abundantly used in some key positions strong fantastic elements to a clearly cognitive and most illuminating effect. If Marx and Kafka could, why not others?

Let me therefore revoke, probably to general regret, my blanket rejection of fantastic fiction. The divide between cognitive (pleasantly useful) and non-cognitive (useless) does not run between SF and fantastic fiction but inside each – though in rather different ways and in different proportions, for there are more obstacles to liberating cognition in the latter.

Finally, I confess at the outset I've been unable to do even partial justice to the burgeoning commercial genre of Fantasy, whose spread and my partial assayings from it have contributed to convince me we should indeed bother about this field, in a way that Cabell, Lovecraft or even Dunsany could not convince me. Indeed, one of the problems of the term "Fantasy" is that it almost inextricably stands for three corpuses of different historical scope: 1/ the post-Tolkien corpus of "heroic" plus "horror" fantasy; 2/ the Morris-to-just-after Tolkien corpus of what may by now be called "classical" Fantasy, up to say the mid-1970s; and 3/ the tradition that can be retrospectively identified as having shaped these corpuses, beginning in Gothic novels and German Romantics and continuing in a phase of inserting the fantastic novum into realistic surroundings after 1830–40 (Gogol, Poe, Hawthorne, etc.). Most of my examples come from the second corpus: I cannot delve into the world's most successful writer Stephen King (120 million copies sold worldwide by 1996) nor, in fact, accomplish the necessary mapping of Fantasy at present. I hope here merely to indicate some pertinent historical and theoretical parameters for doing it. While fantastic fiction always and necessarily introduces forces that suggest some powerful, other dimension or world, it is only in phase #2 that this suggestion crystallises into articulated Secondary Worlds. My impression is that such parameters and elements are in present-day Fantasy again recombined with everyday and also with past settings, indicating greater historical urgencies confronting the reader (this too was pioneered by Wells, in stories such as *The Wonderful Visit* or "The Door in the Wall"). But perhaps some of my findings may be used for somebody else's investigation of a field grown so huge that I may not be able to survey it in this one life.

This essay is therefore what the root meaning of that word implies: it is frankly an experimental assay to see whether whatever sense I may draw from the accumulated splendors and miseries of fantastic fiction mostly until the mid-70s, and from the secondary literature up to our days, can begin to make sense also for corpus #1 above. I'm not sure this can succeed, for the pressures of the Post-Fordist mutation of capitalism may have produced a burst of fictional Fantasy mutations that would need further mediations (for example, a context incorporating the rise of occultism, as attempted by Ben-Yehuda). But even if my experiment fails, a "negative experiment" may be cognitively useful, indicating what roads not to take.

1. Some Preconditions for Approaching Fantasy

Our motto must therefore be: Reform of consciousness not through dogmas, but through analyzing the mystical consciousness, the consciousness which is unclear

> *to itself, whether it appears in religious or political form. Then it will transpire that the world has long been dreaming of something that it can acquire if only it becomes conscious of it.*
>
> Marx, letter to Ruge 1844

1.1. Patrick Parrinder wrote in 1982 a brief essay, "The Age of Fantasy," which begins by noting that "Fantasy, a word with a long history, has recently emerged as a name of a loosely conceived literary mode or genre.... [Its] commercial exploitation...has spread from advertising to pornography... and other forms of mass entertainment. Billion-dollar horror and science-fiction movies satisfy a double taste for wish-fulfilment and for a mild dose of the occult..." (109–10). Parrinder notes that Fantasy begins where deep belief ends, and relates Herbert Spencer's somewhat invidious but not wholly unjust terms, in which "barbarism and superstition, having been eradicated by advancing civilisation, take on a new kind of social utility as the subjects of pleasing tales [... about] witches, monsters, ghosts, wizards, devils, and the like" (109). Beside the historical point which I shall discuss later, this may to begin with serve to remind us that one should take with due seriousness the tons of murderous gore blithely justified in Conan the Barbarian or the high-minded racist Tolkien,[3] and of course in most horror tales down to Peter Straub and Clive Barker. But then, it is also high time for me to remember Benjamin's great historical insight which makes civilisation (read: class society as presently constituted) coextensive with its hidden face of barbarism, and to eradicate any kinship with Spencer's Whig triumphalism. First because it implied that civilisation was synonymous with bourgeois horizons, and second because it implied that it had finally and irreversibly won out over obscurantism. I am diametrically opposed to both of these positions. But though I never shared them, having experienced what the bourgeoisie leads to in Fascism and the Second World War, in retrospect the horizon of *MOSF* can be seen as mutedly triumphalist, expecting a long and difficult but ultimately probable socialist victory. This hope was rapidly becoming untenable even as I was wrapping up *MOSF* in the 1970s. Today it is clear that the present horizons require an agonising rethinking of all such positions – though not of final orientations. I see our global horizons as at best a struggle lasting for several generations against the amok runs of financial capitalism with a bestial face that rapidly spreads hunger, wars, druggings, brainwashing, and prostitution, and at worst a descent into full super-technoscientific barbarism. This rethinking does not at all mean an abandonment of ethical ideals and political imperatives, but it does mean a re-examination of all tools and mediations. Advancing on firm ground one can scorn rafts, but amid a deluge one has to use all means at hand, however flimsy.

1.2. Parrinder proposes to link Fantasy strategically with desire; and already Tolkien had recognised that Fantasy stories "were plainly not primarily concerned with possibility, but with desirability" (40). What desires were responsible for Tolkien, Conan, and Co. having encountered such favourable ground in the US and then European – for example French – counter-culture of the 1960s? A very brief answer would be that at that point a revolt had spread in depth and breadth against a stifling military-cum-bureaucratic Establishment, whose main institutionalised ideology was (and with suitable changes still is) technoscientific rationality subservient to profit-making. Probably the best depth diagnosis of it was given by the prescient Karl Marx who in the 1850s pinpointed the central building block of the alienated mega-oppressive apparatuses of capitalist industry and organisation of life (market intertwined with State), in general overview as well as in its central cell, the industrial shop-floor:

> In the machine, and even more in machinery as an automatic system, the use-value, that is the material quality of the means of labour, is transformed into an existence corresponding to fixed capital.... The worker's activity, reduced to a mere abstraction, is determined and regulated on all sides by the movement of the machinery, and not the opposite. The science which compels the inanimate limbs of the machinery to act purposefully, by its construction, like an automaton, that science does not exist in the worker's consciousness but rather acts upon him through the machine as an alien power, as the power of the machine itself. Living labour [is appropriated] by the objectified labour inherent in the concept of capital.... (*Grundrisse* 692–93, transl. modified)

The worker becomes "a mere living accessory" of the machinery, which includes the bureaucratic private and public apparatuses, measured against which any personal "value-creating power ... is an infinitesimal, vanishing magnitude" and which "destroys every connection of the product with the direct need of the producer ..." (693–94). The domination over Nature by technoscientific apparatuses is consubstantial with their domination over the producers or creators: "The right of property originally appeared to be based on one's own labour. Property now appears as the right to alien labour, and as the impossibility of labour appropriating its own product" (458). Machinery (fixed capital) is objectified past labour, now dead, that zombie-like seizes the living. The program announced by the young Marx in the epigraph to this section has to cope with this demonic possession.

Thus, for all the mealy-mouthed celebrations of reason, rationality decayed, in the practice that determined the life of a huge majority, from the Enlightenment hopes and decomposed into what was reasonable and perfectly functional in terms of personal and sensual goals for individuals and large classes of people (self-determination, shorter working time, psychophysical use-values) but irrational to the ends of the ruling apparatuses – and vice versa, into what was an apparatus type of reasoning perfectly meshing with the military-bureaucratic complex (cf. Gorz 53 and passim). The rationality claimed by bureaucracy and technoscience is an impoverished pseudo-rationality: for example, a huge quantitative and functional improvement of means for genocide and ecocide. This could not but give reason a bad name. The immense potentialities of science and technology for making people's lives easier are themselves as alienated as the people affected by them. In war, the condensation of everyday politics by other means – and there were over 30 wars in 1999 alone! – dehumanised humanity looks through the media "at its own annihilation as an esthetic pleasure of the first order" (Benjamin GS I: 508). It is scarcely surprising, even if not healthy, that some strata of the population began to place their hopes in all kinds of occult sciences, magic, or a return to reactionarily refunctioned religious beliefs, flying from alienated reason to unfalsifiable doctrine. As dogmas go, the Invisible Hand of the Free Market making for universal contentment was no better than being washed in the Blood of the Lamb or the UFOs.

In particular, sad to say, technoscientific culture as developed in, by, and for capitalism is as a rule non-culture in relation to all that is not technoscientific: not merely arts, but all non-violent and sensual activities. Post-Modernist cultists often claim that the new "clean" techniques of the computer have changed all that. Well, they certainly have not changed the horrible exploitation of the young Chinese women producing microchips. Have they changed the life of us users? The jury is still out about the effect on intellectuals such as myself, though it is already clear the computer and the Web have deepened the chasm between global North and South. On the industrial shop floor, computerisation has made plant operation much less transparent to the workers, whose erstwhile skills have largely been frozen onto the software instructing the machines, which they do not understand. The abstracting or "ephemerisation" of work is even clearer in the "service" sectors and offices, where "the product itself is abstract" (Chapman 307). In sum, *technologies without self-management from below* "have boxed far more people into a life of artificial, animated stupefaction. To these people... [l]ife becomes a kind of phantasmagoria of...technological features" (idem 308). Technoscientific culture subservient to the profit principle necessarily disregards the cost to the environment and to the degradation of human senses (such as the hearing faculty subjected to the bellowing amps). It has proved incompatible with respecting fleshly bodies of other people or exalting their sensitivity and pleasure (cf. Gorz 113), which is the only way to exalt one's own sensitivity and pleasure. True, for a privileged mercenary minority in the field of, say, molecular genetics or informatics, "[f]etishism has never been more fun, as undead substitutes and surrogates proliferate.... Ask any biodiversity lawyer whether genes are sources of 'value' these days, and the sources of commodity fetishism will come clear" (Haraway 134). But treating workers or employees as means to a misnamed "productive" end, as mere labour-power, is a repression of the subalterns' as well as of the masters' sense and sensitivity. Beside the workplace, this is evident in our housing, urbanism, noise, pollution, lighting, materials, and other matters over which the ordinary citizen has no control, including most education. Marx's diagnosis has been confirmed in spades.

The culture of ruling institutionalised violence is thus, deep down, a barbaric culture. In such circumstances, which dominate most people since the Industrial Revolution, life outside work ("leisure") becomes the opposite of and compensation for life at work. The exploited human and non-human nature rebel: but only humans can do so in a conscious, goal-oriented way. How can we, from this vantage point, view the delight in Conan and similar less brawny heroes? As a complex mixture of ideology and utopia, I'd suggest: on the one hand a condensed reproduction and reaffirmation of cruelties from the readers' alienated reality, and on the other a compensatory glimpse of use-value qualities which that reality lacked. The Heroic Fantasy stories have at least the merit of, first, showing this openly, second, marrying it to individual initiative and sensuality, and third, holding at arm's length the particular causal nexus of the violence around the reader or moviegoer which has made the simplified circumstances of Iron Age life seem less alienating. This does not cancel out their overall stultifying, sometimes frankly semi-fascist, horizons. So we must weigh the pros and cons.

2. Preliminary Delimitations: On What Fantastic Fiction Is Not

> *This novel is set in a world where there are no television talk shows, no income taxes, no commuter trains, no air pollution, no nuclear crises or campus riots or midi skirts. – A world blissfully innocent of detergent commercials, thirty-cent subway fares, Spiro T. Agnew speeches, freeze-dried coffee, electric toothbrushes, pornographic movies from Denmark, draft dodgers, Women's Lib, and the Los Angeles Freeway. – It is a world that never was but certainly should have been.*
>
> Lin Carter, 1971 (the book is dedicated "To the greatest living creator of wordplay-and-sorcery, J.R.R. Tolkien")

2.1. Once again, I find myself considering how to define what we're talking about. Labels and categories are not sufficient to dispose of any matter; but they are indispensable to begin with. I start from the hypothesis that fantastic fiction is a literary genre (more probably, a family of genres), and adopt Jameson's pragmatic approach to historical genres which mediate between formal analysis of texts and their history as social life; as cited fully in "Kick-off" above, for this approach genres are literary institutions, or social contracts between a group of writers and a public, which specify the proper use of a particular cultural artifact. To my mind this stance happily and unavoidably brings about a number of simplifications for the inevitable initial concern of whoever wishes to speak about genres: how can one restrict one's field so as to make it both synoptically manageable and true to one's bedrock prejudices and pragmatic evidences about the existing lay of the fictional land. We are dealing here with two interpenetrating jungles: a jungle of existing genres is rendered almost impassable by the jungle of approaches.

So my concern is, to begin with, what a generic approach to Fantasy does *not* have to deal in. As to corpus, we don't have to include much self-conscious "high lit." Modernism, any and all Post-Modernism, or anything before about the end of 18th Century. As to approach, we don't need to deal with "realism," with psychoanalytic explanations nor with "the Fantastic."

2.2. *Fantastic fiction is entirely* – and more clearly than other genres – *a creature of history*. Everybody from Walter Scott on agrees that it is not thinkable before overriding mythological or religious belief suffers an epochal political breakdown, as a consequence of which some of its aspects and elements become available for fictional manipulation. Its beginnings can be dated – at various times in various countries – to a time when the bourgeois laicising cleavage into natural vs. supernatural begins to dominate at least in the literate classes, and yet the alternative to realism is no longer straightforward allegory. The puzzles begin as to what do the manipulated signifiers come to signify when imported into the various new semiotic wholes, beside the meta-signifier that the author's hegemonic reality is being held at arm's length as insufficient or outright disgusting. The first, or diachronic, paradox of Fantasy (and what I've called in *MOSF* the other "metaphysical" genres such as fairy-tale and horror tale) is that it begins where deep belief in supernatural values disappears: Dante or Milton didn't write fantastic fiction but religious, political, cosmological epics. A present-day reader looking backward at the epic of *Gilgamesh* or Spenser could for some purposes – such as building a list of reusable Fantasy props – licitly treat it as Fantasy (Lin Carter and C.M. Manlove do so illicitly). But a heavy toll is paid for flattening out historical imagination. Except that they are, evidently, not illusionistic realism of the middle-class type, in no historical sense are the function, intent, audience, and all other aspects of Homer, animal fables (cf. Tolkien 15–16), Malory, Hamlet's father or any other writings before (roughly) Pre-Romanticism commensurable with fantastic fiction as discussed here. When Tolkien reuses elements from *Beowulf* or the *Nibelungenlied*, and Eddison from Ariosto, they have been digested and metamorphosised.

The relationship of modern Fantasy to many other genres of fantastic fiction, such as Gothic fiction and ghost stories, is equally unclear. There are indications that these could be treated primarily as early horror stories of given social imaginations, for example, the Gothic of the generation before and after the French Revolution (cf. Lévy, Punter, Monleón, Ringe, and Runcini *Paura* for the Gothic, and Briggs for the ghost story). "Fantastic fiction" might conveniently be divided into the historical phases suggested above, very roughly allotted to ca. 1764–1830, 1830–1880, 1880–1960 (the high modernist phase), and the contemporary, post-Tolkien moment. The massification and acceleration of capitalist reification is evident in this filiation. I shall mention here two elements: first, success brought increasing autonomy to fantasy fiction's themes and figures: a vampire or werewolf could be treated ironically, science-fictionally, or just neutrally, as an adventure prop. Second, the scope grew. Before ca. 1880, horror tales used the malevolent intrusion as primarily a local one; as late as Wilde's *Dorian Gray*, it destroys simply the – no doubt representative but still singular – protagonist. There seem to have been very few equivalents to a completely different country or world: the great pioneers were, I think, the fairy tales, and then the *Alice* books and the national, continental, and finally global SF after the Future Wars, *Flatland*, and the dystopias/eutopias of Jefferies, Bellamy, and Morris. It is reasonable to suppose that a major (the major?) impulse toward fantastic fiction is the violence engendered by capitalist violations of personality, spreading from the countryside, city, and shop floor to the shrinking world map. And it is certain that at least one major source of globalisation, consubstantial with global economic nets of exploitation, is the advent of incredibly massive world wars, with all the political and technoscientific revolutions they bring along – faced more directly in SF from Wells on and by eversion in Fantasy. This would provide a handle to explain the shift of Fantasy's center of gravity from the old imperial countries of England and France to the USA, so that even the medievalist nostalgia of Tolkien could only there find a mass resonance and become a form-building impetus (cf. Aldiss 136). It is there, after the same First World War which shaped Tolkien, that Lovecraft advanced from a haunted house (building and dynasty), wood or village to a whole town, and by slow discovery our whole contaminated world.

From all such fascinating topics, here I can enter only upon some central matters after ca. 1848 in Europe and the USA, when the state of affairs described in Marx's above X-ray of industrial society begins to impinge on writers and readers. Were I writing a history I would certainly start with Poe and Morris, and probably even with Walpole and Hoffmann, and put the Kafka-Borges vs. Tolkien opposition at the beginning of a further phase characteristic for this century.

As to the *Alice* books by Lewis Carroll. I shall here limit myself to indicating that I'd allot them to a separate genre of fantastic fiction, which Clute in the Clute-Grant *Encyclopedia* calls Wonderland (1030) but does not fully define. I'd interpret Rabkin's discussion of reversal in *Alice* (109–12), or possibly broaden it, so as to envisage Wonderland as a playful subversion of scientifico-logical rule-making (primarily categorisation) and gamesmanship, such as had passed into contemporary commonsense. Elements of Carroll's unique fusion of dream story, akin to nonsense in poetry, with strict rules (as in the games of cards and chess) were often imitated but never even distantly equalled. Heroic fantasy from Tolkien on is in a strange "zero way" parasitic on the model of fully separate and self-contained, yet quite non-religious, Secondary World in Wonderland, and by way of stronger opposition on the horror tale and SF too (Tolkien could be described as twisting Wells through Tasso, *Alice*, and *Beowulf*).

Finally, I adopt two important delimiting arguments by Clute. The first is of a general nature, stressing as it does that any fantastic fiction must be a coherent, "thick" narrative in order to render believably present the "impossibility" impinging upon this world or the "otherworld" (cf. Heinlein 23 and Tolkien 37). It needs a plot whose figures traverse a landscape that possesses enough consistency so as to evoke the illusion of an inhabitable place modelled – with the pertinent modifications – on our familiar "zero world." This rules out non-narrative verse and shorter lyrical prose, for example of Surrealism, and dream tales (cf. Tolkien 13–14). The second is historical, noting that much 20th-Century fiction found "mimetic" illusionism insufficient, but that to call Fantasy such "enterprises of Modernism and Postmodernism [is] to strip the term 'fantasy' of any specific meaning" (in Clute-Grant 338). Insofar as Post-Modernist writers follow their programmatic denial of ontological stability in reality, so that the norms of their narrative universe are undecidable, the question of genre cannot be posed for them (how far program accounts for practice is another matter). However, I shall, while adopting this for my initial enquiry, take leave to doubt it for some products of Modernism, such as Kafka and the Latin-American "magic realism," or Woolf's proto-feminist estrangement of history in *Orlando*, where the norms are clear and their tenor discussable as parable. I do acknowledge that much more work and insight is needed to probe the interaction of fantastic fiction and Modernism.

2.3. As to approach: first, it was pragmatically unavoidable for the practice of all "estranged" writing as of (say) late 18th Century to relate by contraries to the absolutely dominant bourgeois positivism. In literature and the arts this meant a more and more narrowly conceived realism, naturalism or mimesis, and in that historical sense fantastic fiction is the coeval mirror twin of "realism." The early theory was constrained to follow this. But for quite some time now it has not been helpful to define SF simply as "the other side of realism" (Clareson) or fantastic fiction as all non-realistic writings minus (maybe) SF and the fairy-tale. Such an extensive *omnium gatherum* allowed only a delimitation by contraries: I tried to protest in *VSF* against "confusing SF and supernatural fantasy on the purely negative basis that their imagined realities are not identical with the author's empirical reality" (91). Since no definition *ex negativo* can be theoretically defended, theoreticians have often preferred employing a kind of essence or meta-principle of The Fantastic opposed to banal illusionism. Yet meta-principles need the most solid historical anchorage in order to make any sense. I shall continue this discussion in my third section.

Second, as Joanna Russ once complained about criticism of supernatural stories (*To Write* 60; cf. Carroll 168–77), psychoanalytic explanations are in most cases insufficient or totally unapplicable. I mean by this the orthodox Freudian limitation to ahistorical individual psychology, though Jung's ahistorical collectivism (not without influence in Fantasy) is still worse and academic "cognitive science" quite irrelevant. Neither the unconscious nor archetypes can deal with institutions, social contracts or proper uses of artifacts. Obversely, any psychology will be able to deal with everything in suitably impoverished terms: so there's no difference between fantastic fiction and any other fictional (or indeed non-fictional) text or semiotic artifact as to its phallic vs. castrating or animus vs. anima tenor. Spacetime forces me to let these stand as a more or less self-evident, undefended though highly defensible, propositions. I hastily add that I love reading Freud's novels (certainly more than Tolkien's) and that cognitive illuminations from his or other analysts' shrewd observations about particular texts or syndromes – such as the uncanny – may prove useful in their proper place.

Instead, I'd follow the path ably pioneered by Jack Zipes in his investigation of the cognate estranged genre of fairy-tale. He shows clearly how its tradition began in 17th-18th Century France as a co-optation of current folktales. Their plebeian concerns were with counteracting ruling power and brutal oppression by means of magic possibilities allied with the daring and self-reliance of the Third Son or Young Girl. No superordinated other world appears: the magical and miraculous "represent metaphorically the conscious and unconscious desires of the lower classes to seize power," to affirm a more just outcome at least for the hero/ine (8). This was superseded by Perrault's male-dominated upper-class didacticism, socialising children into the absolutist compromise between the Court aristocracy and the high bourgeoisie, which was at the same time pitilessly murdering thousands of reputed witches and werewolves as well as religious and political heretics. Perrault's, and later the Grimm Brothers', codification was a clearcut cultural politics which presented an image of properly acceptable behaviour for the readers, adhering to the new code of bourgeois moralism: domestic industry and self-sacrifice for girls, courage, competition, and acquisitiveness for boys (Zipes 8ff., 28ff., 46ff.). I conclude from this that the parallel world of the fairy-tale can be seen as a spread of possibilities between the poles of a subversion bringing out the social repressed (the political unconscious?) and a use that reaffirms and "naturalises" repression.

Third, on "The Fantastic" as meta-principle. This is a German-cum-French Romantic invention, recoded by Todorov's influential 1970 book rendered into English with that title. As his whole earlier phase, the book is vivacious and stimulating, but also held within rigid limits of quasi-linguistic doctrine (structuralist poetics) and national corpus. I won't here delve into the peculiar linguistic imperialism, which for example relegates SF to an ill-advised footnote or two, except to indicate that it seems to me the founding wrong swerve of all modern appeals to The Fantastic divorced from a corpus of stories. More modestly, I would argue that Todorov draws exclusively on possibilities present in French fiction 1650–1950 (including what can be fitted into it from German Romantics, primarily some Hoffmann) and codified in French literary criticism from Nodier on. The validity of his categorisation into uncanny vs. marvellous plus oscillation between them is therefore very small for the Anglophone and even German traditions, it is restricted to cases where some of those writings – for example James's *Turn of the Screw* – operate within ideological conventions similar to the French ones. This is not to prejudge whether a non-generic quality of *le fantastique* may not be of use for some purposes, as was for example attempted by Rabkin and Jackson. But just as confusing utopianism with utopian fiction has led to direst critical aberrations (cf. *MOSF* chapter 3), and it eventually turned out that utopianism could only be discussed with some hope of clarity after delimiting utopian fiction, so in my opinion uses of "the fantastic" can only be fruitfully envisaged *after* the actual classes of fantastic fiction and Fantasy have been at least centrally identified and discussed with some degree of exhaustiveness. If one attempts to discuss both at the same time, one risks doing too much (as Rabkin's fantastic in detective fiction, pornography or English architecture) and also too little as far as generic precision goes. Finally, any human qualities are historical. They may be long-duration affects or horizons, but they cannot be a spirit above the waters of history – an Idealist beast of a hypostasis.[4]

In my own first clearing of the ground I cannot pretend to any thorough argumentation, only to methodological consistency. I shall attempt to discuss what I take to be defining parameters for Fantasy, and what follows from them.

3. *In medias res*: The Genres of Ahistorical Alternative Worlds

History is a nightmare from which I am trying to awake.

A character in James Joyce, 1922

History is a laboratory in which we learn that nothing works, or ever can.

A character in Michael Swanwick, 1991

In such a Case they talk in Tropes,
And, by their Fears express their Hopes...

Jonathan Swift, 1731

3.1. What I have in *MOSF* called the "metaphysical" stories present worlds of "arresting strangeness" (Tolkien 47–48), that is, not vouched for by empirical observation or common sense: though inevitably using most elements – events, existents, and relationships – from the author's "zero world." Within this group, how may fantastic fiction be differentiated from fairy tales or old myths and folktales?

The main differential parameter that fantasy fiction, in the widest of my three senses, is supposed to be necessarily defined by is in scholarly debates usually called *the impossible*. Almost everybody and his grandmother up to and including the first wave of writings on it – for example Delany, Irwin, Manlove, Rabkin, with Tolkien as the Great Ancestor of Fantasy theory – make use of it (the exception would be some Jungian, occultist or neo-fascist myth peddlers in Europe). But what does this mean? As Gary Wolfe observed in a thoughtful essay almost 10 years ago, without much echo in theoreticians, "the notion of the impossible itself raises a number of intriguing questions, not all of which can be adequately addressed by the resources of literary scholarship" (2). I won't go either into the ontological niceties of "possible" or into the esthetic debates about verisimilitude from Aristotle on, but turn to C.N. Manlove, a textual analyst not surefooted in the fields of theory who therefore shows the resulting aporias more clearly than (say) the sophisticated Rabkin. Manlove requires that "a fantasy" contain "a substantial and irreducible element of supernatural or impossible worlds, beings or objects..." ("Nature" 16 – the parts I left out here seem to me unnecessary). Is impossible the same as supernatural – the latter meaning, I suppose, whatever does not accord with the laws of physics and other "hard" sciences? Manlove denies this by citing Peake's *Gormenghas*t books whose world is simply laterally alternative to ours but has no supernatural elements, Gary Wolfe adds to this Peter Dickinson's *The Blue Hawk*, and one could cite a number of further alternative worlds without magic in the English tradition of some W.H. Hudson, Norman Douglas, Saki, and Rex Warner, or in Maurice Maeterlinck's turn of the century plays of gloomy castles and woods (such as *Pelléas et Mélisande*) – and on. True, there might always be a suspicion that the worlds of Peake or Douglas might exist in an exceedingly odd and out of the way corner of our world, whose main historical tendencies happen to have passed it by. But if there is no internal evidence to that, and/or if the coherence and quality of strangeness are sufficiently marked, they cannot be put into a kind of grotesque Ruritania. For most of these writings the suspicion won't hold, and we are left with what I'd call *historically unanchored worlds*, without any changes in cosmic ontologies or natural laws. Even the horror fantasy's intervention of a second world with different, maleficent laws into the realistic world does not mean that the former must be a supernatural world – say in most Poe and in many of his followers, from Lovecraft to King. The anchors are then ideological, mainly in the guise of the protagonists' psychological reactions.

Sufficiently valid exceptions demolish a presumed rule, and these examples demolish the identification of "impossible in our empirical world" with supernatural. If we still wanted to go on in these terms, then impossible would have to be superordinated to supernatural, and there would be a supernatural and a natural impossible... What then is impossible in Peake and Hudson, or complementarily in Poe and Lovecraft, if it is not different ontologies or physical laws? If the fantastic fiction's "unreality" is "unlikeness to the Primary World" and "freedom from the domination of observed 'fact,'" as Tolkien held (47), what kind of unlikeness is at work here?

The way out may be found if the schema of fantasy fiction is compared to the Alternative Histories of SF, where at some nexus point – say, of a key battle or invention – history has diverged from our "normal" Terran history. Discussing the rise of this subgenre after 1871 in the UK, I defined it as "an alternative but believable locus used to articulate different possible solutions of problems possessing a sufficient magnitude to alter the overall history of the narrated world (intertext – all the varieties of historiography)" (*VSF* 394–95). In that light, I submit that what Fantasy reacts against, and as a result inscribes itself into, has primarily to do with *experiences of everyday life, arising out of ongoing socio-economic history, that stifle central aspects of personality*. The laws of gravity, biological aging, intra-atomic composition or speed of light can be challenged in SF; Fantasy's worlds as a rule do *not* delve into them – though gods or magicians when necessary may overcome them by higher (unexplained) powers.

Fantasy's alternative locus presents an alternative concept of "history," or better flow of human affairs, usually reduced to personal power relationships around or among the principal narrative agents: it is only within such relationships that interest in abrogating our empirical physical laws can be found. It is *not* used to articulate any major – or even minor – problems from the reader's history: this is why Delany's *Nevèrÿon* books, concerned with such historical matters as gender ironies, slave revolt, and the rise of patriarchy and of AIDS, fit uneasily into, or to my mind mostly fall out of, Fantasy (cf. Clute, in Clute-Grant 916). It is also why the (to my limited knowledge) best text by Fantasy authors I've read in the 90s, Steven Brust's and Emma Bull's *Freedom and Necessity*, is not Fantasy – nor SF – but a historical novel. Fantasy creates a world where one or more all-important individuals *intimately interact with a spacetime* not only radically different from the author's historical moment of social life but also, and primarily, *denying history as socio-economic lawfulness*. This is effected in two complementary ways, giving rise to two different genres of Fantasy. A gradual discovery of evil and superior forces occulted (as a rule literally) underneath the "realistic" textures of existence and taking those textures over has for its *telos* the thrill of a peculiar type of fear, and shapes the horror tale; "...or else, [stories are] cast altogether in the realm of phantasy, [...an] exotic world of unreality beyond space and time..." (Lovecraft 87), shaping the "heroic fantasy." While identifying both genres, I shall focus mainly on this second one; and I shall, as set out at the beginning, have to leave out all the recent narrative interferences between these "pure" paradigms and the empirical present and past life-worlds.

In Fantasy, the spacetime or world is consubstantial with a plot traversing a landscape so as to evoke the illusion of an inhabitable place modelled on our familiar "zero world," and by the same token boldfacing the differences to it by arriving into a different and radically simplified, *expurgated* Otherwhere. This movement is the founding gesture of cleavage and distancing as constitutive of Fantasy as is in SF King Utopus's cutting off the New Island of Utopia from the old continent or Cyrano's flight to the Moon and the Sun. It is explicitly foregrounded in the influential (if mainly SF) model of Burroughs's John Carter leaving 19th-Century USA for Mars; a number of early Fantasy tales (for example, the *Alice* books and Eddison's *The Worm Ouroboros*) also use this transfer opening, until it passed into the generic memory and could be more elegantly dispensed with. Howard's (et al.) Hyborian Age or Cabell's Poictesme or Tolkien's Middle-earth are not Alternative Histories in the sense of the eponymous SF subgenre, but Alternative Worlds forsaking the author's history and society, asking our own social time to have a stop and start again in some other way (usually running in a circle or on the spot), with a new deal of the cards for the individuals unhappy in our social history.

3.2. A powerful exception to – or is it variant on? – the arrested history seem to be the works of a writer of considerable power and grace, J.R.R. Tolkien.[5] Though there is no overt religious activity in this book, it is because the Catholic apologetics are omnipresent in its temporality and agential system. Catholic ideology is predominantly, since the Council of Trent if not since Constantine, conservative providential collectivism: the history of the whole human species has a preordained sense with a happy ending, what Tolkien called a "eucatastrophe." There are admirable aspects to its grand sweep and, at best, its feeling for incarnate beauty which makes all natural (including imaginary) creatures kin and which Tolkien possessed in no small measure. But in the doctrinal Master Plot the forces of Good and Evil, working through natural as well as supernatural existents, must battle it out between a Fall and the Happy Ending; and for purposes of both wonder and persuasion this may be shown in a "thick" Alternate World where no capitalist economics – neither the pesky human labour nor finance and technology – cloud our sight of what's really essential. The turn to medievalism and quasi-pastoral (it could be a new category for Empson's varieties of pastoral), where you can go in meticulously for landscapes, battles, and psychological states, fits both anti-technological ruralised nostalgia and the need to reconcile persuasive description with evacuation of economic collectivism. One could formulate the problem with Tolkien by isolating two aspects of his writing, say as the graceful and the rigid. He often writes with a powerful simplicity, a hate of ugliness, and a deep love of not only some Fantasy creatures – the melancholy, non-fallen but also non-redeemable Elves, the magnificent Ents – but also, as he said, of "the earth, and all things that are in it: tree and bird, water and stone, wine and bread, and ourselves, mortal men, when we are enchanted" (9). Here he is comparable to that atheist lover of a kindred poetic enchantment and even greater master of Fantasy, whom he somehow manages never to mention in his considerations, fellow-Oxonian William Morris.

Yet the comparison of these two anti-propertarians is most revealing. No doubt, Tolkien has a right to his own doctrinal premise about forces of history, and it is quite refreshing to see them converge upon a happy ending. But once a reader refuses to swallow their posited constellation and unavoidable goal, Tolkien's bold simplification begins to seem useless – how to talk about evil without talking about wage slavery? – and indeed bloody-minded. They can only work within a polarisation in which all industry is the province of Sauron and Saruman, while the good pole is a Disraeli-like "historical block" whose legitimacy comes from dynastic descent of the old landowning and pastoral rulers renewed by blood-and-fire baptism (Aragorn), and allied with the little people (Frodo) against the upstart modernisers (see Zanger 232–

35 for that tradition in English Fantasy). Furthermore, there are strong hints that, for all their creatural failings, the Good heroes are providentially enabled to triumph (cf. Manlove, *Modern* 168–93). Now since this is the ideational backbone for everything in the narrative, it will contain and largely override its graceful aspect. Thus, I must contest the quality of Tolkien's admirably combative partisanship. Given that we do not live in the age of Sigurd the Volsung or Beowulf vs. Grendel but in the age of capitalist world wars, which deeply affected the trench officer Tolkien (see Jones 70, Turner 11–12), the blithe wiping out of entire armies or races may make us pause before the pervasive horizons of his text.

Of a piece with it is the total shutting out of labour, scarcity of women figures (see Zipes, *Breaking* 154), as well as sensuality and erotics in general, which feeds into the sharp allotment of black vs. white moral evaluations to separate species – as in the Morlock-like Orcs, proletarians seen as sex-maniac and ant-heap ogres (cf. Helms 69 and Glover 203–07). Racially too, the goodies are pale-skinned, mostly also beautiful and tall Northerners – were it not for Hobbits, Elves, and Ents, the cast would be really cloying – and the baddies are swarthy skulkers, while all of them together seem adolescents playing splendid games (cf. Turner 19 and 23–24). This seems benighted by the standards of Morris, never mind of 1940. The sum effect of a kind of short-circuit between these dogmatic rigidities and his techniques of believability is that these "almost *secretly* transform readers from secular appreciators of a text into something like parishioners" (Clute, in Clute-Grant 953), as we've seen in his fan clubs and many descendants including *Star Wars*. To despise – as Tolkien himself rightly did – the practice of Henry Ford or Adolf Hitler, and yet to exalt the cleansing violence of his type of Crusade, clearly a variant of "state ideology" (Jones 67), would seem contradictory. That he was taken up by the anti-Vietnam War generation of the 1960s is highly ironic, and testifies to its internal contradictions, or is it soft core?

The Tolkien model, then, structures its narrative time in strict analogy to Christian temporality, in which the arrow of creature-made history is finally a relatively brief interval in the Creator's cycle. The climax at the end of the Third Age is borrowed from the battle at the end of the time against the Great Enemy: Sauron is a figure of the Antichrist with industrial power coded as magic. The preordained victory of the Good finally rejoins the more banal one of arrested history: there was a crisis but it is necessarily resolved in "eucatastrophe" (cf. Jones 70). The price may have been high, and there is an appealing elegiac note making good use of the paradoxes attending beauty and loyalty in the Fallen World as the Elves leave Middle-earth taking Frodo along, but "recovery and consolation" triumph, bringing time back to its cyclical nature. The Eucatastrophe is rather what Brian Aldiss has called a "cozy catastrophe," a scare ending in coziness and a dinner at the pub (see Wilson, and Turner 20). Safe again in Ye Merrie Olde Englande!

3.3. Not wishing to further the Babylonian confusion of critical tongues, I am following the convention of calling this genre *Heroic Fantasy* (though "hero fantasy" might be, as Clute suggests, just as or more appropriate, see Clute-Grant 464). Its world is not, as SF, a development of historical – technological, overtly political or other – tendencies within the reader's environment; rather, it salvages from it only ideology and strong affects in search of a loyalty. It is a modified type of history organised around an individual (or in Tolkien a collective) hero within a correlatively simplified landscape. Heroic Fantasy may have some elements in common with, yet it is centrally different from, the horror tale à la Poe, Stoker, Lovecraft or King – which is what, following Caillois, I actually had in mind when I spoke in *MOSF* of a "genre committed to the interposition of anti-cognitive laws into the empirical environment." The elements that may be common to both (principally, the supernatural forces) are in Heroic Fantasy not horrifically inserted into a simulacrum of the reader's empirical world. In Heroic Fantasy the "intimate interaction" from my definition in 3.1 is to be specified as *decisive intervention* by the hero into his world, while in the Horror Fantasy it is to be specified as *decisive impingement* of hidden malevolent powers in the world upon the "hero." The horror tale must operate with superior, usually supernatural, entities such as gods, magicians, demons, werewolves, witches, vampires (and after Freud the occult powers may shift into the psyche). This can only be cognitively recuperated by an allegorical tenor, as happens in much "high lit." from Gogol's *Nose* to Wilde's *Dorian Gray* or in Klein's pioneering interpretation of Lovecraft as horror of the individualist subject at the coming about of the monopoly phase of capitalism (130 and passim; to my mind, the real novum of a story such as "The Shadow over Innsmouth" is not only the extension of point-like horror to a whole civic microcosm but also the gentleman-narrator's realisation of his family or class complicity with it). The rather different Heroic Fantasy ontologies in Tolkien, Norman Douglas or the *Conan* stories may or may not use magic or gods – my judgment for those three cases would be yes, no, and sometimes. How the supernatural factor is manipulated makes for important differences in the wished-for effect and some key elements in the story; but this does not seem to me the founding *differentia generica* of Heroic Fantasy. As Heinlein noted long ago, "a fantasy story is one which denies in its premise some [I would add sufficiently significant, DS] feature of the real world, it may be quite humdrum in all other respects" (23).

Thus, the defining parameter of Heroic Fantasy is that the presented world is definitely neither the author's and original (or subsequent) reader's historical web of forces, nor even any attempt at a reasonably representative "encyclopedia" of them. To the contrary, it is *an alternative, opposed and radically expurgated, structure of human relationships bereft of technology, ignoring capitalism*. Magic or supernatural forces are then a formal and ideological addition that strikingly emphasises the otherness by enlisting the precapitalist aura of such beliefs and ideologemes. The determining parameter of Heroic Fantasy is the satisfyingly simplified alternate world, as a rule akin to reverie or daydream by situating the reader "in a world and not in a society" (Bachelard, cited in Wolfe 7). I would argue this is the case with Fantasy in general, since the Horror Fantasy's necessarily monomaniacal concentration on revealing the horrible forces which invade the empirical world also simplifies and degrades it to their arena. I shall take an example from the deeply reactionary but not ineffective rhetorics of perhaps the most politically committed Fantasy after Tolkien, Norman's *Gor* series. It usually contains an emblematic obligatory scene of *anagnorisis*: the come-uppance for our bluestocking feminist miss, who had refused to understand that she is no more in her Terran environment of egalitarianism frustrating both the men and herself, but with the super-macho warrior hero on an anti-Terra where delicious female enslavement fosters full S/M erotics (since the *proton pseudos* or founding lie here is that women can only enjoy when they're physically dominated). Both the enslaved woman and the enabling literary device (*priëm*) of a reversed world – in that sense, Rabkin is right – are in that moment shown naked to the reader (cf. on recognition Clute in Clute-Grant 901). As other Fantasy, this world is not ontologically but politically adrift: not a cosmological but a historical anti-Terra.

We have, I think, so far identified at least three full-fledged genres within fantastic fiction: Wonderland, Heroic Fantasy, and occult or Horror Fantasy.[6] None of them is either an archivally registered locus from, or a tendentially possible locus directly continuous with, our social history. But of course they are just as closely (perhaps more closely) related to it: as an *a limine* refusal of that social history, yet condemned to use elements abstracted from it as seed for its anti-world. The more emphatic a negation of X, the stronger some kind of determination by X.

3.4. The forms of Heroic Fantasy are much richer than these first delimitations. I shall mention here some of the most salient aspects and elements from its phenomenology.

The reader's imaginative transfer from her empirical or "zero" world to the Heroic Fantasy world has to be given a landing point. The ahistorical otherwhere has of course a geography – one is tempted to say: the less history the more geography. Geographic gigantism, the flight from time to space, runs rampant in the invention of huge worlds with most bizarre races, for example in Vance or in Tolkien's huge epic landscape with men, orcs, ghosts, Elves, Ents, wizards, dwarves, hobbits, and supernatural Entities. But Fantasy sometimes has a secondary or other history (strongly so in Tolkien, almost none in the dreamy Cabell or present-oriented Leiber). The Russian Formalists called this the "motivation" (which has fortunately nothing to do with psychology, but may be rendered as justification) of the new environment. It may be a never-never land, whether legendarily incantatory or humdrum, in the spread Dunsany – Cabell – Peake; or situated in a legendary age before our recorded one, as in *Conan* or in Tolkien; or in a legendary age after and at the end of our history, usually totally gloomy, as in W.H. Hodgson's *The Night Land*; contrariwise, activist and go-getting, strongly admixed with SF, on other planets or at the Earth's core (Burroughs's Mars, Venus, and Pellucidar cycles); ascending from legendary spacetime to "higher planes" of beings with godlike powers, as in the Corum cycle by Moorcock and some similar almost-SF by Farmer. Or it may dispense with a precise spacetime reference and simply adopt a barbaric Iron Age and as it were settle the arrested moment, as with Leiber's pair of appealing rogues attempting to survive in it, the Two Musketeers as underdogs in Conan-land. Etc.

But such variations are less important than the "*intertexts*" on which various kinds of Heroic Fantasy lean, and which as a rule decisively mediate its "relationship to our reality" (the latter a key notion which will recur in this essay). I have suggested the intertext is sometimes SF, mostly in its planetary romance form, but this tends to diminish with increasing genre differentiation between SF and Fantasy up to the 1970s and then – I think – get recontaminated or "crosshatched" (Clute). Other, more frequent candidates to take the place historiography occupies in Alternative Histories are, singly or often admixed, the nostalgia of Medievalism and of the clean pastoral or yeoman existence. Catholics and Anglo-Catholics such as the Inklings are particularly prone to this, but the radical socialist Morris proves how national extremes may meet, whereas the US slam-bang tradition (intertext: Westerns, pirate and other adventure stories) is prone to "hard" primitivism (Conan). It is difficult to imagine a technological Fantasy, since in it the current runs strongly against technology and "cold reason"; nevertheless, these can be found transposed into the power of baleful magicians in Heroic Fantasy or of the superior gods in Horror Fantasy. Retaining a sense of power-conflicts over the use of technology tilts the story into SF, as in Marion Zimmer Bradley's fine Darkover series, which has even progressed to strong feminist themes. The quite high technology of the steel blade or ocean-going vessels is admissible, I suppose because of the neutralising intertext of Arabian Nights. But just as in SF, and quite different from myths, we never meet a working smith or shipwright in Fantasy, the field of production is under a total anti-proletarian taboo; while adventuresses, like C.L. Moore's Jirel of Joiry, are few and far between before Joanna Russ. "Oriental stories" as mediated by European imagination are the intertext for most cities, always far from the heart's desire (never mind Tolkien's hellish industrial district, a nonce appearance in Fantasy I suspect): they are doomed to decay in Dunsany, or alienatingly aseptic like the Zamyatinesque one Titus finds leaving Gormenghast, or simply givens of barbaric scenery, set against the ubiquitous deserts and glaciers (Jameson might rightly call them aspects of Fantasy's strongly marked world-reduction). *Fertility*, whether in women or jungles, is very rare, and then short-lived and/or menacing.

As different from Horror Fantasy, usually narrated from the vantage-point of the impinged upon, often with an initial disbelief in the malevolent incursion (cf. Clute, in Clute-Grant 909), Heroic Fantasy is organised around the *hero/es* for whom their world is as a rule familiar. This protagonist role is as a rule taken by a single individual (Conan) and on the other end of the spectrum Tolkien's (and Eddison's) anti-individualist throwback to a heroic group – say with war leader and ethical leader – where the torch of leadership can pass from one group member to another. The individualist heroes have brawn and martial – plus sexual – prowess (as Conan), or swordsmanship and cleverness (as in Leiber), or faith and dogged overcoming of obstacles in serving the Good (as in Tolkien). In his "salvational history" variant, the scope of their intervention is epoch-making (Frodo, Aragorn) but this is an exception; on a lower level of naked power struggle Conan supposedly makes a difference in the Hyborian Age; or the protagonists are, more realistically, marginal to life in the story's world (the Leiber duo). In Heroic Fantasy the hero "does not age in the mind's eye; he or she fights on, for ever ..." (Clute, in Clute-Grant 915), a swashbuckler updated from Dumas, pirate stories or the Douglas Fairbanks movies, if not from comics.

The *supernatural* element may include benevolent forces or figures in the rare religiously oriented writers of the Tolkien type; it may even be neutral and used for comic effect, as in Thorne Smith's *The Night Life of the Gods*; but most often in Heroic Fantasy and always in Horror Fantasy, it is malevolent (especially when it represents crushing cosmic indifference to humanity, as in Lovecraft's Old Ones, or mocking disregard, as in Machen). It always impinges upon the protagonist, it is there to aid or combat him, a cypher – often multiply removed – of the historical forces the Fantasy thinks it escapes. In Horror Fantasy malevolent forces always invade empirical space, they are absolutely or strongly dominant. In Heroic Fantasy, as argued earlier, they may be absent in the Peake-Douglas variant or many Dunsany stories, on and off present in the languid irony and elegant effrontery of Cabell, a more or less important part of the scenery as in Conan and Leiber, or all-important as the Enemy in Tolkien. It must be techno-bureaucratic rationalism or bourgeois positivism (aided in places by religious orthodoxy) which impelled taxonomists to make of the supernatural the be-all and end-all of Fantasy.

Indeed, taking magic or the supernatural in general at its face value seems to have prevented depth investigation of its signifying tenor. Its operators or "shifters" are after all kidnapped props bereft of the sense – the doctrine and the ritual – which they had in their original systems, so that they necessarily become cyphers for our concerns today (for example Pan usually connotes the lust and/or innocence of sex as against Christianity, cf. Merivale). My impression is that as a rule the gods connote power beyond the individual's influence and signify the capriciousness or malevolence of our power apparati; they can be used to show strongly the affects of the individual at their mercy but they show very little of the causal nexus that brought the power about and could conceivably counteract it. Magicians however, when not simply plot devices, often connote human power (through manipulation of transcendental forces for empirical ends) and even revolt.[7] Except for some late feminist sympathy for witches, and the rare cases where magician equals struggling artist, as in Le Guin and Moorcock, magic as a rule stands as cypher of evil to be defeated and marks Fantasy's ambivalence toward, or panic flight from, not simply technology but all superindividual struggle for power. We should meditate on the implications and drawbacks of Leiber's pithy synonym for Heroic Fantasy, "sword and sorcery," and why it has stuck.

3.5. I do not enjoy the role of Roman censor, and I abhor the pedantically hidebound schoolmaster. I would much rather, in Tom Moylan's terms, deal in annunciations than in denunciations. But Cato was right, within his premises, to insist that Carthago must absolutely be destroyed, and while I do not share Fichte's supernaturalist terminology, his insistence that in our historical period we are living in a state of "perfect sinfulness" translates an insight much deeper than Tolkien's. In this world, denials are not only the logical complement of each and every affirmation but also the pride and glory of an intellectual. Saying No! in thunder to anything that makes for a "degraded, enslaved, abandoned, contemptible [human] being" (Marx, "Critique" 18) remains the ABC of what I see as proper, civic professionalism. Nonetheless, there are twenty-odd letters after C, and I am, out of respect for the sufferings inscribed in Fantasy, attempting to bend over backwards and weigh it not only justly but even mercifully. Yet I arrive now to "*science fantasy*," where I cannot forbear a more radical refusal.

The uncouth term names a hybrid sub-genre mixing elements and motivations from SF and Fantasy in more or less arbitrary manner. This subgenre goes at least from Stevenson's *Dr. Jekyll and Mr. Hyde*, through a lot of genre writers from the 1920s on like Abraham Merritt, and a whole wave from the late 1960s on that culminates perhaps in the various ambitious and lexically innovative series by Gene Wolfe, beginning with *The Book of the New Sun* tetralogy from the early 1980s. In *MOSF*, I noted that the narrative logic of Stevenson's famous tale cheats where the cause of the Jekyll-to-Hyde switch is concerned: it begins by means of a chemical concoction, not explained but presented as continuous with accepted Positivist science; but this is soon shelved in favour of Hyde's "returning" simply by force of desire and habit, which foregrounds the muck-raking allegory of the bourgeois professional hiding abjection under respectability (69). This unclear oscillation between a horror tale and older moral-cum-religious allegory undercuts any allotting of responsibility for Hyde's horrible deeds, using the alibi and red herring of a science dangerous by and in itself rather than by who uses it how and for/against whom (perhaps what I miss may become clear if we compare it to both Timothy Leary's experiments on himself with LSD and to the CIA's and KGB's experiments with such psycho-drugs on defenceless human guinea-pigs). While Stevenson's deft footwork then shifts to detection from various points of view, I cited approvingly James Blish's opinion that in "science fantasy" as a rule "plausibility is specifically invoked" for an important part of the story "but may be cast aside in patches at the author's whim...[in] a blind and grateful *abandonment* of the life of the mind" (68).

I'd here only partly qualify this strong medicine by allowing for several kinds of exceptions based, *first* of all, on whether the two incompatible plausibilities or verisimilitudes are situated in the vehicle or the tenor. The story with an unclear tenor, as in Stevenson and to my mind (if I understand him) in Wolfe, may have all kinds of incidental felicities and intriguing, even splendid, aspects, but it finally cannot be esthetically, and therefore also ethically, exemplary. Yet the use of, for example, telepathy, in many stories from Bester through Le Guin and on, seems to me as a rule a fairly clear parable of the yearning for collective understanding and/or for a balance of rational and emotional in contacts with animals (Norton) and other Others (women vs. men, or humans vs. the elfin *chieri* in Bradley), which I'd have no problems of reading as SF or as superior Fantasy. To the contrary, much of the "science fantasy" I went on to discuss in *VSF* (90–94), culminating in the Christian occultism of Marie Corelli, led me to conclude that her type of narration (echoing down to C.S. Lewis and present-day US "militia" ideologies) is a fraudulent reconciling of a totally superordinated – here religious – world with currently dominant sexual, religious, and political taboos, whose narrative logic is simply overt ideology within a proto-fascist horizon plus quasi-Freudian erotic patterns. This genre convergence can be explained as a strong obfuscatory ideological necessity of given social classes, but it does not seem to me either valid SF or valid Fantasy.

That is my major complaint against this hybridisation. It is perfectly legitimate that not only the sociopolitical role but, even more, the epistemological "deep structures" of Galilean science, evident from Bacon on, should be held up to pitiless scrutiny, say in Nietzsche's vein of showing up its umbilical cord to power structures. To do that, it is not enough to show revulsion against "materialist civilisation" or similar bogeys, but rather to show an intimate understanding of that epistemology and respect for its achievements (would most of us really wish to throw electricity overboard?). As different from SF, Fantasy seems poorly equipped for that; and "science fantasy" runs the risk of having the worst rather than the best of the two worlds between which it sits (cf. Le Guin, *Language* 134–35). It seems then to reproduce the post-1848 bourgeois compromise between reason and occultism – say in Maupassant's exemplary "Horla" or Meyrink's *Golem*. At its best, it may warn against overmuch meddling into our delicate life-world by scientists blindly following the hegemonic liberal assumptions about linear perfectibility (compare, just as one example, today's molecular geneticists building up billions for pharmaceutic companies and unknown horrors for us), and develop this into "thick" descriptions of the fruits by which the intervention should be judged, as in Le Guin's *Lathe of Heaven*; or it may examine how useful are some old myths today, as in Delany's *The Einstein Intersection* (significantly, both cases lean toward an SF explanation of the fantastic aspect).

Second, the SF-Fantasy blend may be clearly overriden by comedy (from humour to satire), by adventure (as in Varley's *Titan/ Wizard/ Demon* trilogy), and for aught I know by other narrative modes. In such cases it should be judged by the success of the dominant mode (considerable in Varley, as different – say – from most E.R. Burroughs), and the Biblical injunction not to begrudge their fill – the minor "science fantasy" element – to the kine who do there thresh the corn should be charitably followed in lieu of Cato's grimness. Finally, *third*, we may be seeing a reversion to and/ or innovation on allegory, as in the case of the tortured Gnostic psycho-allegory of David Lindsay's *A Voyage to Arcturus*, a work I admire as I would any great failed experiment – for its intensity and consistency – without sharing its premises.

Useful critical spadework has come out of the post-Tolkien swell of "fat-volumed trilogies detailing marvelous exploits of gods, warriors and wizards – a thing which is with us still, and which in recent years... has taken on the overtones of ersatz scripture" (Zelazny 59); and some of it deals with "science fantasy." I wish to briefly consider two overviews arguing for it, written since my *VSF* strictures, Brian Attebery's article of 1981 and Carl D. Malmgren's chapter (final form 1991). I'm afraid I cannot find much in Attebery to agree with. His erudite listing of a number of works starts from the premise that "Whereas science fiction portrays a universe ordered by logic, fantasy revives the outlook of a child or savage" (236); but I doubt that his exemplars – such as Norton, Crowley, Delany, Zelazny or Wolfe – can be usefully interpreted as halfway to reviving a childish and/or savage outlook. It is simply too easy to set up a strawman consisting of official rationalism, "hard" science, and schematic logic, and call any interference between this type of norm and a world which does not fit such norms "science fantasy."

As for Malmgren's rich discussion, it goes in for David Allen's definition of "science fantasy" as stories that assume an orderly universe but "propose that the natural laws are different from those we derive from our current sciences" (cited on 140). I find this too fuzzy for use, for two reasons. First, the "different" laws may or may not be continuous in *method* with our long-duration cultural logic. If they are not, then the story is probably straightforward Fantasy, to be evaluated by criteria proper to it. And if they are, then the story is probably squarely (as all Alternative Histories) or mostly (as McCaffery's Dragonrider series) within SF, to be evaluated by criteria proper to it. Second, and just as important, the narrative proportions and balances of the story – the way it is read – are not mentioned here. This, I think, is acknowledged in a number of instances by

Malmgren's careful dissections – for example, of the time-travel story, which may be "science fantasy" only when it is not a narrative enabling device of marginal importance. Thus, of Malmgren's two "test cases," Lem's *The Investigation* and Leiber's *Conjure Wife*, the first one refuses any and all laws for the epidemic of disappearing corpses, while in the second one "[t]he scientific explanation of magic is based on analogy and is not particularly convincing" (144); either alternative can scarcely aspire to the dignity of Allen's and Malmgren's "different natural laws." The article claims all of Doc Smith as well as Sturgeon's *More than Human* and Dick's *The Man in the High Castle* as "science fantasy"; if this were so, what would be left as SF (the literature of R&D?) would scarcely be worth the bother: in which case, hybrid forms wouldn't matter either.

I've been sometimes suspected of over-theorising, and I confess there are some spidery lures in the proper spinning of a conceptual web, as in any exercise of craft mastery. But I've never thought of myself as a theoretician, only as a historian deeply conscious that all our "seeing as" (Wittgenstein) is always already theoretical (as well as historical). The only chance to articulate our histories critically was then to foreground the theory according to which it is seen as X. However, this has to my mind entailed as much explicit theory as necessary – but no more. In the case of "science fantasy" we may have arrived at the limit of necessity (Occam's Razor). The search for a clear definition of what Blish saw as a patchy and whimsical narrative form may be trying to pin down a will-o'-the-wisp. Is there anything we can understand better by using this category rather than by saying that there are some marginal forms of SF (and of Fantasy?) using elements of the other genre? If there isn't, might it not be better to give it up?

4. Some Dilemmas on Uses and Values of Fantasy

> *I ... come to the last and most important of the three questions: what, if any, are the values and functions of fairy-stories* now*?*
>
> Tolkien, 1947

4.0. Since by "fairy-stories" Tolkien meant more or less what is today called Fantasy, I shall come to my end by speculating about this overriding question.

Tolkien also presents one of the first and still one of the best arguments in favour of Fantasy, with a family resemblance to Brecht's simultaneous plea for an "estrangement effect":

> ... we need recovery. We should look at the green again, and be startled anew (but not blinded) by blue and yellow and red. We should meet the centaur and the dragon, and then perhaps suddenly behold... sheep, and dogs, and horses – and wolves.... Recovery (which includes return and renewal of health) is a re-gaining – regaining of a clear view...; so that the things seen clearly may be freed from the drab blur of triteness or familiarity – from possessiveness.... [T]he things that are trite... are the things that we have appropriated, legally or mentally. (57–58)

This is seconded by Rabkin and Jackson, who sound in their books a clarion call in favour of fantastic fiction as a general epistemological subversion of encrusted habits of thinking and perceiving; but since this clearly doesn't apply to much of banal Fantasy, it is then restricted to some subset ("high lit." Modernism in Jackson) or indeed to the principle of "being fantastic." From the Marxist side this was shared by Zipes's work on fairy tales and by Runcini's plea for understanding *il fantastico*, which he intriguingly saw as situated between the religious and the erotic discourses ("È possibile"; cf. also Ceserani's parallel to romantic love). And lately this uplifting horizon has been as it were codified by Clute's crucial claim that Fantasy characters may be "good to think with." Now, let me generously add to his claim all other pertinent narrative elements, such as landscapes or plots, and let me further, as against the Puritanical or business barbarians' discomfort at or even hate of new stories, wholeheartedly agree that narrative, because it is "the most important mode, from times immemorial, chosen by humans for the conveyance of meaning," is *potentially* "a primary technique... for the inculcation of lessons inimical to the Thought Control Police who... notoriously hate and fear the anarchic, freeing power of the raw tale" (Clute 899). Indeed, I've argued, on the traces of Jameson, that storytelling is a privileged cognitive method, *al pari* with and irreducible to the conceptual abstractions of philosophers or politicians. In my pantheon, narrative is (together with image) one of the Supreme Goods. But the corruption of the best is the worst, and capitalism is notoriously the social formation most efficient at co-opting potentialities into Darth Vaders. It is therefore useful to confront Tolkien's argument with Freud's in *Civilization and Its Discontents*:

> Life as we find it is too hard for us; it entails too much pain, too many disappointments, impossible tasks. We cannot do without palliative remedies...: powerful diversions of interest, which lead us to care little about our misery; substitutive gratifications, which lessen it; and intoxicating substances, which make us insensitive to it. (25)

I won't argue here whether Freud enumerated the "palliatives" either fully or quite precisely but only attempt to situate his categories on a good-bad scale, which I take to mean "enhancing vs. poisoning life". Let me note that I'm much in favour of gratifications, or even of any momentary escape from unbearable pain. But I'm here asking about the price all of us pay for any of them. The diversions paralyse doing anything against the impossible hardships of being, so that I'd situate them toward the bad end. Even worse are the intoxicating substances, drugging ourselves into insensibility. The substitutive gratifications are ambiguous: good if their lessening of pain doesn't entail buying more pain in the long run for most of us, bad in proportion to their entailing such swelling of pain. Insofar as the play-acting of Fantasy's worlds is taken seriously as diversion, they are debilitating drugs. They then fall within "fantasy" as antagonistically defined by Simone Weil: "a proliferation of... self-centered aims and images... in the service of consolation, domination, anxiety, and aggrandisement... [, protecting the psyche] from insight" (Ruddick 358). Only insofar as the everted gratifications of Fantasy may not only momentarily ease and dull the pain of being but also contribute to deeper or more lasting eradication of pain, can they be seen as salutary.

Granted, as Le Guin has repeatedly reminded us, what Tolkien's pun called a recovery can be thought of at one level as play: "a pure pretense with no ulterior motive whatever.... the game played for the game's sake." But in our extremely threatened times, as competing new and very rough beasts slouch toward Bethlehem, the kind of critic most of us are (and I certainly am) must insist on the other level: "a game played for very high stakes.... an alternative technique for apprehending and coping with existence" (*Language* 84). I call this level *political* (a more ingratiating name would be civic, but that to me lacks the epistemic component favoured by Tolkien and Brecht). Fantasy is – and seems to have historically always been – a literature for "the time of troubles" (cf. Jameson, *Political* 118) when central authority is markedly weakened, gangs of official and unofficial brigands abound, and ideological hegemonies totter: millenarian sects and false prophets arise and all of us search for new sacred books, so that in art too individualism gives ground to "additive and composite" creativity (Eco 502, whom see for all the above). Surely almost all Fantasy comes out of experiences of subaltern social groups.

What for me does not follow – as it does for the optimistic Elkins and Rabkin, and with some hesitation for Jackson and for Zipes's earlier works used here – is the romantic idea that the repressions in and of the lower and the middle classes (the latter being particularly prone to self-deception, cf. Benjamin GS III: 220) *have to* result in cognitive liberation rather than – say – in a black mimicry of hierarchic oppression. Writings that articulate anti-hierarchic self-determination, surely present in the spread of Fantasy – for example, Le Guin's *Earthsea Tetralogy* or some works of C.J. Cherryh – do not, alas, seem to me too frequent in the orgies of new hierarchies, suffered as fate in Horror Fantasy or gladly reimposed in the swashbuckling Heroic Fantasy and even in Gene Wolfe. My criterion to test Clute's "good to think with," or Le Guin's claim that Fantasy "tries to hint at an order and clarity underlying existence" (*Language* 87), is: Do the narrative structures and their upshot (tenor) hinder or help the reader to orient herself in her everyday world? Do they supply what I'd call points of intervention or application (as a lever must be applied at a point to gain purchase, or as a surgeon must cut at a precise point)? Is Fantasy as a tradition and present institution a tool of the reigning ideology of wars for profit, *locking out cognition* (in Kracauer's phrase) as workers are locked out when demanding an economic basis for dignity, or is it an induction of cognition, however partial and metaphoric? Hurray for an escape from alienation: but is, or is not, the "escape from the phony" also one into a mirror-image phony (Le Guin, *Language* 205)? Isn't very often a degraded pseudo-utopianism at work here (see Marin, and Suvin "Utopianism")? This has to be decided for each text or grouping of texts.

4.1. But then, what would be the context and criteria for analyzing any group of Fantasy texts? They should probably center around the implications of *transgression*, of a Fantasy text going beyond the spacetime of capitalist history; Jackson has called it, with much exaggeration, "a desire for...all that is in opposition to the capitalist and patriarchal order" (176), one that puts this order in doubt by estranging it. But if this oppositional verbiage is seriously meant, such imaginary transgressions will be seen as situated between the poles of a *compensation substituting for* vs. an *exploration preparing for* (or at least *allowing for*) empirical oppositional *action*. The former favours alternative, rigid hierarchies founded on individual power in a simplified world, the latter alternative, supple causalities founded in the dialectics between a resisting world and collective action (so far best shown by Tolkien, who however then subsumes the action under preordained historical cycles). Benjamin opposes in another context the dream of the anesthesised patient with the intervention of the surgeon: the former has no distance to the events, the latter has the distance needed for perspective and prospects (GS IV/1: 131). This seems a proper image for the two poles.

According to the useful Lotman, literary functions may be divided into two main groups: the active forces and the obstacles. Roughly up to the middle of 18th Century, consubstantial with the laicisation discussed at the beginning, the obstacles are non-human and superhuman forces which can at best be ethically queried by the tragic hero and author but which cannot be influenced by either. Such a mighty obstacle, called in semiotics the actant of Arbiter determining the outcome (cf. my "Can People"), is literally transcendental: so that whether it may in a given culture be called The Gods, God, Destiny, Nature or even History is for that culture perhaps crucial but in a "long duration" perspective secondary. The great enlightening act of the ascending bourgeoisie was to have reduced the world to people, that is, to relations among human groups and institutions, which among other matters meant the identification of obstacles with reachable and possibly removable people or human classes. Accordingly, I would pose two consubstantial central questions about Fantasy texts: what kind of *Destiny* and what *plot structures* obtain in it? My very general answer would be that in Horror Fantasy Destiny is absolutely superordinated and plot structure is subordinated to inducing the affect of fear and horror; while in Heroic Fantasy Destiny is within the hero's will to power and plot structure a serial manifestation of that will which could go indefinitely on (it would even be possible to write further Tolkienian epics about his First, Second and Fourth Age). In both cases, impotence and omnipotence, the plot is cyclical, whether the cycle closes with a whimper or goes on indefinitely. This differs from SF, where the struggle against Destiny may succeed or fail, depending on the constellation around its novum, but its outcome is not preordained – there may be a bang. The norm for a protagonist in a Horror Fantasy is that he must gruesomely fail, and in a "heroic" tale heroically succeed; in an SF tale, she depends on the mutable forces of the thick history being challenged: the plot opens up the closed, mythical cycle. Historically speaking, I'd still suspect that those who want to purge More, Swift, and Cyrano – that is, utopia, satire, and wit – from the roots of SF reduce it to an R&D ideology (or horror thereat, as in Mary Shelley), while there's no possible doubt that fantastic fiction cannot be imagined before mid-18th Century.

To specify further what happens between the poles we could begin, as I broached in 3.1, by noting what may Fantasy's ideational structures legitimately be or not be set *against*. Many critics have noted a central characteristic of Fantasy is its lacunary and *en creux* character. The central energy shaping its narrative is a strange, sometimes banal and sometimes most ingenious, anamorphic modelling: the concave inversions and eversions are moulded by the convex pressures impinging upon personalities in high capitalism. From a humanist perspective this was early on (from the Romantics to Marx) identified as capitalist alienation, then as technological hyper-urbanisation (Morris), bureaucratic rationalism and disenchantment (Weber); and most intricately, updating Marx's hard-headed analysis of the springs of capitalism, as the total invasion of our life-world by commodity relationships hand in hand with the hype and brainwashing, from advertising to the "entertainment industry," that covers it up and makes it palatable (Benjamin and Jameson). But it has remained, to my mind, quite unclear how the esthetic aversions inside a Fantasy narrative relate to quite different pragmatic subversions outside the narrative. Well-meaning critics of various shades of pink, from liberals to humanist Marxists, have simply assumed an equation between Fantasy's semantic range or elasticity on the one hand, and political openness on the other hand, as a matter of faith, as a – dare I say? – magical effect. Alas, no such short-circuit obtains.

Negt and Kluge note about the experience of alienated labour that "[t]he unbearable real situation experienced by the worker leads to the creation of a defense mechanism," but that the faculty of fantasy is, as a blind libidinal counterweight, not only "an unconscious practical critique of alienation" but also an inverted expression of this alienation (33). Thus, what if the esthetic gratifications in our commercial, Disneyfied, dehistoricised arrested moment of history use the "fantastic" alienation as a substitute and pre-emption of efficient critique? So that (as Jameson said about the cognate Post-Mod genre of "fabulation") "the making up of unreal history is a substitute for the making of the real kind"? As an inveterate formalist and lover of tales, I would say this does not have to happen – Jameson continues by noting that the "new multiple or alternate strings of events rattle the bars of the national tradition and the history manuals" (*Postmodernism* 369) – but how come it usually does? To put it most bluntly, why should Tolkien or the Conan stories or the frenziedly racist Lovecraft not be legitimately usable by neo-fascism (as its ideologists in Europe have vociferously claimed)? If Hoess, the commander of Auschwitz, relaxed by playing Haydn, why could not a future Hoess of genetico-electronic oppression be a fan of Dunsany, Tolkien or *The Exorcist* movie? Is there anything intrinsic to Fantasy that militates against it? Has it not, after all, been used several times by the most bloody oppression, in Hitler's Wagnerian Valhallas and Werewolves or the Ku Klux Klan's Imperial Wizards?

Thus, I believe we need more precision about which elements or aspects of capitalist rationality, commodification or organisation does Fantasy usually react against. What ways out of them does it take, to living or dead ends? And as the end-all, what is the *main effect* of its (perhaps various) ways out?

4.2. The common denominator of Fantasy seems to me the resolute *refusal of any technology, urbanisation, and finances associated with the capitalism of Industrial Revolution* and "paleotechnic" (Mumford) machinery, as well as the *refusal of the opacity and sheer loss of synoptic overview which follow for all efforts to understand relationships between people*. This is of a piece with the full evacuation of both the constraints and of what Jameson calls the object world of late capitalism. Carried over from the everyday pressures are, I think, three factors, which follow in ascending order of shape-shifting in relation to the reader's empirical world.

First is the omnipresent hugely *endangered status of life and liberty*, stemming from our global avalanches of unemployment, hunger, epidemics, wars – you name it.

Second, power politics are installed in place of any overarching historical laws, whether of bourgeois "progress" or of socialist sublation of capitalism that retains the achievements of industrialism; even the nostalgic collectivists of the Tolkien kind cannot show a monotheistic religion or Saviour. Heroic Fantasy and Horror Fantasy divide according to whether personal salvation through the action of saviour-heroes is on the agenda or not. If it is, the reader's alienation is countered by the attempt to wipe the historical slate clean and try the pursuit of happiness in a rougher but more understandable environment, the landscapes and cities using 18th-Century Arabian Tales or similarly filtered legends of "harder" primitivism, and often intermingled with power from polytheistic godheads and wizardry; if it is not, the power politics are transmuted into the intervention of immeasurably superior crushing godheads or entities into everyday spacetime, which yokes the reader's alienation into the pleasure of esthetised horror. In a further ideational compromise characteristic for our history of scaled-down hopes, parts of Heroic Fantasy may also be seen as shelving the very thought of salvation in favour of little oases of privatised survival, either still against the backdrop of a whole age (Conan) or simply in the interstices of a city (Leiber).

Third, and for this initial hypothesis final, the most keenly felt disenchantment (Weber) or loss of aura (Benjamin) pervading all aspects of capitalist hegemony, is replaced by *new thrills or affects*. Even Lovecraftian horror maps a kind of demented causality that is more bearable than the isolation, fragmentariness, and alienation imposed by bureaucratised rationality yoked to the profit principle – and even more so the re-enchantments of Dunsany or Tolkien.

There is no doubt the sociological bearer of Fantasy is a large group of alienated readers at the margins of the Post-Fordist social hegemony, drawn from the marginalised intellectuals, the young, the lower classes, and the women, and that a good part of them would be Benjamin's narcotised dreamers escaping its pain. Hugh Duncan exemplified this for the USA in the 1960s as follows: "[t]he American Negro, the poor [W]hite, the impecunious adolescent, are urged daily and hourly, by some of the most persuasive magicians known to history, to want everything that money can buy, yet because they are black, unskilled, or too young, they cannot satisfy those exhortations.... they must repress [their] desires" (in Elkins 25–26, and cf. Russ *To Write* 61). But how are we to update this for the last quarter century?

My hypothesis is: The long-range structural crisis of capitalism coincides with the mass growth of fantastic fiction in and at the end of the high modernist phase (see 2.2), in direct parallel to the widening of its readership from the Poe-to-Morris disaffected intellectuals into a mass appeal to the marginalised social groups. In particular, this includes a large segment of the young generation whom the collapse of the Welfare State and all other organised opposition to savage capitalism has left without economic and ideological anchorage. The hugely encroaching commodification of everything means that when work is obtained, it is very rarely related to pleasure any more. Subjectivity has been bereft of most private oases (work, family) which used to alleviate subjection and marginalisation: it is now sold like Peter Schlemihl's shadow. This results in a huge rise of everyday humiliations in shamelessly exploited labour buttressed by sexism and racism – culminating in a score of extremely dirty wars that openly institute global surveillance and reduce people to data, murdering or being murdered, but carefully occult the motives. One resentful response is then hugely swelling yearning for a world where goods are not commodities and people are not alienated by the all-pervasive machinery of bourgeois war of each against each, or at least the reader's representative is top dog. In them, the sympathetic heroes are often pirates or thieves (in *Conan* and Leiber), or average people faced with inexplicable opportunities or resentfully yoked to overwhelming horrors (as in King's *Carrie*). To the empirical world out of joint there are opposed inverse worlds "in joint," though as a rule in a simplified joint (plaster cast?). Ever since the Romantic predilection for fantastic fiction, Bessière notes, "the fracture of history is resolved in a kind of narcissism of the imaginary" (44); "the fantastic is called for to indicate the absoluteness of exclusion, the overarching perversion of human reality" (222).

Building on Klein, I'd think SF appeals to social groups with confidence that something can at present be done about a collective, historical future – if only as dire warnings. This entails as a rule a comfortable neighbourliness toward, and mostly actual alliance with or indeed commitment to technoscience (Morris was representative of possibilities of exception). To the contrary, in a situation where people's entire life-world has in the meanwhile undergone much further tentacular and capillary colonisation, Fantasy's appeal is to uncertain social classes or fractions who have been cast adrift and lost that confidence, so that they face their own present and future with horror or a resolve to have a good time before the Deluge – or both. There seems to be wide agreement among editors and writers, based on polls, that Fantasy is read predominantly by younger people, perhaps up to their mid-30s and 70% male (Kelso 440 and 445), who have internalised the experience of lacking safe and permanent employment. A number of them are university graduates (as in SF), but in Post-Fordism this no longer ensures entry into the professional-managerial class; and a number seem to be already the de-schooled generation – certainly the quality of their education is markedly inferior, especially in science subjects, to the pre-1960s. Therefore the epistemology of SF can appeal to the cognitive universalism of natural and/or social laws, however renewed, while an individualistic and pluralist epistemology of Fantasy appeals to occultism, whimsy or magic, opposing the SF model while leaning on it. As the ideologically pioneering anthropology began, with Lévi-Strauss, delving into "cool" "societies without history," short-circuiting myth and mind outside of history, the young people of the urban middle classes, mostly employees and university educated, rejected normative (or any) cause-and-effect relations (Ben-Yehuda 75–77, 85).

Both Klein and Ben-Yehuda note how exactly parallel in time and largely overlapping in horizons are the rise of occultism and the new developments in what is by now all lumped together into the mystifying category of "speculative fiction": the SF in the wake of *Dune*, and all Fantasy. Though everybody from Klein to Kelso lacks hard data, it is clear Ben-Yehuda is correct when he cites as enabling conditions for this, first, the decomposition of the political horizons of the 60s' counter-culture – or any other oppositional mass politics – and the privatisation of organising belief, and second, the tremendous loss of prestige by technoscience because of wars and ecological disasters (87–88, 98–102). It is not by chance that Freud's hypothesis of an unconscious out of time was published in 1915, while an entire generation was being slaughtered in the horrible stasis of the World War 1 trenches. But in these straits, SF has to my mind on the surface three but in fact only two sustainable options. The first option is to continue with what Stableford calls "futuristic costume dramas," erasing more and more their difference with Fantasy as to any rational credibility or causality involved; the best writer of this option – which can now claim the cachet of a Post-Modern sensibility – is surely, as of *Dhalgren*, Samuel Delany. The second option is to defiantly embrace the imperial NASA use of hard sciences as the only rightful claim to SCIENCE Fiction – let me call it the Ben Bova school. But this is then going to become not perhaps totally extinct, as Stableford prophesies, but the fiction of those engineering and science students who still read fiction – a dwindling group. For the genre as a whole, it is no option. The third is the Le Guin to K.S. Robinson line: which, whatever its present politics, must be called a Left-wing one insofar as it has inherited from European philosophy and the Welfare State age (from Lenin to Keynes) a commitment to the use of reason to effect radical changes in the way people live together (this practically means today enmity to the new NATO-cum-WTO/IMF supremacy). I would include here all thoughtful and self-critical feminist SF from early Russ through Charnas and Pamela Sargent to C.J. Cherryh and Gwyneth Jones. In sum: either SF will become integrally critical, or it will eventually be outflanked by Fantasy and fail as a mass genre.

4.3. Any imaginative world is defined by notions of probable or verisimilar *causality*. How this is handled may be a crucial test for Fantasy. Let me stress again, as I did in Section 1, that to my mind cognition is much richer than, and in some ways even opposed to, scientific rationalism, so that I do not wish to apply the latter to Fantasy (or to SF). I'm quite out of sympathy with exaltations of bureaucratic or any other rationality as against emotion[8], or of unhistorical Truth in any dogmatic sense, be it religious or "scientific." My main watershed criterion for the use of reason would be: does it "include people" (Kracauer 57), do singular people have each a name and a face in that Truth? That is: is it couched exclusively in terms of the no doubt indispensable but also insufficient abstractions (the "god words" Science, History, Nation, Gender, Race – you add to it), or does it gather in the interests and desires of embodied people and their groupings (classes)? Defining those desires is notoriously tricky – who has an infallible definition? – so that I can only give some suggestive examples. Are we talking about blind Justice, forbidding with equal majesty the millionaire and the beggar to sleep under the bridge (as Anatole France put it), or about the possibility of gaining a reasonable livelihood for all working people? About Loyalty or the need to live with the people you choose irrespective of any above god word (you can find this affirmed in *We* or *The Left Hand of Darkness* but denied in *Lord of the Rings*)? About Piety or the desire to subject even our most cherished assumptions to the test of doubt?

I recognise that Fantasy, in opposing its "fulgurant and precise immediacy" to "normal perception," departs from "conventional causality" (Bessière 180–81), but at least the reactions of the protagonist necessarily participate in some flexible causality (not necessarily of the "positive" linear and monocausal kind). This allows, at best, some articulation of the pros and cons of various forms of pressure and resistance to be tried out for the delight and instruction of the reader needing tools against Clute's Thought Police. In Benjamin's late work a powerful sociopsychological theory can be found of capitalist modernity as a hypnotic dream-world; the Weberian disenchantment of the world provokes a compensatory collective dream that Benjamin, like Marx, wanted to interrupt by "dissolving mythology into the space of history" (GS V: 1014; cf. also Buck-Morss, chap. 8 on Benjamin's "Dream World of Mass Culture"). If not, what would Fantasy deal in? It could be simply adventure, from mild thrills of surface novelty to sensationalism, which is in my experience the case of a majority of writings in Fantasy (and SF). This fits very well into the enduring US tradition of "romance," characterised – as against, say, the French, English or Russian, but also against a whole other strand of the US "novel" – by "an assumed freedom from the ordinary novelistic requirements of verisimilitude, development, and continuity; a tendency toward melodrama and idyll; a more or less formal abstractness and... a tendency to plunge into the underside of consciousness; a willingness to abandon moral questions *or to ignore the spectacle of man in society, or to consider these things only indirectly and abstractly*" (Chase ix, underlined DS), to sacrifice the thickness of relations between people in favour of a dream world elsewhere.

But in that case Fantasy's undoubted inventiveness turns repetitive and banally underdeveloped, a simple obverse of empirical taboos, and the forces impeding personal development can no longer be beheld or articulated. In Spinoza's words, "their idea of freedom is simply the ignorance of any cause for their actions" (86, transl. modified). Fantasy then often intersects with what Joanna Russ has called "dream literature": an attempt "to turn the work of art into vicarious experience – to arouse emotion or appetite directly without the inevitable alloy of reflection given by art and without any of the embarrassments of thought or the mixedness of real experience" ("Dream" 13). On the non-cognitive end of the spectrum, such monophonic sensationalism easily generates texts complicitous with war lust and power lust in general and plotted as individualistic (often "superman") enforcing of same. In the US context, the latter texts can be seen as the literature of potential or actual armies, including semi- or three-quarter-fascist Aryan militias, that rely on an undebatable system of belief (whether religious, openly magical or occultist – that is, racist – is here not central). They violently enforce ruined certainties of bourgeois Family, Self, Nation or Race. The most brilliant critical book I know of in the field, Irène Bessière's, seems to conclude (if I read her richly deceptive clarity correctly) in the same vein: "... the Fantastic is not the place of a liberated writing (because the text would gain independence from the current extra-textual conventions), but of a writing (*écriture*) of non-pertinence.... In fact, we are here dealing with a literature of lack" (240). In view of the new Leviathan in whose belly we must live, capitalism without a human face, I do not think the total refusal of Fantasy by illustrious critics, such as Aldiss or Klein, is useful any longer. Yet all of the above suffices perhaps to explain why I impenitently see as hugely sociopathic one pole of Fantasy's mass effect – both in itself as well as its swallowing up SF that had in the era of civic and youth protest developed considerable anti-hegemonic and truly subversive tools of cognitive estrangement (cf. McClintock 35). The effect of such Fantasy is to contain SF by redirecting attention and money away from it.

4.4. And what is the relation of emotion, *affect* or desire – put on our agenda by the pioneering work of Rabkin, Bessière, and Runcini – to cognition? Alas, we know even less about emotions than about most other matters discussed in this essay. Emotion is a survival tool, no more sacred than any other: it may be life-furthering or genosuicidal, and I have argued (in "Cognitive" and "Haltung"), following Brecht and some feminists, that it can only be the former if it is articulated and clarified. Is it to be treated as a license to dispense with narrative coherence and richness of figures – that is, as inimical to cognition – rather than intertwining with them as an aspect of integral cognition? Is the explosion of Fantasy to be strategically linked with desire as the great buzzword of Post-Fordist cultural theory, and in particular with narcissism à la Christopher Lasch's thesis in the 1970s that Americans were driven to act out of self-regarding assertion in lieu of historical continuity and social justice, and that this is based on the highly ideological assumption – touted by PR merchandising – that "the individual and his or her desires were the only tangible reality" (Parrinder 110)? I refuse to believe that the stringent diagnosis of Bessière's (meant mainly for classical horror tales): "[t]o the absence of meaning (*sens*) corresponds a totalisation through the effect of fear or anxiety," as a "substitute of signification" (198), is necessarily constitutive of all fantastic fiction; substituting usually rather primitive and banal affects for all cognitive logic seems a total dead end both in esthetics and in ethics. For, semantic organisation is a model derived and modified from but relating to the readers' orientation toward and within pragmatic organisations of work, buying and selling, "leisure," etc., which largely determines what happens to them. A signifying organisation is crucial if we want to talk about causal nexus permitting orientation in the interests of working people: especially for people in mass societies, "organisation is the proper medium within which the reification of human relationships is played out" (Benjamin GS III: 221, and see the discussions with Brecht recorded in his diary, GS VI: 525–29). The point seems to me not simply to call "the fantastic" an affect (Rabkin 213) but to find which dosages of which affects in Fantasy dovetail (quite inevitably) with which semantic, sense-making propositions, and to which end. As a rule, primitive or muddy emotions correspond to primitive and muddy concepts; and obversely, I cannot think of any conceptually and semantically clear articulation that doesn't also require and generate clarified emotions – and vice versa.

A case in point would be the strong affect of horror, which combines fear and disgust. I've suggested earlier a possible defence of Lovecraft (cf. also Klein, and Russ, *To Write* 60ff.). A first approach to the reasons for horror tales was given by Edmund Wilson – whom I consider one of the premier critics of the 20th Century, a man of great erudition and acumen, as well as a distinguished novelist himself. They are

> first, the longing for mystic experience which seems always to manifest itself in periods of social confusion, when political progress is blocked: as soon as we feel that our own world has failed us, we try to find evidence for another world; second, the instinct to inoculate ourselves against panic at the real horrors loose on earth... by injections of imaginary horror, which soothe us with the momentary illusion that the forces of madness and murder may be tamed and compelled to provide us with mere dramatic entertainment. (173)

Wilson's first reason applies to all Fantasy. For Horror Fantasy in particular, I'd call the reasons, a bit more sympathetically, a longing for salvation and a homeopathic accommodation. But both remain ambiguous: fake salvation easily slides to perdition, and poisoning oneself in small, safe doses easily escalates to shoreless craving. Two polar possibilities seem again to present themselves, which I'll call, following Russ, *subversion* and *addiction*. On the one end, as Benjamin argued about Baudelaire, our empirical world may be cognised as horrible: go into any bank and look at the strained faces of the not yet "rationalised away" employees, or listen to the talk in any campus pub, and you'll see where naked fear comes from. Seeing the profit system not merely "as" victorious but "as" life-destroying is subversive. Or on the other end, as is usually the case, horror literature and film has nothing to do with an interest-bound estrangement but tends to sensationalist addiction, heaping gore upon gore, slanting the story – as Lovecraft recommended – towards a culmination in fear, which has been properly called an anti-cognitive or "cognition hindering" estrangement (Fischer 16). The price paid for the explanation of a lone person's fear and horror seems to me too high if it inures us to the perpetuation and indeed escalation of that horror.[9]

Curiously and most characteristically, even though the "taproot" medieval or Antiquity texts from which Fantasy abundantly draws comprise some of the most significant love stories we know (Tristan and Isolde, say), erotics are scant in it. Horror Fantasy finds little or no place for it, so that Poe thought the death of a lovely maiden was the most affecting story possible; but even in Heroic Fantasy erotics are (at least up to the '80s) usually stiff, derived from melodramatic subliterature of realism, as in Tolkien – if not derived from bourgeois harem fantasies and rape pornography.

4.5. I arrive now at my final, unresolved point: the place of Kafka. In spite or maybe because of its extreme pessimism and bleakness, the Kafkian parable may have – within a generic space not too far from Fantasy – come nearest to a useful diagnosis inimical to the organisational forces policing us. Its sad and grave humility does not pretend the lone subaltern individual, caught like a bedbug or other endangered animal in the cages and burrows that define it, can miraculously transcend the nightmare of Father-society. On the contrary, it "places the fantastic as a determinate, marked *absence* at the heart of the secular world" (Jameson, *Political* 134) – and at its best identifies this absence with the pressures of the institutions (of family, judicial system or the ruling "castle" power) which dehumanise the tracked little man. In a characteristically complicated twist, Kafka seems to me to go back to the Bakhtinian carnival which – just like satire – identified the enemy: it is a black, Boschian carnival, but the communal values are at least its absent horizon. Obversely, Fantasy seems constitutively inclined to treat armies, guilds or any other good or bad community only as backdrops for "hero fiction." In the SF of Le Guin – whom I take to stand for the best in our field – the reader can find a lot about the effects of gender reorganisation in *The Left Hand of Darkness*, and about the interaction of political and planetary organisation in *The Dispossessed* and *The Word for World Is Forest*. In the splendid *Earthsea* series, the best of her "psychomyths," she seems in comparison to deal in individualist anxieties of the nuclear Self, cathartically healed after a lapse: the mage school is a backdrop, the wonderfully apposite archipelago world a necessary allegorical equivalent to the stations of Ged's progress but not a "thick" society as in the SF novels. For the rest, she could have said with Flaubert: "Ged c'est moi" and what she did say is that "The trilogy is, in one aspect, about the artist" (53); while about the protagonist of *The Dispossessed* she rightly said "J'aime Shevek mais je ne suis pas Shevek" (I love Shevek but I am not Shevek – *Words* 22). No genre Fantasy I know has advanced from empathy into and identification with the protagonist-hero to rich critical sympathy possible in the best SF. No doubt, this our narrative representative needs defending, but how far will this be accomplished by reducing the K. vs. Castle tension – an investigation of obscure causalities – to K. alone?

I'm here getting at one of the central contradictions of the bourgeois horizons: <u>an officially individualist society without a space for the individual</u>. It is a twist on one of the oldest problems of philosophy, the subject-object relation: "[The fantastic tale] can no longer pose simultaneously the reality of the Ego and of the World" (Bessière 68). Its transfer into worlds that have been bereft of our history and world means it is no longer believable that "everyday life contained a probability of a free relationship of subject to society" (idem 222). And since we've arrived at political philosophy, the rise of Fantasy doesn't coincide only with that of occultism but also with the Foucault moment (though no writer except Delany was conscious of this). Both Fantasy and Foucault – and after him, the deluge of French Deconstructionists, repackaged for wider consumption in the US – now worked up the collapse of Leninist socialism and of the Rooseveltian (Keynesian) response to it, or in short of any overarching renovation of society. What remains on the ruined battlefield is no longer strivings of entire dominant and dominated classes, it is their reduction to simple will to power: "Once hypostatised as a new First Principle, Zarathustra-style, power loses any historical determination: there are no longer specific holders of power, nor any specific goals which its exercise serves" (Anderson 51). At this point the Welfare State horizon of history as long duration gives pride of place to "getting a thrill," "the intensity of the instant" (Virilio and Lotringer 99, and see 98–102). The undoubtedly always present power struggles lose their historical anchorage and rich causal overdetermination: enter Conan & Co.

The Kafka model (to which, *mutatis mutandis*, many Latin Americans like the more playful Cortazar may be adjoined) loses on the one hand the thrilling safety of vicarious fear from Horror Fantasy and on the other hand the overt compensations in the manageable worlds of Heroic Fantasy: the judgment on this will depend on just how threatened we feel to be in these grim times. A Kafkian parable is also indirect, delving below the reified "positive" surfaces. But its indirections then delve directly into at least some characteristics and manifestations of the forces of oppression, without too much energy expended on the separate world. A burrow or an office waiting room suffice; the abnormal powers, huge and menacing, reside in the familiar but not understood (Hegel's *bekannt aber nicht erkannt*) world. Kafka does not transfer the endangered individual out of our thick, multiply causal, institutionally reified, entangled history: the nightmare from which we cannot awaken into a dream.

Notes

* My thanks go to my old friend Romolo Runcini for inviting me to the conference "Orizzonti del fantastico" in Procida, Oct. 1999, without which this essay would have been written much later, if at all; and to Alessandra Contenti for a collateral invitation to present "Problems in the Theory of Fantasy Fiction" to a group of colleagues at Comparative Literature of Univ. di Roma III, and for much other help. My attendance at these two invitations was rendered possible by the assistance of the Dept. of Foreign Trade and International Affairs of Canada. Sylvia Kelso, an excellent knower of contemporary Fantasy and debates around it, did her best to open my ears to its sounds and railed at me for not listening to them better; but even her own essays arriving by snail and e-mail could not overcome some of my prejudgements. Doug Porpora discussed Tolkien and other matters with me during a wondrous weekend, and Tom Moylan gave much good counsel. My thanks also go to John Clute, Patrick Parrinder, and Robin Bloxsidge of Liverpool UP for kindly sending me some writings used herein, and to Clute and Jack Zipes for some comments that I heeded. I owe thanks for further arguments to Matt Beaumont and Stan Robinson, while the anonymous reader of *Extrapolation* alerted me to a number of details I've corrected.

I hope I've taken cognisance of the main writings in English and French (from Scott and Nodier on) as well as a large sample of writings in German and Italian dealing centrally with what is here called Fantasy, but I shall adduce only those on which I rely by citing or accepting arguments.

1 The term is probably unfortunate but we're stuck with it. All the multiplicitous earlier meanings of "fantasy" as a mental faculty are irrelevant, and so are the claims that this faculty is more present in Balzać's *Peau de chagrin (Wild Ass's Skin)* than in his *Père Goriot (Old Goriot)*. If one throws into the mix phantasy or fancy (from 19th Century to Herbert Read) or even imagination – as if this wasn't what made the stone stony – the confusion is compounded and we are in a Borgesian labyrinth. A sexy new recipe for expressive hollowness in the second half of our century, from Judith Merrill and the New Wave on, is "speculation," prophetic of the present stockmarket.

2 Clute 18; he endearingly adds: "For this writer, bad sf can be seen as a category of trash, and can be junked at sight. Bad fantasy...is <u>*junk-food*</u>, an addictive mockery of the true meal, which sticks to the stomach, and eats it." But I must caution here that nobody has a solid statistical basis: Clute's as well as Hartwell's data are between 7 and 20 years old.

3 The somewhat one-sided Alpers is right on this crucial point.

4 See on this Jameson's strictures in his "Magical Narratives" essay (*Political* 115–17), indispensable for situating Fantasy. It belongs squarely to Jameson's Romance, the

preconditions of which he identifies as "the category of worldness, the ideologeme of good and evil felt as magical forces, a salvational historicity" (ibidem 148) – with my proposed added parameter of "ahistorical historicity" as *differentia specifica*.

5 I shall concentrate on Tolkien's *The Lord of the Rings* to the detriment of the cognate C.S. Lewis, whose planetary trilogy seems to me a slide from SF to Fantasy. I can posit all the more easily that Lewis's strengths are subsumed in Tolkien after the remarkably apt demolition job done by Gwyneth Jones, who sees in all of Lewis's fantastic fiction "the same taint... a deliberate investigation of pain and shame, ... but distinctly, childishly orgiastic," always in service of conversion to his Anglo-Catholicism (63). This entails huge Neo-Platonic narrative improbabilities (66, 72) and, more important, leads into Hollywoodian moral oversimplifications: "you can tell the Good creatures because they are Beautiful" (66).

6 Once a literary genre, figure or other convention is established, it can be treated comically or ironically. We should probably also allow for the rather rare <u>*comical Fantasy*</u>, for example of Thorne Smith, Max Beerbohm or of W.S. Gilbert's *Iolanthe* play, and nowadays of Terry Pratchett; this borders on the more somber and less rare grotesque, such as Gogol's *Nose*. And there are other cognate forms, as Russ argues in the case of "the Modern Gothic," which may be different from Horror Fantasy (*To Write* 94–119).

7 The definition of magic in the parenthesis, as opposed to religion, is adapted from O'Dea 7. By the way, Tolkien agrees that the object of the magic by Magicians is power (and therefore dislikes it as meddling domination, which is theologically quite proper - 10 and 52–53).

The eminent Italian historian of religion Di Nola identifies the relation of poor peasants in past ages – or indeed of modern oppressed marginal groups – who turn to witchcraft/wizardry or "the horned god" (Satanism) in order to deny the majority's belief systems as oppressive and incapable of salvific efficacy, as <u>*inversion of traditional religious beliefs*</u>. Such magic functions both as homeopathic therapy and occult ritual (discussed in Runcini, *Paura* 166–67). The diametrically opposed polarities of use would for me here be simple inversion (for example black vs. white magic), which keeps the unverifiable structure of what it inverts and thus reproduces the hegemony it contests, as against a spiral twist into the unknown new relations by means of old but anti-hegemonic symbols, which is potentially cognitive.

8 See my writings refusing this dichotomy ("Cognitive," "Utopianism," and "Haltung"). I hope to work further on this.

9 Carroll's book-length investigation of what he calls "art-horror" notes how its threatening and impure bearers (monstrosities) defy our commonplace categorisation, so that they are often connoted by locales outside – or, even worse, at the margins – of the "normal" world of social intercourse. The esthetic frame, the verbal or cinematic story, lets the audience share in the characters' disgust without themselves being "really" threatened. This builds on much similar speculation, whose fountainhead is Burke's book on the Sublime and Beautiful, where he attributes our comfort at tragic or horrible fiction to "the contemplation of our own freedom from the evils which we see represented," 41 and ff., also 36–37 and 123.

Indeed, Carroll poses there is a centrally cognitive pleasure in the process of discovering what was so far occulted and then (most often) cathartically evacuating the monster. I doubt the virtues of catharsis, and I think Carroll doesn't see that any genuine cognition must subordinate disgust to imaginative contact with the fearful novum (as, say in the original Creature of *Frankenstein*, or today with the necessity of understanding Post-Fordist orchestration of impoverishment). I'd allot more weight than he does to Stephen King's argument that horror fiction is deeply conservative: "as Republican as a banker in a three-piece suit," "a reaffirmation of the order" (quoted on 199). Nonetheless, Carroll's spadework is important, not least in his insistence that emotion includes beliefs and thoughts.

Works Cited

Aldiss, Brian W. *The Detached Retina*. Liverpool UP, 1995.

Alpers, Hans Joachim. "Loincloth, Double Ax, and Magic." *Science-Fiction Studies* 5.1 (1978): 19–32.

Anderson, Perry. *In the Tracks of Historical Materialism*. U of Chicago P, 1984.

Attebery, Brian. "Science Fantasy," in D. Cowart and T.L. Wymer eds., *Twentieth-Century American Science-Fiction Writers, Part 2: M-Z. Dictionary of Literary Biography*. Gale Research, 1981, 8: 236–42.

Benjamin, Walter. *Gesammelte Schriften*. Suhrkamp, 1980ff. [abbreviated as GS].

Ben-Yehuda, Nachman. *Deviance and Moral Boundaries*. U of Chicago P, 1985.

Bessière, Irène. *Le Récit fantastique*. Libr. Larousse, 1974.

Briggs, Julia. *Night Visitors*. Faber & Faber, 1977.

Buck-Morss, Susan. *The Dialectics of Seeing*. The MIT P, 1995.

Burke, Edmund. *A Philosophical Enquiry into the Origin of our Ideas of the Sublime and Beautiful*. Oxford UP, 1998.

Carroll, Noël. *The Philosophy of Horror*. Routledge, 1990.

Carter, Lin. "Introduction" to *Conan the Buccaneer*. Lancer Books, 1971, 9–18.

Ceserani, Remo. "Le radici storiche di un modo narrativo," in *La Narrazione fantastica*. Nistri-Lischi, 1983, 24–34.

Chapman, Gary. "Taming the Computer," in M. Dery ed., *Flame Wars*. Duke UP, 1994, 297–319.

Chase, Richard. *The American Novel and Its Tradition*. Doubleday, 1957.

Clute, John. *Look at the Evidence*. Liverpool UP, 1995.

Clute, John, and John Grant eds. *The Encyclopedia of Fantasy*. St Martin's P, 1997.

Delany, Samuel R. "About 5,175 Words," in T.D. Clareson ed., *SF: The Other Side of Realism*. Bowling Green U Popular P, 1971, 130–46 [original publ. 1969].

Eco, Umberto. "Towards a New Middle Ages," in M. Blonsky ed., *In Signs*. Johns Hopkins UP, 1985, 488–504.

Elkins, Charles. "An Approach to the Social Functions of Science Fiction and Fantasy," in R.A. Collins and H.D. Pearce eds., *The Scope of the Fantastic*. Greenwood P, 1985, 23–31.

Fischer, Jens Malte. "Science Fiction - Phantastik - Fantasy," in K. Emmert ed., *Neugier oder Flucht?* Klett, 1980, 8–17.

Freud, Sigmund. *Civilization and Its Discontents*. Hogarth P, 1951 [original publ. 1930].

Glover, David. "Utopia and Fantasy in the Late 1960's," in C. Pawling ed., *Popular Fiction and Social Change*. St. Martin's P, 1984, 185–211.

Gorz, André. *Métamorphoses du travail - Quête du sens*. Galilée, 1988.

Haraway, Donna J. *Modest Witness @ Second Millennium*. Routledge, 1997.

Hartwell, David. *Age of Wonders*. Walker, 1984.

Heinlein, Robert A. "Science Fiction: Its Nature, Faults and Virtues," in [B. Davenport ed.,] *The Science Fiction Novel.* Advent, 1964, 16–63 [original publ. 1959].
Helms, Randel. *Tolkien's World.* Houghton Mifflin, 1974.
Jackson, Rosemary. *Fantasy: The Literature of Subversion.* Methuen, 1981.
Jameson, Fredric. *The Political Unconscious.* Cornell UP, 1981.
Jameson, Fredric. *Postmodernism.* Duke UP, 1992.
Jones, Gwyneth. *Deconstructing the Starships.* Liverpool UP, 1999.
Kelso, Sylvia. "Whadd'ya Mean, 'Narrative'?" *Para.Doxa* 4.11 (1998): 431–51.
Klein, Gérard. "Trames et moirés," in M. Thaon et al., *Science-fiction et psychanalyse.* Dunod, 1986, 47–151.
Kracauer, Siegfried. *Das Ornament der Masse.* Suhrkamp, 1977.
Le Guin, Ursula K. *The Language of the Night.* Putnam's, 1979.
Le Guin, Ursula K. *Words Are My Matter.* Small Beer P, 2016.
Lévy, Maurice. *Le Roman gothique anglais, 1764–1824.* FLSH, 1968.
Lotman, Jurij M. *The Structure of the Artistic Text.* Michigan Slavic Contributions, 1977.
Lovecraft, Howard Phillips. *Supernatural Horror in Literature.* Dover Publ., 1973 [original publ. 1924].
Malmgren, Carl D. *Worlds Apart.* Indiana UP, 1991.
Manlove, C.N. *Modern Fantasy.* Cambridge UP, 1975.
Manlove, C.N. "On the Nature of Fantasy," in R.C. Schlobin ed., *The Aesthetics of Fantasy Literature and Art.* U of Notre Dame P and Harvester P, 1982, 16–35.
Marin, Louis. *Utopiques: jeux d'espaces.* Minuit, 1973.
Marx, Karl. "Critique of Hegel's *Philosophy of Right,*" in R.C. Tucker ed., *The Marx-Engels Reader.* Norton, 1972, 11–23.
Marx, Karl. *Grundrisse.* Trans. M. Nicolaus. Vintage Books, 1973.
McClintock, Michael W. "High Tech and High Sorcery," in in G.E. Slusser and E.S. Rabkin eds., *Intersections: Fantasy and Science Fiction.* S. Illinois UP, 1987, 26–35.
Merivale, Patricia. *Pan the Goat-God: His Myth in Modern Times.* Harvard UP, 1969.
Monleón, José B. *A Specter Is Haunting Europe.* Princeton UP, 1990.
Negt, Oskar, and Alexander Kluge. *Public Sphere and Experience.* Trans. P. Labanyi et al. U of Minnesota P, 1993.
O'Dea, Thomas. *The Sociology of Religion.* Prentice Hall, 1966.
Parrinder, Patrick. "The Age of Fantasy," in his *The Failure of Theory.* Harvester P, 1987, 109–14 and 214.
Punter, David. *The Literature of Terror.* Longman, 1980.
Rabkin, Eric S. *The Fantastic in Literature.* Princeton UP, 1976.
Ringe, Donald A. *American Gothic.* U of Kentucky P, 1982.
Ruddick, Sara. "Maternal Thinking." *Feminist Studies* 6.2 (1980): 342–67.
Runcini, Romolo. "È possibile un'analisi marxista del fantastico?" *Alternatives* 2 (1995): 107–18.
Runcini, Romolo. *La Paura e l'immaginario sociale nella letteratura.* Liguori, 1984.
Russ, Joanna. "Dream Literature." *Extrapolation* 11.1 (1969): 6–14.
Russ, Joanna. *To Write Like a Woman.* Indiana UP, 1995.
Scholes, Robert. "Boiling Roses," in Slusser and Rabkin eds. [see under McClintock], 3–18.
Spinoza, Baruch. *The Ethics....* Transl. S. Shirley, ed. S. Feldman. Hackett, 1996.
Stableford, Brian. "The Final Chapter of the Sociology of Science Fiction." *Foundation* no. 79 (2000): 41–58.

Suvin, Darko. "Can People Be (Re)Presented in Fiction?" in C. Nelson and L. Grossberg eds., *Marxism and the Interpretation of Culture*. U of Illinois P, 1988, 663–96.

Suvin, Darko. "On Cognitive Emotions and Topological Imagination." *Versus* no. 68–69 (1994): 165–201.

Suvin, Darko. "*Haltung* (Bearing) and Emotions: Brecht's Refunctioning of Conservative Metaphors for Agency," in T. Jung ed., *Zweifel - Fragen - Vorschläge: Bertolt Brecht*. Lang V, 1999, 43–58.

Suvin, Darko. *Metamorphoses of Science Fiction*. Yale UP, 1979.

Suvin, Darko. *Positions and Presuppositions in Science Fiction*. Macmillan and Kent State UP, 1988.

Suvin, Darko. "Transubstantiation of Production and Creation." *The Minnesota R* no. 18 (1982): 102–15.

Suvin, Darko. "Utopianism from Orientation to Agency: What Are We Intellectuals under Post-Fordism To Do?" now in his *DBH*. P. Lang, 2010, 217–67.

Suvin, Darko. *Victorian Science Fiction in the UK*. Boston: Hall, 1983.

Suvin, Darko, with Marc Angenot. "Uses of Marx: The Implicit of the Manifested (Or, Demystification and Critique)." *Rab-Rab* [Helsinki] no. 3 (2016): 35–72 [earlier versions 1979, 1997].

Todorov, Tzvetan. *Introduction à la littérature fantastique*. Seuil, 1970.

Tolkien, J.R.R. "On Fairy-Stories," in *The Tolkien Reader*. Ballantine, 1973, 3–84.

Turner, Jenny. "Reasons for Liking Tolkien." *London R of Books* 23.22 (2001): 1–28.

Virilio, Paul, and Sylvère Lotringer. *Pure War*. Semiotext(e), 1983.

Wilson, Edmund. "A Treatise on Tales of Horror," in his *Classics and Commercials*. Noonday P, 1967, 172–81 [original publ. 1944].

Wilson, Edmund. "Oo, Those Awful Orcs." *Nation* April 14, 1956: 312–14.

Wolfe, Gary K. "The Encounter with Fantasy," in Schlobin ed. [see under Manlove above], 1–15.

Zanger, Jules. "Heroic Fantasy and Social Reality," in Schlobin ed. [see under Manlove above], 226–36.

Zelazny, Roger. "Fantasy and Science Fiction," in Slusser and Rabkin eds. [see under McClintock], 55–61.

Zipes, Jack. *Breaking the Magic Spell*. U of Texas P, 1979.

Zipes, Jack. *Fairy Tales and the Art of Subversion*. Wildman P, 1983.

5

Going into a New Century: Sociopolitical Prospects for Utopia (2000)

Note 2020: *The following were answers to a questionnaire for the New York Public Library "Utopia" website in 2000. How little it either understood or cared for utopia/nism is revealed in the fact that out of their five questions four were about the Internet. I therefore refrain from citing the ideological nonsense of Question 3 to 5, which in fact I didn't answer but appended to these answers my entry (here enriched) "Horizon (Utopian)," from "Lexicon: 20th Century A.D.," in Public [Toronto] no. 19: 72-75 (Spring 2000).*

Q1: Of the utopias that have been conceived – in theory, in literature, in reality, on the Internet – which do you find the most appealing, and why? Of the dystopias that have been conceived, which do you find the most terrifying or unpleasant, and why?

A1: Most appealing to me would be the diametrical opposite to present-day capitalism without a human face (or is it showing its real face now that it fears communism no longer?). That is, a type of relationships between people which would use the stupendous productivity developed by capitalism to ensure a by now quite possible life of dignity for each human being. Dignity means first and foremost getting rid of the totally unnecessary starvation, epidemics, drugging, and other brainwashings enforced by the war of each against each, breaking out into innumerable small wars (such as in the streets of many US cities) and medium wars between states. In my opinion this could only come about by a rigorous introduction of direct democracy from below, extending Jeffersonian ideas to all genders, ages, and races. The nearest one can today get to obviously abbreviated depictions of such states is in the "warm" utopian tradition of William Morris's *News from Nowhere*, supplemented by more practical economics as in Ursula K. Le Guin's impoverished anarcho-communist planet in *The Dispossessed* or Marge Piercy good future in *Woman at the Edge of Time*. A number of practical attempts should also be mentioned, from utopian colonies in the US of the last 200 years to the popular socialist beginnings of major revolutions of this century, from Lenin and Trotsky's Russia through Tito's Yugoslavia and Mao's China to Castro's Cuba, which were however all more or less ossified and stifled by poverty from within and military and economic pressure from without.

I'm not sure whether the worst dystopia is the one in which 85% of people in today's world live physically and perhaps 98% psychically, or what is to come after its not too distant breakdown. Being an optimist, I opt for the earlier. Again, approximate descriptions can be found in Science Fiction, from the US New Maps of Hell in the 1950s to the present.

Q2: Is an ideal "community" made of virtual identities worth calling a utopia? Are physical bodies necessary to the creation of a utopian society, or can one be populated solely by alternate online identities? Does the Internet provide a "place" where a utopian community can be created? Why or why not?

A2: While "virtual reality" or "cyberspace" is an interesting and potentially promising, as well as badly misusable, invention, I cannot imagine a purely ratiocinative bliss, one without sensory and motor feedback to the brain. As you know, beside the sense of a "radically better place" or "place with radically better relations between its inhabitants," the term of utopia can also be used in the negative sense of unreal cobwebs in the brain, what Lord Macaulay – an expert on colonies – sneeringly referred to when he affirmed that possessing an acre near London is better than a principality in the land of Utopia. For one thing, the Internet excludes the three quarters of humanity who do not have proper electricity and phone supply lines – say all my former students from India, China or Africa – nor can they hope to have it in the present organisation of economics that enforces widening division between the relatively rich, mainly in the North, and the abysmally poor, mainly but not only in the South of our globe. I use the Internet in my professional work, and I have nothing against isolated and alienated individuals (as all of us are in this hugely privatised age) getting succor from wherever they can. But to pretend it is a Messiah coming to save us all, in lieu of focussing on how it could be used for lightening life outside the Internet, seems to me utopian in the bad sense: unrealistic and misleading. We should refrain from using this bourgeois or capitalist sense.

My counterproposal on how to use utopia/nism follows:

Horizon (utopian)

The concept and image of horizon comes from phenomenology (Husserl, Merleau-Ponty, Ricoeur) and it was refunctioned by Ernst Bloch into a consciously sociopolitical tool within his "warm stream" Marxism. It is a spatial metaphor necessarily associated with the cognate spatial concepts and images of locus and orientation; these are "the Urforms[s] of theoretical work," with roots in astronomy (Negt and Kluge 1002) and geography. Beyond that, the roots reach into the desire for understanding and the ancient metaphoric cluster in which seeing, guaranteeing an ability to purposefully move and act, stands for cognition. "Locus" is the place of the agent who is moving; "horizon" that toward which the agent is moving; and "orientation" a vector that conjoins locus and horizon. The horizon changes with the location of the moving agent, as was exhaustively argued by Giordano Bruno. But orientation can through all the changes of locus remain a constant vector of desire and cognition.

The use of these terms is predicated on an analogy with the empirical world. The claim of the "Possible Worlds" approach to fiction, as well as to all other forms of social imagination, is that people's imaginative structures are necessarily taken from "natural worlds" (that is dominant conceptions thereof). For "the term of 'world' is not a manner of speaking: it means that the 'mental' or cultural life borrows its structures from natural life" (Merleau-Ponty 225), our here-and-now has a preferential status. "The natural world, as an organised and perceptually structured spatiotemporal ensemble, constitutes the original text... of all possible discourse, its 'origin' and its constitutive environment.... All possible discourse is enunciated only against the ground of the perceived world's significant space, by which it is surrounded..." (Marin 167 and 175). The fact that we can meaningfully effect this metaphoric analogy from practice to signic constructs constitutes itself a highly significant meta-meaning.

The freedom of the users (originators and addressee-modifiers) of Possible Worlds consists in the fundamental fact that the worlds can be and are expressly modified in the newly articulated signic constellations. I shall discuss this further on the example (valid with suitable modifications for other uses too) of utopian fiction and imagination.

The goal of utopia is in principle not an already localised or fixed humaneness but an ongoing not-yet-manifest type of human relationships, a hominisation in Engels's or Teilhard's sense. This is "a depth dimension of the Onwards" (Bloch, *Tübinger* 147); from which it follows that there can be no final, "classical" or canonic locus of utopianism. This can be systematised as the dominance of Horizon over Locus. Locus does not coincide with but interacts with Horizon: this makes for a dynamic, open utopia (for example, Platonov's *Chevengur*, Le Guin's *The Dispossessed*). Action and agents embody here the orientation toward a moving – in these cases, an anarcho-communist – utopian horizon. In this ideal case of a dynamic utopia, locus constantly tends toward and yet never fuses with horizon, as at the end of Brecht's *Caucasian Chalk Circle*.

The second possibility is that Locus coincides with or swallows Horizon: this makes for a dogmatic, static, closed utopia (for example, Plato's *Commonwealth*, Campanella's *City of the Sun*, Cabet's *Voyage en Icarie*). Such a doctrinaire or dogmatic text "asserts the utopian focus as 'ultimate' and drastically limits the possibilities of the utopian horizon; an open-ended text, on the other hand, portrays a utopian locus as a mere phase in the infinite unfolding of the utopian horizon, thereby abolishing the limits imposed on it by classical utopian fiction" (Somay 26). After the Industrial Revolution, static utopias turn quickly reactionary and into an impediment to disalienation. For the readers of those (our) times, utopias stressing order over freedom are, retroactively, also such.

The third possibility is Locus by itself, without a utopian Horizon (which means it is a pseudo-utopian locus): this makes for heterotopia. The best theoretical example is Foucault, and the best fictional one his explicit would-be disciple's Samuel Delany's *Triton*, which is also a direct – and to my mind mistaken – polemic with

The Dispossessed's "ambiguous utopia." While both novels refuse "the doctrinaire identification of the utopian locus with the utopian horizon, Delany... also does away with the utopian horizon itself.... [The utopian] horizon and the urge are [in Delany] absent, and that absence leaves his characters purposeless and confused" (Somay 33).

The final logico-combinatorial possibility is to have in a text Horizon alone, without a utopian Locus. This is where non-localised "utopian thought" belongs, such as all the abstract blueprints, utopian programs, etc. I have difficulty in seeing how a horizon without concrete locus – without Bakhtin's chronotope – can be a fictional narration in any strict (not ironic or loosely metaphoric) sense.

To sum up the above locus/horizon combinatorics:

1/ H > L: open-ended or dynamic utopia;
2/ L = H or L > H: closed or static utopia;
3/ L (H = 0): heterotopia;
4/ H (L = 0): abstract or non-narrative utopia(nism).

These terms (as well as a further set of agential terms, see Suvin "Utopianism") might be applied as analytic tools to the whole range of utopian studies – fictions, projects, and colonies.

Finally, the interaction of locus and horizon in the dynamic utopia constitutes it as not too dissimilar from – possibly as a special case of – Eco's definition of a semiotic encyclopedia:

> It appears not as a finished object but rather as an open project: not a utopia as *terminus ad quem*, that is a state of perfection to be reached, but a utopia as a regulating idea, as a project *ante quem*, whose force stems precisely from the fact that it cannot and should not be realised in any definitive form. (Eco 108)

Eco himself identifies such an open utopia with a rhizomatic encyclopedia only, which I would rather liken to my possibility #3. I would not share the Post-Modernist taboo on global (or indeed provisionally, here-and-now total) organisation of knowledge as in my utopia #1 above: on condition that this totality is conscious of itself as a synchronic cross-cut for well-defined interests and with a limited pertinence. There is no reason that would necessarily prevent such a dynamic utopia from defining strategically central cognitive trees available for action aimed at radical change at any given point.

Thus I would conclude, with Bloch, that we should hold a steadfast orientation toward the open ocean of possibility that surrounds the actual and that is so immeasurably larger than the actuality. True, terrors lurk in that ocean: but those terrors are primarily and centrally not the terrors of the not-yet-existing, but on the contrary simple extrapolations of the existing actuality of war, hunger, degradation, and exploitation of people and planets. In order to understand how to approach such open adventist possibilities, we may have first to learn the lesson of the dynamic utopias, where locus constantly tends toward and yet never fuses with horizon.

These are spatial metaphors. Caution and flexibility are much needed for their temporal use, with periodical reappraisals - corroborative or agonising, as the case may require.

Works Cited

Bloch, Ernst. *Das Prinzip Hoffnung*. Suhrkamp, 1959.

Bloch, Ernst. *Tübinger Einleitung in die Philosophie*, Vol. 11. Suhrkamp, 1970.

Eco, Umberto. "Quattro forme di enciclopedia...." *Quaderni d'italianistica* 2.2 (1981): 105–22.

Marin, Louis. "Pour une théorie du texte parabolique," in Claude Chabrol et al. eds., *Le Récit évangélique*. Aubier Montaigne, 1974.

Merleau-Ponty, M[aurice]. *Phénoménologie de la perception*. nrf, 1945.

Negt, Oskar, and Alexander Kluge. *Geschichte und Eigensinn*. Zweitausendeins, 1981.

Somay, Bülent. "Towards an Open-Ended Utopia." *Science-Fiction Studies* 11.1 (1984): 25–38.

Suvin, Darko. "Utopianism from Orientation to Agency," now in his *DBH*. P. Lang, 2010, 217–67.

6

A Colloquium with Darko Suvin: Interview with *Science Fiction* Magazine, Australia (2000–02)

Note 2020: The interview was done electronically, with a list of questions sent to me by the editor, Van Ikin, compiled by him and his fellow SF critics Russell Blackford and Sylvia Kelso. I conflated the questions into several groups, made a résumé for each group, and later strongly edited it both to avoid repetition from my other writings and to add some matters. The original was reprinted in Warriors of the Tao, Borgo P, 2011, 243-87.

Q.1–2 and 4: RELATIONSHIPS BETWEEN "NATURAL" SCIENCES, "CULTURAL" SCIENCES, AND "THE POLITICALLY COMMITTED LIFE"; THE EXAMPLES OF FOUCAULT AND CHOMSKY

> Salus reipublicae suprema lex *(The health/salvation of the commonwealth is the supreme law)*
>
> Old Roman maxim

Russell, I've come to deeply disbelieve our dominant institutional carving up of the domain of knowledge and commitment (belief). Its historically first step, the laicisation of Descartes – I've written on this extensively and will return to it in answer to another question – was defensible as a politically liberating turf war between theologians and philosophers, though Descartes himself conceded the final say to the Church and (what is even more pernicious) took over its split between body and soul – the latter renamed mind by the new philosophers – to the ongoing detriment of the body. The next step by Galileo and Newton was then to mathematise "natural philosophy," call it science, and allot to it the same dual role of Queen of Cognition and Supreme Good as was formerly held by theology. This shut out (or better: pretended to shut out) the Subject in favour of the Object, emotion in favour of reason, female knowers in favour of male – see Donna Haraway on the early Royal Society in England or the encroachment of MDs on the delivery of babies – *etc. et sim. ad nauseam*. The less crassly Philistine traditions of France and Germany kept an assistant Supreme Good, whose cognitive role was however unclear: Art or Poesy (from painting to verse: prose fiction joined this only in C18–19).

So if we today ask, as a young man called Volodya Ulyanov did at the beginning of the great but unfortunate 20th century, "What Is to Be Done," the hegemony of the last quarter millennium has brainwashed us to answer: whatever it may be, it must be by means of, under the flag of SCIENCE. (And of course the only true sciences are the mathematisable ones, while the "social sciences," involved in messy human affairs which refuse to be totally quantified, are womanly soft as opposed to hard male reason; the contempt felt by the "hard" for the cringing "softies" can be wonderfully heard if you've been even at the margins of funding debates in a university Senate or a government granting body!) This is a powerful answer, seductive precisely for the intellectuals we need, yet on the whole a misleading one. Transmuted into technoscience, it intervenes with exponential force and speed into everybody's daily life.

Let us then further ask, on pain of extinction: What does science do? How does it do what it does? Is the power of intervention gained by this method worth the price we're paying for it (genocide, ecocide, hunger, wars)?

When "science" separated itself out of wisdom – whose backbone is *care* for health and salvation, theology's strongest trump card – on the basis of quantifying, it displaced the wrong qualities of theological knowledge, for example Aristotelian "qualitative physics." But it also displaced the supreme law of the commonwealth's *salus*. It dispensed with any quality, except the quality of being quantified. It thus divorced scientific fact from value. The price seemed right for 300 years. It became too high with the triumph of the Industrial Revolution (say ca. 1848), and has grown exorbitantly ever since. The project of human survival is consubstantial with a return of "specialised" sciences – most urgently the most powerful ones – into their matrix of cognitive wisdom. Truly democratic science, by and for (the) people, has to espouse being publicly taken to account as to each and every of its uses and consequences: which would be no more dictatorial than the strict control relentlessly exercised over it today by and for profit, debasing all that's not instantly marketable as quantified bytes of "information."

Modern natural science itself has given us hints how to do this spirally, not by abolishing Newton but by subsuming him under Einstein as a specialised case. As just noted, human affairs are certainly messier than the Lorentz algebraic transformations which can quantify that particular subsumption. We shall have to declare that big chunks or aspects equivalent to Newton (Bacon, Descartes...) are counterproductive and not usable after a given point of people's relationships with each other and with the environment, such as 1848 in the rich North. Use-value qualities are by now an intrinsic and inalienable part of facts. For example, as a fact for us air is only air if breathable and water only water if drinkable. Chunks or aspects of science compatible with this may be – must be – subsumed. Genetic manipulation in the present profit-mad state of society is much too risky: soon the filthy rich shall have chimaeras and sphinxes as pets, and the military sentient weapons. Any prudent society would ban it, just like research into nuclear, bacteriological, and any other weapons of mass destruction, until we grow wiser (after the Revolution).

But I'm not ready to concede science to the Pournelles and Bovas, or to the Tellers and Von Brauns. My answer is: not against science but for a science saturated with consciously chosen survival (to begin with, anti-military) values. Not back to Aristotle but forward from Marx and Nietzsche.

Thus, I refuse the carving up of wisdom into science, religion, politics, economics, and similar. What today (meaning in the last 30 years) passes for politics I have the deepest contempt for, be it Blair-Clinton or Reagan-Thatcher or the various bloody sects rightly (but in wrong ways) reacting against capitalism without a human face, triumphantly astride a wrongly united planet. The liberatory force of the only bearable politics, radical socialism or communism or anarchism, was defeated from without and within in the half century after 1917. I participated in it, as a Titoist (from 1945 to the mid-60s), still believe in its original aims and achievements, and would participate again if I found it anywhere. In the meantime, we are all privatised and have to do the best we can. Chomsky does very well (better in politics than in linguistics, I think), Foucault did much less well, for his tergiversations and outright obfuscations possibly hindered as much as helped, but he tried, partly succeeded, and should be honoured for that. I could give other names: Trotsky, Raymond Williams, Stuart Hall, Edward Said... But I should end with a warning: alienated politics are clearly at odds with disalienating (that is viable) art. Artists (poets) can best help by being idiosyncratically within but at the margins of fighting, liberatory movements (Brecht, Picasso...). For example, by writing about the implications of genetic research by means of narrative cognition (stories). Perhaps you can find some further positions in the following Appendix, written as an entry into an encyclopedia of the 20th Century.

APPENDIX ON SCIENCE (see more in my "Horizons," also in "Considering," sections 1.2, 4.2, and passim)

Who in the 20th Century used the scientific method, how, in whose interest, and with what results? It was used by intellectuals as a rule in the service of capitalist collectivities (States or corporations). In the guise of "technology," it has become a directly intervening and decisive force of production. The fruits thereof are contradictory: technology could be, if used by the people and for the people, potentially liberating, but the results of capitalist technology are today at best mixed, and at worst catastrophic, with a good chance at destroying vertebrate life on this planet through profiteering and militarism.

The dynamics of developing sciences seem opposed to the sudden durable revelation of religion. But they are poles of the same globe. True, there is a real difference between them, of a piece with the difference between pre-capitalist social formations based on agricultural space and capitalism based on industrial time and then financial spacetime. Yet, the dogmatic pretension of science to get – in however deferred and lengthy ways – to a final capital-T Truth about the universe partakes of the same long-durational, class-society delusion that history and human interests and evaluations in it can be brought to a stop: or that, in a Platonic-Christian vein, history is only a manifestation of the unchanging Truth.

There are by now few respectable thinkers who would not concede that of the two main kinds of scientific knowledge, "facts" and "theories," the theories – say of chemical valence – are self-evidently useful fictions and the facts an unholy amalgam of sensual evidence and semantics plus theory (that is, fiction). Let me take Harré's example for a factual sentence, "A blue precipitate appeared at 28°C" (80), and note that its referent would be rendered quite differently in cultures which see blue as not different from green (there are many such cultures), which would instead of degrees Celsius use a qualitative scale (say, "it blushed"), and which would instead of "precipitate appears" say "Mercury has been revealed" (as the alchemists would). Is the sentence "Mercury is revealed when water blushes green" really translatable into Harré's lab language without remnants? If a sentence (as any linguist would know) includes presuppositions as well as positions, it is not. Is the untranslatable part simply magical mumbo-jumbo that can be suppressed? This would depend on what additional cognition it might contain: for example, "Mercury" may well be more specific (as to its look or curative powers) than "precipitate" and thus contain more bytes of information. And what about great cultures which instead of the subject-object syntax use mainly contiguity and richer if less univocal relationships, and say something like "East Dragon – green – sudden event – blush – liquid," as I fantasise the Chinese would? How come they invented gunpowder, printing, and the South-pointing compass needle?

In sum, "Many, indeed infinitely many, different sets of hypotheses can be found from which statements describing the known facts can be deduced..." (Harré 87). As a whole current of philosophers has maintained since Gassendi, theories are not true or false but good or bad instruments for research. Formally speaking, "atom" is the name of an agent in a story about "chemistry," just as "Mr Pickwick" is the name of an agent in a story about "the Pickwick Club" (Harré 89), notwithstanding some different rules of storytelling in the two cases. "[Theoretical f]ictions must have some degree of plausibility, which they gain by being constructed in the likeness of real things," concludes the middle-of-the-road Harré (98). In other words, literary and scientific "realism" are consubstantial products of the same attitude, the quantifying immanentism of bourgeois society. Yet institutionally sanctified technoscience persists in claiming it can provide the truth, a socially enforced certainty, while the apparently "weaker" and certainly more modest Dickens did not. The philosophic and other systems of belief arising out of (and constituting) science remain stuck on this two-dimensional surface. As a planet's map is regulated and shaped by the grid of cartographic projection, so is any such system based on a principle, for example the Aristotelian excluded middle or the Hegelian necessarily resolved dialectical contradiction. And this principle is also a kind of (obviously circular) meta-reflection about, or methodic key of the system that is in turn founded on and more or less necessarily deduced from it, and that exfoliates in the form of a finite series of propositions culminating in a rounded-off certainty. This form is finally not too different from the 19th-century "well-made," illusionistic stage play; no wonder, they both flow out of the Positivist orientation. *The Lady with the Camelias* and the Laws of Thermodynamics are sisters under the skin: both show a beautifully necessary death.

Therefore, cognition is not only open-ended but also codetermined by the social subject and societal interests looking for it. The way science has been practiced since Galileo is not only a cultural revolution but also a latent or patent _political_ upheaval.

The ready subservience of science to capitalist destruction of life – in theory, the crude but still very powerful scientific Positivism and philosophical Objectivism – must be decisively abandoned if we are to preserve the human species and most life as we know it.

Q. 3 and 5: DID MY VIEW OF SF CHANGE?; ON ENLIGHTENMENT

Sylvia, there seem to be two questions you posed here. The latter one, having to do with Fantasy or "fantastic fiction," I have dealt with, as you know, in a forthcoming long piece ("Considering"), so I better respectfully refer your readers to it. I'll focus on your first question, whether my *Foundation* 1997 article, "Novum Is as Novum Does," represents (in your words) "a shift in the view of SF originally constructed in *Metamorphoses*, as a rationally based, cognitively organised, 'intellectual' genre...."

In brief, no and yes. Centrally, my view was a blend of description of SF possibilities and a prescription of which of those I deem the best (most sane and politically useful) horizon for it. This has NOT changed: the only sane way of survival for our and other vertebrate species – the cockroaches and worms will with any luck survive the worst Homo sapiens will inflict on the planet – is a society without classes rooted in political economy, which is some form of communism (socialism, anarchism, or whatever better name we'll find for it in the future). This is best known to SF readers from the desert Kropotkinian variant in *The Dispossessed*, or differently variant approximations in Marge Piercy, Stan Robinson, and others (a languidly beautiful variant refusing machine rhythms is of course William Morris's *News from Nowhere*, in an echo of which the alternative title to my above article was "News from the Novum").

What has changed is the historical reality, devolving from the Welfare State to a new beast slouching toward Bethlehem: Global Capitalism without a Human Face. Therefore the short-range prospects into which this long-range view of mine was immersed have also changed, and entail much rethinking. Trying this for the last 15 years or so, I've concluded that – since we have to have terms by means of which to handle the new experiences of huge human groups, interpenetrating within and comprising in different ways all of us – the foci of this change can be stenographically analyzed as two questions: in the present to which all of us belong, "What is this present?" and "Who are we?" My working hypotheses for a first delimitation, without the ifs and buts no doubt necessary for further understanding, are: The what is *Post-Fordism*; the we is *intellectuals*. Again, I've had to write about this extensively, both in the article you mention and in "Utopianism from Orientation to Agency."

This also means – to finally face Sylvia Kelso's initial question – that I think my project in *MOSF* is being quite misread if it is taken simply as a plea for "cold" reason as against emotion, interests, and similar. Perhaps I ought to have spent even more space on defining my terms: and for other reasons I've in the meantime done so (in "Cognitive"). For, it was quite clear in my mind that I switched from the use of "science" to "cognition" precisely in order to prevent the subservience to and disciplining of SF by institutionalised science of the militarised technology kind or of the cheerleading futurology kind – both US and Soviet. Sylvia is right in seeing within my rethinking of the 1990s an even stronger delimitation against these, for they have in the meantime grown both stronger and more obviously complicitous with our ruling wreckers. Therefore I insist today more on the distinction between the fake and the true novum (radically diminishing vs. radically enhancing the potentialities of life). But I hold that valid emotion is both articulated and in a feedback with categories of reason: as is proper for a cognitive faculty.

Q. 9–10: ON A CHANGED HUMAN ("POSTHUMAN") NATURE IN FUTURE AND HOW DOES SF COPE WITH THIS

Russell, many thanks for sending me the text of the Symposium on "Posthuman SF" chaired by you at Aussiecon '99 (now as "Symposium…" in *Foundation* 2000). I confess that ere you sent it I was stumped by your question. Posthuman? It seemed *déjà vu*: Foucault at end of the 60s? – and then the interminable tomes of everybody else in Paris recycling their Nietzsche, best in the Guattari-Deleuze hundreds of pages jumping from plateau to plateau amid the playful rhizomes? Well, there's a limited number of fashions, so after recycling those of (say) 1920s and 30s why not advance to the *haute couture* of the 1960s – especially when you can disguise this in the shiny new material of teflonised cyberspace when walking down the catwalk and hoping to rake in millions from the *New Yorker* yuppies? So where are now the discussions about the death of SF after the Hiroshima bomb, or after landing on the Moon, or after the end of US protests from Selma to the Kent State University shootings (say 1961–73, the true Golden Age of US SF in that quarter-revolution)? But where are the snows of yesteryear? What will you discuss, Russell, when you get (as I hope you do) an equally brilliant panel in 2002? I'd lay you a little bet: not "Posthuman Nature in SF"…

This is not to say that hidden somewhere within this ultra-violet herring there are no real, even central problems facing us; and I think your panelists ably dug many of them up. As everybody knows – unless irremediably taken in by the fake extrapolation ballyhoo legitimating SF as bellwether for US capitalist technoscience and promoted by the Bova-Pournelle wing in SF – these are matters that have practically nothing to do with any far future but take the muddled white-grey-smoggy light of our everyday life through the SF cognitive system of parabolic mirrors or prisms so as to analyse it into clear, *pro analysi* component colours. I'll focus here only on the downfall of the nuclear Self and the correlative or consubstantial global political economy.

I do believe the bourgeois nuclear Self is fast receding on our horizons, and the adventures of nuclear physics from Rutherford on can be read as an exact image of that "long, melancholy withdrawing roar" and splitting (let us pause for a moment and think why – to begin with, the same brains stamped with the same historical horizons were delving into either). I wrote seven years ago a long essay, whose full title might hint at my position: "Polity or Disaster: From Individualist Self toward Personal Valences and Collective Subjects." It evinced much sympathy for arguments from the most diverse quarters (one of them is Marvin Minsky's work on AI cited in your Symposium, but some of my main arguments were drawn from the Chinese cultural sphere where there never was a Self in the individualist sense – just as there wasn't one in Antiquity and not fully in the Middle Ages) that finally amounted to saying that, if there ever was an unsplittable Self between Descartes and Mach, or Robinson Crusoe and Stephen Dedalus, it is now an assemblage of quarks and charms and whatever. That does NOT at all mean there are no Subjects or personalities: Chinese or Japanese or Hellenic history is full of them. It just means that the Individuum (non-divisible-essence-of-personality) is a historical invention – the English historical semantics for that invention are admirably disentangled in Raymond Williams's *Keywords* – for which praise and blame ought to be given to two major forces: first, the Christian idea of a soul with interiority in direct communication to God, eschewing all Earthly City loyalties such as clan, city, State or other non-godly and therefore ungodly collectivities. The problem is that this is tenable only in times of dire threat to life by war and starvation, when such collectivities are seen to work badly if at all (we're getting there again, thank you). But it does not cope with the need of halfway equal citizenship in a reasonably livable affluence. This need gets met, second, by the bourgeoisie of Machiavelli's, Luther's, Bacon's, and Descartes's time that transferred such inner loyalties to the new godhead of market competition, flatteringly usurping the ancient nickname of "freedom." True, the Invisible Right Hand of market competition often got into inexplicable trouble and needed to be rescued by State protection (the Left Hand of Darkness indeed), so a collateral invention came to be the Nation.

We're now, in my diagnosis, already more than halfway to new collectivities, the top-down ones: the "senator from Boeing" from Bester's *Tiger, Tiger* has been with us almost forever (Clinton seems to have been the president from the abominable broiler-chicken industry). The Cartesian delusion, culminating in Kant or Mill, is over. The only question is: will this be a bottom-up, democratic collectivism – such as envisaged by Jefferson, Marx or Kropotkin – or a top-down, oligarchic one? Commune and co-op, or dictatorial war-camp? Alas, I wouldn't bet any big part of my pension funds on the former: as More said at the end of his *Utopia*, I rather hope than believe it. In other words, will our "psychic" charms and quarks be able to recombine according to our bodily interests, as in Piercy's Mattapoisett or Robinson's Mars, or will they be straitjacketed into the terrorism of Bill Gates, Wall Street, and the World Bank, mortifying our flesh in the new corporate and feudal capitalisms? You can find this too in Gibson, Piercy, Gwyneth Jones, and many others in SF, probably the best X-ray instrument we have within fiction. So the dislike of the body, rampant from cyberpunk to Ken MacLeod, seems to me a very bad sign. To split mind from body, sensorium from senses, is Cartesianism gone crazy. And Maureen Kincaid Speller rightly made the crucial parallel between the traditionally (in Christianity) "lower" body and the lower classes:

> ...all these portrayals of a transhuman or posthuman existence... show privileged societies, peopled by an elite who can afford to cut loose from their flesh containers and play throughout the Universe.... Who maintains this existence for them? .. .who tends the machine or grows the new body? One is left to posit a mysterious invisible underclass,... rather like the servants running a Victorian country house, or the Hispanic gardeners and maids in Los Angeles. The emphasis is on choice, but choice is governed by material wealth, and that is surely no choice at all. ("Symposium" 89)

The lower classes traditionally (magically) include women, the lowest creatures on any religious scale. Since we don't have SF critics from the global periphery or from working classes (bar one or two maybe, I am from the semi-periphery), the female and feminist critics are as a rule most attuned to this. Not only Speller but also Helen Merrick rightly notes how "women, people of colour, and gay people" are accustomed to thinking of their bodies as constructed, usually by others ("Symposium" 96). Speller's Hispanic maids serve here an admirable triple purpose: they identify ethnicity, class, and gender of the oppressed and exploited, the immigrants from the colonised periphery of the global capitalist system into its core, who bring with them (in a fine show of poetic justice) the overt violence exported by the empires into their countries and classes one or two centuries ago. But of course, the economy and daily life of the rich would collapse without the working and consuming poor: so their immigration, legal or not, is tacitly or openly encouraged, while taking good care they do not get the economico-political rights of the unionised workers they're helping to displace and vanquish.

Finally, what does this do to the techniques of writing and reading SF? Not much, I'd think. Whatever Greg Egan's or anybody else's scientific and futuristic ideas, they still inevitably write for today's readers. The problem of "round characters" à la E.M. Forster, taken from 19th-Century Realism and propagated (but not practiced) in SF by Le Guin, seems to me no problem: SF does not have them, nor should it, nor can it: for it is a parabolic or emblematic and not a mimetic or naturalistic genre. Kingsley Amis had it right long ago: Gulliver cannot be a mariner out of Joseph Conrad – that is, an individual seen simultaneously from without and within, which gives the stereometric effect. All the interesting, indeed most ingenious variations involving non-human entities, for example, the "demons" of Walter Jon Williams's *Aristos*, are simply metaphors or emblems for existing facets (charms and quarks) of the Subjects or personalities today. Personality has, as pointed out by your panelists, always been fabricated: there is no original Rousseauist Noble Savage whom we have lost through capitalist technology. True, the pace of change enforced by computerised stock-markets seems unprecedented in duration and in global scope – the direst stresses of Auschwitz or Vorkuta or the Ithaca NY jail were less extensive. The fragmentation thrown up by the Subjects in answer to such stress will surely present some new recombinations, not necessarily pleasant. While it is only fair to try and get the best out of any situation one finds oneself in, its particular potential delights, the yuppie delight in them, well noticed (say) in Gwyneth Jones's review of Stephenson's *Snow Crash*, seems to me much too exaggerated, one-sided, and more than somewhat irresponsible. And the reader of 2001 or 2010 will be able to accept and understand more fragmentation than before, not so much because Prigogine or Foucault have by now percolated into the intelligentsia but because the reader's life will be increasingly such: run where the corporations wants you, when it wants, and how it wants; and the wants change with the profit winds. But a story will still have a beginning, middle, and end, simulacra of people and of landscapes in time, and so on. In the evolution of Homo sapiens, the 4,000 years from Homer and Gilgamesh are not such a big deal.

But we do kill and maim more efficiently.

Q. 11–12: ON D. SUVIN, HIS PATH IN SF, AND SF CRITICISM AT PRESENT

Thanks for the kind questions, Van! Well, I think the civic *persona* of Darko Suvin is only interesting because certain historical shapings happen to have crossed and possibly fused in his flesh (including the brain). As best I can make sense of those shapings, they were first of all my family ambience. My father was an MD specialising in dental prosthetics, who had the good fortune to have lived through a socialist (well, semi-socialist maybe, but that was an awful lot then and there) revolution during and after the Yugoslav, and world, anti-fascist Second World War 1941–45. He had studied in Vienna (for Zagreb, our native city, to my childhood home in which I still think back fondly, was in his youth a part of the rotting Austro-Hungarian empire), and there tried for the very newfangled Freudian psychiatry, only to be told by an assistant of Freud that he had no talent for discovering the proper symptoms and complexes – so I have a family inheritance (I guess) of suspicion toward individualist psychology and its facile circles and wedges. Though very small and gracile, he managed to survive two years as a Partisan doctor and eventually was a main founder of the Stomatological Faculty at the University of Zagreb, dying revered by his pupils, then deans and professors – happier than we are in foul PoMo times where having master-teachers is considered irksome (so much the worse for all of us and our craft). I might have inherited from him my scholarly side, for he published many articles and books on prosthetic dentistry. But as usual for sons – and Hitler's rise to power saw to it that I remained an only child – the most important shaping came from my mother, a strong and worldly-wise personality, who from a young bourgeois lady before WW2 evolved into somebody saving her nuclear family during the war under three Fascist states (Croatia, Germany and Italy) and then into a chief secretary of a research institute – one of those really running the place – in socialist Yugoslavia. Those interested in my feelings at her death can find it in my book of verse *The Long March*, in the poem "Be Still in Peace" and the shorter "The Watch Given to the Verse-Smith by Trude": for I've been writing poetry on and off from 1951 (and short prose even longer), first in Croato-Serbian and then (after I began dreaming in English in the 70s, so Freud had some good insights) in English.

I was a translator and interpreter (English-Italian) already as a very young boy who had fled with his mother in a fishing boat from a Dalmatian island across the mine-infested and German bomber-infested Adriatic Sea to the newly liberated southern

Italy in October 1943. I remember spurning the offer to learn the piano at the age of 7 or so (my father played Vienna waltzes on it, very rarely) and choosing to learn languages instead, which resulted in an intense and lifelong but totally consumerist love of music, Bach to Bartok and the Beatles and not much further I'm afraid – one's sensibility does close down at 40 or so, which is how I explain Lukács's misunderstanding of Brecht. I was enrolled in the daringly progressive Montessori kindergarten in Zagreb at the age of 4 I think (English and French) – and yes, I come from the bourgeois intelligentsia (my two grandfathers were respectively a small "colonial goods" merchant and a bank chief bookkeeper) whose nose was in the Fascist times rubbed into the betrayals our class shamefully wreaked on its own whilom ideals, Milton to Mill to Mazzini, so that they found abode with Marx. So the (temporally) second main influence on me is the profound plebeian antifascist liberation movement I saw and felt, viscerally indeed, both in Dalmatia and indirectly in liberated Italy. Marxism as a theory came upon its heels; it has its own huge intellectual delights but it was never (I hope) for me a bloodless dance of concepts, Parisian style; which is why I don't feel a need to jettison the still crucial insights of Marxism when the historical movement – for a time – collapsed (though I've been working a lot on just what needs to be modified in it, such as 19th-Century scientism).

I read the *Communist Manifesto* when back in Zagreb in my early teens at the end of 1945 – in a wartime printing by a Partisan brigade agitprop section I got from my father – and I still remember the passage about the proletariat not being able to liberate itself without upending the whole structure of bourgeois life as vividly as I do my first love (at age 10) and my first sex experience (much later): "yes," I said to myself excitedly, "that's it"! I didn't quite know – not having yet studied the Roman kings – what the proletariat was, but I knew they were the poor, oppressed, and persecuted, so surely I belonged with them (for the Fascists had dispossessed us of everything but life and the pursuit of happiness) just as much as the peasants in Yugoslav Army uniforms. I joined the still mysterious and hush-hush Young Communist League at the end of the same year, in high school, and in 1948, during Tito's break with Stalin, I was as it were drafted – protesting my unworthiness – into a Communist Party preparing a mass basis for that tough struggle (which also meant that if the Russians occupied Yugoslavia, as was quite possible, I would have been a good candidate for one of the grapes they would hang on the city lamp-posts). I did get, as I discovered later, both into the KGB and the CIA files at the time. Well, you sheltered and cosseted people from the upper "Western" 10% of the globe can maybe see this is a quite normal – or indeed an extraordinarily lucky – East (or better Southeast) European biography: a German bomb fell 50 meters from me, and if their technoscience had been up to the Vietnam War standards (never mind today), I wouldn't have gone on to "the pinnacle of international 20th-Century criticism," as the flattering Dr. Ikin puts it, or anyplace else but a small rocky grave for my pre-teen fragments. Living on borrowed time your whole life – and seeing that other children like me in Korea or Vietnam or Angola or the Black ghettoes of the US of A may not be so lucky – wonderfully clears the mind.

And how did I get to SF? Not by way of Sumatran jungles like Brian Aldiss or the skyscraper bureaucracies of New York like Fred Pohl or the campus oases into which a dying Native wanders like Ursula Le Guin (to mention only three people I know well enough to speculate biographically about), but by way of having lived in say six years (1940–46) in 5 regimes: a monarchist despotism, two Fascist states of militarised terror, the "Western" allies in Italy 1943–45 with some insight in the corrupt business of profiting from feeding hungry Italy, and the peasant communist revolution in postwar Zagreb... And I have no words, even after a lifetime, to describe the outrageous sense of annihilating psychophysical anxiety and heart-constricting persecution a small boy in fear for his existence can feel when subjected to the monstrous threats from which the Revolution was the only salvation. Thence I guess my assiduous reading of utopias from More on (eventually SF from Lucian on) to Wells, of course preceded at age 11 or so by every European child's hefty dose of Jules Verne. I wrote an extrapolative mini-utopia of a united classless world for a high-school assignment in I think 1948 (just an anatomy without characters, I fear, though I think it did have a point-of-view narrator zooming around daringly between continents in an airplane), which I have alas failed to find among the school papers my wife Nena retrieved last year from a friend's attic in Zagreb. But of course I studied "high lit," there was nothing else (except sciences, in which I first did a 6-year degree): English and French – German was still too painful, though reading Hegel, Karl Marx, and Karl May, as well as a pretty young redhead with green eyes from Munich on the Adriatic, eventually cured me of that. I specialised (if that's the word – I've always been easily bored and going on to new fields) in Drama, having studied that also at Bristol UK, the Sorbonne in Paris, and eventually Yale for one semester or year in each place, as an indigent foreigner unwillingly imitating the *vie de bohème*.

I suppose Van Ikin's formulation, that SF (he also mentions literary, and I'd add cultural, theory) was "a destiny chosen for me, rather than by me" has a good share of truth: we are given only a few choices by History (my name for destiny), and if wise we choose the one we were having elective affinities toward anyway, before conscious choice. Theater was for me utopian oases of storytelling in the fleshly present: but I've always had a commonsense, I guess bourgeois intellectual, distrust of crassly intrusive collectivities, having gone through my share of them (I remember with some horror visiting Chip Delany around 1970 in a NYC commune where he was living and which he has recently so beautifully described), and I've never ventured into the whip-wielding-cum-cajoling role of a theatre or maybe movie director, so that the nearest I came was dramaturge (art director?) of a student theatre: and of course critic, historian, theoretician first of drama and then even of performance. But this faded after moving from Europe, my great and untranscended shows of the 1950s–60s' Golden Age in Stratford, London, Paris, Milano, Berlin... SF, always considered as between the utopian and antiutopian horizon, as – I decided later – a sort of parable for us, was then what we weren't but could perhaps be, or at least could explore analogs of us as being. You'll understand that there's a certain importance and urgency about such a business, not simply competing (as Poul Anderson put it) for the idiot multitude's beer money.

Again, History intervened. I discovered that the revolutionary afflatus was fading back home, I dimly felt the Party bureaucracy had let the self-management project – in which I'd been involved – slide when it got too close to (their) power; I had a falling out with the dominant forces at my Faculty of Arts in Zagreb (the Nationalists hated me and the Party people didn't defend me), so I decided I could be an alienated intellectual anywhere I could fruitfully work. The only proper job I could get was first in Amherst MA in 1967, and then at McGill University in Canada from 1968 on (I retired in 1999). Students had been rioting there too, demanding power, French-language teaching, and more interesting courses – including SF. They didn't get the first two, but they got a "Marxist" teaching drama and – on and off – an SF course: some who later became my friends confessed to an immense disappointment when the Marxist appeared in suit and tie! But I'm a European committed to the life of the mind and dislike drugs of any sort, from tobacco and marijuana to Scotch and Disneyland (I do have a small chink for white wine and Italian brandy). What I taught the first 10 years can be partly seen in the *MOSF*, which however doesn't include the oodles of contemporary SF I was teaching, Heinlein to Le Guin and Dick, better seen in *Science Fiction Studies* (*SFS*) at the time. So I never had academic problems in teaching SF, this was riding the wave of the epoch and became a recognised niche in academia – I even got Fredric Jameson to write for *SFS* and sit on its Board with Northrop Frye and sundry academic worthies. Just luck. And I continued in tandem to write about Brecht and Beckett and John Arden.

Q. 13: SF CRITICISM AT PRESENT, LACUNAE

> *Let us, in the interests of propaganda, compile a list of problems we do not pretend to have solved.*
>
> Brecht

Of course I won't compile a Brechtian list here either for SF criticism in general (Marc Angenot and I gave it a shot in the essay "Not Only but Also," in my *Positions*, 44–60, but this was in another country and the wench is dead) or for mine own. For one thing, it might be too long. For another, a single person cannot do it, only a group; and I should stress here that I deeply disbelieve in copyrights and geniuses, so that whatever strengths my criticism may have truly derives from my having – in a doubtless truncated way, dictated by our social (dis)organisation – functioned as a focuser and formulator of group debate, incorporating selected hints, insights, scoldings, proposals... by, say, the co-editors (Dale Mullen, and then Marc Angenot) and almost the whole board of consultants of *SFS* during my 1973–81 tenure – just as half of the contributions in that period of *SFS* bear traces of my hands-on editing. I simply wish to indicate the most glaring gaps, which prey most on my mind. From what is to be done in SF criticism, I pick out one matter which seems to me a key: *the parable as the strategic (creative and critical) tool* – which then logically entails a reconsideration of Fantasy.

When Patrick Parrinder (as editor) and I were discussing a possible title for a volume of essays by various hands at the occasion of my retirement, due out this Summer from Liverpool and Duke UP, I suggested that instead of "Cognition and Estrangement" it really ought to be "Cognition, Estrangement, the Novum, and the Parable." This was an only semi-joking proposal, for my (teleologically) final essay in the *Positions* book advances a view of SF that takes a new tack in comparison to the first three terms from *MOSF*, though

I trust it is not incompatible with them, as a further analogy or variant of flexibilised allegory. In art rather than science, the nearest analogy may be the "moment of Cubism" (thus Picasso rather than Einstein), which John Berger dates ca. 1910–14, but in his sense of a horizon where all was possible I'd extend it to the new generation after 1917, to the Left Modernism of Joyce, Chaplin, Eisenstein, and Brecht. It would not be too difficult to correlate this with the debates between the open and closed interpretations of Marx (Bloch's "warm stream vs. cold stream," say Luxemburg or Gramsci vs. Kautsky or Stalin), in which the "cold" pole eschewed the scandal of dialectics in favour of the comforting Newtonian predictive element ("iron laws") inherited but also transcended by Marx.

I cannot here retraverse the theory of parable, but may only in the most abbreviated way (to be filled in by the kind reader reaching for the old essay) repeat that the parable has perennially been the privileged genre – and even more: the privileged *method*, which can therefore extend to stories of any length – of fruitfully marrying textual seduction (in the "vehicle") and cognitive consummation (in the "tenor"). You'll note it is a highly affective, nay erotic, way of bringing about what Brecht called "the gentle might/ authority/ violence of reason" (*die sanfte gewalt der vernunft*), the feedback between the universal and the singular that constitutes any cognition. This way may be sneered at by people who cannot imagine that reason may be seductive – poor they! For they are weighed in the balance against Aristophanes, countless *mashal*-writing rabbis, Jehoshua of Nazareth, Gautama the Enlightened, Swift, Lessing, and so many others: "I had not thought death has undone so many" (T.S. Eliot).

All very well, I hear the dogmatic Post-Modernists reply, we know Bellamy wrote impressive parables and Wells stories which are narrativised parables (as "The Country of the Blind"), but what has this to do with us in the new dispensation? Well, maybe little with you – though I read much Derrida and Guattari-Deleuze as parables, and in fact the whole Post-Modern vulgate-text is one mega-allegory of the lovehate at the loss of Master Narrative and of the clever hysteria of Hegel's Serf without a Master – but a lot with the state of affairs we're trying to understand today. The parable is the most complex, refined, and populist form of allegory, opposed to the elitist theological combats of Virtues and Vices, those black-and-white exorcisms. The overall horizons of allegory to my mind deal with the horizons of the relationships of art to truth, or of narrative and metaphoric imagination to conceptualised, normative doctrine. In other words, allegory has to do with the interplay between what is in social hegemony held to be true (and thus in a way privileged and indeed sacred) and what is held to be feigned (and what has therefore, historically, oscillated uncomfortably between being unholy, just entertaining, or a second mode of privileged cognition). This has become more complex and exacerbated after the capitalist Industrial Revolution, which both installed inescapable social dynamics and yet held fast to the ruling-class traditional belief that history is at a qualitative end, and – in the new bourgeois variant – only quantitative growth remains (as in sports' records or computer software: faster, higher, more). What then is the role of new creativity, which is as it were generically discontinuous from the privileged body of normatively "true" texts, which is fiction or heresy rather than fact or orthodoxy?

I have argued in a brief old text (Suvin, "Preliminary") that all allegory, verbal or otherwise, is a more or less admitted relationship between a new proposition and an existing privileged set of normative and ruling propositions that the allegory re-produces (*egoria*) in a variant and other (*allos*, dare I say estranged?) way; and it might be apparent how discussions of the novum necessarily intertwine with allegorical horizons. I noted there an inherent tension in a dynamic bourgeois society between piety and creativity, the static tradition of doctrine and the deviating pressure of experience, so that a modern parable can only be faithful after its own fashion: even the most believing creators are uncomfortable allies for priests, I concluded on the basis of my own heretical Titoist experience. Within such horizons, the small forms of proverb, riddle, animal (or Alien) fable, and parable will be more open to a conflict of authority than the "large forms" of mythical and religious systems, which are inexorably drawn into a confirmation of (sometimes new) authority.

The parable is, then, traditionally a way of intimately relating doctrine to fiction – and vice versa. The traditional politico-religious point of the parable is to open the listener's ears to the irruption of (often new) understanding, Bloch's "aha-effect": "O now I see that the tiny grain of mustard seed growing into the biggest bush of them all is Christ's Word about the Kingdom of Heavens growing into my heaven-reaching faith in it!" Theoretically, one might expect the parable not to survive the death of God in the 20th Century, the rise of competing macro-godheads and tribal godlets which entailed the slaughters of tens of millions as well as the starving of and psychic terror over, and thus evacuation of imaginative reason from, hundreds of millions, that have between them irretrievably sullied the alternatives of ideology and the Id. But practice is always slyer than theory, and while Old Nobodaddy might be dead, the parable has managed to survive in two ways, identified with Kafka and Brecht (not counting nostalgic reactions back to reach-me-down Romanticism). Kafka managed to write parables – as Beckett managed to write Mystery-plays – against a backdrop of "zero doctrine," that is, the painful absence of community values and interhuman sense that was traditionally codified into a more or less religious doctrine, so that his isolated protagonist became a grotesque lone creature (my favourites are the animal fables of "The Burrow" or "Josephine the Songstress" rather than the clearer almost-SF of "The Penal Colony," but the overt thumbnail sketch is in "The Door of the Law"). Brecht on the whole successfully navigated the whirlpools between the Scylla of nihilism (Kafka) and Charybdis of pseudo-religious Marxism as belief-into-scientific-destiny (not confined to Stalin) in order to approach a paradoxically experimental doctrine in which it is the method of fitting the sight to the situation seen that matters and not any system. The allegorical Little Man Schweik finally meets the allegorical Ruler Hitler at the end of one of Brecht's most engaging parables of how to survive despotism, and Hitler fails: he is not prepared for Winter... Neither is Joan Dark in the slaughterhouses of locked-out Chicago, an awful warning – the first "new map of hell," in fact – how the unemployed and dispossessed have to stick to each other or miserably die (*St. Joan of the Slaughterhouses*). It's a cold world, my masters, and you better be prepared – by slyness, wit, and method.

As I was arguing, after Marx and Nietzsche it's no go for parables – or any other allegories – which trust in the Transcendental Signifier, the doctrinal tenor as soul or static essence, to which is then adjusted the imaged story, the vehicle as sensual body: they cannot satisfy. If there is to be any soul or essence (I argue in "Two Cheers" that a dynamic, changeable essence is necessarily to be posited in order to speak about anything), it can only be decisively co-constituted by the body – here the story with its figures and metaphors. Surely all flesh is grass and in a way perhaps the vanity of vanities, but it's the last line of defence and offence, delight and memory, left to us. In fact, if the Platonic-Idealist doctrine of two realities is thereby refused – the soul being either a changeable disposition of flesh or nothing at all – it is no longer quite true that the vehicle is concrete (plant) and the tenor abstract (belief in the Kingdom), and we might even pose the question whether this understanding of allegory is not characteristic of German Idealism and Romanticism, a late and degenerate form. Was King Pluto concrete but riches an abstract concept for Aristophanes, was Christ's Kingdom To Come really abstract for medieval believers? In this intimate interaction, the fact that the tenor is being elicited by such-and-such a Possible World cannot be simply subsumed by the tenor's concept or even its image and then forgotten, otherwise we'd have to equate any such fictional text to a leading article written against the same horizon. (This is my problem with the useful "discourse theory," debated for years now with Marc Angenot.) An irreducible surplus is engendered by the humanising features of World, Figuration, and Narration of their interactions.

To exemplify it by contraries: the contingent grain of mustard-seed gives rise to a stout suspicion that whatever tenor is built by means of it may get into trouble once the world of the listener is sufficiently removed from Mediterranean agriculture. A post-industrial Kingdom of Heavens may have to cease being a Kingdom and in Heavens, acquire a dynamic vector, etc. Post-industrial cognition can only proceed by experimental construction out of "nature's" (the production mode's) constriction, the main constriction or resistance as well as source of strength in capitalism being the money economy (on which Balzac's realism is founded). Thus science, which anyway stems from human relationships that it then strongly inflects, is the philosophical – or better, methodological – model for steering their dynamics.

In storytelling terms, this means no explicit "moral" of the fable or tenor of the parable is imaginable and thus tellable today, unless it be the moral of open-endedness: History does not end, and this is no small matter when all the *gleichgeschaltet* media tell us it's ended definitely (and as we can see badly). And conversely, the "show" of vehicle is to be much "thicker," much more validated by material(ist) details or "realistic," much more livable-in and seductively ostended, than the usually laconic and somehow reticent, wry European brevity of Brecht's or indeed Kafka's. Both of them knew roughly or precisely what to expect; we today do not know: we must not believe Kafka, we cannot believe Brecht (who is politically equivalent to a warm halfway house between Lenin and Luxemburg). Yet the most important matter remains that in any such ongoing history Kafka's and Brecht's Judgments are inescapable, and the Trial may be upon us sooner than we think.

Works Cited

Amis, Kingsley. *New Maps of Hell*. Harcourt, Brace, 1975 [original 1960].

Broderick, Damien. *Reading by Starlight*. Routledge, 1995.

Calvino, Italo. "Per Fourier," in his *Una pietra sopra*. Einaudi, 1980.

Debray, Régis. *Le Pouvoir intellectuel en France*. Ramsay, 1979.

Harré, R[on]. *The Philosophies of Science*. Oxford UP, 1972.

Human Development Report 1996. Ed. UN Development Programme. Oxford UP, 1996.

Jones, Gwyneth. *Deconstructing the Starships*. Liverpool UP, 1999.

Suvin, Darko. "On Cognitive Emotions and Topological Imagination." *Versus* no. 68–69 (1994): 165–201.

Suvin, Darko. "Considering the Sense of 'Fantasy' or 'Fantastic Fiction.'" *Extrapolation* 41.3 (2000): 209–47 [chapter 4 of this book].

Suvin, Darko. "On the Horizons of Epistemology and Science." *Critical Quarterly* 52.1 (2010): 68–101.

Suvin, Darko. *The Long March: Notes on the Way 1981–1984*. Hounslow ON, 1987.

Suvin, Darko. "Novum Is as Novum Does," in K. Sayer and J. Moore eds., *Science Fiction, Critical Frontiers*. Macmillan and St. Martin's, 2000, 3–22.

Suvin, Darko. "Polity or Disaster: From Individualist Self toward Personal Valences and Collective Subjects." *Discours Social/Social Discourse* 6.1–2 (1994): 181–210.

Suvin, Darko. *Positions and Presuppositions in Science Fiction*. Macmillan and Kent State UP, 1988.

Suvin, Darko. "Preliminary Theses on Allegory." *Umjetnost riječi* no. 1–3 (1977): 197–9.

Suvin, Darko. "Two Cheers for Essentialism and Totality: On Marx's Oscillation and Its Limits (As Well As on the Taboos of Post-Modernism)." *Rethinking Marxism* 10.1 (1998): 66–82.

Suvin, Darko. "Utopianism from Orientation to Agency: What Are We Intellectuals under PostFordism to Do?" now in his *DBH*. P. Lang, 2010, 217–67.

Williams, Raymond. *Keywords*. Oxford UP, 1985.

7

Poems of Old Age I (2000–04)*

FOUR DEPARTURES FROM HEINE

2.

In the forest in the gloaming
I was given a strange vision
The Queen of Fairies was a-roaming
Clearly seen, without misprision.

Round & round me her train went
& she turned & flashed a smile
Tell me, O Queen, just what this meant
Spare me, Mab, the miss a mile.

Did you stage it for my learning?
To reward my fealty?
Does it mean a love returning?
Does it mean the death of me?

3.

Red-eyed bloody business weather!
One-eyed profit-ordered town!
How i wonder when – not whether –
Earthquakes rise to break you down.

5.

For on this rock we shall erect
The Church that works from downside up
The Third Age church of Holy Bodies
Both personal & congregational:

See: hunger, killings are not needful
The pie in TV skies deceives
Give us today our daily sweets
Give us down here the sacred hearts & sense.

Return to body its merry pump
Rid of the fat that has enclogged it
The overeating brought by hunger
The ulcers caused by profit slash & burns.

Return to brain its hormonal bath
Disturbed by wolfish enmities
To people & birds & beauteous trees –
When heart & brain work well, we shall be saved.

If you, O masters, will not let us
Be saved, entirely we must
Remove you: profit is the fat
In bloodstream, profit brings the early stroke.

Your lying church will be dismantled
Our Earth at last inhabitable,
Polluted eyes may see no godheads
The cleansed may go to many-coloured stars.

When holiness meets wholeness
& the people absolute,
Washed clean of Class Division Sin
We may aspire to the cosmic Lute.

14. (Doctrine)

Drummer, drum on & have no fear
& kiss the bare-breast Liberty!
This is the whole of science & art
The sum of all philosophy.

Drum & inveigle the drowsy people
Send the snake's hiss & roar of lions,
One step in front, ready to die,
This is the sum of art & science.

This is old Karl's dialectics
Of all philosophy it is the Summa.

I've understood it because i'm not stupid,
& saw the Revolution one Summer.
6-14700

LE CENERI DI TITO (BERLIN DAY, END OF C20)

German winter   elder ladies with mink coats
Peroxide hair   too much makeup
Lines slashing from both mouth corners down & out
I burrow into sleep quietly on morning islands
At the bottom of the ocean schools of fish
Soft murmur of weary voices
They are bombing Beograd & Novi Sad
No more theatre festivals in springtime
Blood silting up all rivers.

Whispering of fish   jealousy of fish
If sharks were men
Big gangsters eat little gangsters
Peasants are burned out of their villages
City people bombed out of their homes
Thousands of Munch faces screaming
Humans   from their womb humanity forcibly ripped
By progressive technology & humanism
Demanding oceans of blood

Western brainwashed in uniform shoot at Balkan brainwashed
The center doesn't tolerate too much periphery
Top dollar American mercenaries bomb scared Serbian draftees
Bristly bearded gangsters from Beograd cleaning Albanians out of medieval monasteries
They are madly in love with the Serbian destiny to suffer
Smooth shaven gangsters from Washington upgrading armament technology
They are madly in love with the profits of arms industries
Booms in Balkan skies   booms on the stockmarkets
Communicating slaughterhouse vessels

Oceans of blood   oceans of profit
Who is king of the world jungle must be made quite clear
Sharks are not so clever   except in fable

Now you can touch what we lost with Tito's brotherhood & unity
Now you see how a people's revolution is eradicated

One million & three quarters dead in the partizan war
A ton of TNT to wipe out every dead partizan
These dead are dangerous they must be killed again by bombs & lies
Counter-revolution by the center against the periphery
Blood on stone blood & stones
Thou shalt not get out from under world banks fish mouth silently

This is Moses & the prophets

700-251200

AUTOBIOGRAPHY 2004: DE DARCI NATURA

With thanks to brother Nazim Hikmet

Beginnings

I was born in 1930, amphibious year in between disasters
I've left my native city for good in '67
I left it many times before & returned many times since,
Until that year, it was 1991
when it left me
Alone with my writings, Nena,
a few friends, smouldering memories,
Mourning, indignation.

When i was 11 i fled from the killers speaking my language
Already i had begun learning other languages
I had refused to learn playing the piano, some obscure
Daimon led me to say
"I'll learn languages instead", deciding
Daimon, his bitter tears
at age eight into my soup scotched
All talk of going to Palestine.

When i was 11 i heard it on the radio
the Germans were bombing Beograd
When i was 69 i saw it on television
the US were bombing Beograd
Between the bombings my life was spared
i owe it to the dead
To speak up against fear: articles for Wall Newspapers
First utopian sketch at 17, first poem at 21

On a May First, already

Elegiac, a girl was leaving me, the Party was leaving me
(I knew the first & was to learn the other). When
I was 13 i changed from
                    a refugee in my carved-up country
To refugee sundered from my country
                                        amid another language
Crossing a narrow sea with hundreds in a fishing boat, seriously
Holding on to the one suitcase

Too young to be afraid amid minefields, under Nazi bombers
No more anxious than usual for a *confinato*
Whose parents could be shot any morning. So i crossed from occupation
To liberation, into the city of Bari
                                    marvellous to youthful eyes
Where horse-drawn coaches had a plank
                                    at the back between the wheels
For daring schoolboys to jump on.

When i was 21 my daimon decided, stubborn daimon,
Walking the sunlit streets of a Spring Sunday
To quit the repetitive certainties of engineering for the discoveries
Of arts & letters, of the planks
                                that mean unforeseeable life
People in student theatre
                                won out over things in the lab
With my heart in my throat.

Thus it all took shape, in the yellow afternoons of Zagreb
In the sunlight blazing back blue from Adriatic wavelets
Between the lines of Balzac
                            & Shakespeare, the Russians & Krleža,
Tito & Hegel, Engels
                    & Lenin on the two souls
All irretrievable now, the communist
                                        youth, confident hopes,
& i was on my Way.

Reflections

Some grow up to know well the names & kinds of trees, others
Of city streets (friend Mirkec knew all those of Zagreb
Better than any taxi-driver)

i grew up knowing departures
Thru guarded borders, but reading Dante, & Bert, & Nazim
Understood i was one of the demographic tens of millions
Exiled by injustice.

I am lucky: i've slept mostly in my own bed, even if at times
In poor rented rooms, & only twice, briefly, in friendly
Camps for refugees, a pet nightmare
like the car backfires
Bursting upon my ear like German bombs;
i haven't really hungered
Tho near enough to guess at it

& quite near enough to understand terror & humiliation
& how reason is the only shield & sword
In proletarian hands, labour-power
sellers of brawn & brain
Like BB, my example in politics:
"a party consisting of one person"
(His writings, friends, his unforgotten memories)
"Closely allied to communists".

I've loved many women of my time, loved the best image
Of my possible self in & together with them
Monogamy comes to me as a kitten purring at my
Ankle, i stroke its head
distractedly, with real affection.
I'm changeable but always loyal, i envy only the dead
Milton, Marx & such ilk.

I rode a bicycle around Zvonimirova Street as a boy
A Vespa around Zagreb & an NSU scooter to Lošinj
At the age of 30 i flew
for the first time, Dubrovnik to Beograd
I've had three small cars, two accidents, & left driving gladly
Preferring to steer my thots down unforeseen roads
I've survived the worst of capitalist *realia*, bombs & cars
I've broken off relations with the megapowers
of cellulars & iPods
I've been lucky

To escape & learn to know much Europe, much North
America, the warm seas & breezes of the Caribbean

& Mediterranean, & above all Japan
                that princess descended from the Moon
Cruel & kind; & i learned from the gods of the sea waves
                                of the Sava
& Thames & Avon & the Seine, Saint-Laurent & the Spree,
The plangent fates of humanity

& returned to the waves some insights i learned. My poems
In two languages, published in obscure places
On three continents, have been read by a few friends, so many
Numbers for the absent biographer
                    the poems are the best me
& the best i can say for myself is
                    i kept the faith comrades
In this sad & wondrous time.

<u>Retrospect</u>

What did i want? The pursuit of happiness when young, but more & more
One thing: to live this brief life on beauteous Earth
Not like exploited tenant
                buckling down to parasite bosses
or like landlord, but like steward
                    handing on to those coming after
Our family house preserved, cleansed from the worst vermin
Maybe even repainted.

I wanted to believe, as brother Nazim, in the trees,
The wheat, but above all the sea – *thalassa, thalassa*!
& in my strange fellow forked
                animals, man unkind,
In my own class, presumed intellectuals: alas, i could not
Even women not rarely failed me
                    or i failed them, class
Corruption runs deep...

I grew discontented with the worsening
                        times, not happy to be
A nay-sayer like mad Swift, but making the best of a bad obligation
As the addictive drug of destruction
                    spread our rulers among,
Disliking not merely our murdering set-up but on top of it

The cruel gods of our small cosmic sector, the sadistic
Godlet of blind biology. Systems stand together no more.

Surely other universes must be better made, surely
We could make even this botched world better!
More similar to Mozart
                                        beauteous like Botticelli
Stern & compassionate like all great teachers, a forgiving mother
Infinite like the wine-coloured sea.

264-1504

Note

* All my poems have at the end an abbreviated form of *the date*: "i stamp them with history as calves on a ranch," said my master Brecht. "Le Ceneri di" means "The Ashes of" and associates to Pasolini's great poem *Le Ceneri di Gramsci.*

8

Circumstances and Stances: A Retrospect (2004)

Note 2020: *The editor of PMLA asked me to write a brief article (wordage precisely limited) for the end section of their issue on SF, and supplied some lead-ins to which I respond below.*

You asked me about the "particular cultural and political circumstances in which I write." They have changed decisively several times in my life. I have been several times an expatriate and finally an émigré from Yugoslavia, and am now an expatriate from Canada: my life has made me very attuned to global material and moral changes. I shall focus on the changes that I personally, being laggard, felt as inciding deeply on my professional work only in the last 10 years or so, the watershed for me being the illegal and immoral bombing of Serbia led by the United States. By then I had published three books on SF: *MOSF* (1979), *VSF* (1983), and *Positions* (1988) – and written enough further essays for a fourth book, which was scrapped when Liverpool University Press had its budget cut and/or fell out of love with me. The changes make me, alas, the bearer of bad news, for as I see it our rulers have in practice destroyed the wall that our disciplines wrongly thought existed between culture and political economics, and we had better draw the consequences. And yet the gesture and bearing (see Suvin "Haltung") of writing this report also imply a hope that, with much clarity, work, and luck, we intellectuals – writers and then critics – can make an important difference.

1. In this world of late aggressive capitalism without a human face, what we are allowed or denied to teach by its politicians and managers, what monies we are given or refused for research, intervenes into our daily lives in unprecedented, capillary ways. A primary factor shaping our situation is the bending of all technological and other cultural innovations to the purposes of capitalism as a totalising system. Two-thirds of the Gross National Product in the societies of the capitalist North today derive from the mental labour of the new middle classes, whose core is constituted by intellectuals. Richard Ohmann's classical book about the role of English in America notes, "Knowledge (technical, scientific, managerial) is accountable, not only for the material triumphs of [the capitalist] system, but for the all-encompassing control it has over the way we live" (273). Through copyright and patent legislation, often through piratical plunder of non-patented knowledge, mental labour is being more and more

subsumed under exploitable property. We live in a "knowledge society": alas, one in which useful knowledge and perniciously fake knowledge are closely intertwined. Knowledge as use-value for living is being evicted by knowledge as exchange-value for profits, with its logical end in "smart bombs" for mass killings.

What, then, is knowledge? And what is the function of us intellectuals as bearers of knowledge? As to the first question, the economic collapse of Fordism and the political collapse of Leninism plus Keynesianism have shaken our epistemology: how come we thought we knew what we knew, when a good part of what we thought we knew beyond a peradventure in (say) 1945–74 has turned out to be inaccurate? Some certainties have become thoroughly uncertain, and I do not see how we can now gauge the correctness of any new hypothesis without establishing first a great deal about how do we know what we believe we know, about what is the *bon usage* of knowing and in knowing. There is no way around focusing on some knots within epistemology. I adopt the definition of epistemology as the theory of knowledge, dealing with the possibilities and limits of human knowledge, with the analysis of conceptual and other (e.g., affective) cognitive systems, and in particular with the critique of language and other sign systems as concrete consciousness.

For a starter: any epistemic tool of ours defines equally its object-types and its subject-wielders *as* something and *to (for)* something; its embodied adoption co-defines our access to the world of signifying and significant potential actions. Any understanding intervenes into life to a certain degree – if only by refusing to intervene. In brief, it is imperative that we realise, as the feminists have, that epistemology does not function without our asking the political question "What for?" or *cui bono* (in whose interest?). Interests and values decisively *shape* all perception: it was Marx's great insight that no theory or method can be understood without the practice of social groups to which it corresponds. Thus our answers can be found only in feedback with potential action. As Vico argued, whatever we cannot intervene into, we cannot understand: it follows that *the epistemological and the political intertwine*. Those who do not put an explicitly defensible civic cognition at the heart of their professional cognition at best adopt the dominant epistemology of the time when they were students, and at worst adapt their cognition to the new epistemology of the Powers-That-Be.

I cannot here articulate properly an answer to the second question: our deeply contradictory situation as intellectuals, impacted like a split tooth. I have discussed this elsewhere ("Utopianism," "Novum," and "What May"), concluding that we are essential to the production of new knowledge but largely kept out of the strategic decision-making about our universities and about dissemination of our artifacts. Therefore, our civic concerns are not something we might hold, as it were, privately: indeed, we can only understand what our professional work may be if we understand how and why it is being shaped by identifiable national and international forces. The age of the Welfare-and-Warfare State saw the culmination of the cut from the global surplus we "middle" 10–15% – "administrators, technicians, scientists, educators" (Wallerstein 83–84) – were getting; and "the shouts of triumph of this 'middle' sector over the reduction of their gap with the upper one per cent have masked the realities of the growing gap between them and the other [85–90%]" (ibidem 104–05). This trend is since the 1970s being reversed, with much acceleration.

We cannot escape being involved in the politics and economics of knowledge. Like Gulliver, in Laputa.

2. What does this sharp change of circumstances mean for me? I have two answers; one is spatial and existential, the other temporal and professional.

First, I chose to retire in 1999–2000 and transferred back to Europe, not only my birthplace but – for all my admiration of many North American achievements and gratitude to Canada – my spiritual home. My move was also a political decision. Not only is it much easier to be a "senior citizen" where there are still chinks in consumer capitalism. It is also that, as Arnold Toynbee remarked half a century ago, "America is today the leader of a world-wide anti-revolutionary movement in defense of vested interests. She now stands for what Rome stood for. Rome consistently supported the rich against the poor in all foreign communities that fell under her sway..." (92–93). Paradoxically, I have to defend "America" – that is, the USA known from the media and the military – from most of my European intellectual friends, who are thoroughly disgusted at the reigning discourse in it and at the actions the discourse seeks to justify; I try to point out that from Jefferson and Thoreau to the present day the best and strongest critiques of the United States came from inside: in SF, some examples are Thomas Disch's forgotten masterpiece *334* (which draws a parallel between the US and the Late Roman Empire), and then the many splendid women writers from Joanna Russ and Ursula K. Le Guin on, and then the great dystopian tradition from the 1940s-50s "new maps of hell" on, and then... and then...

Finally, what do the new world circumstances mean for my work as a critic of SF? Criticism is for me still more of an art than anything else, and prescriptions ill fit a fast evolving state of art. Thus I may best answer your question by giving you examples of the shifts I found myself resorting to.[1]

First, they include not writing only about fiction but also taking on with philological tools, according to one's competence and conscience (both of which can be trained), the Orwellian discourse about war, errorism, immigrants, and similar issues – exactly what the MLA Delegate Assembly refused to discuss in 2002. This investigation further entails returning to our most kindred ancestral period, to my mind 1917–45, and writing about Benjamin's messianism, Brecht's combative hopes, as well as the role of German academics under Nazism.

Second, when writing about SF and neighbouring genres (such as the burgeoning Fantasy of both the "heroic" and "horror" varieties, overwhelmingly to my mind a bad involution that today dominates over SF on the library and bookstore shelves), I focused on the interaction of fictional scenarios and our pressing concerns. This work should not be taken for sociopolitical or philosophical criticism as extrinsic to literary or formal criticism, but for an integral epistemological rethinking similar to what the best activist critics (liberals in the 19th Century, socialists and feminists in the 20th) have always done, yet striving for new epistemico-political tools to face new necessities. The tools have to be invented. I tried out one such method in revisiting the first and probably still the best SF dystopia, Evgeniy Zamyatin's *My (We)*, so that my essay, I like to think, mimics the DNA double helix: it braids alternate sections of, on the one hand, how the text looks differently after the fall of the centralised State Leviathan which was its *raison d'être*, and, on the other hand, when we look at the new Leviathan of capitalist immiseration and plunder of Russia in order to find out why our eyes have changed. The result is certainly preferable to formalism on its own (still the ABC of our wisdom) but possibly too mechanical to claim the status of a model. I attempted something similar in an essay about the discourse of cloning in SF and science. Third, in the discussions of utopianism, I concentrated either on its relation to action or on dystopia, the state we are presently living in and can therefore understand well; furthermore, I strove to differentiate within dystopia between what is and what is not an antiutopia, that is: a piece of antiutopian writing, explicitly designated to refute a literary and political utopian horizon (such as some anti-Bellamy novels following on his *Looking Backward*, and similar manifestations from about 1917 on). Fourth, I investigated also within SF analogues to Benjamin's way out, which can be found in many places, such as the later writing of Philip K. Dick – its descent into total police-State dystopia (*A Scanner Darkly*) and its attempt to imagine salvation through a complex and in places ironic divine intervention (the VALIS cycle) – or the best SF writer who has to my mind emerged from the 1990s, K.S. Robinson.

Note

1 See my titles in Works Cited, especially "Considering," "Goodbye," "Reflections," "Science Fiction Parables," "Theses," and "With Sober." After some hesitation, it finally seemed advantageous to have them identified for those who would want to look some up.

Works Cited

Ohmann, Richard. *English in America*. 1976 [rpt. with new retrospective "Introduction" Wesleyan UP, 1996].

Suvin, Darko. "Considering the Sense of 'Fantasy' or 'Fantastic Fiction.'" *Extrapolation* 41 (2000): 209–47 [chapter 4 of this book].

Suvin, Darko. "Goodbye and Hello: Differentiating within the Later P.K. Dick." *Extrapolation* 43.4 (2002): 368–97.

Suvin, Darko. "*Haltung* (Bearing) and Emotions: Brecht's Refunctioning of Conservative Metaphors for Agency," in T. Jung ed., *Zweifel – Fragen – Vorschläge*. Lang V, 1999, 43–58.

Suvin, Darko. "Novum Is as Novum Does," in K. Sayer and J. Moore eds., *Science Fiction, Critical Frontiers*. Macmillan and St. Martin's, 2000, 3–22.

Suvin, Darko. "Reflections on What Remains of Zamyatin's *We* after the Change of Leviathans: Must Collectivism Be Against People?" in M. Barr ed., *Envisioning the Future: Science Fiction and the Next Millennium*. Wesleyan UP, 2003, 51–81.

Suvin, Darko. "Science Fiction Parables of Mutation and Cloning as/and Cognition," in D. Pastourmatzi ed., *Biotechnological and Medical Themes in Science Fiction*. University Studio, 2002, 131–51.

Suvin, Darko. "Theses on Dystopia," in R. Baccolini and T. Moylan eds., *Dark Horizons: Science Fiction and the Dystopian Imagination*. Routledge, 2003, 187–201.

Suvin, Darko. "Utopianism from Orientation to Agency: What Are We Intellectuals under Post-Fordism To Do?" *Utopian Studies* 9.2 (1998): 162–90.

Suvin, Darko. "What May the 20th Century Amount to: Initial Theses." *Critical Q* 44.2 (2002): 84–104.

Suvin, Darko. "With Sober, Estranging Eyes," Afterword to P. Parrinder ed., *Learning from Other Worlds: Estrangement, Cognition and the Politics of Science Fiction and Utopia*. Liverpool UP, 2000, and Duke UP, 2001, 233–71.

Toynbee, Arnold. *America and the World Revolution and Other Lectures*. Oxford UP, 1962.

Wallerstein, Immanuel. *Geopolitics and Geoculture*. Cambridge UP, 1992.

9

Of Starship Troopers and Refuseniks: War and Militarism in US Science Fiction (An Overview)* (2005)

For John and Judith Clute, 30 years of memories of Camden Town

To be whole is to be part.

Inscription on Odo's grave in *The Dispossessed*

"Do we get to win this time?"

Rambo's query in one of Stallone's movies

1. To Begin with: Some Generalities (Notions and Delimitations)

...autopsies are the place in which new lessons about anatomy are learned.

Fredric Jameson, *Postmodernism*

1.0. Why bother with Science Fiction[1] that deals centrally with war and/or militarism, and even devote to it a whole volume of *Fictions: Studi sulla narratività*? For one thing, because we live in a world increasingly determined by the unholy feedback between politico-economic militarisation and war: war as Clausewitz's continuation of politics by other means gives pride of place to war as the substitute for politics and unacknowledged pillar of the dominant system. For another thing, because SF has as its best always been a very interesting early warning system carrying cognitions and understanding otherwise accessible only in very specialised ways; and furthermore, even in its middle reaches, SF – read in the USA both by schoolboys and airforce generals, and by now also by many young women – is often a very good indicator of its readers' intimate preoccupations.

My favourite (alas) anecdote at this historical juncture is the following apocryphal one: Shklovsky said to Trotsky, "As a literary critic, I'm not interested in war." Trotsky responded, "But war is interested in you."

Thus, when we intellectuals from the richer world area shy away from understanding the immensely menacing context of our dwindling privileges, the pleasures of reading SF may be yoked to cognition.

1.1. About Science Fiction

Now, in good logic, when faced with such complex terms and notions as SF, War, and Militarism, not accessible by common sense or intuition, one should begin by devoting a lot of effort to define and delimit each of them. I can do so only partly, for a book would be required for each.

As concerns SF, however, I have written several books (*MOSF, Positions, VSF*) and subsequent considerations, and must respectfully ask the reader to look them up. I shall only mention that if one holds, as I roughly still do, that SF is a literary (etc.) genre *defined by the interaction of estrangement and historical cognition, and whose main formal device is a narrative chronotope and/or agents alternative to the author's empirical world*, then Hero Fantasy of the Tolkien and Co. type and Horror Fantasy of the Poe-through-Lovecraft-to-Stephen-King type each is another beast, which is not dealt with in this volume or introduction (I attempted to discuss their ahistorical worlds in "Considering").

1.2. Some Words on War

My definition of war, taken from my "Capitalism," in which detailed discussions and references can be found, is: *a coherent sequence of conflicts, involving physical combats between large organised groups of people that include the armed forces of at least one State, which aim to exercise political and economic control over a given territory*. This includes both wars between State-like entities and within one. However, one or more fights or skirmishes, even between groups of people such as mafia gangs, do not qualify. Though to my mind antagonistic competition regardless of human lives is the heartbeat of capitalism, for the present analytical purposes war does *not* include only metaphoric oppositions (for example Hobbes's everyday civil war, "where every man is enemy of every man"). The aim of war was originally the forcible expropriation in favour of a given social class – sometimes tribal or ethnic group – of booty, land, and/or labour power from the vanquished. However, in developed ("civilised") class societies war has also always been *ultima ratio regum*, a means to evade inner revolutionary tension by outer conquest, while in a multi-State system other indirect and intermediary (but crucial) aims may be added, such as securing advantages for coming tensions and conflicts – for example, dominion over sea lanes or oil resources – and the destruction of commodities and people.

Continuous warfare has *never ceased* under capitalism: "Warfare has been... central to capitalism and the nation-state system" (Kaldor 285). Definitions of war differ, but believable estimates put the number of killed in 20th-Century wars at 120 million, with many more than that wounded, persecuted, and traumatised. Between 1945 and 1993 at least 160 wars have raged with 30 million people killed (cf. Dal Lago, "La guerra"

16). The frantic search of the US corporate-military class for enemies that might justify further hundreds of billions out of the pockets of taxpayers shows the USA-USSR competition was largely a welcome excuse for "a permanent war economy" (phrase coined by Charles Wilson of General Electric in 1944, *in* Lens 14). We are already within the most terrible Hundred Years' War in human history. Just as capitalism came about in plunder wars, there is no evidence it could climb out of economic depressions without huge military spending, a "war mega-dividend" (best examples: the 1930s and the 1990s - cf. Kalecki, Amin, and Keegan). This was always understood in the workers' and socialist movement: Jean Jaurès phrased it as "le capitalisme porte la guerre comme la nuée porte l'orage" (capitalism brings war as the cloud brings the tempest). Much before Lenin, who took Russia out of World War 1, the socialists' slogan was "war upon war" (see Angenot, *Antimilitarisme*).

Finally, some words on the paradoxical relationship of war to political economy and production of goods. On the one hand, "A simple definition of a warrior might be a person who survives by taking what others have or have produced" (Love and Shanklin 283); yet on another, from the inception of the modern State and market, wars have always been "the greatest and the most profitable of investments" (Lefebvre, *Production* 275). Since the 1930s, the war industry on our planet has been engaged in unprecedentedly enormous production, circulation, and consumption-by-annihilation of commodities. In the '80s-90s, official military spending oscillated between 2.5% and 5% of world GNP but some estimates place the share of production due to the war industry at four times as much, while the share of research and its financing devoted to military R&D is believed to have *surpassed 50% worldwide*: both are growing rapidly, most notably in major powers such as the USA. In any case, research and procurements for war are *indispensable* for the stability of the economic and political system. A huge part of these trillions goes to the superprofits of "Northern" corporations, and a smaller but appreciable part for the maintenance of practically all the ruling mafias and classes in the world. As Gowan summed it up: "for the US to play the role of guardian and manager of the entire core [of capitalist powers after the Second World War] required militarising the American state on a permanent basis. But that in turn looked as if it might help resolve tricky problems of the domestic political economy" ("US" 25). The war economy palpably marks the divorce between capitalism and civic responsibility for other people and for the planet. But the stakes are even higher: if "the enduring, primary symbiosis between capitalism and war" (Kolko 474) means that wars are indeed necessary for the survival of this social formation, then the capitalist social formation has truly, as McMurtry argues, entered a "Cancer Stage."

Material production impinges directly on SF that deals with war: either overtly, in a few best cases (some Vonnegut and the borderline SF example of Pynchon seem to me untranscended) or, as a rule, by excision into the *non-dit* that however limns what is told in the narration as the ocean limns an island. It is a peculiar instance of Jameson's "effacement of the traces of production" which is a part of the taboo-field of repressing thinking about a possible role of classes within production as societal mega-groups with different and often conflicting interests (*Postmodernism* 314–15). No doubt, this disregard of production comes naturally to the armed forces whose task is destructive consumption (clearing the ground for new and more murderous production and profits), even though they are saturated with the newest devices for faster and larger mass killing lovingly described and extolled in all militarist SF from Heinlein on. Such production is simply considered a *deus ex machina* called "technology" (or today, more properly, technoscience). This reality of contemporary war machines is not far from the discourse of and on SF, which has in the USA since its mass coming about, which began with Gernsbackian science popularization, been enmeshed with what Joanna Russ has with angry perceptivity seen as "SF and Technology as Mystification" (*To Write* 26ff.), and indeed as the addiction of US capitalism – Russ would say patriarchy, and I'd say both are correct – to the technological fix. As she observed about academic work, the mystification of and addiction to technoscience "has allowed a lot of folks to go through the motions of thought and scholarship without ever touching such unpleasant and disturbing matters as what we all have to do to make a living" (26): but that would hold in spades for the effacement of who produces and appropriates what under which conditions in the military-industrial complex that sets up armed forces of all countries. Such repression and removal of production is then faithfully recorded, without making of it a problem, in the narrative depiction of an only slightly estranged war machine by surface realism in most SF under discussion (in better cases, when we're not in thinly veiled fairy tale or Western).

1.3. Even Fewer Words on Militarism

The military-industrial establishments of corporate capitalism, primarily in the USA, which produce "life-killing commodities" as the most profitable part of global trade (cf. McMurtry *Understanding*), are not only the strongest factor of organised international violence, but also possibly the strongest factor enforcing a world cultural revolution for the total colonisation of human life-worlds and eco-systems by the commodity economy.

Economically but also culturally, as the great US maverick Veblen found more than a century ago:

> The direct cultural value of a warlike business policy is unequivocal. It makes for a conservative animus on the part of the populace. During wartime, and within military organisation at all times, civil rights are in abeyance.... [T]he members of the community [will]... learn to think in warlike terms of rank, authority, and subordination, and to grow progressively more patient of encroachments on their civil rights.... Warfare, with the stress on subordination and mastery and the insistence on gradations of dignity and honor... has always proved an effective school in barbarian methods of thought. (391–93)

The strictly political fall-out of militarisation is, so far as I can see, only beginning to be properly assessed (but cf. beside the classic Mills *Power* now Burk ed., Busch, Caplow-Vennesson, van Creveld, Dal Lago *Polizia*, Herberg-Rothe, Joxe, Klare, Lyon). To maintain its power and profits, the Never-Ending Warfare needs, first, to constantly stress dangerous enemies, with or without a real basis. Second, it needs to efface the divide between peace and war, as well as between external and internal enemies. With the excuse of security, democracy can be suspended at will for all but a minority of the privileged, and citizen armies are jettisoned in favour of professional soldiers and mercenaries (and since the difference between them is supposed to be the presence of a permanent loyalty, that line too has grown ever thinner). If war is a police action, then it does not need democratic debate and approval; and obversely, a navy can be employed to prevent illicit immigration (say in the Mediterranean, cf. Busch). A first approximation to delimit the understanding of *militarism* may be discussions reviewed by Jabri (99–103), from which the following conclusions may be drawn: 1/ militarist practices (and their legitimation) conceal social contradictions through emphasis on conformity across the social divide; 2/ militarism means a proclivity of the rulers to propound military solutions to issues which could be solved by other means, and to organise acceptance of such solutions by "lower ranks"; 3/ in consequence, militarism leads to sharp rise of intolerance towards dissent and of manipulation of all information channels to preclude other solutions.

Militarisation then means a reorganisation of society to enforce militarism (cf. also Berghahn, Leone-Anrig, Mann, Mills, Tirman ed., and – too late to be taken into account here – Bacevich). *Militarisation is suspension of central civil liberties and subordination of all aspects of civil society to militarist "security" imperatives even in times of official peace.* Before colonial liberation movements, dictatorships enforced by bayonet and gun muzzle were the rule in all imperial possessions; in the 20th century such rule has become more common in nominally independent States than at any time since the rise of the bourgeoisie, marking well its degeneration. This is technically facilitated by the enormous elaboration of armaments, accessible only to large economic systems, and it is underpinned by the spread of both organisational complexity and of the brainwashing industries such as the mass press and media. As a result, "the new balance of forces has eroded rights won in earlier periods. The extraction of surplus value meets less resistance, and capital loses what civilising effects it might have had" (Schwarz 32). This explains how come we can be returning, as Eco's pioneering essay found, "Towards a New Middle Ages," with huge insecurity palliated by private armies and drugs, with nomads, mystics, and (I'd add) the neo-medieval genre of SF!

Thus we have to fall back on some understanding from the more civilised and hopeful time of Enlightenment, and I can today do no better than give you my two favourite citations, which were sent me by friends careless of proper bibliographical sources:

> ...Anyone can understand that war and conquest without and the encroachment of despotism within mutually support each other; that money and people are habitually taken at will from a people of slaves to bring others beneath the same yoke; and that conversely war furnishes a pretext for exactions of money and... for keeping large armies constantly afoot.... In a word, anyone can see that aggressive rulers wage war at least as much on their subjects as on their enemies,

> and that the conquering nation is left no better off than the conquered. (Jean Jacques Rousseau, *Abstract and Judgment of Saint-Pierre's Project for Perpetual Peace*, 1761)

> Of all the enemies to public liberty war is, perhaps, the most to be dreaded because it comprises and develops the germ of every other. War is the parent of armies; from these proceed debts and taxes. And armies, and debts, and taxes are the known instruments for bringing the many under the domination of the few.... No nation could preserve its freedom in the midst of continual warfare. (James Madison, 1795)

And we should always remember the great slogans of the Anglo-American dictatorship from *1984*, "WAR IS PEACE. IGNORANCE IS STRENGTH. FREEDOM IS SLAVERY": as Rousseau and Madison – and the whole anti-militarist tradition, from Enlightenment to the early 20th-Century socialists – knew, war, militarist subjection to an entrenched power clique, and brainwashing are aspects of the same depth process.[2]

Militarism necessarily implies the horizons of war as its justification. Obversely however, warmongering did not, before modern mass and total societies, necessarily imply militarism – Social-Darwinist or Hobbesian warfare sufficed.

1.4. Corpus

Having set up a few orienting beacons, how is one to get a handle on the sprawling SF texts dealing with War and/or Militarism? One has to start with a series of enforced manoeuvres for limiting this huge corpus. The first delimitation is to focus on the last 60 years – in which we today inevitably read premonitions of, and sometimes resistances to, a not only discursive putting into place of Never-Ending Holy Warfare in the era of the Bush Dynasty, the unhappy reason for all our dealings with such a matter in the first place. The second delimitation is to focus on literary fictions rather than on TV, movies, comics, videos, and computer games – see about them the contributions in the Suvin ed. *Fictions* issue, which this essay was originally introducing – that may be sociopolitically more important as immediate shapers of people's minds. Indeed, following Jameson's startling analyses, perhaps we ought to talk about architecture or more generally about command of space consubstantial with war and militarisation, with its "dialectics of privilege and shelter" (*Postmodernism* 289) shaping social power, evident for example in long distance killings as well as in redlined housing districts by "race."

The third delimitation is to focus on US SF, as befits the hugely dominant position of US-based warfare and military, as well as on analyses of either that SF or US culture: Gramsci's concepts of hegemony and historical alliance, but also of Fordism (which then leads to Post-Fordism), as continued in the post-60s' analyses, come immediately to mind as indispensable tools for approaching such a discussion. Finally, it is both impossible and unnecessary to deal exhaustively with any mention of war (and/or militarism) in SF; also, the mere presence of a marginal SF invention or trope in a non-SF story about war will not suffice. It is enough to make a few exemplary choices among narratives in which war (and/or militarism) are either the dominant theme or at least one of the central foci – though to my mind if a marginal treatment has some specially interesting features, if it is articulated especially well, then one should not be dogmatic and use whatever helps one's argument. But the stress has to fall on SF that deals with war/militarism as its central theme, and in such a way as to either: articulate that theme seriously beyond the clichés current in the author's locus; and/or present and articulate a take on, or stance toward, the theme that is not usually found. (Either would be what I consider at least in part a novum.)

These delimitations enclose an area for putative large-scale research. From it, I shall here have to mention vast segments only to say I shall not be focusing on them. This holds most of all for what has for good reasons constituted probably the bulk of both SF and SF criticism about war from the 40s to the 80s: *nuclear warfare*, the militarisation of society needed for it, the ensuing holocaust, and the probable dark age of breakdown in technoscientific civilisation and reversion to open Hobbesian warring for survival. True, nuclear warfare is, all experts know, quite possible again in the form of tactical mini-nukes used by the US – and possibly Israeli – armed forces under the post-Vietnam doctrine that "our" casualties must be very small so as not to upset short-range electoral politics, while casualties of the Enemy (whoever may be proclaimed as such) must be as huge as possible in as short a time as possible; in the future, non-State groups may well join this proliferating "club." To my mind, in a somewhat longer perspective, "normal" strength or Hiroshima-and-larger nuclear strikes are not at all impossible either: the end of 2004 brought reports of a renewed nuclear bombs' race between the USA and Russia, there are simmering conflicts which involve other nuclear powers (such as Pakistan and India, or Israel and Iran), while the mega-war between USA and China, openly envisaged in the US Righwingers' plans, looms in a still longer perspective. Yet this balance of MAD (Mutually Assured Destruction), apt to affect the whole planet, is at the moment – and in the whole period from, say, Reagan's times on – not the focus of either military reality or SF written under its goad. If it does re-enter the focus, we shall have to rethink matters. In the meantime, the reader interested in nuclear war can be referred to the work of Bruce Franklin, including the 1984 anthology he edited, and the secondary bibliography in Suvin ed., containing items Dr. Proietti and I culled from a much vaster critical literature, including the overviews in the Brians and Burns items. One hopes all of this will not be too rigid, so that for example UK-based writings will lurk in the background to contrast with the US-based ones, that there will be no ban on mentioning SF movies or fiction between Chesney and Heinlein,[3] and so on. But even after such maneuvers, the field remains huge; more than usually, any approach or set of approaches will have to acknowledge from the start its premises and its nature of a bet justified by possible cognitive results.

2. Singularities I: Historical Texts 1959–74, an Ambiguous Ascent

The old order is not yet dead, the new order cannot be born. In the half-light monsters arise.

Antonio Gramsci

2.0. The Two Souls of US SF

For the purpose of orientation at this uncommonly endangered point of history, I am proposing as a hypothesis (homologous to the discussion of intellectuals at the end) that there are two souls or stances within US SF. As any attempt at encompassing hundreds of texts in several generations, this digital hypothesis is more simplified than would be a full analogical spread, accounting for the ifs and buts and grey zones, which would however need a research institute with the budget of, say, one-fiftieth of an atomic submarine. At one extreme is, then, the stance that mass slaughters – with all weapons imaginable and regardless of the military-civilian divide, and with a concomitant militarisation of society – are inevitable for the salvation of the commonwealth, and should therefore be seen in a spread between sad necessity and cynical glee. Its characteristic seems to be that it refuses to even envisage possible causes making for war and militarisation, which would therefore be avoidable by uprooting such causes. At the other extreme is the stance that while dangers and lures of mass warfare and militarisation are real and have deep systemic roots, they ought to be resisted in all possible ways because the commonwealth would thereby either not be saved and/or corrupted into something not worth saving. Its characteristic is that it attempts to understand war and militarism by establishing a feedback between them and the social and historical currents inducing them: which then issues either in forebodings of doom or in possible and better alternatives. This hypothesis will be picked up in the final Section 4.

The two stances can in SF be more or less overt or hidden; I do not believe this feature is an indication either of esthetic success, especially in an estranged and allegorical genre, or of political affiliation (see the discussion of Heinlein's, Dick's, and Le Guin's novels in this section). However, I believe it is much healthier for a culture when splits within it are brought to the surface, where they can be openly discussed with a chance for understanding as a precondition to resolution. And in fact, open polarisation coincided with sociopolitically liberatory periods, such as 1940–50 and 1960–74 (when the two souls came openly out in the famous double ad in *Galaxy Science Fiction* of June 1968, listing SF writers for and against the Vietnam War), whereas social taboos and sometimes penalties against dissent from warmongering and militarism characterise the regressive periods of the 1950s and from the 1980s to the present.

2.1. From Twain to Heinlein

The two souls can be followed from the inception of the US writing that eventually constituted itself as the SF genre. Bruce Franklin has shown (in *War Stars*, especially chap. 3) how in the latter part of the 19th Century the immense prestige of Edison, among other things the pioneer of technologised warfare and government consultant, was opposed by the grim forebodings of Mark Twain's *Connecticut Yankee in King Arthur's Court*, in which the high technology party is buried beneath the rubble of the final battle together with the vanquished. Twain's "philosophical fable" of progress is in bitter contrast to that genre's usual cheer; its "theory of capitalism and ... interpretation of the historical process that has brought it into being" (H.N. Smith 39) issues into radical pessimism. As in much foregoing 19th-Century SF, from Mary Shelley through Hawthorne to Jules Verne, the only sustainable novelties are destructive ones (I argue this at length in *MOSF* chap. 8).

The dichotomy might be called one between the believers in "Onward and Upward to Conquest by High Technology" and the doubters, from pessimism to alternate vision. Changing what needs to be changed, it obtains again between the two World Wars and with especial force after 1945 between the war-exalting SF wing of, say, Jenkins ("Murray Leinster"), who picked up the genocide torch from Williamson and Hamilton, and the much better narratives by refuseniks, from Fredric Brown and Chan Davis to Tenn or Bradbury (see on all Franklin, *War* chap. 13). Judith Merril's story "That Only a Mother" and her novel *Shadow on the Hearth* brings the cost of an atomic war literally home, as seen there by a woman; Fritz Leiber's "Foxholes of Mars" is a remarkable, brief sketch of the coming about of a galactic Hitler out of the rage of warfare; while the refusal of global-scale slaughtering is perhaps most explicit in Theodore Sturgeon's prescient plea in "Thunder and Roses" (1947) – more or less simultaneous with Heinlein's ambiguous early stories about the nuclear menace – that allegiance to survival of mankind or indeed of biological life on Earth is superior to any national allegiance or even to "western civilisation." The US Congressional repression of dissent from 1947 on and the ensuing Cold War hysteria meant that the balance, especially in the strictly watched movies, shifted in the 50s either toward the warmongers or toward coded events in the other spacetimes of the "new maps of hell." Overt anti-war or anti-militarist artefacts will emerge again only around 1959: the movies from *On the Beach* and *Fail-Safe* on, culminating in Kubrick's gallows-humour masterpiece *Dr. Strangelove* (1964), and a larger spate of literary fictions beginning with the two 1959 anti-nuclear-war classics, Walter M. Miller Jr.'s *A Canticle for Leibowitz* and Mordecai Roshwald's *Level 7*, and going on to the works of Dick, Disch, Spinrad, and others in the golden SF age after 1960.

But despite growing anti-war sentiment, the dominant context of the time was one of frantic Cold War rearmament, with multiple overkill capacities geared to titanic corporate profits (hundreds of billions of dollars, it seems) and to economic, and therefore political, stability of the status quo. Within it, Robert A. Heinlein's *Starship Troopers* (1959) became the ancestral text of US SF militarism, that inflected and to an important degree shaped the implicit and explicit debate ever since. I propose to read it here as a paradigm of US classical republicanism gone sour in the age of imperial expansion. The tenets of classical republicanism have been summarised by Carroll Smith-Rosenberg, writing about the 1790s, as follows:

> Courage, self-reliance, and love of liberty were essential for the practice of civic virtue: modernity – commerce, consumerism, and fashionable life – would corrupt aspiring republicans and plunge their republics into tyranny (Pocock, chap. 13). Yet it was the modernising world of commerce, consumerism, and fashion that America's urban classes seemed bent on embracing.... (1331)[4]

Heinlein's story begins, alternating slam-bang action and didactic explanations, as a routine "drop" combat mission of a group of space marines on a supposedly enemy planet seen through our first-person protagonist, but then immediately flashes back to a conflict between him and his rich businessman father, which leads him to a snap decision to enlist. So much for "commerce, consumerism, and fashionable life," about which we practically hear no more in this unsubtle though powerful black-and-white paean to combat life. (The father too joins the armed forces after the war has been brought home to the Terran Federation and eventually becomes the officer son's trusty top sergeant, in a variant of the Heinlein *topos* where the hero becomes his own father.) Through all kinds of self-doubts and tests, from boot camp to officer career, our protagonist grows in the courage and self-reliance needed to protect liberty. The armed forces, spearheaded by the space marines or "starship troopers" (this is either Heinlein's deliberately provocative reference to Hitler's "storm troopers" or alternatively a Freudian slip), are the only full citizens entitled to vote in the brave new world of the future that came about after the collapse of the soft USA and a third World War. They are the only locus of belonging and spiritual safety for "a real man" (8/89), far superior to the tolerated market or money economy. The central conflict of the novel is therefore only apparently between Humans and Aliens – the Bugs, extrapolated from the Chinese in the Korean War (11/121), who remain faceless pulp monsters of the ant-hive communist stripe fit only for slaughter[5]: the conflict is between consumerist-cum-commercial individualism, the "producing-consuming animal," and "man" (12/36) in the proper hierarchical collective of the military. Even that opposition is after a few exemplary incidents backgrounded in favour of an accomplished agitprop exaltation, the education of our hero into military values and honour, where there can be only emulation between good and better (startlingly parallel to the utopian communist ideal, for example in Yefremov or the early Strugatskys, or Le Guin's anarcho-communist "to be whole is to be part").

The rule by veterans' election is supposed to ensure "plac[ing] the welfare of the group ahead of personal advantage" (12/145). I find this a very worthy goal, especially when faced with the Post-Modern rulers and their cynical greed, but the premise is flawed, as in every static meritocracy: veterans' groups turn as a rule after one or two decades into crusty defenders of the status quo from the last-but-one war. Thus the most welcome, and to my mind right-on stress on the responsibilities of citizenship, on the citizen as the active subject constituting the State or nation, results only in his (literal) cyborgisation into a fighting machine. Such cosmic – or any Earthly – politics are for Heinlein impelled by naked Social Darwinism or imperial *Lebensraum*: "Man is... a wild animal"; "All wars arise from population pressure" (12/147). As Franklin points out, though among the generic ancestors of this novel "are those World War 2 movies idealising the military lives," yet "this is not about a mass conscript army called up in a war to defend democracy" (*Heinlein* 103). Heinlein effected a new twist on the subgenre, which was also his response to antimilitarism in novels such as Norman Mailer's *The Naked and the Dead*, and later those by James Jones, Heller or Pynchon. It resulted in a remarkably prescient forecast of a super-technological elite army (in his fiction: spaceships plus powered combat suits), which was to be more and more implemented after Vietnam. In our historical world, while mouthing slogans from republican virtue that by now only sound Orwellian, the military fused with the "producing-consuming animal" as its executive arm, to enforce capitalism by martial law where market law is not enough. This test by history might explain why Heinlein's last phase is constituted by longwinded escapist novels about immortality, sex, and transferral to younger bodies.

Nonetheless, Heinlein remains (to my mind) overall the most significant SF writer of the 1939–1961 epoch, and certainly one of its two or three most popular and influential ones. His stance in *Starship Troopers* is one of his many ambiguous and extreme, but also radically divergent, thought experiments from 1939 on. Franklin calls the story "Logic of Empire" (1941), in which a monopolist Earth company is based on interplanetary slave labour, Heinlein's "most radically 'left' story" (*Heinlein* 22), and in other stories of the somewhat makeshift "Future History" cycle it leads, not without clear echoes from Twain, London, and Orwell, to a replay of the 1776 War of Independence, evoked also in the interplanetary war of *The Moon Is a Harsh Mistress* (1965–66). Yet already his early novel *Sixth Column* was a racist paean to the "white" resistance movement against the Pan-Asian horde, a cross between the Red and the Yellow Peril, and its invasion theme was reused in the heyday of the anti-communist hysteria as *The Puppet Masters* (1951), with the enemy allegorised as hive-mind alien slugs who take over US bodies and minds, so that civil liberties must be suspended in favour of loyalty checks. Most important for our purpose are two stories: "Solution Unsatisfactory" (1941), the first US reflection on world politics under atomic weaponry, where in the choice between a global US empire and a Wellsian elite world dictatorship, the New-Deal Era Heinlein surprisingly opts for the latter; and "The Long Watch" (1949), where a military putsch to take over the world by means of atomic bombs is foiled by the sacrifice of a democratic junior officer. The tension between the two souls of republican virtue and elitist (or indeed quasi-Calvinistically predestined) meritocracy will remain a constant feature of all good Heinlein narrations – his best novels, those that opt for inclusiveness and liberation, being to my mind some juveniles and *Double Star*.

Heinlein's strength is a hard-nosed preoccupation with precisely observed power and authority, and indeed with the place of the father (cf. Aldiss 229):

> In a style which exuded assurance and savvy, [his] early writing blended slang, folk aphorism, technical jargon, clever understatement, apparent casualness, a concentration on people rather than gadgets, and a sense that the world described was real.... His characters were competent men of action, equally at home with their fists and a slide-rule and actively involved in the processes and procedures (political, legal, military, industrial, etc.) which make the world turn.

However, such strength is achieved at a very high cost. As of this novel, Heinlein's "dialogue and action become traps in which any opposing versions of reality were hamstrung by the author's aggrieved partiality" (both quotes from Pringle and Clute). And Franklin remarks how in Heinlein "Earth is beautiful only when viewed from a distance, where people and their civilisation cannot be seen" (*Heinlein* 20). I would expand these two observations to the thesis that the major strength and flaw in *Starship Troopers* is *world-excision*.[6] Not only is there no civilian life in it, but any and all "animality" outside of fighting – that is, the normal bodily life of producing and consuming – is also excised. It may be secondary, and, in view of Heinlein's writing from *Stranger in a Strange Land* (1961) on mostly due to publishers' taboos, that there is no sex or eroticism in *Starship Troopers*, except for warm but rigidly asexual affection between battle comrades. However, the excision not only of love but of the female element as such is surely of central significance. True, women too can join the armed forces but they are confined to the – as it were – housing sphere of the Space Navy and largely unseen, though their protection is the biological reason for war (11/125); and the debilitating female influence of the hero's Mom is expunged by having her die in an atomic bombing... Thus the novel's overall position rests on presuppositions announced at length in well-placed interspersed lectures, but tenable only if rebuttals from reality are disallowed.

Now of course no book can contain even a small part of the author's world, but what type of relationships you systematically exclude will define everything else you can say. In particular, Heinlein's concept of historical time-horizons seems a strange medley of political and technological progress with catastrophes (up to *Stranger*, when miraculous interventions abolish linear time). He wants unbridled individual affirmation but here it can only be achieved in military super-corporativism, which separates itself into an elite super-class. His strength is dealing with catastrophes; but they can only confirm the ups and downs of the linear and quantified time of technological bourgeois civilisation. If elite progress is interrupted, the only alternative to slavery of the corporative monopolist or hive-mind type is the anticolonial revolt of 1776 (repressing the fact that after it slavery and extermination of Native Americans went merrily on). No glimpse of a radical difference, the earmark of dissenting SF from London through Sheckley or Le Guin to the alternative histories of K.S. Robinson, is conceivable here, not to speak of the cosmic brotherhood Benjamin glimpsed in Scheerbart's *Lesabéndio*, where technological construction liberates peaceful creativity and – in the vein of Fourier, Percy Shelley or the later Stapledon – fuses people with stars (Benjamin II/2: 630–32 and 618–20, see also his "On the Concept of History," I/2: 691–703).

2.2. The Intertextual Tradition of US SF: Edisonade in Lieu of History

How is that huge blind spot, the tunnel-vision allowing an all-around view and precise orientation only in wholesale planetary destruction of the *Starship Troopers* kind, to be explained? It is not an individual failing, for Heinlein was a well-informed, intelligent, and original mind within a given framework, and moreover more consistent than most other SF writers of his heyday. At the beginning of the 20th Century, Henry James explained it in *The American Scene* as the US society's orientation to quantification within not to be doubted limits of technological progress, the "perpetual increase of everything," which will have to be paid for at some point in some way. His shrewd diagnosis, not unworthy of Tocqueville, is that the USA attempts to supply through money what can only be achieved by historical experience – which includes suffering and, one supposes, qualitative wisdom instead of merely quantitative increase.[7] Linear time within quantified history, even when or perhaps especially when the cash nexus is repressed, necessarily leads within Heinlein's relentless logic ("Logic of Empire" is only one example of his superb titling, among the best in SF) to the same maneuver early Christianity had to resort to in order to explain how come that divine descent did not triumph: the invention of the potent and ever-ready Enemy. Progress is the supreme good; in technology it has potent weapons at hand; and yet only an elite minority is committed to it, and it is constantly faced with the majority's indifference, backslidings, even outright defeats. For the Supreme Good to win, therefore, the enemy has to be rooted out by wholesale indiscriminate slaughter, as in the Parable of the Tares.

From Edgar Allan Poe on (the argument may be found in my *MOSF*), a characteristic of US SF has been its infantile gosh-wow, slam-bang aspect: sensationalism and sentimentality. Now "infantile" is not necessarily a cuss-word, it may have connotations of fresh, naive or innocent, and it is at any rate more promising than "senile" – a symmetrical cuss-word often flung at Europe by US visitors, Twainian innocents abroad, horrified by its post-feudal up-front hierarchies (as his Yankee was by Arthurian slavery and Walt Whitman by Shakespeare). One could argue that the most mature US SF was shaped by the awful suspicion, first adumbrated in the Gothic admixture up to Poe and Hawthorne and then more precisely in Twain's *Connecticut Yankee*, that US innocence is withering into a premature senility. The most powerful "new maps of hell," culminating beyond the '50s in the horror transmutations of Disch and Dick, and then in Gibson's cyberpunk and Spinrad, belong to this hermeneutics of suspicion. Nonetheless, up to the mid-60s SF remained almost exclusively "white boy's fiction" (cf. Russ 79), and even after the notable influx of first-rate (and then of some not-so-first-rate) women writers and therefore of women readers in the last 40 years or so, this aspect of SF is probably dominant to this day. Now the main activities of white boys have in the USA, before computers and video-games, traditionally been sports – including gun sports – and science. Sports fans do not read much fiction, which leaves us with science.

At this point I would have to write a whole essay devoted to the co-optation of modern science by capitalist profit and in particular the war industry: at least half of all US scientists and engineers work today for military priorities (cf. C.H. Gray and Tirman ed.), so that "by and large, technoscience is part of a war machine and should be studied as such," with ca. 80% of US federal obligations for research and development already in 1986 devoted to "defense" (Latour 171–72). This subjection breeds arrogant scientism of inevitable progress, defined by Le Guin as "technological edge mistaken for moral superiority" ("Introduction" 4) and by Wallerstein as a pivot of "[that] truth which reflected the power realities and economic imperatives of historical capitalism" (89). But I can only refer the interested reader to further discussions and the bibliographies in my essays "What May" and "Science Fiction Parables," and concentrate on John Clute's argument in the brilliant article "Edisonade" (from which I take all quotes in these two paragraphs, but cf. also Franklin, *War* 54–77).

Edisonades are Clute's most apt neologism for SF narrations focussed on "a young US male inventor hero who uses his ingenuity to extricate himself from tight spots and who, by so doing, saves himself from defeat and corruption and his friends and nation from foreign oppressors"; typically, what he invents is a war weapon plus a means of transport. The name derives from the public image of Edison as potential inventor of fearsome and decisive war gadgets, enthusiastically fostered by him to the edge of charlatanism (possibly satirised both as Sir Boss in Twain and the Wizard of Oz in Frank Baum) and taken up by much popular early SF from dime novels to Serviss's *Edison's Conquest of Mars* – serialised in a newspaper as counterblast to Wells's pessimism in *War of the Worlds* – where "Thomas Alva heads to Mars, where he commits triumphant genocide before granting the survivors colonial status." The edisonade was then given a huge boost by space opera, beginning with "E.E. Smith's *Skylark* sequence [which gave it] the Galaxy as playground and estate, provided an infinity of frontiers to penetrate, territories to stumble into and to claim, and entrepreneurial empires to build in all innocence. The Smithian edisonade remains central to entertainment space opera to this day." Especially destructive between the World Wars were the space operas of Jack Williamson and of Edmond Hamilton, who was known as the "world wrecker" and did not disdain genocide either.

Clute's thesis is that when Heinlein and his followers began to make explicit ideological claims for the new Edisons:

> innocence fled.... Once looked at with an eye to the main chance, it turns sour, self-serving and entrepreneurial, and we find ourselves in the land of some Hard-SF writers of the 1980s, whose protagonists are never poor, and never lose, and never give; nor would it perhaps be stretching the term too far to find in the ruthless protagonists of much survivalist fiction ghostly and solipsistic echoes of the edisonades of a more innocent time – when the hero did not have to understand the consequences of his triumphs.

My reading of history is different here: I think innocence had fled by the time of Mark Twain, as he well knew.[8] At any rate, Heinlein's novel fuses the 1930s' everyday realism with a collectivised edisonade: the inventing both of the capsule and of military education in civics has been done by the space marines, and all that remains for our protagonist is to fill the slot assigned him and thereby save his soul and humanity.

2.3. The Golden Age, 1960–74

The period of ca. 1960–74, the true and untranscended Golden Age of Anglophone – US and UK – SF, is in relation to our theme marked by two factors: first, its main preoccupation was not war and militarism (Vietnam began to be fictionally digested only toward the end) but envisaging alternate, usually better, possibilities of human relationships; second, to the extent that there were some remarkable instances of concern, they were predominantly anti-war and anti-militaristic.

It could be claimed with some justification that a good part of the most important writings obliquely reflected the Cold War, nuclear arms race, growing involvement in and protest against large-scale slaughtering such as the war in Vietnam, and the growing militarisation and alienation this produced in individuals and the fabric of civil society (as again today). This may be most clearly seen in such masterpieces as Ballard's *The Atrocity Exhibition* (1970, US title *Love and Napalm: Export USA*) – pulped in its first printing by the US publisher – or the "Daily Life in Late Roman Empire" strand of Disch's *334* (1972). However, I shall keep to overt articulations. What one may call the "Heinlein wing" is built on the axiom of a peculiar "species racism," namely that humans are individuals, and therefore elite specimens better fitted to win wars and occupy the Galaxy. Bad enough by itself, it is as a rule a fig-leaf analogy for "Western" capitalist individualism. This is the common denominator of Poul Anderson (of his "Dominic Flandry" Cold War series begun in the 1950s and his novel *The Star Fox*, with their considerable anti-pacifist acrimony but more subtlety than usually found in this wing, including an attempt at lyricism) as well as of admirations of military virtues in two long-running and somewhat repetitive series begun at that time. These were Saberhagen's "Berserker" episodes of galactic conflict with ruthless killing machines, and Gordon Dickson's more complex variant of an elite super-individual in the early novels of the "Dorsai" series, where a seemingly quite junior officer, who is however a strategic genius plus physical near-superman, comes to save all humanity in the galaxy and gets the beautiful recalcitrant girl to boot. At the time of the Vietnam War he turned in *Soldier, Ask Not* (1964–67) towards an examination of the protagonist's own destructive impulses, albeit seen only as a matter of individual ethics. As ambiguous as this last novel was Frank Herbert's far more sprawling and heterogeneous *Dune* (1963–65), astutely set in a desert environment with a vital scarce resource, extrapolated from Arabia, which posits a universe of unceasing cynical warfare for that resource as well as a galactic jihad and political Messianism. This strongly elitist and authoritarian, if not semi-fascist blend was not only a progenitor of much too long continuations but also a trend-setting harbinger of many uncouth blends of all-out war and New Age religiousness intermixed with secret societies, parapsychology, and occult sciences.

The anti-war and sometimes anti-militarist writings of this period were richer, more coherent, and more innovative. Among the most important were one novel each by Disch and Spinrad, some novels by Dick, some black stories by Malzberg, and of course the Tralfamadore strand of Vonnegut's novels, most impressively reactualising war in his *Slaughterhouse-5*. This current was also reflected in Delany's first trilogy, with vivid episodes of urban conflict, and Harrison's rather inconsequential farce *Bill, the Galactic Hero*. One of the civically most committed writers to the Campaign for Nuclear Disarmament was *John Brunner*, who wrote the song for its UK protest marches. When in the late 60s his prolific space operas started being reprinted, so that he could for 4–5 years write one instead of three titles per year (personal communication), he entered upon his plateau period, with more than a nod to Dos Passos's '30s' radicalism. In *The Jagged Orbit* the cool Cubist technique works well, depicting a near-future USA which has segregated blacks in enclaves, gone in for universal private high-tech armament, and become a huge armed madhouse, splitting emotion and reason.

A similar tack is taken by Thomas M. Disch's *Camp Concentration*, which recounts its "conchie" (conscientious objector) narrator Sacchetti's experiences in a near-future, Dantesque US concentration camp for criminals but also for political prisoners who are, during a nuclear, bacteriological, and chemical war in Malaysia, used by the military as guinea-pigs. They come to realise their experimental super-syphilis treatment heightens human intelligence to make them usable as the military's think-tank, but causes death within months. The inmates perform Mann's *Doctor Faustus* as well as a rejuvenation put-on, Sacchetti writes a comedy about Auschwitz, and there is a *deus ex machina* salvation at the end out of pulp SF rather than Dante. Except for this awkward close, which shows Disch is stronger in describing phenomena than finding causes or suggesting ways out, it is a fine piece of work, baroquely convincing in its erudition, poetry, and manic-depressive tone, all of them well motivated by the nature of the experiment. The underlying preparations of the US government for such camps – possibly with some echoes from Disch – are also the subject of the splendid movie by Peter Watkins, *Punishment Park*.

Norman Spinrad's grotesque cannibalistic dictatorship and a guerrilla revolution coming from the jungle within a second-rate melodrama in *The Men in the Jungle* was already a far-off echo of Cuba or Vietnam. But in the remarkable *Iron Dream* he achieved the startlingly revealing though uncomfortable blend of the whole US Superman SF trend – from dime-novels and edisonades through comics to the less civic-minded followers of Heinlein's militarism – with the racist ideology and practice of Hitler, who is in this parallel world the author of the novel (called by him *Lord of the Swastika* and detailing the racial Leader's exultant genocides). This is a two-way street: it points out how Hitler as an immigrant writer in prewar USA would have fitted exceedingly well into its space-opera brand of SF, akin to and indeed crossing over into sword-and sorcery Heroic Fantasy of the Conan or even Tolkien type, with various stinking under-species taking the place of Jews and Soviets and a Nietzschean Blond Beast hero as the fanatic and always successful defender of racial purity against post-nuclear-war mutations. In other words, the fictional plots of such SF-cum-Fantasy were homologous with the insane super-Wagnerian plots of the actual Third Reich. Obversely, Nazi reality was shaped by kitsch out of the occult sciences of Aryan cosmology, allied to capitalist high technology. However, the tongue-in-cheek impersonation of frenzied genetic superiority and phallic slaughter (no sex and in fact no women are to be found in Hitler's novel) within such kitsch stylistic exaltations may be too good, or at least too sophisticated for the typical US SF reader, kept blissfully ignorant of that practice by the mass media and educational system following NATOs reuse of Nazis in the Cold War. Thus, the translation in West Germany ran afoul of the anti-racial-hatred norms and was cited in judgment there...

Parallels between the increasingly militaristic and repressive USA and Nazi Germany, in a "thick" insight into the affinities between politics borne by the same classes of big speculators and small shopkeepers, were frequent in Philip K. Dick. He had already in mid-50s broached the horrors of Cold War paranoia, militarism, mass hysteria organised by politicians, and encroaching government surveillance (for example in "Breakfast at Twilight," "War Veteran" or "Second Variety"), and this was to remain a constant theme of his. *The Man in the High Castle* is the first high point of such dystopianism, situated in a world where the USA has been divided among the occupying Nazis and Japanese, where Africa has been wiped out, and a world war between the victors is brewing. The novel's startling insights into Fascist psychology, just as the insight in *The Penultimate Truth* into political manipulation by totally pervasive media enclosing people into an underworld (as already in one of his best short stories, "Foster, You Are Dead") is offset, with typical Dickian vagary, by the blithe use of a post-holocaust setting as a Berkeley pastoral in *Dr Bloodmoney*. The political edge is further blunted by Dick's shift in the latter '60s from epistemology to ontology, where reality is not veiled by big business and big State but truly changing; yet it returns with a vengeance in *A Scanner Darkly* (see for longer argumentations Suvin, essay 9 in *Positions* and "Goodbye"). In Dick's dystopian clear-sightedness, while the rich live offstage "in their fortified huge apartment complexes" (chap. 2), the little people are trapped in a total surveillance State where hologram cameras are routinely used, every pay phone is tapped, supersonic tight beams are used for police assassinations, and the closest friends inform on each other. What I have called Dick's "second plateau" extends to *Radio Free Albemuth*, written in 1976, in which a police State is instituted by a President – a blend of Nixon, McCarthy, and Hitler – come to power in 1969 (a coded SF way of saying that in the author's spacetime freedom has already been lost). The protagonist's resistance group is shot and he survives condemned to perpetual hard labour, with an opening toward brighter perspectives re-established in the novel's coda.

2.4. The Furthest Reaches and Culminations: Refusing the Linear Time

The two undoubted culminations of the Vietnam War and civil protest era SF are works by Le Guin and Haldeman. They are rather dissimilar, but could be seen as two different strategies for refusing or distorting linear time that knows only progress or regress – "development" or "under-development" in our politicians' pernicious lingo.

Joe Haldeman's *Forever War* is divided into four sections, "Private," "Sergeant," "Lieutenant," and "Major Mandella," strung out along dozens and then hundreds of years from 1977 to 3143 courtesy of Einsteinian time-dilation in combat jumps between galaxies, so that the initial reluctant draftee aged 22 physiologically grows only to middle age; in a brief coda he has married a conveniently surviving army love and expects a first baby on an Edenic planet. Except for the plentiful drugs and sex in the gender-integrated army (though galactic humanity becomes homosexual, which stabilises population) and some updated technology, the "Private Mandella" part is flat-out Heinlein-style training and combat stuff – the soldiers are in "fighting suits," each of which is "an investment of over a million dollars" (1.7/25) – with two major differences: no civic propaganda and no villainous enemies. The Taurans' blood is red, for "all God's children got hemoglobin," and the close-range combat is mass slaughter, ironically called "just following orders" as in Vietnam (1.6/61 and 64), so that our hero hesitates between his whilom peace-loving self and the "killing machine" programming (2.3/78). In other words, "Vietnam and Sinai" (2.6/97), marijuana, Woodstock, and the anti-war movement have intervened between Heinlein and Haldeman. Earth grows into a fairly horrendous centralised bureaucracy, the initial conscription law gets extended in every section, and understanding civilians, who are born one or many generations later, is practically impossible, which means that for the needed elite soldiers this becomes a "forever war" and the army is the only home left. But after 11 centuries it is discovered the Human-Tauran war was a misunderstanding and a political necessity: "Earth's economy needed a war, and this one was ideal. It gave a nice hole to throw buckets of money into, but would unify humanity...." (4.8/215). The Taurans are still collectivist clones, but the Humans also turn to cloning and peace is established.

Ursula K. Le Guin's *The Word for World Is Forest* is what would in Europe be called a red-green novel, one that combines acute sensitivity to ecology not only with the condemnation of a colonial war but also with an in-depth search for its psychological equivalents in the macho mentality that wants to tame and rape the environment as well as women. The short novel is structured by the allegorical juxtaposition of the three focal characters, the memorable, and even frightening, "conquistador" career officer Davidson (one of the most acid psychological studies of that type, to be put beside similar portraits by Mailer or Heller), the liberal scientist Lyubov who puts humanity above Terra, and the native leader Selver, easily the most complex of them. The human-derived planet natives, who live in independent forest clans, practice a feedback between "dream time" or The Men's Tongue, in which insight and psychological stability is achieved, and "world time" or The Women's Tongue of empirical reality, in which community and ecological stability is achieved; the double time-horizon also provides an effective "war-barrier" (3/61), although it may make for a static balance with the environment. This feedback and balance they find notably lacking in the psychically poisoned Terran "yumens." Selver becomes one of the rare finders of major collective insight or a – non-theistic – "god," a translator between the dream-time and world-time, when he learns war killing from the invaders, defeating them at their game (shades of Ho Chi-minh – but realistically, there's also a final hint of the price to be paid).

The novel is wrought in a combination of textural artistry – say the colour scheme rooted in vegetation, conveying the delicate beauty of the New Tahiti planet and its ruthless destruction, or the different and complementary stances within both invaders and natives – with very effective composition of cinematic cross-cutting, which is rare not only in SF and marks Le Guin's position at the crossroads of SF, poetry, and classical Realism (gender and power psychology). If there is a cognitive limit to it, this may be found in Le Guin's constant aversion toward political economy, so that devastated Terra's desperate need for logging the new-found forest planet is easily defeated by insight. But the strong yet delicate delving into the psychic roots of war and domination is what allows us to go on and envisage such a limit and the ultimate causal horizons (which are to my mind a blend of politico-economic pressures and type psychology). It is, so far as I can see, the furthest cognitive outpost to which SF has arrived insofar as the war and militarism theme is concerned.

Le Guin's "plateau period" in SF – omitting her work outside this genre – might be found in the magnificent 1969–75 interval going from *Left Hand of Darkness* to *The Dispossessed*, but extending to my mind also to the story "New Atlantis" (cf. also my "Parables of De-Alienation" in *Positions*). Its yin and yang are two interlocking narrations. The old Atlantis, rushing to its doom, is a near-future "corporative State," a well-identified US variant of admass fascism as an all-embracing bureaucracy, with Gulag-style Rehabilitation Camps and Federal Hospitals for dissidents. When an illegal group invents direct energy conversion which undercuts the need for any centralised State, it is repressed. This militarist repression strand in "New Atlantis" subsumes the real life experiences and warnings of the US Left and English-language SF, from early Heinlein or Chan Davis's "To Still the Drums" and other SF of the '40s, before Congressional intimidation clamped down, up to Leo Szilard's – the atom bomb's initiator's – "My Trial as a War Criminal," and writings or movies discussed in 2.3, such as those by Disch and Dick (cf. Franklin *Vietnam*). The emerging Atlantis is a shimmering undersea creation, just coming into being and self-understanding, a beautiful new genesis of perception and cognition – of time, space, number, and universe – by means of fitful lights. True, the new Genesis is an impure one, its light-bearing creatures are still in the process of swallowing each other, "tiny monsters burning with bright hunger, who brought us back to life." Yet the hungry lights define a city being recreated and raised by immense geological pressures (Le Guin's substitute for history), whose emergence seems at hand. I read this symbolistic New Atlantis, narrated in a collective "we" form, as a new life-form and creation of beauty and cognition symmetrically opposed to the perishing US republic, narrated in the "I" form. Nonetheless, at the end the new creation is also a "yearning music" that asks the US one "Where have you gone?" – a lament for our lost potentialities, for all the lives gone under in our wars, diseases, and starvations.

A comparison of Le Guin's and Haldeman's final horizons might be of use here. Haldeman's novel is generally thought to be an anti-*Starship-Troopers* text, and in many ways this is correct. But though war is no longer either just or necessary, it is for our focus group unavoidable (except for the happy ending). And if it is a cynical political ploy-cum-error, no deeper possible causes – such as long-term system stability – are envisaged or thinkable. The US Space-Age Soldier has become disillusioned and left Heinlein's, or any other, civic salvationism behind, but he (now updated to s/he) is still an obedient cog in the senseless killing machine, drugged by pills and misinformation. In Le Guin's novel, the well-meaning Liberal commits the error of playing along with the colonising Army while sending in his critical reports, not knowing they would never get into the public sphere unless a native uprising happened. But a new allegorical type appears in it and in the story "New Atlantis" (poetically and facelessly in the latter): a radical, other Insurgent who refuses the rules of the powerful but vulnerable Oppressor. This is entirely lacking in Haldeman, where the best our hero can hope for is an oasis outside of time and space, not too dissimilar from the Tralfamadorian zoo of Vonnegut's where Billy Pilgrim ends up with the buxom Hollywood star. In brief,

Haldeman is against war but ambiguous about the military (cf. also Gwyneth Jones); Le Guin is both against war and against militarism.

And yet there is one weighty factor these works by Le Guin and Haldeman have in common: the *refusal of a linear time of progress*, where knowledge is divorced from responsibility and the furthest frontiers of technological triumphs mean more killing: senseless wars abroad and bureaucratic-cum-militarist oppression at home. This may be the common denominator of the anti-slaughter stance: in Disch's "Daily Life in the Late Roman Empire" sequence from *334* it's evident in the interferences between that age and the time of a near-future Manhattan; in Spinrad, in the all-pervasive tonal contradiction between "his" and "Hitler's" novel which involves also opposed time-horizons; in Dick's *A Scanner*, in the technologically and politically enforced total split between the two personalities and the two names for the same person of the police spy vs. the spied upon; and it would not be difficult to go on about Vonnegut's "chronoclasm" (time-break) or the other texts. In Le Guin's novel, genocide as well as rape of women and planet both end with the arrival of the ansible, ushering in the "simulsequential," post-Einsteinian time; in Haldeman's, the Forever War is more ambiguously ended by renouncing heterosexual procreation that biologically bore linear human time. In Le Guin, opposition to the murderous "progress" is possible (however ambiguous the consequences might be); in Haldeman, only evasion. While my preference is clearly for the first, both options come from and return into our real world-time, and might be in different circumstances acceptable solutions for different persons.

3. Singularities II: Historical Texts 1975–2001, a Deluge with Exceptions

> *Americans have a peculiar chronic blind spot when thinking about war... – they always imagine [it] as taking place somewhere else.*
>
> Lois Bujold

3.0. The Coastlines of Atlantis Erode

From the mid-70s on, the lay of the land around and within US SF suffered a sea-change. The US government cut in 1973–75 its losses in Vietnam, leaving that country devastated by more high explosives than were used against the Axis in World War 2 and by chemical warfare (the most believable count of Vietnamese civilians killed is around two million), and clamped down on any dissent going beyond the peace plank; hence the Le Guin story and the two late Dick novels discussed above. Analogous, only cruder, repression was going on in the Soviet bloc after the 1968 invasion overthrowing the reformists in Czechoslovakia – and it had similar, if more heavily coded, echoes in the SF of the Strugatskys. The arms race, huge military procurements, and proxy wars or armed interventions did not at all abate, witness the 1973 US-organised overthrow of the Allende government in Chile, the ongoing clashes in Africa, then in the late 70s the clerical revolution in Iran and the Left revolution in Afghanistan, followed by the alliance of the USA and fundamentalist "islamists" against it and the Soviet intervention with its symmetrical mini-Vietnam. After the defeat of the '60s' movements and all independent Leftism, the US governing classes were on a steady counteroffensive to regain the terrain lost through Keynesian compromise with labour and decolonisation in the global South, which had culminated in the peace movement and the Vietnamese liberation struggle. The rise of Reaganism and Thatcherism was an abrupt shift to the Right, going on ever since. From communists to true liberals, the Left was in a material and moral disarray, which (strangely enough) became terminal after the collapse of USSR in 1989, and savage despoiling of the Welfare State went on full swing, East and West. Intellectuals adjusted, at best concluding with Foucault, Deleuze, and Derrida there was nothing outside epistemic power, infinite rhizomes, and micro-differe/ances, at worst denouncing any systematic understanding in favour of "weak" thought. The only politics they deigned to notice was the micro-politics of, say, gay rights or "textual politics" – emblematically, in Delany's important *Triton* a "gravity war" between planets is pooh-poohed in order to concentrate on choice of life-styles and genders, however useful this latter narrowing may be for some limited purposes and in response to violent lesion of their rights.[9] Even the feminist movement, within which by far the best modern SF satires (such as Joanna Russ's splendid agitprop novel *The Female Man*, in which one of the strands presents an actual gender war) and open-ended utopias (such as Le Guin's unsurpassed *The Dispossessed*) had been written in the 1960–75 period, was split and then contained along those lines.

The main instrument in the systematic climb to power of the Right in metropolitan capitalism without a human face was the strengthening of the State's repressive functions at the expense of its welfare functions, and at the cost of hundreds of billions of dollars going from taxes to armament corporations (see Suvin "Capitalism"). This was centered in the USA, by then a permanent Warfare State which led a global reorientation of technology and economics toward armaments (cf. Hirsch and Roth 126–28 and passim). As the strategic keystone in the ongoing "commodification of everything" (Wallerstein 90) and in sustaining profit accumulation, spiralling State procurements for the military were the easiest and most lucrative way of keeping the economy going, even when consumer demand stagnated due to the assault on permanent employment. By the time of the First Gulf War, a conservative estimate of spending for military purposes was nearly a trillion (one million millions) US$ annually, or between 2 and 2.5 billion dollars daily, and this is now growing by leaps and bounds, so that after 2001 the US military budget was back on Cold War levels. The Pentagon and Department of Defense became thus the US equivalent of the State planning commission, with built-in enormous and omnipresent expense transgressions for key research and technologies (the best portrayal of such procedures in SF may be found in K.S. Robinson's *The Gold Coast*, and of organised warmongering already in the splendid 1967 *Report from Iron Mountain*).

A grim prospect opens up: the deflection of more than half of the world's research and of its financing into profitable commodities for killing makes a sham of democratic control and decision-making. As Wallerstein has repeatedly argued, ideological and economic "liberalism" is incompatible with democracy. Externally, the rise to power of the oil-centered fraction of US corporations under the Bush regimes meant that the post-Cold-War struggle for raw materials was openly entrusted to "gunship diplomacy" and where need be smart bombs. Internally, as mentioned in 2.3, the political fall-out of the Warfare State "is the spread of military rule and militarisation that subordinate all other aspects of civil society to its barbarity not only during wars but in times of official 'peace'" (Suvin, "Capitalism" 104). This necessarily leads to large powers for the top bureaucracy and the military in relation to civilians and to a corresponding degradation of democratic institutions and practices; the military-industrial complex has also become "the single greatest source of environment destruction in the USA" (McMurtry, *Cancer* 174). The divide between military and police actions and power (and also between the military incarcerated and those subject to normal law) grew more and more permeable even before the welcome excuse of anti-terrorism; it is by now employable at will against all real or supposed, present or future enemies of the US world hegemony, such as the Genua protesters of 2001 (see Dal Lago, *Polizia* 71–90).

3.1. The Deluge Begins

In SF, the frenzied drive for not simply profits but "big profits! this year!" intervened first of all with the lure of Hollywood and dumbing down to bestseller level for it. Looking at our radar screens, the editors of *Science-Fiction Studies* in 1979 put it this way (I believe the phrasing was mine):

> It is our impression that the bestseller mentality invading the market is a clear example of how the potentialities of this genre are co-opted and sterilised by economic and ideological forces. This has already resulted in vastly overblown novels, poorly organised and without much else to show for itself except for reducing the level of SF to that of the bestseller reader. ("Editorial" 7–8)

By vastly overblown novels I, at least, was alluding to Pournelle and Niven's *The Mote in God's Eye.* We thought it was an aberrant trend. Maybe so, but it became the dominant trend.

In spite of what we critics usually focus upon, SF is not only a literary genre. It was first widespread in comics – it was "that Buck Rogers (or Flash Gordon) stuff" – and then in both Wells-derived and comics-derived movies, not to mention *Frankenstein* and *King Kong*. But after Kubrick's two movies of the 60s, *Dr. Strangelove* and *2001*, after *The Planet of the Apes* and its sequels, and especially after the smash hit of a safely dumbed-down, fairytale and Manichean, kind of fake SF in Lucas's *Star Wars* from 1977 on – a technospectacular fairy-tale with the horizon of showdown in the OK Corral – Hollywood had become gung-ho for SF (see Fitting's and La Polla's articles in Suvin ed., *Fictions*). Stories of copyright advances in six or seven digits to Heinlein and other SF luminaries began floating around the SF community. Extremely few were chosen (cf. Fitting's filmography in idem), but very many felt called to write respecting

Sam Goldwyn's immortal statement "Nobody ever went broke underestimating the great American public." Thus, by the end of the 80s the SF film boom had subsided in "the filmic equivalent of fast food, offering no lasting satisfaction. Also, too much US product seemed to more astringent foreign tastes to be suffused with an oversweet sentimentality..." (Nicholls). Even so, its impact persisted. Many SF writers wrote scenarios or tie-ins for the *Star Trek* series, which has from its semi-liberal beginnings in the 60s oscillated wildly in quality, SF content, and ideological orientation (the 1968 episode "A Private Little War" clearly justifies the US war on Vietnam); other SF on TV was more staggeringly brainless. There is little doubt that military and warmongering SF revived in *Star Wars* and *Star Trek* before they did in SF writing.

Possibly even more important was the impact of computers (the first IBM mass PC hit the market in 1981), and the increasingly violent video games cultivating killing lust in the 80s. Both grew exponentially, and their users were disproportionately concentrated in the social stratum that also supplies SF readers. On the highest level, computers and internet were the ambience for cyberpunk, the most important SF movement of the '80s which included at least two masters, William Gibson and Pat Cadigan. Within a post-Vietnam revulsion from nationalism, it shrewdly concentrated on the small people caught in the merciless metaphorical, virtual, and real wars of neo-feudal corporativism, using cyberspace as a virtual reality oscillating between mastery and escape.

A further mega-trend directly splitting or hollowing out SF writers and readers was the rise of Hero Fantasy, following in much inferior ways the success of Tolkien's *Lord of the Rings* and the *Conan* movies, and then of Horror Fantasy culminating in the world's best selling writer, Stephen King. Science was compromised by wars, ecological degradation, and capitalist rationality, so that New Age "spirituality" bloomed in lush old and new variants; alert critics had already in the '60s begun to downgrade SF in favour of "speculative fabulation" which might mean anything that was not suburban realism. My above overview concluded that Fantasy's readers are a large group drawn from the presently marginalised intellectuals, the young, and the lower classes, mainly male and precariously or desultorily employed. It is centrally shaped by a refusal of ongoing social history – the technology, urbanisation, finances, and human relationships that came about in modern capitalism. But no alternative project of historical self-governance is allowed: "in Horror Fantasy the power of destiny is absolutely superordinated and plot is subordinated to inducing the affect of fear and horror, while in Heroic Fantasy destiny is within the hero's will to power and plot is a serial manifestation of that will which could go indefinitely on" – as it does in the never-ending warfare series both in Fantasy and SF. My hypothesis was that "SF appeals to social groups with confidence that something can at present be done about a collective, historical future – if only as dire warnings.... To the contrary, when the entire life-world has undergone much further tentacular and capillary colonisation, Fantasy's appeal is to uncertain social classes or fractions who have been cast adrift and lost that confidence," so that they face their own present and future with a resolve to use vicarious horror or heroism – or both – as a safe thrill before the deluge ("Considering" 235 and 238). The deluge was coming apace, and another way to strike out seemed military imperialism.

True, SF literature was stagnating quantitatively, losing much ground, abruptly lowering its quality eyeing the movies, and even falling behind the number of titles in Hero and Horror Fantasy. Still, SF sales were probably aided by the movies, and readers not wishing to read only (or any) Fantasy were still an ideological and commercial force to be reckoned with. As the Left drooped – including for SF in particular its feminist vanguard – the Right, supported by huge financial and power networks, mobilised. The narrative center of SF was inundated and largely occupied – in publication fact rather than in cognitive and formal value – by an organised Right-wing effort to roll back the anti-war sentiment by a new Cold War literature insisting in numerous ideological tracts first on space exploration and rearmament (see Proietti, "Saving," Section 4) and soon thereafter on warfare as measure for Man. This translated into SF as space wars of unbridled Social Darwinism, which differed from prior individualist entrepreneurship, in swashbuckling colonialism of the Anderson type or in sword-and-sorcery Fantasy, by resolutely praising space technology, US military imperialism (often – as already in *Star Trek* – tenuously masked as multiracial Earthmen, see the wonderfully acerbic analysis by Gwyneth Jones), and strict hierarchy. The major new writer of this trend was Larry Niven, in whom the passage from the Soviet to the "Third World" threat may be seen (see Jameson, "Science Fiction"), and its major entrepreneur Jerry E. Pournelle.

Niven had started in the mid-60s to introduce his Man-Kzin Wars universe, and in the 1973 novel *The Protector* his tough frontiersman hero becomes a "superman" monster, literally exchanging such human characteristics as sex for brains, lips for beak, hands for claws, and skin for armour in order to save humanity from incoming Aliens, and incidentally wiping out a whole planetful of Martian natives. The mad logic of militarism, "in order to save this town (country, world), we had to destroy it," is fully dominant here, sparked by vengeful fury at the Vietnam defeat. In several further novels, all coauthored with Pournelle, beautiful space battles wiping out entire armadas are described with juvenile glee (in a pedigree that descends from Italian Futurists and Fascists); the enemies are always cruel and underhanded – in Pournelle the genocide targets are often dark races, or indeed the lowest class as in *Mercenary* – and it is war to the last survivor. Two further collaborations transfer the story overtly to Earth. *Lucifer's Hammer* picks up the torch from Heinlein's survivalist template in *Farnham's Freehold* by repeating the horde of (cannibal!) Blacks that attack the civilised White stronghold, in order to be luckily decimated by poison gas and the remnant enslaved – as near fascism as SF had got by the end of the 70s.[10] In the Californian class war of *The Oath of Fealty*, a rich enclave, ruled by an infallible hierarchy and a brilliant leader, defeats assorted eco-freaks and terrorists. The relatively best but still indigest Niven-Pournelle collaboration is the already mentioned *A Mote in God's Eye*, where the interesting encountered aliens (Niven's best work is the "Ringworld" series where this interest was not yet yoked under militarist ideology) provide a modicum of mystery, only to be explained as dastardry and awful threat. The follow-up novel, *The Moat around Murcheson's Eye*, is to my mind even more interesting, for it abandons head-on conflict for an attempt to differentiate between groups that will and will not co-operate with "us," parallel to evolving US policy toward West Asia. The precondition for co-operating, though, is that it happen on "our" terms, here induced prevention of breeding rate. Alas, the first *Mote* became a paragon for the next decades.

My appended Bibliography of SF Narrations may give an idea (it by no means supplies a full list) of the mushrooming of such militarist SF series. How do these function? Several narrations situated in the same spacetime – a device which economically supplied venues for a series of different, yet connected, events as well as means of reader identification – have been an organising SF device since the dime-novels and early space-operas in the pulp tradition of E.R. Burroughs and E.E. Smith, mimicking the epic drive of Realistic narrations after Balzac. They were either organised simply around the adventuring hero, a descendant of Ulysses or Aeneas, or more interestingly around a sequence of compatible types in a future history. But the potential breakthrough of SF after the *Star Wars* into financial big time, beyond the up-to-one-cent-per-word stage, set loose a startling avalanche of publishing mutations identified in the new vocabulary of "shared worlds" and various other "ties" or tie-ins (single novels or shared-world anthologies) of a "sharecropping" kind. Shared worlds are narrations by various authors in a pre-set sociohistorical and planetary spacetime, usually more or less loosely defined by the venue's copyright owner – original author or indeed corporation – in a set of instructions called a "bible," which often accretes beyond its core "genetic code" supplementary backgrounds, including maps, tables, genealogies, etc.; Pournelle's "War World" bible seems to have been one of the larger concentric growths, though the concept was traced back to the late '70s. The bible can be partly or largely derived from earlier SF literature, film, TV, games or cartoons – say from *Star Wars, Star Trek* or the genetic warrior-class propaganda of "BattleTech" games – and the tied-in developments, as a rule written for hire, are called sharecrops (cf. Clute, "Shared," also Proietti, "Saving," section 5).

Such "ties" are deeply ambiguous: they tie the writers to pre-set limits, usually for modest money offset by promises of visibility; yet they could potentially be occasions for creative ingenuousness and collective co-operation in what one might call world-thickening. Thus, the ties could be innovative manifestations of a shared collective ethos, which would have been called evil empires had the bible been proposed and enforced by a Communist Party Agitprop section or by a Ministry of Propaganda instead of by market carrots and whips. In reality, I suspect (since financial and other negotiations are secret) they are quite often instances of subaltern drudgery and disempowerment, as happens to exploited sharecroppers in agriculture. I found that the "Darkover" tie-ins by M. Z. Bradley and Mercedes Lackey within a feminist ethos, which include interesting variations on Bradley's "Free Amazons," approximate the creative pole. On the opposite pole are the very numerous aggressive, warmongering and/or militarist concoctions by Niven, Pournelle, Saberhagen, and down to David Drake. There may be a few less uniform exceptions here and there, and to my mind the idea of serial collaboration may still in the (rare) right circumstances offer promising possibilities. But on the whole, in them and their authors Heinleinian "species racism" was reborn in the blood of wars and moved center stage.

3.2. Islands of Higher Ground: From Card to Haldeman II

As Proietti rightly concludes, writings propagating war and military-centered social organisation have from the '70s on so inflected SF "as to become one of [its] default images" ("Saving," section 4). By my count from a reliable SF bookstore catalogue in 2004, 30–40% of new US SF titles published were "military SF." The crucial offensive that resulted in this capture of the SF center may have started in 1979, when the impetus of Reaganism and of *Star Wars* (the two were in 1983 successfully fused in the public mind by Reagan's "Star Wars" speech) had begun to bear fruit, so that three major warmongering series by Bretnor, Drake, and Pournelle were started by central SF publishers, reinforcing Pournelle's pioneering "Co-Dominium" series of 1971. In the '80s the series multiplied further, and a proper SF pro-military group was constituted lobbying for Star Defense armaments and wars. I cannot add much to the story already well told by Franklin (*War* 200–01, 211, and passim), Proietti ("Saving," esp. section 4), and other critics to be found in the Proietti-Suvin secondary Bibliography. From the early 80s on, SF movies also bettered the *Rocky* series or other mundane hypermasculine warriors in the "hardened" cyborgs of *Terminator*, *Robocop*, *Cyborg*, and similar.

Eventually, in the militarist SF the torch began to pass from Pournelle's pioneering zest to the more routine activities of the entrepreneur-writer David Drake, who ranges from heroic planetary mercenaries to rewriting the battles of the Roman Empire with help of Aliens. However, I shall rather as briefly as possible concentrate on some works within the middle (and thus relatively much higher) ground of an SF weighing the pros and cons of war, militarism, and their price for people. The complex but considerable talent of C.J. Cherryh, who started publishing SF in 1977, though she deals much with aliens and conflict and seems to me as interesting as anybody else after that time, stands to my mind aslant to our polarised theme and will regretfully not be dealt with. This holds also for major contemporary UK writers, from James White's thoughtful "Sector General" sequence of novels on medicine and aliens (1962ff.) to Gwyneth Jones and Iain M. Banks from the '80s on and Ken MacLeod from the '90s on, who can be rightly opposed to the prevailing black-and-white simplicities hugely preponderant in US SF. Finally, from the middle ground of what Jones rightly identifies as the feminised military SF series after 1985, I shall here discuss only their best writer, Lois M. Bujold, and refer the reader to Jones's discussion (in Suvin ed.) of what I'd see as the lower forms from the still enjoyable Elizabeth Moon to David Feintuch and David Weber.

Orson Scott Card's *Ender's Game* is both one of the most important SF novels of the '80s and a broken-backed piece in many respects – possibly characteristic in that too. For 296 out of 324 pages, it looks like a remarkable use of kids' spacewar videogames as training for real space warfare with merciless Heinleinian Buggers. Exactly such behaviour by kids was praised at the time by President Reagan (see Fitting, note 18) and channelled to the same effect in the movie *The Last Starfighter*, where a teenage videogame champion saves the galaxy; it was at the time also popularised by the furore – and movies, one called *Wargames* – about teenage hackers. In the coda of 28 pages, our genius protagonist is told he and his child helper-friends actually fought and annihilated the whole species of Buggers. Thus the initial 91% look like a Cold War militarist scenario renewed by the point of view of an inmate of a very youthful military academy being dehumanised into a tool (if need be a "despicable" one – 4/35) for humankind's survival. This would be an interesting piece of cynicism on its own, but it is suddenly unhinged in the 9% ending by Ender's guilt and horror at what he and the Terrans have wrought. Gwyneth Jones goes incisively to the novel's heart by noting that its basic move is "Ender annihilates rival: sheds crocodile tears; Ender annihilates rival: sheds crocodile tears…" (Section 1) – and I'd add that in Card's well-crafted writing this simultaneously formal and ideological gambit operates both within briefer segments and in the novel as a whole. The only question is, are they really crocodile tears, that is, hypocritic sorrows?

To my mind they are and aren't: Card attempts to have it both ways. True, when after each near-murderous or fully murderous triumph Ender feels terrible and indulges in moral agonising, this could be written off as standard Puritan hypocrisy within a power trip. Haldeman has noted how "This childlike, more or less boy-like, fascination with machines is a dominant motif in SF, especially the subgenre of military sf.... Like most American boys of my generation and previous ones, I had a childhood dominated by weapons-oriented play" (94). On the one hand, then, the body of Card's novel yokes convincingly such a (slightly extrapolated) psychology of usually defenceless children to the blind needs of the huge war machine: the individual is predisposed towards it but has, in this period which Jones shrewdly identifies as the "pause" (between Vietnam and the Twin Towers), to be persuaded to assume all of its murders, up to Pournellian genocide of a whole alien species and civilisation. But on the other hand – and here Card's religious antecedents come into play – the most arresting passages of the novel are Ender's encounters with what seems a kind of own externalised subconscious in the school computer game; in the ending, after Ender refuses to lead another war, it turns out these were attempts by the Buggers to communicate with him. He finds the cocoon of the last Bugger hive-queen, potential progenitrix of a renewed species, and gathers from telepathic messages the two species had been alike unable to understand there could be any thinking (psychozoic) Other. He writes a book detailing "all the good and all the evil" (15/322) of the Bugger hive, and becomes a Speaker for the Dead, a habit that catches on among humans. This unashamedly utopian and pacifist ending is then transferred to Ender's further cosmic travels which in following novels (*Speaker for the Dead* and *Xenocide*) result in finding a planet for the cocoon and averting another potentially genocidal interspecies misunderstanding. Ender's qualms in the first novel remain belated and quite insufficient to balance a genocide, but its ending and the sequels forbid treating them as hypocrisy. They share the blind spots of all religious pacifism: to end war, they define it as due to misunderstandings rather than interest conflicts (no nations or classes exist for Card), and they put their faith in a super-charismatic Saviour to effect the necessary moral contagion; but at least they want to end them.

Gwyneth Jones argues that Card's *Ender's Game* is in a way near to Haldeman's *Forever War*, since both of their authors are working off the influence of the '60s, evident in the horror at the loss of innocence in and because of inescapable war. The point is well taken – both protagonists "light out for the Territory" (far-off planets), working out their personal destiny and leaving Earth to rot on its own – though the divergencies between a Vietnam veteran turned pacifist and a Mormon missionary to Brazil should not be minimised either. Card notes the ravages of irreversible linear time, only partly stanched by male comradeship and heterosexual erotics; Haldeman uses Einsteinian time-dilation to string on it planets like beads in the earnest (and sexless) Messianic quest among strange tribes. In the interval, something has been gained, mainly in "thicker" description; much has been lost.

Lucius Shepard's *Life during Wartime*, though, is clearly a throwback to the spirit of the 60s – youth culture, drugs, and all: primarily to the beat of its music. Its narrative texture reads like a feverish hijack of Mailer's (or indeed Pynchon's) war absurdities into early Spinrad country. His protagonist is a rock-loving soldier in an interminable Central American jungle war (a melding of Vietnam and the dirty "little wars" the US government was fighting in Latin America before and after it, usually by proxy mercenaries). Its first part describes in vivid vernacular detail the drug-saturated atmosphere and confused decay in and around the army, and Mingolla's[11] eventual ethical revulsion from such dehumanisation; but then it founders in an overlong confusion of ESP, love, and treachery, and a politically illiterate attribution of global power struggles and protracted wars to an *Illuminatus*-type conspiracy, based yet on two Panamanian families in control of a rare drug source…

A similar problem besets John Shirley's in many ways rich and extraordinary "A Song Called Youth" or "Eclipse" trilogy (*Eclipse, Eclipse Penumbra*, and *Eclipse Corona*). Like the politically aware SF of the '60s, and indeed the '40s, but isolated in the latter half of the '80s, his writing is engaged in antifascist resistance, this time against a Right-wing US Christian variant of fascism called SA, which is taking over Europe with the connivance of NATO during a protracted stalemate within a limited nuclear war against the USSR. Various protagonists, notably the rock musician Rickenharp (who composes the Song Called Youth) meet, fight, and die under the leadership of a maverick Israeli in an unequal underground struggle, mainly in Paris but ranging widely over the Old World, and there is a parallel subplot on an orbital colony. Impressive accounts of technical advances in warfare and communication, including cyberpunk-type jacking in, and of political skulduggery on both sides are intercut to form a broad global overview, within which an antifascist coalition ranging from punk anarchists and communists to liberals unmasks the dastards before the UN, and our main protagonist Danny or Hard-Eyes can go off and enjoy true love in orbital free-fall. The long and deft plot is vastly superior in political savvy to Shepard and indeed most US SF, which has since Spinrad and Le Guin become mainly addicted to navel-gazing; Shirley even prefigures the '90s' youth and antiwar movements, which have again had extremely few echoes in SF. Yet his narrative is still naive about the sea-change in world politics and militarism that was developing in the USA. If Shepard's novel is a drug-perfected ESP story used for anti-war purposes, Shirley's smoother trilogy is a somewhat macho youth-culture revolt mingling Chicago in 1968 with the anti-Nazi resistance in retro ways. Both narratives have their heart in the right (1960s') place but their head has not been updated, and both in retrospect seem anachronistic. Even so, eschewing rosy sentimentality and feel-good inwardness to delve into disturbing yet essential matters of collective survival, they have not had nearly the popularity of much inferior writings.

After Kelso's essay "Loud Achievements" and the brilliant pages by Jones devoted to Lois McMaster Bujold, I can be briefer about her improbable but successful marriage of the sentimental and military narratives than it would deserve. The marriage can be read either as militarism with a human face, gathering new SF readers from the kinder and gentler wing (mainly women) who may perhaps then go on to sterner stuff, or as a subtle subversion weaning readers away from war and militarism. In the absence of a full dissection of her dozen volumes in and around the "Vorkosigan Saga," my impression is that Bujold modulates from one position to the other within each work but that within the development of the series she leans more strongly toward the non-militarist horizon. Kelso argues that, from the second novel on, the dominant military space opera slowly gives way, within the education of our quite central hero, Miles Vorkosigan, to what I'd call sentimental-cum-political intrigue, so that in the second quinquennium of publication – from *Barrayar* (1991) on – which effects a "deeper pass over the landscape of the earlier books" ("Loud" 12), the taking back of militarism on the whole predominates. This is symbolised by Miles's death and rebirth in *Mirror Dance* (1994), and becomes unmistakable when he in *Memory* (1996) resigns from the military, and the "saga" shifts into the civilian mode. Furthermore, by a series of binary manoeuvres Bujold has shifted Miles right from the beginning out of the Pournelle-to-Drake patriarchal killer type, hugely predominant in US SF.

The first such manoeuvre is his descent from a strong "progressive" mother, Cordelia Naismith, and an honourable ruling-class officer in the first and possibly untranscended volume, *Shards of Honor* (1986). Even the title is doubly binary: honour (an important value in and out of the military) is in shards, but even if broken up they are still shards of honour. Indeed, *Shards* and *Barrayar* have been retrospectively, but not without reason, reunited in a dilogy called *Cordelia's Honor*, which not only underscores the original focus on Cordelia and sympathetic parenting but makes it obvious how Miles too is a blend with the "feminine" qualities predominating. The second manoeuvre is Miles's being poisoned as fetus by enemies of his father's reformism, which results in brittle bones, small stature, and a distinctly non macho, even slightly comical appearance. This has the advantage of triggering the Ugly Duckling or folktale pattern, where the seemingly poor and downtrodden hero at the end wins, here by a combination of brains and valour, enlisting the empathy of readers. The third binary is Miles's double role as junior officer (who is in reality a privileged imperial spy) and swashbuckling admiral of a mercenary fleet doing the empire's dirty business among far galaxies. The fourth is a foregrounding of the doubling or mirroring device in the interaction with his clone brother Mark, and less obtrusively with the trajectory of one of his loves, Elena Bothari; and one could doubtless go on (say about the name Miles, both archetypal Latin soldier and Twain's pauper that passes for prince – Kelso, "Loud" 12, and Proietti, "Saving" note 12). One could even suspect that such doublings anamorphically reproduce and negotiate Bujold's double allegiance to psychological SF of the Le Guin type (half a dozen subsidiary characters are deftly sketched in) and to military SF of the galactic space-opera type: to exploring malleable gender identities within the rigid line-up of the military.

There are drawbacks to Bujold's meld: Miles is often the hero of a Regency romance, improbably charming, resourceful, even sexy – Rochester masquerading as Jane Eyre. Conversely, gory interstellar warfare is hollowed out but also accepted as inevitable – this is well symbolised by the marriage of Miles's liberal mother to his heretic warrior father. Within Bujold's briskly competent narrative drive, her writing encompasses both felicitous nuggets and what I'd call some (not quite purple but) rosy prose. While planets are – somewhat vaguely – differentiated by ideological traditions, any vertical social tension is absent (Kelso cites Bujold's remark that the home Vorkosigan planet is the "white-bread suburb of the galaxy" – "Loud" 14). However, it should not be forgotten that in two somewhat marginal novels, foremost in *Falling Free*, she managed to broach a working-class exploited as slave labour, the genetically modified "quaddies," disguised as childlike innocents in a love story of modest pretensions. And the great final chapter of *Shards*, finding and washing the space dead, to my mind transcends Card's focus on the heroic protagonist's guilt and reparation: it encapsulates Bujold's concern with the simultaneously collective and individual price of war to ordinary people, whom it destroys.

A more overt antiwar-cum-feminist voice is to be found in Joan Slonczewski's *A Door into Ocean* (1986). It is a variant on Le Guin's untranscended template in *The Dispossessed* of an exploitative planet, whose inhabitants are possessed by "propertarianism," vs. an egalitarian moon, here with several go-betweens of different stature. In place of the greedy rich planet as against the poor egalitarians, here the hard-dry-stony, aggressively militarist and feudal, hi-tech planet is opposed to the soft-wet-silken water-covered moon, inhabited by ecobiologically oriented and parthenogenetic women, while the rule and mores of a highly destructive and repressive patriarchy is opposed to the "lovesharer" women, who live in a cross between modern basis-democracy anarchism, early Quakers sharing unanimity, tribal communism, and a feminist sister-gathering. Furthermore, instead of the non-interfering estrangement in *The Dispossessed* between the opposed camps, *A Door* is halfway to *The Word for World Is Forest* in that a more realistic military invasion of the hard imperialists takes place and has to be thwarted with great losses to the seemingly soft but unyielding pacifists. A major strength of Slonczewski's is the creation of a very full world ecology, in the imaginative and liberating tradition of explicitly anthropological SF – among others by Oliver, Blish or Bishop – which does not take place in the linear clarity of Le Guin's (or Herbert's) desert but in the rich depths and interstices of the planet-wide ocean. The politics of the conflict are supplied dialectically rather than black and white (the worst military torturer is a woman), but to my mind the respectably Gandhian premise of the ocean-dwellers' victory is much too optimistic. Yet if this novel, one of the masterpieces of the '80s, is a throwback to the US '60s, it also carries forward its "make love not war" theme, being reborn in the protests against the ravages of global eco-destruction.

Perhaps this is the place to mention briefly works of two SF authors I consider to be second to none in their respective generations, and indeed our major beacons, Ursula K. Le Guin and K.S. Robinson. But both have given their major contributions to our theme outside of this period, Le Guin in 1972, as argued in 2.4, and Robinson in 2002 with the *Years of Rice and Salt*, so that their partial incidence on our theme will here be dealt with briefly. Within Le Guin's titanically multifaceted and splendid work *Always Coming Home* – perhaps the most impressive summa of soft primitivism we have had in utopia or SF – the astoundingly rich pastoral recreation of tribalism and ecological balance is systematically violated only by the slave-owning warring male horde of Condors in the "Stone Telling" sections, for whose militarism only rapacious machismo seems responsible. But this is marginal within the mosaic-like work, and a sickness that ebbs away by itself. While this may be acceptable in that (so to speak) renewed prelapsarian world, it is of little help with the readers' immediate concerns becoming more pressing every year.

K.S. Robinson has in the Dennis McPherson-Stewart Lemon strand of his multi-plotted *The Gold Coast* given us the best inside description of skulduggery in (very slightly extrapolated) Pentagon procurements deals, which have "all the trappings of an objective rational process, but [are] at the same time fairly easy to manipulate to whatever ends are desired" (42/213) and the crazy self-serving world of the military-industrial complex. As an exasperated engineer grumbles:

> Need a boost – military spending – it's been the method of choice ever since World War Two got them out of The Great Depression. Hard times? Start a war! Or pump money into weapons whether there's a war or not. It's like we use weapons as a drug, snort some up and stimulate the old economy. Best upper known to man. (42/220)

Within a novel centered on drug-taking, this is the most potent drug. And Robinson went on to his masterpiece of the 90s, the "Mars" trilogy, which to my mind made him the torch bearer of the historicising SF that Le Guin had by then largely forsaken for other interests. It is the richest and most believable history – slightly anamorphic to Terra, as when our "green" movement is on Mars (of course) the "red" one – of both corporate struggles against people who actually create a livable planet and ecological struggles of conservation vs. transformation. Revolution and repression, militarisation and resistance happen here too, but the occasional shooting is given unrivalled scope and breadth by the multiple and criss-crossing causes and consequences, allowing the reader the greatest of all freedoms: to think through and about it, as an estranged history with alternate time-streams whose coming into being as collective history is the work of praxis (cf. Jameson, "If I Find").

Disclaimers similar to what I can discuss here from the opuses of Le Guin and Robinson are due for another as important writer, Marge Piercy. Quite reasonably, she bet in the 1991 *He, She and It* on a future of ecological mega-breakdown and, before the full takeover by Bushism and the Warfare State, on the passage of power to a few mega-corporations with wastelands and gang-ruled urban sprawls in between. Corporation centers and a few "free cities" supplying indispensable specialised know-how live under domes, one of them being our focal Jewish city of Tikvah (which is lay and cyber-oriented – Israel has been destroyed in an atomic war). Life in the mega-corporation cities is indistinguishable from total militarisation in the name of technoscience, whereas their conflicts between each other and the free cities at times erupt into mini-wars conducted by both internet and reality warfare. This is the case after our protagonists in Tikvah succeed to produce the perfect defense cyborg Yod, who is programmed both with the male and female stance, with power and deviance, and thus also a perfect, considerate and tireless, lover (a parallel plot, which I shall slight here, concerns the Golem Joseph defending the Jewish ghetto in Baroque Prague). The successful defense of Tikvah flows at the end into a tentative alliance with the politicised gangs in the sprawl on the ex-US East Coast. This rich novel focusses not only on female scientists but presents also, most cognate to our theme, two female underground fighters, the info pirate Rivkah and the enhanced cyborgised Nili from an Israeli-Palestinian women's enclave surviving hidden in the radioactive zone. It is an exemplarily intelligent SF integration of warfare into the concerns of her earlier two SF novels *Dance the Eagle to Sleep* (youth revolutionary resistance and feminism) and *Woman on the Edge of Time* (ecology and political economy). Its scenario is at the moment not on the historical agenda, but may return to it if Bushism is defeated and/or the ecology massively breaks down.

My final exhibit here is another novel by Haldeman, *Forever Peace*. It is nearest to us in time, so that it can incorporate both the latest technoscience and the urgency of getting out of Bushist warfare. It has the, to my mind enormous, advantage of attempting to show that the war-cum-militarist universe could be ended by action, but an ambiguously utopian and finally unbelievable way to get out of it. The premises are scientifically impeccable, though by now overoptimistic: a nanotechnology which determines both the protracted North-South global-cum-civil, class-cum-race war in the first part of the novel and (in its ability to create any objects out of water and sand) the "Universal Welfare State" with "electrocash" economy on the US side of the war divide. The warfare is fought mainly by highly trained university people on their three-year-minimum draft, "combat-jacking" into invulnerable war-robots – thus melding the SF traditions of Heinleinian suits and cyberpunk. The interesting psychological aspects of a platoon of ten soldiers with interconnected brains, making for a new morality but also vulnerability, is carried over into the "civilian" part, which begins as a scientific puzzle about building a planet-sized particle accelerator on Jupiter and ends as a political thriller. It turns out that the Jupiter Project, supposed to recreate the Big Bang conditions, would also destroy the known universe, but that a Fundamentalist Christian End of the World sect blocks its suspension for religious reasons. Our heroes, who are by convenient coincidence also colleagues of the top US scientists, find out that prolonged collective jacking-in renders people incapable of hurting others. Though the sect's hard core has infiltrated the government and army command, our heroes' derring-do (they occupy the neuralgic center of power in Washington DC and subject its inmates to the pacifist jack-in) prevails, and we all live happily ever after in a saved universe and pacifist world.

It is not clear why the "nano-forges" are kept a US Government secret when their worldwide use would obviate all scarcity and the need for unending wars, but this is perhaps politically believable; more to the point, it is not believable they could remain a secret. Furthermore, while a plot by scientists to save both peace and the universe by changing the brains of the generals is a very welcome utopia, this unfortunately encompasses both its meanings of a better place and of an impossible no-place. The story's beginning of super-cyborgised jungle warfare remains a believable anti-war tale, its middle a rare SF warning about the misuses and huge dangers of technoscience, and its end a very early prescient alarm at one of the main pillars of present US administration, the so-called Christian Zionists who do hold a belief that one should hasten Armageddon. It is also a rare example, just like Haldeman's earlier novel, of a story adopting the usual military and technoscientific grounds (cyberwarfare, huge scientific projects) but then hollowing them out in an, as it were, self-criticism from within. But like some other narratives based on miraculous nanotechnology (say one by Greg Bear), it degrades at end into a fairy tale.

4. Particularities

> *Clear thinking [about war prevention] becomes more at a premium than ever, plus the need for the clear-thinkers to write it all down and teach it to others. False models of thinking about each other, of human beings who are in conflict, are as deadly as false maps to the tactician.... The anti-war thought that I've encountered in both fiction and real life has been so far too much addicted to feelings and not enough to convincing analysis.*
>
> Lois Bujold

4.0. "Gentlemen, You Are mad!"

It is instructive to confront a famous outcry from 1946 to a publisher's blurb in 2004 as a measure of what has (and has not) happened at the center of our subject-matter, and what defines its horizons.

In 1946, after the atomic bombs on Japan and sensing the winds of the arms race, the great utopologist Lewis Mumford published an article in the prestigious *Saturday Review of Literature* with the title "Gentlemen, you are mad!" The "gentlemen" are the US leaders who lead toward global suicide while convinced they are rationally working for peace and security. The madmen, however, are also all of us, letting them get away with it, indeed "view[ing] the madness of our leaders as if it expressed traditional wisdom and common sense" (qtd. in Franklin, *War* 4).

At the end of 2004, a lost manuscript of Heinlein's first utopian SF novel was published; from dozens of his SF titles, he was on its front page identified as "author of *Starship Troopers*." This is the hour chiming on the readers' clock. It is also the hour on the TV and movie watchers' clock: innumerable movies and series about the military are resulting as I write (February 2005) in the introduction of a TV "Military Channel," with an unbelievably propagandistic US program, and with a "Military History Channel" in preview. The Pentagon budget for 2006 is foreseen to top 600 billion dollars, which together with the ongoing costs of the Afghan and Iraqi wars will amount to around 30% of the US Federal outlay. As an offshoot, the MIT has opened in 2002 an Institute for military nano-technology with huge grants by the Defence Department. What a devolution, what a fall, have the US and the world reality and imagination experienced in 60 years! Mumford's mad leaders spend hundreds of millions of dollars to get re-elected so they can spend hundreds of billions in war procurements to enrich a few corporations, and maybe one percent of the US population, and fight a holy war for power and profits. The rest of us allow this. It is a variant of what Marcuse analyzed for the US Secret Service as the Nazi "rationalising of the irrational (in which the latter retains its power but flows into the process of rationalisation), the continuous to-and-fro between mythology and technology" (49).

US "Military SF" (one of five subgroups for SF in the Catalogue I referred to in 3.2) is a small though meaningful epicycle on the mega-cycle of imaginatively organising and then really fighting this never-ending war. What does it matter that it is as a rule poorly written, monotonous, repetitive, and addictive? Or, perhaps even more strikingly, that it defies elementary rules of sense, such as when, in *Star Trek: Nemesis* of 2002 (though mass media are always more brainless than the corresponding level of written fiction), the final conflict between huge spaceships is still a pirate-style boarding and fistfight? It sells well and confirms audience expectations. I have to be the bearer of bad news: obviously, a large part – most probably a majority – of the main audience that has historically nurtured SF after Wells, the US youth and intellectuals, has undergone what is in Italian nicely called *imbarbarimento*, descent into barbarism, or in US idiom dumbing down. Gwyneth Jones pithily characterises the core that reads military SF as "the rich-poor (materially rich, poor in every marker of high culture) of the USA" (in Suvin ed.). The causes would include huge existential pressures on the spottily employed and systematically humiliated youth as well as the huge monophonic propaganda machines of all the media, turning aggression and rage against foreign scapegoats.[12] In the middle of this process (still ongoing), Rifkin concluded that the USA is becoming:

> a country populated by a small cosmopolitan elite of affluent Americans enclosed inside a larger country of increasingly impoverished workers and unemployed persons. The middle class, once the signature of American prosperity, is fast fading.... In 1989 the top 1 percent of families... owned... 50.3 percent of the net financial assets of the country. (173; see on the horrendous statistics of "The Other America" and "The New Reserve Army" of increasing poverty 177–94).

However, a kind of "cold Civil War" that raged in many US cities of the '60s–70s, and still characterised much cyberpunk in the '80s, has been turned to growing criminality and drug-consumption – though not at all to greater urban security. Not only the richest capitalists and executives but also the new elite professionals or "symbolic analysts" – "distinguished from the rest of the population by their global linkages, comfortable lifestyles,... and abundance of security guards" – went in for secession into isolated enclaves (Robert Reich, cited in Rifkin 177), lauded early on by a Pournelle-Niven novel and best depicted by the latter Ballard (cf. Proietti "Chiusure"). On the fringes of such symbolisers, subject to the same pressures as their readers, most SF writers have joined the engineers of material and human resources, the admen and design professionals, the new bishops and cardinals of the media clerisy, most lawyers, and the teeming swarms of supervisors as the Post-Fordist "organic" mercenaries. They have sincerely or cynically jumped aboard and refused to think about the price of war and militarism, in US and abroad. They are engaging in what Le Guin has, already in less extreme contexts, called "[a] denial of authorial responsibility, a[n elitist,] willed unconsciousness" ("Introduction" 5). We are lucky to still have niches for the Robinsons and Slonczewskis, voices going against the current, as well as SF from the UK. In the climate of increasing repression, with laws in USA (also UK and France) already allowing for secret, unlimited, and judicially unreviewed detention of any stranger plus suspect "sympathiser," I can only hope such niches will last. But the overall frenzied propaganda for war and militarism will obviously go on in the USA until the macro-political climate changes.

In the meantime, we should strive to understand. All of this is being done in a feedback system of writers and readers, our colleagues, our classmates (if I may use this term). How, how come?

4.1. On Intellectuals and Death

Who writes to whom, and *therefore* *about what and how*, in the US SF since 1945 – or since 1959, the year of Heinlein's *Starship Troopers*? It is a nice and unresolved point just which class/es is SF written for, in the commercial and ideological sense. At any rate, it circulates almost entirely within some middle classes of the White North. I have expounded on this at length (Suvin "Utopianism," cf. also "Novum" and "What May," with large bibliographies), and will repeat here that in my opinion the addressor and addressee subjects are various contending fractions of what may be loosely called intellectuals – including what I'd call "apprentice intellectuals," the famous SF core consisting of 13-to-25-year-old readers, no longer overwhelmingly male. Intellectuals are people who work mainly with images, concepts or narrations and "produce, distribute and preserve distinct forms of consciousness" (Mills, *White* 142 – cf. more precisely Mills, Noble, and the Ehrenreichs). Hobsbawm calculates that two thirds of the GNP in the societies of the capitalist North are now derived from their labour, though their proportion within the population is much inferior, globally perhaps 10–15%. Politically, they (we) may be very roughly divided into servants of the capitalist bureaucratic State, servants of large corporations, self-proclaimed "apolitical" or "esthetic" free-floaters, and radicals taking the plebeian side. The funds for this whole congeries of "cadre" classes – "administrators, technicians, scientists, educators.... have been drawn from the global [exploitation] surplus": none of us has clean hands. The Fordist welfare-and-warfare-State saw the culmination of the "cut" from this surplus we "middle" 10–15% were getting; and "the shouts of triumph of this 'middle' sector over the reduction of their gap with the upper one per cent have masked the realities of the growing gap between them and the other [85–90%]" (Wallerstein 83–84 and 104–05).

As different from this Fordist dispensation of roughly 1915–73, the new collectivism from top down, while mouthing individualist slogans stripped of State worship, needs fully other-directed intellectuals whom Post-Modernist cynicism has dispensed from alibis. Post-Fordism has had quite some success in making intellectual "services" more marketable, a simulacrum of profit-making. This began in sciences and engineering: industrial production since ca. the 1880s is the story of how "the capitalist, having expropriated the worker's property, gradually expropriated his technical knowledge as well" (Lasch xi, and see Noble). In the age of World Wars this sucks in law, medicine, and "soft-science" consulting in the swarms of "professional experts." Nowadays those who buck the market better get themselves to a nunnery. The class aggression by big corporations against the immediate producers, corporeal and intellectual, means that Jack London's dystopian division of workers under the Iron Heel into a minority of indispensable Mercenaries and a mass of downtrodden proletarians (updated by Piercy in *He, She and It*) has a good chance of being realised.

On the one hand, as Marx famously chided, "the bourgeoisie has stripped of its halo every occupation hitherto honoured and looked up to with reverent awe. It has turned the physician, the lawyer, the priest, the poet, the scientist, into its paid wage-labourers" (*The Communist Manifesto*). On the other hand, the constitution of intellectuals into professions is impossible without a measure of autonomy: of corporative self-government and, most important, control over one's work. No doubt, this constitution was enabled by the fact that the salaried are "the assistants of authority" (Mills, *White* 74), but no authority can abide without their assistance. We share to an exasperated degree the tug-of-war between wage labour and self-determination. Even the poorest intellectual participates in privilege through her "educational capital"; even the richest manager or commanding general may not be able to rid himself of the uncomfortable itch of thinking. In a living contradiction, we are essential to the *encadrement* and policing of workers, but we are ourselves workers. Excogitating ever new ways to sell our expertise as "services" in producing and enforcing marketing images of happiness and safety, we decisively contribute to the decline of people's self-determination and non-professionalised expertise. We are essential to the production of new knowledge and ideology, but we are totally kept out of establishing the framework into which, and mostly kept from directing the uses to which, the production and the producers are put. We cannot function without a good deal of self-government in our classes or artefacts, but we do not control the strategic decisions about universities, research or dissemination of artefacts. The marginalised and pauperised humanists and teachers – increasingly adjunct policemen keeping the kids off the streets – are disproportionately constituted by women and non-"Whites," a sure index of subalternity.

Already before World War 2, Siegfried Kracauer – an important student of culture beyond his famous analysis of the pre-Nazi horror movies – gave us, I believe, two keys we can use to understand the in-depth processes shaping the mainstream of "Military SF" (and a series of analogous manifestations in US culture) in our Post-Fordist existential squeeze. First, he observed most middle-class professionals, including students and intellectuals, live in personal isolation and a lack of sense, where belief is merely conceptual and the main danger is the *horror vacui*. From these vacuities, sects and mysticisms both religious and lay draw their appeal (106–12). In a second essay, discussing the US illustrated magazines (such as *Life*), he concluded they were one of the most powerful weapons for "locking out understanding": "In them, the spectators see a world, the perception of which is hindered by what they see" (34). He attributed the success of their images to the spectators' fear of thinking about death (I found the same of Disneyland, in "Utopianism"). While we might today, after further experience, broaden the causal system behind his phenomena, the dangerous denial of reality would remain. Even Kracauer's observation that in such magazines the way to banish death was the multiplication of a certain kind of image remains valid. In psychological terms, what we are talking about here is whether, when, how, and how much intellectuals engage in death-lust, while pretending to ignore death.

To illuminate this, we have to posit a spectrum of roles and stances between the poles of what Foucault calls "the 'universal' intellectual" of the Voltaire-to-Zola tradition (usually a writer hurling his political "J'accuse" at the injustices of huge apparatuses and other ruling class privileges) and "the 'specific' intellectual." The latter is the expert that emerged as dominant in the Manhattan Project's atomic scientists and other physicists and has continued down to today's molecular biologists and security theoreticians, whose high prestige – pay and status – is due to the meshing of technoscientific knowledge with "the economic and strategic domain" (122–23). Such a polarisation slights the existence of grey zones in between in order to focus on the indispensable value-judgment in the overarching matters of the survival of millions, perhaps billions, of people under war, and of all of us under militarisation. A condition of proper usage for this heuristic polarisation is that it has to be checked by feedback from particular texts, while taking into account that the most interesting ones are not those of the outright Social-Darwinist warmongers of Pournelle's type but those Jameson would nominate for ambivalent political confusion.

For, to understand intellectual production – not only in arts, even in mathematics – I believe the no doubt useful sociopolitical definitions of intellectuals, from Mills and Foucault to Bourdieu's revealing description as "a dominated fraction of the dominant class" ("Intellectual" 145 and *Other* 319ff.; cf. Guillory 118ff.), are insufficient. We also need an axiological definition, which to my mind would be something on the order of: "people who interpret the past and ongoing flow of cultural production as articulations of a beauty that keeps alive the necessity of justice." This feeds back into approaching SF, as defined at the beginning of this essay: for I agree with Keats and Scarry that beauty is potentially cognitive.

4.2. Allegorical Types, Spacetimes, and Stances

This to my mind means that various fractions of intellectuals, between the poles of Le Guin's responsible (or Foucault's universal) ones and the irresponsible or specific or embedded ones, talk to each other in the symbolic analyses of art. In military SF, a great majority of titles and writers belong to the latter pole. The balance between the two groups in the subgenre may be skewed in comparison to all SF, for many prominent writers and critics have such a distaste for anything associated with war, and therefore the military, that they refuse this framework *a limine*. I must confess this was my optimistic stance too, but when what seemed transient aberrations grow into a quarter-century trend occupying the center of a genre, realities must be faced and contradictions within them uncovered. The key question is: how is such a dialogue conducted, in what ways and forms? In fiction, by means of a narration employing agents, chronotopes, and stances. My hypothesis is that in SF, and even more clearly in such a schematised subgenre as military SF, they are all to some degree (and in novel ways) allegorical: that their reason for being is to refract societal stances, choices or structures of feeling.[13] I shall briefly discuss their novelty, then adduce some examples and attempt to sound them for stances.

Agents in this corpus such as Triumphant Leader, Dupe, Victim or Resistant Other are allegorical roles or types; however, they differ from classical allegory before mass capitalism, say from Buddha and Aristophanes to Bunyan, by abandoning the one-to-one relation between vehicle and tenor, in which a semiotically presented body stands for a pre-existent notion (as Plutus for riches and Ares or Ira for war). When a body (a type) came to be overdetermined by standing for several notions – say the Miles Gloriosus of later Antiquity or the Renaissance Capitano for military inscription, cowardice, magniloquence, and so on – it was not too difficult for Renaissance realism to inject into its constituent notions a truly contradictory one, say the affection for a younger man as opposed to Epicurean sensuality in Falstaff's relation to Prince Hal, and thus to evoke that illusion of soulful depth or three-dimensionality which we came to call a "character." In that sense, I have argued that all the characters of Realism have a backbone of type (Suvin "Can People"): the naive *amoroso* of comedy underlies Stendhal's Fabrice del Dongo, uncomprehendingly lost on the battlefield of Waterloo. But the allegory was backgrounded and indeed came to be theoretically blackballed by most Romantics in their flight into the depths of the stressed individual – though their revolutionary wing produced the best allegorical poem in modern English, Shelley's "Mask of Anarchy."

In doctrinaire individualism the individual is a Robinson Crusoe on his desert island, communicating with other such island-dwellers by means of ground-to-ground missiles in offense or alliance. Though Defoe's Robinson came with a huge baggage of implements and notions from the society that shaped him, the bourgeois ideological mirage blanked this out. The senseless Romantic opposition between the valuable individual as an unsplittable atom opposed to the soullessly mechanical collectivity underlies even the ancestral, and possibly still best, dystopia – Zamyatin's *We*, mimicked then by Orwell's *1984*. As usual, it was taken to its extreme by the Nazis, who agreed with Klages that the intellect is "the enemy of the soul" (cf. Glaser 99). Yet it not only seems that the Leviathan of centralised State is fading in favour of the Leviathan of globalising corporations (I argue such points in "Reflections"), but the overdetermination initiated by Realism has by now grown much more intimate and complex. Joanna Russ's pioneering encapsulation goes:

> Perhaps SF is one symptom of a change in sensibility (and culture) as profound as that of the Renaissance. Despite its ultra-American, individualistic muscle-flexing, SF (largely American in origin and influence) is collective in outlook, didactic, materialist, and, paradoxically, often intensely religious or mystical. (*To Write* 10–11)

In fact, the allegorical type had surfaced already in the very unromantic experiences of crowded cities and then crowded battlefields (in Balzac the two can be scarcely distinguished), where roles such as Young Upstart and Courtesan, rather than nuclear individuality, became again determining frameworks for success and survival. The individual Young Woman or World War Soldier was thereby not denied but slotted, and the slot determined to a significant degree – sometimes bearable but sometimes overwhelming – her freedom of choice. The narrative agent had a face and as a rule a non-allegorical name, but also a deep structure of type(s) – as Shelley's poem mentioning his period's prime minister begins: "I met Murder on the way,/ He had a mask like Castlereagh." The spaceship containing various ranks of diplomats, military, and ragtag civilians is only a further development of the drawing room, hotel or sanatorium of the Realistic tradition, where such neo-allegorical, that is, parable types – social roles, ages, genders or nationalities – could believably mingle. This mingling then leads to enrichment but also to confusion. Enrichment, because a narrative agent can evolve or shuttle between traits and roles, be US, woman, militaristic, ethnically socialised, traumatised by repressed rape in adolescence, upwardly mobile, and a genius – in fact a superwoman singlehandedly winning a galactic battle – all in one fell swoop (fans will recognise here Elizabeth Moon's Esmay Suiza). Confusion, because almost all such agents in recent SF, from Heinlein's archetypal Space Soldier called Johnny Rico on, repose on an irreconcilable contradiction. The individualist stress on the narrative protagonist-hero/ine, who is – with wens and all, as Cromwell said to his painter – the reader's narrative focus and guide, is at odds with the collective framework into which modern mass organisations (the bureaucracy, but most notably the executive, Catch-22 bureaucracy-in-arms of an army or interstellar navy) and the consubstantial mass technology inevitably put her. What Jameson would call the personal and the tale of the tribe are simultaneously contrary to each other and a source of potential cross-over strength. In military SF, you must be both a hero and an interchangeable cog in the all-encompassing machine. Thus the price is very high: the collectivity no longer stands for participatory democracy from below upward but for militarised hierarchy.

A basic choice presents itself here, which is part and parcel of the perennial "two souls" of US SF, polarised between the thoughtful Twain-to-Le Guin and the gung-ho edisonade-to-Heinlein paths. The poles differentiate warmongers from the war critics. To pick up on my discussion of James's *American Scene*, is there a moral and material price – increasingly inescapable as ecological destruction – to the US linear accumulation of the "perpetual increase of everything" or not? Will the authorial stance focus on the inevitable or even exhilarating nature of war, boyishly – and after the '80s also girlishly – foregrounding the nifty technology and ranging through all the times and spaces of actual or imaginable history, or will it focus on its historical price in atrocious psychophysical suffering of victims, whether enemies or "our" soldiers, and the destruction of things and values? If the former, is there any redeeming element to be found within imperial trash indulging in destruction? If the latter, is there any indication as to the causes of war and militarism which would help the reader to understand how these might be prevented?

Often, as noted by Franklin and Jameson, the refusal to envisage the price in blood and suffering means a shift from army to navy locales, and in the extreme cases to space equivalents of the Strategic Air Command (cf. Franklin, *War* 95–108; Jameson, "Science Fiction" 36) busting planets into smithereens. When the Marines have to descend to slugging it out on the ground, the technological wonders of "suits" isolate combatants from the gory mess, even more so when battles are followed from spaceships on virtual space screens in pretty streaks of colour – as inaugurated by *Star Trek* and *Star Wars*, which spoke to the adolescent "love for shiny gadgets, spiffy uniforms, authoritative-sounding technotalk and a hot rod that shoots really cool laser blasts" (Corliss). But such militarist SF mainstream, from Pournelle to Drake or sometimes even Moon, is rather dreary (and furthermore much of it is discussed in the essays by Jones and Proietti). As a rule, the pro-war writings are *only* about the war/military, plus some crude identificatory ego-psychology. To the contrary, as a rule the anti-war writings are *only partly* about the war, that is, also about much more around the war. Though this makes them difficult to summarise, I shall focus on a few narrative as well as ideological characteristics of the better SF about war and militarism, mainly in the "pause" period 1974–2001, discussed in more detail in 3.2. First, about the *narrative agents* and their consubstantial *chronotopes*: and centrally, do victims have faces here?

Militarist and pro-war SF works are at best, say in Heinlein, allegories of socialising the reader – at first only male, as of the mid-'80s also female (see on that much more in Jones) – into triumphant warfare and the military. As opposed to them, in anti-war works the voice, stance or view of, and at their best from, the plebeian *underdogs and victims* is incorporated to various degrees and in various ways. This latches on to the Twainian tradition of Sturgeon, Disch, Le Guin, Dick, and others mentioned earlier. The underdogs – as a rule, overtly or covertly, US characters – are variants of either duped soldiers in the field (in both Haldeman titles and Shepard) or of the refuseniks who understand they're other, as already Sturgeon's soldier and Cordwainer Smith's Commander did: some of Shirley's, Robinson's, Le Guin's (in "New Atlantis") or Haldeman's (in *Peace*) underground members or subversives, Slonczewski's collectivist women, and Piercy's alliance of women, cyborg, and underground (surprisingly, Poul Anderson has an exceptional refusal of genocide in "Dereliction"). Card's Ender begins as a dupe with an aptitude for ruthlessness plus agonising about it, but at the end bursts that chrysalis, as it were, and becomes a religious and super-elite refusenik. As in other aspects, Card is having it both ways: Ender is a child, for most of the narration much sinned against, but also a genius and White as in the most Right-wing militarist SF. Yet as a rule, our protagonist to be identified with is a draft-age male, and such SF rehearses from the late '60s on the alternatives posed in all clarity for the Vietnam War generation. In some significant exceptions, the protagonist is not single but serial/collective and/or female, as in Slonczewski and Robinson (Piercy adds the ambidextrous cyborg).

Haldeman's *Peace* seems inscribed into "hard SF," written for and about scientists and academics, but subversively speaks out of this community and about the dangers of technoscience; Piercy is equally immersed into cyber-programming but here science is again (also) a weapon for freedom. At the "soft" end of this spectrum, in Le Guin, Slonczewski, Robinson, and Piercy, the status of women (and of sane erotics) is, as usual in the Left tradition, a measure of both power and victimization: rape precedes and signals genocide. As the Italian Futurists' Manifesto of 1909 pithily put it, on the eve of the season of World Wars: "We shall glorify war – the world's only hygiene – militarism, patriotism, the destructive gesture of freedom-bringers, beautiful ideas worth dying for, and scorn for women" (Marinetti 41–42).

To the contrary, with a very few exceptions such as Haldeman and Piercy, in the war critics technoscience is slighted in favour of psychological and even political argument. The presence of a hospital (quite frequent in Bujold) is a signal of heterodoxy, concentrating on the bodily price of war, and even more so the rare presence of burial ceremonies (as at the end of Bujold's *Shards* and in a way of Card) or of sacrifice (in Piercy). Both may show the raw presence of mangled bodies, this final vulnerable rampart of humanity, excised in pro-war writing beginning with Heinlein (see 2.1 above, and much more in Proietti, "Saving"). Finally, the victims we are shown can be supposed enemies and outright Aliens – a difficult feat, managed only in Le Guin's creechies in *The Word*, Piercy's cyborg, or at a remove in Card's Bugger queen, though I suppose the parthenogenetic collectivist women of Slonczewski's are the truly alien Other to the mercantile patriarchy. The family resemblance between terms for such derided and disposable people, taken from the dominant lingo which the SF shows up as alienating, reveals to my mind their root in political deviance: creechies (the natives) are homeomorphic to Disch's conchies (conscientious objectors) and even earlier Pohl-Kornbluth's consies (conservationists), the template for all of them being the post-1945 witchhunt commies (communists).

Whatever else the epoch following on, say, the 1911 Balkan Wars and Mexican Revolution may be, it has two red threads. First, it is 100 years of never-ending mass warfare, internal or international, of which the two World Wars were only the tempestuously noticeable peaks; the lulls in the North around the two World Wars were a local illusion. World War 2 was fought in good part to end the internal dangers of the US and then global Depression, and it can be argued the USA is since the early 1960s exporting its low-grade urban warfare precisely in the form of militarised "police actions" (cf. Dal Lago, *Polizia*) – certainly there's no dearth of prominent SF works arguing that. Second, not coincidentally, this is the epoch of mass bureaucracy, itself born out of war procurements and identified in the pioneering works from the neuralgic areas of imperial Europe East of the Rhine: Weber, Simmel, Kafka... but then also from Gogol to Belyi, Zamyatin, Platonov, Bulgakov, and Co. It is again Jameson, our indispensable Virgil in these infernal *bolgie*, who remarks how Big Brother has in the US-dominated globalisation been supplanted by the language as used by prostitute mass media and experts: "Everyone today is, if not organized then at least organizable," and what has been called "subject-positions" are "the forms of identity afforded by group adherence." The demolition of the nuclear subject has had positive cognitive aspects, bursting the shackles of individualism. But Jameson adds the warning, quite evidently also applicable to militarist SF, that "the dissipation of those illusions [as to the autonomy of thought] may reveal a wholly positivist landscape from which the negative has evaporated altogether, beneath the steady clarity of what has been identified as 'cynical reason'" (*Postmodernism* 322–23).

When people (or their stand-ins, the narrative agents) are inserted into huge organised groups - bureaucratic, technoscientific, military, political - with an overwhelming structure, seemingly as firm and eternal as Saussure's *langue* is when compared to any of its actualizations in *parole*, this is much more than a framework. Just as language, it is an intimately osmotic home (that with startling frequency in this corpus turns also into a prison-house) intervening into or indeed shaping the protagonist's deepest love-hate values. These may be most revealingly analyzed as the knot of belonging, which will lead to stances toward war and militarism. In this knot, the single personality is not only part of a collective, it is made possible and at least co-created by the collective. The best theoretical tool I've found to begin dealing with this is Jameson's "overdetermination in ambivalence," where works and narremes (such as the protagonist) "become endowed with associations at one and the same time 'plebeian' and 'bureaucratic', with the not unexpected political confusion inherent in such ambivalence" (*Postmodernism* 314).

Thus, a crucial parameter in these narrations is the difference in *authorial stance* (usually transferred to central narrative agents) *concerning mass slaughter*, which entails a choice of belonging. Blithely condoning it as either inevitable or even good, and correlatively finding a home in the military, is omnipresent in pro-war SF, which has a special narrative role of "shreddies," minor characters wasted mercilessly and repetitively - though there are exceptions concerning military honour and care for the troops as against *realpolitik*. On the other pole is opposition to slaughter, especially when the line between the killed combatants and civilians becomes unclear, vividly brought out in Shiner, Haldeman's two novels, Robinson, Slonczewski, and Piercy, correlative to which are alternate communities of dissident scientists and even underground fighters (as already in Piercy's *Dance*, Russ's *Female Man*, Le Guin's *Word*, and Dick's *A Scanner Darkly*). In this most alienating world, opposition to war and to the military is not always identical, for the military can be an apparent - and for a while real - surrogate home of soldierly fraternity, as in most Bujold and in the earlier Haldeman (and as, for a while, in the 20th-Century armies arisen from liberation wars or revolutions, from Trotsky's Red Army, Villa, Zapata or Ataturk to the guerrillas and partizans from Spain, Yugoslavia, and China to Cuba, Vietnam, and Africa). The narration's stance - Eco's *intentio operis* - is of a piece with the political setup envisaged. It ranges from direct extrapolation of the Cold War and Vietnam War situations, modulating into Third World threats and then terrorism, say in both of Haldeman's novels, to Bujold's benevolent quasi-feudal empire with local autonomy (not capitalist, but more than a little Ruritanian - however, as different from Cordwainer Smith's not so benevolent and immensely powerful oligarchy, rather rosy than somber); Card characteristically straddles both extrapolation and exoticism. I am tempted to posit as the absolute limit of all US SF about war the fact that politics are *never* caused by economic interests - at the very rare best, in Le Guin's *Word*, Robinson's "Mars" trilogy or Slonczewski, these can be mentioned as one not further examined factor. The economic process is reduced to the destructive consumption in war, while class interests (so obvious in Bushism) do not appear even in an authorial subconscious. In that context, Piercy's setup of economic politics is a glaring exception, correlative to her not writing primarily for the SF readership.

The opposition may range from (loyal or cynical) doubt to outright anti-war stance, beginning with passive resistance. As Haldeman's article exemplarily concluded, illustrating his trajectory to *Forever Peace*:

> I had refused to kill people directly, but wasn't reluctant to apply technology and expertise to the same end.... [M]erely paying income tax made you an accessory to the murder of Vietnamese; civil disobedience was the only moral alternative. If I'd known then what I know now, that may have been the route I'd taken. ("Vietnam" 100–01)

Within such opposition, doubt and passive resistance were rife, but also the quite frequent *deus ex machina* happy ending, as in Haldeman *War*, Card, Shepard, and Shirley. This often makes for what I have called broken-backed narratives. Actual active resistance, if need be an apostasy against one's own country of provenance and original allegiance, arose very rarely: I can think in this period only of Shirley, Le Guin, Robinson, Piercy, and Haldeman's *Peace*. The huge pressures of fannish – and probably publishing – conformism as well as of self-censorship are evident here.

The 1961–74 "Golden Age" culminated in the refusal of linear <u>time</u> of technoscientific progress that led to vaster murdering, by opting out as in Haldeman or by more heroic opposition as in Le Guin. This recurs here too but in muted forms. It may become simply personal evasion, as in Shepard, improbably coupled with political reversal, as in Card, or it may be collective resistance, as in Le Guin's failed group, Robinson's, Slonczewski's, and Piercy's more successful and best articulated mass movements or, midway between them, Haldeman's improvised scientists' cabal. Often, as in Shirley, there is a nostalgic ending having the best of both: after the victory of resistance, the bliss of anti-gravity erotics. Bujold's simpler worlds of space opera avoid the final evasion by structurally incorporating it into the binary tensions between the militarist and sentimental or erotic aspects, yoked together by our victorious but afflicted hero, victim and power-holder in a charmed universe. I would consider all of these narrative strategies, finally revealed at the end of each book, as attempts to find a space for the utopias of pacifism, erotics, and finally of self-determination in a hostile world that often blocks them. Yet narratively and realistically unmotivated utopianism easily degrades into improbable fairy tale, if not Card's outright messianism. Obversely, where alternatives are not only suggested but up to a point believably (which means collectively) shown in "thick" detail, as in Slonczewski, Robinson, and Piercy, utopianism grows what Bloch would call "concrete."

Just like its readers, US SF has not found a believable way out of war and militarism, but at its best it has given us precious articulations and signposts.

Notes

* I am very grateful to John Clute, Fredric Jameson, and Sylvia Kelso for sending me some secondary materials, and to Clute, Alex Fambrini, Jerry Määttä, Salvatore Proietti, Alcena Rogan, Johannes Rüster, and other friends who discussed with me some aspects of this article. Opinions and mistakes are mine.

1 Given the many SF reprints, citations to a title will be by chapter/page.

2 Cf. to begin with Leone-Anrig, and for the extraordinary actuality of Orwell's political analysis in the age of Bushist Never-Ending Warfare, Catani's competent sketch of war in SF. The US Commission on National Security reported in 1999 (before the attack on Twin Towers!) that since the end of the Cold War, the USA has "embarked upon nearly four dozen military interventions... as opposed to only 16 during the entire period of the Cold War" (cited in Gowan, "Instruments" 152).

3 The pivot role of H.G. Wells, from the wars of classes in *The Time Machine* and *When the Sleeper Wakes* through the reverse imperialist *War of the Worlds* to the World War of *War in the Air* will alas be slighted; I hope to be forgiven, the readier as I devoted two chapters to it in *MOSF*.

4 There is of course a whole small library of works on this theme, from which I list only the Pocock referred to in the quotation.

5 The bestialisation of enemies owes nothing to the rise of communism, rather one could say that – as we have experienced since 1989 – the latter was a godsend to fill a pre-established necessity of the system. For one example, see George Washington's quite normal reference to "both [the Savage and the Wolf] being beasts of prey though they differ in shape" (qtd. in Smith-Rosenberg 1326): one could paraphrase Voltaire to the effect "Should Communism – or today, Terrorism – not exist, we would have had to invent it."

6 I take the cue for this term from Jameson's "World Reduction" essay, which speaks about Le Guin and her differing methods, but does mention a "surgical excision of empirical reality" (223).

7 My take on *The American Scene* was sparked by Prof. Giles Gunn's lecture, "The Moral Relevance of America's Greatest Travel Book in an Age of Terror," at the University of Salerno, Dipart. di Studi linguistici e letterari, in October 2004, from which I also take the quote; the interpretation and inferences are mine. An important element for this withering of time-horizons into a two-dimensional arrow is to my mind the successful clamp-down on the immense discontent by working classes, surfacing from the millions of Thoreau's "lives of quiet desperation" into protest movements from Populism to Socialism and unions. These movements are well represented in the US estranged fiction by names such as Donnelly, Baum or London, and in its New Deal phase are clearly co-responsible for the rise of mass SF and refracted in it.

8 I'm here indebted to *The Grolier Multimedia Encyclopedia of Science Fiction* (CD-ROM, 1995), edited by John Clute, and especially his own entries on various writers and aspects, though I might – as in this case – here and there disagree. On rereading my essay, I've spotted a few places where his turns of phrase have seeped into my own, because I could not better them. My dedication to John and his artist-wife Judith by no means implies their responsibility for any opinions in this article.

9 As we know, the story is more complex and contradictory. I am here speaking only about the overall effect of the intellectuals' adjustment, and have written at length about the nuances in "Introduction" and "Polity."

10 On criteria for fascism today, cf. Britt.

On "survivalism": it is the fictional equivalent of the near-fascist or fully fascist "libertarian" militias, religious or lay, which bloomed in the 1980s and into the '90s. Their stories are set in post-holocaust venues where the hated State apparatus and its all-embracing citizenship has disappeared, so that our macho hero must kill or be killed. I would read this as the extrapolation and coming to the fore of what I mention as the smouldering mini-civil-war in the post-1960s USA. It comes in two variants, with group protagonist, usually a political Right-wing tract with dystopian pretensions of eventual world-domination (cf. the pioneering survey by Orth in the Proietti-Suvin Bibliography in Suvin ed.), or with single protagonist, usually a tale of unbridled violence including torture and rape. The latter variant's higher, more or less sanitised reaches may be seen in Kate Wilhelm's *Where Late the Sweet Birds Sang* already in 1976 (discussed in my "Science Fiction"), the *Mad Max* movies and books, and in some fiction by Niven (cf. Franklin *War* 211, Clute "Survivalist," and Proietti, "Saving" section 5). Significantly, as Clute notes, after the first Gulf Oil War in 1991 the fortunes of this subgenre abruptly ebbed, pre-empted by Bushism: this anxiety has been stanched, the war has been exported.

Similarly, the very success and shameless ubiquity of earlier privately employed, secret or supposedly idealistic *mercenaries* (the "mercenaries business" is estimated at 130 billion dollars per year or one sixth of the global military spending, there are over 50,000 of them in Iraq only; cf. "Où," Singer, Traynor, and the wealth of data in "Multinationales") has reduced their visibility in military SF to just another variant or niche, as in Drake's "Hammer's Slammers" or the "Battletech" series.

11 An interesting question is why the Italian names like Mandella and Mingolla. My guess would be that they connoted a semi-peripheral position of their bearers: neither admitted to fully share WASP power like the Irish or the Jewish-Americans, nor on the periphery like the Black, Hispanic, and Asian-Americans.

12 The transferral of rage to Others, when faced with what appears an insoluble existential quandary, is a well-known sickness, present in the US tradition since the first colonisers applied it to Native Americans, see Smith-Rosenberg 1333 and passim. Cf. on rage when a sense of justice is offended Arendt 63–64 and on "the brutalising effects of post-Fordist labor markets" and rage Luckhurst 149 and passim. The best insights into the subject of mass killings and their meaning is to be found in the burgeoning new disciplines of Peace Studies and Sociology of Violence, cf. for an introduction Herberg-Rothe.

13 I adopt and adapt my use of allegory from Fredric Jameson's writings about cultural products, in his *Fables* (cf. chapter 5, esp. 90–104) and *Postmodernism*, also *Seeds*. See an earlier discussion of mine on SF as parable in the final essay of my *Positions*.

Works Referred To

A. Science Fiction Narrations (chronologically by year of first publication)

1889 Twain, Mark. *A Connecticut Yankee in King Arthur's Court.*

1898 Wells, H.G. *War of the Worlds.*

Serviss, Garrett. *Edison's Conquest of Mars.*

1907 London, Jack. *The Iron Heel.*
1912ff. Burroughs, E.R. "Barsoom" (Mars) series of novels (to 1943).
1913 Scheerbart, Paul. *Lesabéndio* (in German).

*****

1928-35 Smith, E.E. Skylark series (with a coda in 1966).
1941 Heinlein, Robert A. "Logic of Empire."
1944 Brown, Fredric. "Arena."
1946 Davis, Chandler. "To Still the Drums."
Jenkins, Will F. *The Murder of the U.S.A.*
1947 Sturgeon, Theodore. "Thunder and Roses."
1949 Heinlein, Robert A. "The Long Watch."
Orwell, George. *1984.*
Szilard, Leo. "My Trial as a War Criminal" (see also his collection of SF stories *The Voice of the Dolphins*, 1961).
1950 Merril, Judith. *Shadow on the Hearth.*
1951 Heinlein, Robert A. *The Puppet Masters.*
Wise, Robert. *The Day the Earth Stood Still* (movie).
1951ff. Anderson, Poul. "Dominic Flandry" series of stories and novels (ongoing with intervals for almost three decades).
1952 Leiber, Fritz. "The Foxholes of Mars"; "The Moon Is Green."
1955 Sohl, Jerry. *Point Ultimate.*
1959 Clarkson, Helen [pseud. of Helen McCoy]. *The Last Day.*
Heinlein, Robert A. *Starship Troopers.*
Kramer, Stanley. *On the Beach* (movie).
Miller, Walter M. Jr. *A Canticle for Leibowitz.*
Roshwald, Mordecai. *Level 7.*
1959ff. Dickson, Gordon R. "Dorsai" series.

*****

1962 Dick, Philip K. *The Man in the High Castle.*
1964 Dick, Philip K. *The Penultimate Truth.*
Heinlein, Robert A. *Farnham's Freehold.*
Kubrick, Stanley. *Dr Strangelove* (movie).
Lumet, Sidney. *Fail-Safe* (movie).
Smith, Cordwainer [pseud. of Paul A.M. Linebarger]. "The Crime and the Glory of Commander Suzdal."
1965 Anderson, Poul. *The Star Fox.*
Dick, Philip K. *Dr Bloodmoney.*
Harrison, Harry. *Bill, the Galactic Hero.*
1966 Heinlein, Robert A. *The Moon Is a Harsh Mistress.*
Watkins, Peter. *The War Game* (movie).
1966-69 (First) Star Trek TV series. Paramount Television/NBC, created by Gene Roddenberry (also executive producer); six movie spin-offs 1979ff. and four succeeding series with different subtitles 1987ff.

1967 Disch, Thomas M. *Camp Concentration.*
Report from Iron Mountain on the Possibility and Desirability of Peace. Introduction (and authorship) Leonard C. Lewin.
1967-73 Niven, Larry. *The Protector.*
1968 O'Donnell, K.M. [pseud. of Barry N. Malzberg]. "Final War."
1963-69 Delany, Samuel R. *The Fall of the Towers* (trilogy).
1969 Brunner, John. *The Jagged Orbit.*
Vonnegut, Kurt Jr. *Slaughterhouse-5.*
1970 Piercy, Marge. *Dance the Eagle to Sleep.*
1971 Watkins, Peter. *Punishment Park* (movie).
1971ff. Pournelle, Jerry E. "Co-Dominium" series.
1972 Disch, Thomas M. *334.*
Le Guin, Ursula K. *The Word for World Is Forest.*
Spinrad, Norman. *The Iron Dream.*
1972-74 Haldeman, Joe. *The Forever War.*
1973 Romero, George A. *The Crazies* (movie).
1974 Niven, Larry, and Jerry Pournelle. *The Mote in God's Eye.*

*****

1975 Le Guin, Ursula K. "The New Atlantis."
Russ, Joanna. *The Female Man.*
1976 Delany, Samuel R. *Triton.*
Dick, Philip K. *Radio Free Albemuth* (publ. 1985).
Piercy, Marge. *Woman on the Edge of Time.*
1977 Dick, Philip K. *A Scanner Darkly.*
Niven, Larry, and Jerry Pournelle. *Lucifer's Hammer.*
Pournelle, Jerry E. *The Mercenary.*
1977ff. Lucas, George. *Star Wars* (movie series).
1979 Hackett, John, et al. *The Third World War.*
1979-80 Bretnor, Reginald ed. "The Future at War" series of pro-war essays and stories.
1979ff. Drake, David. "Hammer's Slammers" series of novels and short fiction on galactic mercenaries.
Pournelle, Jerry E. "Janissaries" series.
1980ff. Brin, David. "Uplift" series of novels of galactic species-conflict.
1981 Ing, Dean. *Systemic Shock.*
Pournelle, Jerry E., and Larry Niven. *The Oath of Fealty.*
1982 Vonnegut, Kurt, Jr. *Deadeye Dick.*
1983ff. Pournelle, Jerry E., and John F. Carr, eds. "There Will Be War!" series of military anthologies.
1984 Castle, Nick, Jr. *The Last Starfighter* (movie).
Delany, Samuel R. *Stars in My Pockets like Grains of Sand.*
Franklin, H. Bruce ed. *Countdown to Midnight* (anthology of stories about nuclear warfare).
Jackson, Mick. *Threads* (TV movie).
1984-85 Le Guin, Ursula K. *Always Coming Home* ("Stone Telling" sections).
1984-87 Naha, Ed ed. "Traveller" survivalist series (mostly written by John Shirley).

1985 Card, Orson Scott. *Ender's Game.*
Niven, Larry, and Jerry E. Pournelle. *Footfall.*
1985-90 Shirley, John. *Eclipse* trilogy.
1986 Card, Orson Scott. *Speaker for the Dead.*
Slonczewski, Joan. *A Door into Ocean.*
1986-87 Shepard, Lucius. *Life during Wartime.*
1986-96 Bujold, Lois M. "Vorkosigan" series of 11 novels and 1 book of short stories (continuing but no longer in a military ambience).
1987 Van Buren Dann, Jeanne, and Jack Dann eds. *In the Field of Fire* (anthology of Vietnam-derived stories).
1987ff. "Battletech," game tie-in series of shared-world novels.
McKinney, Jack [pseud. of Brian Daley and James Luceno]. "Robotech" series (18 vols. so far).
1988 Bujold, Lois M. *Falling Free.*
Robinson, K.S. *The Gold Coast.*
1988-92 G. Harry Stine, "Warbots" series of a dozen short novels.
1988-94 Niven, Larry ed. "Man-Kzin War" series of shared-world anthologies.
1988ff. Pournelle, Jerry E. ed. "War World" series of shared-world anthologies.
Drake, David A., and Bill Fawcett eds. "The Fleet" series of shared-world anthologies.
Drake, David A., and collaborators. "Crisis of Empire" series of tie-in shared-world novels.
1990 Anderson, Poul. "Dereliction," in David Drake and Bill Fawcett eds., *Sworn Allies.*
1990ff. Drake, David A. "Northworld" series.
1991 Card, Orson Scott. *Xenocide.*
Piercy, Marge. *He, She and It.*
1991ff. Drake, David A., and S.M. Stirling. "The General" series of novels.
1992-96 Robinson, K.S. "Mars" trilogy *(Red Mars, Green Mars, Blue Mars).*
1993 Niven, Larry, and Jerry E. Pournelle. *The Moat around Murcheson's Eye.*
1993-2000 Moon, Elizabeth. "The Serrano Legacy" (series of 7 novels).
1996 Emmerich, Roland. *Independence Day* (movie).
1997 Haldeman, Joe. *Forever Peace.*
Verhoeven, Paul. *Starship Troopers* (movie).
1997ff. Skurzynski, Gloria. "Virtual War" series.

B. Secondary Literature Cited

I debated splitting this into two subsections, on SF vs. war, militarism, and everything else, but concluded the overlaps meant it wasn't worth it. About war, see much more in Suvin "Capitalism."

Aldiss, Brian W. *Billion Year Spree.* Weidenfeld & Nicolson, 1973.
Amin, Samir. *Capitalism in the Age of Globalization.* Zed Books, 1997.
Angenot, Marc. *L'antimilitarisme: Idéologie et utopie.* CIADEST, 2000; rpt. P del'U Laval 2003.
Arendt, Hannah. *On Violence.* Harcourt Brace Jovanovich, 1974.
Bacevich, Andrew J. *The New American Militarism.* Oxford UP, 2005.
Benjamin, Walter. *Gesammelte Schriften.* Suhrkamp, 1980.
Bourdieu, Pierre. "The Field of Cultural Production." *Poetics* 12 (1983): 311–56.
Bourdieu, Pierre. *In Other Words.* Trans. M. Anderson. Stanford UP, 1990.

Britt, Laurence W. "Fascism Anyone?" *Free Inquiry* 23.2, at www.secularhumanism.org/library/fi/ britt_23_2.htm.
Bujold, Lois [M.]. "The Future of Warfare." http://lavka.lib.ru/bujold/b_wareng.htm [talk in St. Petersburg 2000].
Burk, James ed. *The Adaptive Military*. Transaction Publ., 1998.
Busch, Heiner. *Grenzenlose Polizei? Neue Grenzen und polizeiliche Zusammenarbeit in Europa*. Westfälisches Dampfboot, 1995.
Caplow, Theodore, and Pascal Vennesson. *Sociologie militaire*. Colin, 2000.
Catani, Vittorio. "Su pei mondi a guerreggiar…," in his *Vengo solo se parlate di Ufi*. Delosbooks, 2004, 232–50.
C[lute], J[ohn]. "Dickson, Gordon R.," in J. Clute and P. Nicholls eds. *The Multimedia Encyclopedia of Science Fiction*, CD-ROM. Grolier Electronic Publ., 1995.
C[lute], J[ohn]. "Edisonade," ibidem.
C[lute], J[ohn]. "Shared Worlds," ibidem.
C[lute], J[ohn]. "Survivalist Fiction," ibidem.
Corliss, Richard. "Our Critic Rides a Time Machine." *Time* Feb. 10, 1997, 55.
van Creveld, Martin. *The Art of War*. Cassell, 2002.
Dal Lago, Alessandro. "La guerra-mondo." *Conflitti globali* no. 1 (2005): 11–31.
Dal Lago, Alessandro. *Polizia globale*. ombre corte, 2003.
Eco, Umberto. "Towards a New Middle Ages," in M. Blonsky ed., *In Signs*. Johns Hopkins UP, 1985, 488–504.
Eco, Umberto. *The Role of the Reader*. Indiana UP, 1979.
"Editorial." *Science-Fiction Studies* 6.1 (1979): 1–8.
Ehrenreich, Barbara, and John Ehrenreich. "The Professional-Managerial Class," in P. Walker ed., *Between Labor and Capital*. South End P, 1979.
Fitting, Peter. "Notes on Future War in SF Movies," in Suvin ed., 21–9.
Foucault, Michel. *Power/Knowledge*. Ed. C. Gordon, trans. idem et al. Pantheon Books, 1980.
Franklin, H. Bruce. *Robert A. Heinlein: America as Science Fiction*. Oxford UP, 1980.
Franklin, H. Bruce. *Vietnam and Other American Fantasies*. U of Massachusetts P, 2000.
Franklin, H. Bruce. *War Stars: The Superweapon and the American Imagination*. Oxford UP, 1988.
Glaser, Hermann. *The Cultural Roots of National Socialism*. Trans. E.A. Menze. U of Texas P, 1978.
Gowan, Peter. "Instruments of Empire." *New Left R* no. 21 (2003): 147–53.
Gowan, Peter. "US: UN." *New Left R* no. 24 (2003): 5–28.
Gray, Chris Hables. *Postmodern War*. Guilford P, 1997.
Guillory, John. "Literary Critics as Intellectuals," in W.C. Dimock and M.T. Gilmore eds., *Rethinking Class*. Columbia UP, 1994, 107–49.
Haldeman, Joe. "Vietnam and Other Alien Worlds," in G. Slusser and E.S. Rabkin eds., *Fights of Fancy*. U of Georgia P, 1993, 92–102.
Herberg-Rothe, Andreas. *Der Krieg*. Campus V, 2003.
Hirsch, Joachim, and Roland Roth. *Das neue Gesicht des Kapitalismus*. VSA, 1986.
Hobsbawm, Eric. *The Age of Extremes*. Pantheon, 1994.
James, Henry. *The American Scene*. Ed. L. Edel. Indiana UP, 1968.
Jameson, Fredric. *Fables of Aggression*. U of California P, 1979.
Jameson, Fredric. "'If I find one good city I will spare the man,'" in P. Parrinder ed., *Learning from Other Worlds*. Liverpool UP, 2000, and Duke UP, 2001, 208–32.

Jameson, Fredric. *Postmodernism, or, The Cultural Logic of Late Capitalism*. Duke UP, 1992.
Jameson, Fredric. "Science Fiction as Politics: Larry Niven." *The New Republic* 175 (Oct. 30, 1976): 34–38.
Jameson, Fredric. *The Seeds of Time*. Columbia UP, 1994.
Jameson, Fredric. "World Reduction in Le Guin." *Science-Fiction Studies* no. 7 (1975): 221–30.
Jones, Gwyneth. "Wild Hearts in Uniform," in Suvin ed., 69–81.
Joxe, Alain. *Voyage aux sources de la guerre*. PUF, 1991.
Kaldor, Mary. *New and Old Wars*. Wiley, 1999.
Kalecki, Michal. *Theory of Economic Dynamics*. Monthly RP, 1954.
Keegan, John. *The Iraq War*. Knopf and Hutchinson, 2004.
Kelso, Sylvia. "Loud Achievements: Lois McMaster Bujold's Science Fiction." *New York R of Science Fiction* no. 122 (1998): 1, 10–16, and 123 (1998): 13–15.
Klare, Michael T. *Resource Wars*. Metropolitan Books, 2001.
Kolko, Gabriel. *Century of War*. New P, 1994.
Kracauer, Siegfried. *Das Ornament der Masse*. Suhrkamp, 1977.
Lasch, Christopher. "Foreword" to Noble [see below], xi–xiii.
Latour, Bruno. *Science in Action*. Harvard UP, 1997.
Lefebvre, Henri. *The Production of Space*. Trans. D. Nicholson-Smith. Blackwell, 1997.
Le Guin, Ursula K. "Introduction" to her *A Fisherman of the Inland Sea*. Harper Collins, 1994, 1–11.
Lens, Sidney. *PermanCent War*. Schocken, 1987.
Leone, Richard C., and Greg Anrig Jr. eds. *The War on Our Freedoms*. Public Affairs, 2003.
Love, Barbara, and Elizabeth Shanklin. "The Answer Is Matriarchy," in J. Treblicot ed., *Mothering*. Rowman & Allanheld, 1984, 275–83.
Luckhurst, Roger. "Going Postal," in V. Hollinger and J. Gordon eds., *Edging into the Future*. U of Pennsylvania P, 2002, 142–56.
Lyon, David. *Surveillance Society: Monitoring Everyday Life*. Open U, 2001.
Marcuse, Herbert. *Feindesanalysen*. zu Klampen, 1998.
Marinetti [, F.T.] *Selected Writings*. Ed. and transl. R.W. Flint and A.A. Coppotelli. Farrar, 1972.
[Marx, Karl.] *Manifesto of the Communist Party*, in Robert C. Tucker ed., *The Marx-Engels Reader*. Norton, 1972, 311–63.
McMurtry, John. *The Cancer Stage of Capitalism*. Pluto P, 1999.
McMurtry, John. *Understanding War*. Science for Peace and Stevens P, 1989.
Mills, C. Wright. *The Power Elite*. Oxford UP, 1956.
Mills, C. Wright. *White Collar*. Oxford UP, 1953.
"Multinationales des mercenaires." www.ifrance.com/intelligence/mercenaires.htm.
N[icholls], P[eter]. "*Cinema*," in J. Clute and P. Nicholls eds. *The Multimedia Encyclopedia of Science Fiction*, CD-ROM. Grolier Electronic Publ., 1995.
Noble, David F. *America by Design*. Knopf, 1977.
"Où l'on reparle des mercenaires." *Le Monde diplomatique* (Nov. 2004): 22–9.
Pocock, J.G.A. *The Machiavellian Moment*. Princeton UP, 1975.
P[ringle], D[avid], and J[ohn] C[lute]. "Robert A. Heinlein," in J. Clute and P. Nicholls eds. [see Nicholls above].
Proietti, Salvatore. "Chiusure americane," in G. Maniscalco Basile and D. Suvin eds., *Nuovissime mappe dell'inferno*. Monolite, 2004, 87–106.
Proietti, Salvatore. "Saving the American Body at War," in Suvin ed., 83–106.

Proietti, Salvatore, and Darko Suvin. "War and Militarism in Science Fiction: A Select Bibliography…," in Suvin ed., 155–63.
Rifkin, Jeremy. *The End of Work*. Putnam's, 1995.
Russ, Joanna. *To Write Like a Woman*. Indiana UP, 1995.
Scarry, Elaine. *On Beauty and Being Just*. Princeton UP, 1999.
Schwarz, Roberto. "Preface with Questions." *New Left R* no. 24 (2003): 31–9.
Singer, Peter W. *The Corporate Warriors*. Cornell UP, 2003.
Smith, Henry Nash. *Mark Twain's Fable of Progress*. Rutgers UP, 1964.
Smith-Rosenberg, Carroll. "Surrogate Americans." *PMLA* 119.4 (2004): 1325–35.
Suvin, Darko. "Can People Be (Re)Presented in Fiction?" in C. Nelson and L. Grossberg eds., *Marxism and the Interpretation of Culture*. U of Illinois P, 1988, 663–96.
Suvin, Darko. "Capitalism Means/Needs War," in his *In Leviathan's Belly: Essays for a Counter-Revolutionary Time*. Wildside P for Borgo P, 2012, 93–134.
Suvin, Darko. "Considering the Sense of 'Fantasy' or 'Fantastic Fiction.'" *Extrapolation* 41.3 (2000): 209–47.
Suvin, Darko. "Goodbye and Hello: Differentiating within the Later P.K. Dick." *Extrapolation* 43.4 (2002): 368–97.
Suvin, Darko. "Introduction to the 'Non-Cartesian Subjects' Issue." *Discours social/ Social Discourse* 6.1–2 (1994): 7–21.
Suvin, Darko. *Metamorphoses of Science Fiction*. Yale UP, 1979.
Suvin, Darko. "Novum Is as Novum Does," in K. Sayer and J. Moore eds., *Science Fiction, Critical Frontiers*. Macmillan and St. Martin's, 2000, 3–22.
Suvin, Darko. "Polity or Disaster: From Individualist Self Toward Personal Valences and Collective Subjects." *Discours Social/Social Discourse* 6.1–2 (1994): 181–210.
Suvin, Darko. *Positions and Presuppositions in Science Fiction*. Macmillan and Kent State UP, 1988.
Suvin, Darko. "Reflections on What Remains of Zamyatin's *We* after the Change of Leviathans: Must Collectivism Be against People?" in M. Barr ed., *Envisioning the Future*. Wesleyan UP, 2003, 51–81.
Suvin, Darko. "Science Fiction Parables of Mutation and Cloning as/and Cognition," in D. Pastourmatzi ed., *Biotechnological and Medical Themes in Science Fiction*. University Studio, 2002, 131–51.
Suvin, Darko. "Utopianism from Orientation to Agency: What Are We Intellectuals under Post-Fordism To Do?" *Utopian Studies* 9.2 (1998): 162–90.
Suvin, Darko. *Victorian Science Fiction in the U.K.: The Discourses of Knowledge and of Power*. G.K. Hall, 1983.
Suvin, Darko. "What May the 20th Century Amount To." *Critical Q* 44.2 (2002): 84–104.
Suvin, Darko, ed. *Fictions*, no. 3, *US Science Fiction and War/Militarism*. IEPI, 2005.
Tirman, John ed. *The Militarization of High Technology*. Ballinger, 1984.
Traynor, Ian. "The Privatisation of War." *The Guardian*, Dec. 10, 2003, www.countercurrents.org/iraq-traynor101203.htm
Veblen, Thorstein. *The Theory of Business Enterprise*. Scribner's, 1904.
Wallerstein, Immanuel. *Historical Capitalism* [with] *Capitalist Civilization*. Verso, 1996.

10

To Remember Stanisław Lem (2006)

Stanisław Lem, Polish fiction writer, critic, and polymath, died in March 2006, in his 85th year. This major writer needs remembering and critically honouring. I shall attempt to first give an overview of his principal works and then to focus on two of them, in a juxtaposition of his weaknesses and strengths.

1. An Overview

What we know about Lem's childhood and adolescence comes from the charming description in the autobiographical *Wysoki zamek/High Castle* (1995 – this and the following dates refer to the first English translation), which is however silent on the fact that of his parents, both well-off doctors and nominally Catholics though evidently atheists, the father was of Jewish origin. His study of medicine was interrupted by the oppressive and dangerous Nazi occupation, when he worked as a car mechanic and welder. His experiences of the immediate postwar years along a path from solitude to sociopolitical meaning (soon soured by Stalinism) closely inform his earliest manuscript *Czas nieutracony/Time Saved*, later shortened as *Szpital Przemienienia/Hospital of the Transfiguration* (1988). In 1946 he moved to Cracow, received his MD, was research assistant in a scientific institute and wrote (besides lyrical verse, apparently youth peccadilloes) essays on scientific methodology until he ran afoul of the Stalinist adulation of the Lamarckian biological theories of Lysenko. He then switched to SF; according to his homepage www.lem.pl/, he has published ca. 30 book titles so far, with translations into more than 40 languages and ca. 27 million copies sold. His early SF novels, *Astronauci/The Astronauts* and *Obłok Magellana/The Magellan Nebula*, are works of a beginner and limited by some of the conventions of "socialist realism," but are still interesting and contain a number of his constant themes (the threat of global destruction and militarism; human identity). Their utopian naivety is shaped by the committed humanism characteristic of one axis of his work. His other axis, a black grotesque tending towards a parable-like narration, appears in *Dzienniki gwiazdowe* (as *The Star Diaries*, 1976, and *Memoirs of a Space Traveller*, 1982).

The dozen years of partial de-stalinisation after the "Polish October" thaw of 1956 were Lem's golden noon. He published 17 titles: five SF novels, of which more below; 10 partly overlapping books of SF short stories including the Pirx cycle

(*Opowieşci o pilocie Pirxie/Tales of Pirx the Pilot*, 1979, *More Tales of Pirx the Pilot*, 1982), the "robotic fairy tales" of *Bajki robotòw/Mortal Engines* (1977) and the "Trurl-Klapaucius" or *Cyberiad* cycle (1974), and other writings including one stage and three TV plays; last but certainly not least, nonfiction including the "cybernetic sociology" of the early *Dialogi*, and the crown of Lem's speculation and in some ways key to his fiction, *Summa technologiae* (German transl. 1976), of which more below – a breathtakingly brilliant and risky survey of possible social, informational, cybernetic, cosmogonic, and biological engineering in Man's game with Nature. The novels *Eden* (1989), *Solaris* (1970, twice filmed), and *Niezwyciezony/The Invincible* (1973) deploy the mysteries of strange beings, events, and localities to educate their protagonists into understanding the limitations and strengths of humanity. These parables for our age are fittingly open-ended: their tenor is that no closed reference system is viable in the age of cybernetics and rival political absolutisms; the protagonists are redeemed by ethical and esthetic insight rather than by hardware, abstract cognition or power.

Thence also Lem's strong but salutary critique of English-language SF for abusing the potentials of the new in gimmicks and disguised fairy-tales in his *Fantastyka i futurologia* (excerpts appeared with other material in his collection of writings on SF in *Microworlds*, 1985), from which I learned much while refusing his one-sidedness. Unbearably simplified excerpts poorly translated by a Cremlinologist led to the cancellation of the honorary membership given him by the SF Writers Association of the USA, and to a bitter debate within its ranks: his critics included P.K. Dick in his ripest paranoiac phase writing the FBI that Lem was a code name for a KGB committee in Cracow (whose agents in North America were Suvin, Fitting, and Jameson). The offended SF writers were joined by renegade Leftists of some prominence, such as Leslie Fiedler, who misread him as an orthodox Marxist at the same time as Lem was identifying Marxism with the corrupt Russo-Polish variant of "really obtaining socialism." That he nonetheless was published and recognised in the USA, and even more fully in West Germany, is due entirely to the intrinsic merits of his writing. Lem's critique of equally anthropomorphic banalities in Soviet SF was effected through his immense popularity and liberating influence there. In between the two leviathans, at his best he used the experience of a *Mitteleuropean* intellectual to fuse a bright, humanistic hope with a bitter, historical warning. This double vision subverts both the "comic inferno" dystopia and a deterministic utopianism by juxtaposing the black flickerings of the former with the bright horizons of the latter. Even his grotesque stories showing up the often disgusting limits of humankind, as in *The Cyberiad*, are informed by such humanising fun, black satire or allegorical iconoclasm.

Signs of an ideological dead-end, if not exhaustion, showed about 1968, prompting further formal experimentation and a furious brilliance in Lem's writing. In *Glós pana/His Master's Voice* (1983), his radical doubts about human self-determination and sovereignty, and therefore about possibilities of communication with other people (not to mention other civilizations), began threatening to decompose the fictional form of the novel into solipsist musings, lectures, and ideational adventure. *His Master's Voice* may have avoided that by a tour de force of narrative tone, but Lem learned some lessons from this near-escape: he turned to a brilliantly innovative series of briefer second-order glosses at the borderland of fiction and treatise. *Doskonala próżnia/A Perfect Vacuum* (1978) – mainly composed of reviews of nonexistent books, which simultaneously characterise and persiflage their targets – and *Wielkość urojona* as well as the later *Golem XIV* (*Imaginary Magnitude*, 1984) range from thumbnail sketches of grisly futuristic follies to developments of the ideas from his *Summa technologiae* on "intellectronics" (artificially heightened intelligence) and "phantomatics" (illusory existence). We find the "life is an illusion" theme, disguised as fashionable drugtaking, as well as Lem's deeply rooted though atheistic theologico-cosmogonic obsessions, in the most grimly hilarious and longest work of this period, the long story *Kongres Futurologiczny/The Futurological Congress* (1974). Probably his last great SF narrative is the mid-70s long story "Maska"/"The Mask" where his long-standing themes of the labyrinth and the double, imaging forth the mysteries and cruel metamorphoses of human cognitive consciousness, reach a culmination. Only in the 1980s, with the awkward but ferocious assault upon human cognitive pretensions contained in *Fiasko/Fiasco* (1987), did Lem briefly return to novel-length structures. I shall leave his work of the last 20 years aside, brilliant as it has in many ways been, for it often leaves SF for Post-Modernist "weak thought" exercises in ontological mystery, and to my mind does not add much to what he had already wrought.

Lem's overflowing linguistic inventiveness, matching his controversial ideational plenty, is partly lost in translation, though the short stories assembled in English as *The Cosmic Carnival of Stanislaw Lem* (1981) and *One Human Minute* (1986) reveal some of the exuberance of the writing. But it remains clear that Lem has a peculiar vantage-point of his own, with clear scientistic limitations and yet with great strengths, which enabled his narrations to transcend both cynical pragmatism and abstract utopianism.

2. Contra and Pro

CONTRA: I'm taking as my ***first*** text here Lem's *Summa Technologiae*, written (astoundingly) around 1960 and published in Polish a few years later. This is a most sweeping, at the time certainly unequalled, sketch of the technological possibilities of future decades and possibly centuries, which includes rich and well-informed speculations about cosmic civilizations, "thinking machines" (intellectronics in Lem's terminology), the construction of artificial worlds much more perfect than today's virtual space (phantomatics), and many other aspects of the "technological evolution." I read it first in the Russian edition of the 1970s and then checked it with the original Polish and the German translation of 1981 based on the third Polish edition; and I have fought in vain for a quarter of a century in the USA to have it translated – nobody wanted to risk money to translate 600 pages of a difficult text in an unknown language by an outsider.[1] But while I assume that we could even today learn much from it, I shall totally neglect its most rich themes and insights in order to concentrate on a key presupposition which defines and limits this work: this is a book about projected grandiose plans which does not spend a single world on who would be its bearers. It is a book without an agential subject.

More precisely, the subject is allegorical: it is a very anemic and abstract actant of humanity (Condorcet would have been proud of it, and in fact Lem once declared the 18th Century is his favourite one, though he was rather thinking of Hume and bishop Berkeley). Its tacit premise is that future humanity will be not only united but also *lacking all the antagonisms between and within the systems existing in the 20th Century*: both what Lem called capitalism in crisis and degenerate socialism (in the 1950s Lem had thought that socialism was the first system with a scientific approach to human society). Another total *non-dit*, as befits agnostic scientism, was religion (or indeed any articulate horizon for values), some aspects of which – theology and ritual, I'd say – fascinated Lem but were here expunged. Any access to the grandiose possibilities envisaged by Lem presupposes the absence of problems such as wars, hunger, poverty, avoidable illnesses (that is, their great majority), interest conflicts between opposed social groups or classes, oppression by huge economico-political apparati such as a bureaucracy, and similar. The implied bearer of Lem's intellectronics, phantomatics, cosmic architectures (rebuilding of solar systems), etc. could only be a technoscientistic competitor to Marx's classless society, in which the communist slogan "from each according to his possibilities, to each according to her necessities" (*Critique of the Gotha Program*) had prevailed. But there is no hint of a link between the readers of 1960–1980 and that future. Thus far had Stalinism emasculated even a first-class thinker such as Lem by poisoning the wells of Marxism.

I hope not to be misunderstood: I have a great sympathy for a number of vistas in *Summa technologiae*, an attempt to update for the cybernetic and space age both a Rationalist *Encyclopedia* and obliquely the *Summa theologiae* by Thomas of Aquino. Had it been translated into English in time, its brilliant ideational fireworks would have spared us many dead ends and unnecessary discussions, or even actions. But I'm bothered by the unargued exclusions of all the real contradictions except those from technical logic and logistics. The volume's premises are presupposed but never posed. To generalise perhaps not too wildly from this doxological masterpiece of Lem's (which he too considered to be such, cf. his *Conversations* with Bereś), we could conclude that this removal of politics and economics, in short of really existing human agency and the collective forces shaping it, is not only Lem's limit, but that it also pollutes and perhaps invalidates a goodly part of the operative premises he did choose. The depravation of almost all technoscientific horizons in the last 30 or more years, totally shaped by profit and war, must make us retrospectively doubt and refuse many previously unsuspected tenets. I'm not talking only of the absolutist and crypto-religious pretensions of science: Lem had a magnificent nose for any absolutism and didn't quite fall into it. But our doubt has, even more radically, to embrace also the *cognitive methodologies* of institutionalised science – most prominently, the absence of a responsible subject – for example in Lem's master-science of cybernetics (its founder, Norbert Wiener came for this reason to doubt it, and his behaviour still shines forth as an example for us). Perhaps glimpsing the problem, Lem talked at some earlier point of "sociological cybernetics": but there is no sociology in the *Summa*. Therefore, to explain war, the society, and political economy as ultimately dependent on cybernetics, as Lem did from his 1950s' *Dialogues* on, seems a quasi-structuralist idealism, useless and more than a little technocratic. True, in the enlarged 1971 edition Lem speaks self-critically of his illusion that cybernetics would become the "new philosopher's stone" for our age; but having lost this particular illusion, he was left with a pessimistic dead end. In his late SF story masquerading as an essay, *Weapons Systems of the 21st Century*, Lem's formulation still is: "the evolution trends of the most important technologies with military application were independent of human thought" (translated from *Waffensysteme des 21. Jahrhunderts* 16–17).

I close with a final, perhaps the most telling doubt: Lem says nothing in the *Summa* about the *kind of person* which was to bring about the magnificent technical inventions and feats therein. Nonetheless, Dostoevsky was one of Lem's favourite writers, and he mentioned more than once his Underground Man. Such a social profile or role, the bearer of a Nietzschean resentment, would certainly be incompatible with the waking dreams of Lem's technocracy and is therefore not at all considered here, not to speak of the parasitic and warmongering stock-marketeers of today's new imperial ventures and their Post-Modernist epicycle. Further, Lem explicitly refused Freudianism (psychoanalysis), though in his narrations he could not but proceed upon the hypothesis of an Unconscious. So far so good, perhaps: but which type of identity or *consciousness* (a key term of Lem's *Dialogues*), which social psychology would be consubstantial to the rich and extreme experiences of the future golden age of grandiose inner and outer spaces? I would posit that the classical explanation of an I imagined as an indivisible atom has fallen by the way together with its analogy from physics. If so, then the dynamic fragmentation and unceasing recomposition of identity into various social roles, into sociopolitical charms and other quarks so to speak, destroys also the principal pillar of the bourgeois or post-Cartesian science, which Lem here does not doubt: the Objectivism which can bracket any subject. In the *Summa* there are no discernible subjects with their own voices and faces: all the allegorical actants are masks of the narrating Objectivist voice; often, they are robots or typical explorers (that in his best fiction then undergo weird non-Objectivist mutations). By the way, this is to my mind also perhaps the main reason for which SF, that cannot use three-dimensional characters, was so congenial to Lem. But for the same reason his socio-scientific doxology seems today, beyond the exhilaration of his ideas and technological vistas, in need of a fundamental rethinking.

PRO: My *second* text is Lem's most famous novel *Solaris*. Beyond its 40 translations and its two movie versions (the second one being less silly than Tarkovsky's travesty, though vastly inferior to the novel) there is a good reason for the fame, for it is not merely shaped by one of the usual brilliant speculations of Lemian fiction, here the allegory of the cosmic contact with the Utterly Other. Like an ellipse with two foci, it is also shaped by a psychological hypothesis, the dream of a second chance for correcting the awful errors of our lives. One could read it as a fertile oscillation or libration between a Lévi-Straussian cognitive optimism and a Schopenhauerian existential pessimism. The two foci fuse in the novel's protagonist, narrator, and point of view, Kris Kelvin. I'm not sure whether Kelvin has (or ought to have) a face but he certainly has a voice, which melds Lem's omnipresent thirst for knowledge, for me his most rewarding and precious trait, and intimate suffering. Kelvin's name can also be read as a loose allegory, for Lem is a writer of modern parables – a mode that intimately fuses narrative "vehicle" and cognitive "tenor" or upshot.[2] "Kelvin" is a scientist's name taken to indicate degrees of absolute temperature, most famous in both theoretical and popular science for the "Zero Kelvin" or absolute cosmic zero – which can only be asymptotically converged toward but never reached (Nernst's theorem, known also as the Third Law of Thermodynamics). As usual in Lem, we have here to do with a partly everted or ironical allegory: neither the Contact with the living Ocean on Solaris planet, nor the "solar" redemption of the failed relationship between Kris and his beloved Harey, lead to a facile happy ending. One could say that in some ways both fail. Yet finally – in the ending presented by the stupendous episode of the "airy handshake" between Kris and the Ocean – a tenuous approximation to such a contact is shown to be possible. The God of the triumphal illusions of Science is in this novel the pretext for a magnificent and sarcastic "phantomatic" simulation of a science, the history of "solaristics", which is one of Lem's major triumphs. This God, and his Grail of a "Holy Contact" with the Aliens, has failed; not so the glimpsed suggestion of an "imperfect god...whose ambitions exceed his powers" (possibly sparked by Lem's enthusiasm for the visionary SF of Olaf Stapledon).

In conclusion, this seems to me an optimal example of what great SF can give us: it shows us our age (for in SF, more clearly than in most other genres, *de nobis fabula narrator* – the story tells of us) as "the time of cruel miracles," an age which bears at least the chance of a skeptical belief. The contradictions kept out of a number of Lem's non-fictional works, and some of his less successful fiction, return here in the description and interpenetration of the black or dystopian horizon, characteristic for, say, the "new maps of hell" of much among the best English-language SF in the 1950s, and the rosy or utopian socialist horizon, characteristic for Lem's first phase, which justly entertained youthful humanist hopes both for science and for politics, in, say, his novel *The Magellan Nebula.* As I concluded looking at Lem's heyday (in "Open-Ended"), his unique place in SF is due to his personal fusing of the bright hope with the bitter experience, the vision of a needed and possible open road into the future with the vision of sure dangers and quite possible defeats inseparable from the risk of openness. No cognition worth of that name is religiously predetermined. In that sense, *Solaris* is, as much SF, a puzzle – enigma or rebus – and a parable; but, halfway between Brecht and Kafka, or perhaps in terms of his reading I should say between Lévi-Strauss and Borges, it is a paradoxically *open* parable. There is no dogmatic system of certainties to which it could recur. To talk in terms of the Polish environment, it has left way behind it the sacred books of Catholicism, and it refuses the sacred books both of Stalinism and of optimist liberalism. Lem's dialectics envisions in his best works the internal contradictions of an endeavour by means of continual shifting between different cognitive levels; this is most obvious in his satires, as in the grotesque "robotic fables" and the cosmic picaresque of his Ion Tichy. This style of wit places Lem in the *contes philosophiques* tradition of Swift or Voltaire, or of his favourite novel, *Don Quixote.* Beyond the puzzle and the parable, I would pay Lem the highest possible tribute of affirming that the approach to understanding – including the understanding of science – exemplified by *Solaris* is a valid cognition of certain important aspects of people living together. Such a cognition is especially valid today, when we are being subjected to the dominion of a profit-oriented science, from armament industry through drug companies to biogenetic and soon nanotechnological manipulations. For, "any wrong understanding of truth is at the same time a wrong understanding of freedom" (Marcuse 147).

It is easy to identify Lem as being – together with the Strugatsky Brothers – the most significant SF writer outside the English language, on a par with the best among the brilliant Anglo-American galaxy of 1940–75. But furthermore, his stubborn warnings against static "final solutions," his position at the crossroads of major European cultures and ideologies joined to an intense internalisation of problems from cybernetics and information theory, his fusion of dilemmas from ultramodern science and the oldest cosmogonic heresies, his dazzling formal virtuosity – all mark him as a distinctive and major voice in world literature.

Notes

1 Editor's note (HCO): since published in English as Lem, Stanisław. *Summa technologiae*. Transl. Joanna Zylinska, U of Minnesota P, 2013.

2 For more on tenor and vehicle relationships in SF see chapter 4 in this book "Considering," and for more on Lem: D. Suvin, *Parables of Freedom and Narrative Logics: Positions and Presuppositions in Science Fiction and Utopianism*, edited by Eric D. Smith, P. Lang, 2021, chapters 15 and 20.

Select Bibliography

The Suvin 1995 entry has a full list of Lem's publications up to 1994 and more criticism in English periodicals, while my original publication of this essay had a bibliography of 18 items about Lem. In the internet age this is no longer necessary, so I keep only the works by Lem, those cited in my essay, and the articles I found most useful; see also the Science Fiction and Fantasy Research Database, ed. by Hal W. Hall, in the Cushing Library, Texas A&M University, //library.tamu.edu/cushing/sffrd.

Balcerzan, Edward. "Seeking Only Man: Language and Ethics in *Solaris*," in R.D. Mullen and D. Suvin eds., *Science-Fiction Studies: Selected Essays on Science Fiction 1973–1975*. G. K. Hall, 1976, 141–45.

Beehler, Michael. "Speculation's Fiasco: Lem, Ethics, and Alternity," in B. Cooke et al. eds., *The Fantastic Other*. Rodopi, 1998.

Bereś, Stanisław. *Rozmòwy ze Stanisławem Lemem*. Wydawnictwo Literackie, 1987.

Csicsery-Ronay, Istvan, Jr. "Modeling the Chaosphere: Stanislaw Lem's Alien Communications," in N. K. Hayles ed., *Chaos and Order*. U of Chicago P, 1991, 244–62.

Jarzębsky, Jerzy. "Stanislaw Lem, Rationalist and Visionary," in R.D. Mullen and D. Suvin eds., *Science-Fiction Studies: Selected Essays on Science Fiction 1976–1977*. G.K. Hall, 1978, 217–33.

Keller, Lech. *Stanislaw Lem's Theory of Science Fiction Literature*. Monash U Polish Studies. 1997.

Lem, Stanislaw. *Microworlds: Writings on Science Fiction and Fantasy*. Ed. F. Rottensteiner, Harcourt Brace, 1984.

Lem, Stanislaw. *Phantastik und Futurologie*, 2 vols. Insel V, 1977–1980.

Lem, Stanislaw. *Science Fiction: Ein hoffnungsloser Fall mit Ausnahmen*. Suhrkamp, 1987.

Marcuse, Herbert. *Feindesanalysen*. zu Klampen, 1998.

Nudelman, Rafail. "Labyrinth, Double and Mask in the Science Fiction of Stanislaw Lem," in P. Parrinder ed., *Learning from Other Worlds*. Liverpool UP, 2000, and Duke UP, 2001, 178–92.

"Stanisław Lem," Special Issue of *Science Fiction Studies*, 13.4 (1986).

Suvin, Darko. "Lem," in *The Encyclopedia of Science Fiction*. Little, Brown, and St. Martin's P, 1993, 710–12; idem, in *Grolier Science Fiction*. Grolier Electronic Publ., 1995 [CD-ROM].

Suvin, Darko. "The Open-Ended Parables of Stanisław Lem and Solaris," Afterword to S. Lem, *Solaris*, Berkley Medallion, 1971, 212–23.

Thomsen, Christian W. "Robot Ethics and Robot Parody: Remarks on Isaac Asimov's *I, Robot* and Some Critical Essays and Short Stories by Stanisław Lem," in T.P. Dunn ed., *The Mechanical God*. Greenwood P, 1982.

11

On U.K. Le Guin's "Second Earthsea Trilogy" and Its Cognitions: A Commentary (2006)*

A commentary presupposes the classic status of the text it speaks about.

Walter Benjamin

To accept a classical writer without changing him/her means to betray her/him.

Heiner Müller

This article arose out of an unease I felt at the ending of my article on Fantasy (chapter 2 in this book), where it now seems to me not only that spacetime forced me to give short shrift to Ursula K. Le Guin's *Earthsea* writings, but that what I said applies only to the first three books, focussed mainly on the protagonist Ged. I want thus to follow the inner logic of her three last books set in Earthsea.[1] My working hypothesis is that these three books (*Tehanu, Tales from Earthsea, The Other Wind*) constitute a "Second Earthsea Trilogy," of high interest precisely because it both continues and strongly modifies the first one. The second trilogy, while operating with the central presuppositions of the first one, amounts to its reconsideration and rewriting. At the end, I wish to discuss what and how may be cognitive in this Second Trilogy.

1. The Creation of Ea(rthsea), Twice

The geographical layout of the Earthsea world, evident in the careful map carefully repeated at the beginning of most single books in what I shall call the "two trilogies," begins with the name of "Earthsea." It is a compressed oxymoron or paradox, akin to binaries such as "the left hand of darkness," repeated as the verse motto from this world's Creation song on, or indeed before, the first page of *Tehanu*:

Only in silence the word,
only in dark the light,
only in dying life:
bright the hawk's flight
on the empty sky.
The Creation of Éa

The verse "only in dark the light" may serve to introduce two of the main components of Le Guin's Earthsea vision: first, the contraries which complement each other such as dark and light; second, an order of preference in each verse which one suspects may harbour a hierarchy. As different from the full Daoist symmetry in *The Left Hand of Darkness* (where light was the left hand of darkness, darkness the right hand of light), the light here comes to be – comes out of – darkness, traditionally in most mythologies Mother Night (cf. also 57). Further, the word (both an all-important matter and an ineradicable beginning for every writer, but in Le Guin even expressly thematised as a magically creative force, for example in the secret "true name" of each person which shares in his/her essence, and therefore mentioned in the very first verse) exists, comes out of, can be heard only against the enveloping, motherly silence. Since light, again traditionally, means knowledge, cognition or understanding, I shall later investigate how far this obtains in the whole Trilogy. As to life, it exists, has meaning, can be distinguished only as it comes to be, as it is ceaselessly shaped against the background of dying (this shall become overwhelmingly important in the last book, *The Other Wind*). And in the second half of the ditty, which the semicolon suggests is also a conclusion, the hawk's course can be seen as bright only (the adverb is here clearly implied) against the empty sky.

However, all the "against" oppositions, the background vs. foreground, were introduced by my comment: instead of what would seem to me the default concept of "against," Le Guin uses "on" or indeed "in." Why? There is a prosodic reason (in this steely delicacy one syllable more would be unbalancing), but I don't think it is the only or main one. "On" – as a line (of flight) on a visual field – is much more intimate, there is contiguity but no express opposition: if there were no sky flying would not be possible, if it were not empty but cluttered with visual "noise," the flight would be visible with difficulty if at all, certainly it would be less important or noteworthy. "On" seems to me here much akin to "a line <u>on</u> paper" – usually a black line on white paper – thus latching on and enriching the first three "in"s: the word (now written), the light, the life (now bright); in fact, is a line on or in the paper? Only the laziness of our look from above prefers "on." The three couples of silence-word, dark-light, and dying-life are thus contraries but not contradictories, not only complementary to but intimately participating in each other. Furthermore, the verses also enforce the primacy of each first term: silence, dark/ness, dying/death; which we can therefore without too much straining call parental, engendering or motherly. The terms word-light-life are then filial, younger, fresher, more evident – or audible – but never to be fully and properly perceived and understood without the co-presence of the parental quality (the opposite doesn't obtain). The three first lines, where the final prosodic foot progressively contracts from three syllables to one, getting thus weightier as the lines go on, imply to me also a value progression: life contains light which contains the word. I shall risk the hypothesis, to be checked against the *Earthsea* cycle as a whole, that this also means life subsumes cognition which in turn subsumes writing. This is the hierarchy which I here find implied in amazing pithiness.

As to the term "Earthsea" itself, *The Creation of Éa* clearly states that before the earth was, the sea was. A glance at the map of the Earthsea world confirms that the measurable islands are bathed in a circumambient Ocean of which we do not know where it begins or ends, very similar to the relation of life to death. This too is (literally) a hierarchy. It may not be very evident in the narrations, which have to concentrate on people mostly living on dry land, but its water element connected to trees and the Old Speech subtly defines and infiltrates the younger element and powers. "The dry land" *par excellence*, that is without any trace of humidity – or sunlight or living contact – is the land of the dead of individualism, which is faced both in *The Farthest Shore* of 1972 and *The Other Wind* 30 years later, the final books of the first and the second trilogy.

The second half of the cited poem, the last two verses, relates to the first half as the particular to the general. First we were given the law of this world, coterminous with its perception. Now comes the course of events. The balance has here shifted: the parental function of the empty sky seems to me minimal, only an enabling function remains, somewhat offset by the emptiness. The stress is on the flight of the protagonist. Now before they stood at the head of *Tehanu*, the cited verses stood at the head of *A Wizard of Earthsea*. In the first trilogy, even in *The Tombs of Atuan*, the hero was Ged, Sparrowhawk, and his end was honourable but, in retrospect, bright only in personal heroism but not necessarily in an opening to the future. The hero re-established a disturbed balance, his function was conservative. Depending on the situation, conservative may not be a swearword, but it now turns out the balance itself is very suspect. Now the hero, focus, and standpoint is a binomial heroine: Tenar, the motherly, who nurtures the life of and brings out into the light Therru as Tehanu, the dragon child who against all odds knows the words of dragons and men. The verses, being identical, affirm the unity of the two trilogies. But since the verses are as of *Tehanu* put into a different context and thus are for the reader different (as Borges's Pierre Ménard found in his word-by-word rewriting of *Don Quixote* in the 19th Century), they also allow for this unity changing between *Earthsea*'s first and second life-cycle. Whatever Le Guin's reason for repeating them in front of what she thought of – at the time of writing it – the fourth and last book of *Earthsea*, it has now, I would argue, turned into a pointer to this radically changed unity. In the two trilogies Earthsea is and is not the same world. The geography and the initial magic framework seem more or less the same. Yet the glance at them has changed (cf. Le Guin's account in *ER* 19–21). What Brecht would call a semi revolution has intervened between the trilogies. A feminist or, as Alice Walker might say, a womanist revision of the first trilogy is here beginning, one that has "at the end of... *Tehanu*" (written at the end of the 1980s) "arrived at what [the author] felt to be *now*" ("Foreword" to *TfE* XI) and will continue by looking into the future – which in a way is a return to the most ancient past, on a higher rung of the spiral. But also (if I may be permitted the word) a dragonist revision.

2. *Tehanu*: What Happens to Tenar

Farmer Flint's widow Goha on the island of Gont rescues in the first chapter the raped and badly fire-scarred child she names Therru. Herself once a somewhat less cruelly abused girl, the erstwhile sacred princess-prisoner Tenar of Atuan is now in the position earlier reserved for her male rescuer, Ged. Her heroism isn't manifest as a showy clash of force but as unceasing courage that, with stealth and other means of negative power, hides Therru until she can grow up. She has no male network to rely on, only the kind island mage Ogion who dies early on, whispering joyfully "Over – all changed" (31, and cf. 52). This is emblematic of the bad "time of ruining, the end of an age" (16, and cf. 79); I would in fact read the death of this friend of Ged's as emblematic of the death, or if you wish the qualitative reappraisal, of (the universe of) the Gedian first Earthsea trilogy, focussed on the Mage – read: Artist – as a Young Man. In the first trilogy Tenar had left power struggles and retreated to the role of the farmer's wife. The world is still dominated by power-mad males but she now makes the crucial decision: "I served them and I left them.... I will not let them have you" (3). Female solidarity shapes this book and wins out – with some crucial help from enlightened dragons and righteous men, thus politically and psychologically much superior to Russ's sectarian vision and narrative in *The Two of Them*. It is also to my mind much better – clearer and tougher – than the abstract abused child and indifferent community in Le Guin's "Those Who Walk Away from Omelas," as well as than the solution indicated in that title. Instead of exodus, there is subversion: "The child irreparably wronged, whose human inheritance has been taken from her – so many children in our world, all over our world now – that child is our guide" (*ER* 25).

The second thing that happens to Goha/Tenar is the return of the battle-scarred Sparrowhawk, who has by now lost all his magical powers and himself opted out of male power-struggles. On the margins of the patriarchy, on a far-off mountainous and rural island, this is also a qualitatively new Ged who can, having descended from the heights of upper-class power, slowly reacquire the capacity for sympathy and sexual love. It was to my mind entirely appropriate that Le Guin held off in the first trilogy from the usual Theseus-Ariadne culmination in erotics, even if this left Tenar without a clear role after fulfilling her narrative function of cohabiting with the Tolkienian Ring (which, together with the Tolkienian just King and the whole standard set-up of "traditional [F]antasy,... a rigid social hierarchy of kings, lords, merchants, peasants" [*ER* 8] I found a useless but fortunately a secondary element in the first *Earthsea* trilogy). It is difficult to say whether she in that trilogy ended up as more of a narrative dropout or of a social dropout, just as it was difficult to say whether Ged had in fact saved the Earthsea world in the normative black-and-white Tolkienian fashion. The politics of women were left unclear, the politics of men – mages – subordinated to personal wholeness. Having rightly come back to find Tenar, Le Guin was in this novel also coming to a modified stance: "...a spark; like the certainty of a conception; a change, a new thing" (51). It turns out that the personal and the political cannot be sundered (the feminists, and earlier the socialists and anarchists, were right so far). The world can perhaps be saved from one acute danger by a feat of heroism, say analogous to the antifascist Second World War, but the pervasive system of cruel power and privilege cannot be righted by one explosive outburst – an ejaculative Tolkienian massing on the battlefield – but only by protracted and complex collaboration for life between women, men, and dragons (and animals and plants). As in the *Creation* song, we begin with the most important, both basic and enveloping, concept of life: a girl's life, which then changes Tenar's and Ged's. Three scarred people, getting whole again, in the interstices of power – though finally saved only by several arrivals of *dei ex machina*. More was lacking to bring together character and events, the personal and the political. This will be the explicit theme of the other two books in the "second trilogy," *Tales from Earthsea* (in particular the long story "The Finder") and *The Other Wind*, but the new outlook, the new glance which focusses on the changing world, was first found and begun exploring here.

3. "The Finder": The Theory of Earthly Politics

The long story "The Finder" could be called "An Ambiguous Utopia enters Earthsea." The adumbrations of *Tehanu* are here fully developed as a radical modification of the first trilogy's "absolute" magery, disguised as the story of how the mage school at Roke came to be. I shall return to the downgrading of magery in a later section. Here I wish to trace the overt equation of magery to gendered power.

What underlies Le Guin's second trilogy, as is so often stressed in it, are rumblings of a huge change in social and cosmic being. The books struggle to understand and render it. The protagonist Otter/Tern/Medra is the focal point for and enabler of that change because he is sensitive to it. Perhaps the closest it intersects with our non-magic and dragonless world is his anguished outburst: "Will the slaves go free? Will beggars eat? Will justice be done?" And further, the classic question of subversive movements, how do we organise against those whose interests are bound up with established power: "We can't do anything without each other.... But it's the greedy ones, the cruel ones who hold together and strengthen each other. And those who won't join them stand alone" (45). A populist counter-power must be developed, based on trust – or solidarity – as prefigured in the beautiful initial episode of Otter and Anieb who, as slaves in the mercury mines, pool their powers to kill the evil magician-cum-mining-boss and win freedom. Otter finds its seed in existence as the secret society of the Hand, "or the women of the Hand, though we're not women only" (46), but it is predicated on living in the interstice of the slaveholders', exploiters', and warlords' power. This thematises the interstitial life of Tenar and Ged on their peripheral island, but this time in the potential centre of Roke, whose dwellers are however hampered by a persuasion analogous to feminist (or any other) separatism. The early Roke is a true refuge and escape haven but, ambiguously, the refuge is also a self-made prison, the escape has led to a larger and more comfortable jail – and thus abetted the injustice addressed by Otter (cf. also 68).

The sign of the Hand is a fist opening palm up as if in an offering. It is not the communist clenched and raised fist but it can be seen as a less triumphant and more dynamic, less scientific and more utopian, slyer and more secret, and certainly more feminine than masculine (as these adjectives are now understood) analogue to it. The debate between Otter and the original Roke women re-enacts Lenin's 1902 question "What is to be done?" and comes, *mutatis mutandis*, to a similar conclusion – an organised counterparty is needed, this time in feedback with a central school on the hidden island: "Roke's freedom lay in offering others freedom" (69).

Enter gender politics, where my stance is one of a critical ally of intelligent feminism.[2] I find the stress on women as the main force of resistance understandable and up to a point just. It is an intelligent stress for it also embraces men of good will: the man Otter and the woman Anieb could only have won freedom together, Anieb as inspirator and teacher, Otter as the accepter and executor. That most men will attack Roke's liberation movement and that some will betray it, that in a class society ruled by men the rulers will have internalised arrogance and conflictuality, I find persuasive. Also that Roke will, even after Otter's success and the rise of a school where women are *primae inter pares*, degenerate from its Arcadian communism into a gender elitism worse than Plato's Guardians because of prideful males, thus leading to the fiercely misogynic setup found by Ged and here hollowed from within. What I do not find persuasive is a kind of equation of women as such with nature and liberation: I would have dearly liked to find a dastardly woman – Earthsea's equivalent of our world's Mrs. Thatcher, the impoverisher of miners, or Indira Gandhi, the steriliser of poor women – who may even do the work of power-mad injustice better than the males. Le Guin knows about them, witness *The Dispossessed*, but she chose not to show it here. (Let me put it this way: could all women talk to dragons?) Obversely, her beautiful stories of heterosexual love – which aroused the ire of "politically correct" Samuel Delany in the case of that novel – and are shown after Tenar and Ged also in Otter and Ember on Roke, in the story "Darkrose and Diamond," and finally in Alder and Lily of the last book in *Earthsea*, testify that the author knows at least as much as the critic (I think: more).

4. *Tehanu* and *Tales from Earthsea*: The Theory of Magic; and an Approximation to Dragons

Magic may be very roughly defined as the possibility of the human mind to act directly and without other outer means on matter. It differs from religion in that it needs no divinities (though contaminations are frequent).

Magic is usually taken as the element differentiating Fantasy from SF. I have argued this is not necessarily so, not a *differentia specifica* ("Considering"), and I take it – very gladly – that the downfall of magic as sacred power in the second *Earthsea* trilogy doesn't hurt my point. Le Guin has long ago asked why Americans fear dragons, and more recently she has eloquently described how people fearing change turn to Fantasy (but not only to it) for

> stability, ancient truths, immutable simplicities. – And the mills of capitalism provide them.... Commodified fantasy... invents nothing, but imitates and trivialises. It proceeds by depriving the old stories of their intellectual and ethical complexity.... Heroes brandish their swords, lasers, wands, as mechanically as combine harvesters, reaping profits.... (see the whole passage in "Foreword" XIV).

Insofar as this obtains for the overwhelming majority of its writings, Fantasy is part and parcel of a blind refusal not only of the horrors but also of the achievements of bourgeois and *citoyen* civilisation – not merely of science and rationality but also of liberty equality and all-encompassing (non-racialised) fraternity, adding to this sorority and filiality – so that perhaps we should call this last revolutionary slogan rather friendliness or conviviality. However, analogous strictures might be advanced against SF (even if often symmetrically obverse due to its technolatry), though – one hopes – perhaps to a somewhat minor degree. What this says about potential as well as really obtaining cognitiveness in Fantasy I leave for a separate consideration at the end.

As Le Guin has always perfectly understood, magic is most intimately bound up with *power*. Thence its aporias: magic started out in the first trilogy as power of mages (supposedly in the interest of all humanity) over nature, but it was always enmeshed with power over human nature too, and in the second trilogy it is revealed as preponderantly male power for dominating nature as female and females as nature. Power is, so argues a wise witch against the naive young Dragonfly in the eponymous short story, "making people do what you want, or pay you" (*TfE* 211). The cynical apprentice mage Ivory then paints her a picture of corrupt power: some "[Roke] Masters... hold aloof, following arcane knowledge... but using their knowledge for nothing. Others hide their ambitions under the grey cloak of wisdom.... And at the center, nothing" (213). And in particular, they refuse female mages, refuse the fact Roke was founded mostly by such and by winnowing the more ancient sacred practices of local witches and wizards – sorcerers – appealing to the "Powers of the Mother" ("Description" 288–89 and 293–96), and claim that refusal of sexuality is needed for magery; all of this results in refusing to admit Dragonfly/Irian, a dragon chrysalis, as they had suppressed and demonised dragons in general. Facing change, they cling to "order, safety, and peace," and therefore see the Roke Rule and world pattern as breakable glass rather than as breath and fire (cf. *TfE* 260). Just like the macho Fortress USA – or for that matter Fortress Europe or China – they haven't learned that the house is safest that opens its doors (265), or at least allows the wind to blow through the windows (*OW* 231).

Not only does Ged forsake magic (or vice versa – in the second trilogy it's anyway a good riddance) but the whole story "Darkrose and Diamond" refuses magery (as well as commerce) in favour of art. Only slightly more allegorically veiled, so does the key strand of Alder in the final novel, crucial for destroying fear of individualist death, that basis of male magery, through the alternate metaphysics of his love for Lily. As Tenar says, she learned Old Speech easily, but "the runes of power, the spells, the rules, the raising of the forces – that was all dead for me. Somebody else's [that is a male warrior's] language" (*Tehanu* 95). What "wizardry" remains after such deconstruction in the second trilogy? It is either a formalizing translation of the craft masteries of finding, weather-working, changing, healing, illusion creating or knowledge of songs (cf. 70), which in a differently described world could dispense with the hypothesis of magic; or it is consubstantial with trees, most particularly the Immanent Grove on Roke, going deep into the motherly earth; or with the Old Speech that remains untouched in the second trilogy (indeed a key to its dénouement), and to which I shall return.

And then:

And then there remain, unexplainable away, <u>*the dragons*</u>.

Near to midway of writing the second trilogy, Le Guin cites the prefigurative incident in *Tehanu* where Tenar is shown a silk fan by an old weaver (*ER* 21). It turns out to have on its back, usually hidden, finely painted dragons grouped in the same spots as the men and women in the capital city on its usually displayed side:

> She... saw the two paintings, made one by the light flowing through the silk, so that the clouds and peaks [from the dragon side] were the towers of the city, and the men and women were winged, and the dragons looked with human eyes.
>
> "You see?"
>
> "I see," she murmured. (*Tehanu* 115)

This is a materialisation of the "double vision" always possessed by Therru, whose one eye has been burned away but in whom the dragon and human nature also coexist, and it is used by Le Guin to formulate what she saw the dragons in her *Earthsea* narrations as, at that point: "Dragons are... a way of knowing.... the dragons of a new world, America, and the visionary forms of an old woman's mind.... In the first three books, I think the dragons were, above all, wildness. What is <u>*not owned*</u>" (*ER* 21–22). The *status quo* rightly sees them as dangerous, for, in *Tehanu* and after it, their wildness grows to be "not only... dangerous beauty but... dangerous anger.... So the dragon is subversion, revolution, change... [against] oppression. It is the wildness of the spirit and of the earth, uprising against misrule. – And it rejects gender" (but see the whole in *ER* 23–24 and further).

Thus the dragon embodies "the other, the not-human." Yet it is also "our own imagining, a speaking spirit, wise, winged, which imagines a new order of freedom" (*ER* 25–26).

How and why did dragons come about on Earthsea? In *Tehanu* (12–13), this is explained as a species divergence, a split from primeval wholeness on the order of Thales's hermaphrodite story (as recounted by Plato): "in the beginning, dragons and people were all one.... one people, one race, winged and speaking the True Language. – They were beautiful, and strong, and wise, and free." Then came the split (*verw nadan*, *Vedurnan*, the Division), a myth of origins not far from Rousseau, between on the one hand the makers-cum-learners, who also became what *The Dispossessed* memorably named the propertarians, and on the other those who wanted to live in a perpetual instant of freedom, "in love with flight and wildness,... ignorant and uncaring [of study and learning, or... houses and cities]"; murderous conflicts arose between them. Eventually they separated to the opposite sides of Earthsea and became two quite different peoples or species, but among the humans and the dragons there are some who remember the ancient kinship. The dragons' True Language of the Making, however, was (partly?) preserved as the wizards' Old Speech. The dragons chose the elements fire and air, the humans earth and water.

I do not quite understand the dragons. It would be possible to argue for some inconsistencies between the vehicle and tenor, for example in the feral young, but I don't think that really matters. It might be simpler to say with Le Guin: "The dragons remain mysterious to me" (*ER 22,* cf. also *TfE* xv: "nobody can explain a dragon"). They are perhaps an intuition that has nothing above itself, which is unconditional and unsurpassable, all that *quo magis non dici potest* (of which more cannot be said), a materialised and irascible numinosity, the principle, the end/ing, the head (cf. Nancy 157). I do understand what I summarised above. And that they are supremely important to Le Guin and the *Earthsea* vision. Still, some worries nag at me. I shall have another try at dragons at the end.

5. *The Other Wind*: Mysteries of Dragons and Last Things

The title comes from the song cited in earlier books:

> Farther west than west
> beyond the land
> my people are dancing
> on the other wind.

But before the happy ending, the final, last, greatest peripety: going Cob's disturbance of the sociocosmic balance in the first trilogy one better. The new, gravest disturbance is signalled by Alder's beloved wife calling him to the "dry land" and not responding there to her "true name" in Old Speech but only to her everyday name of Lily. The peripety turns out to consist in the unanimous urgency of the human dead to be liberated from their status of shades in the "dry land" and to attain Non-being – a kind of Nirvana, in Le Guin's very unorthodox post-Daoist cosmic syncretism. This radically non-individualist catastrophe has no single wicked author: the nature of things, of *the badly made human contract with the cosmos, is rebelling against the contractors*.

It becomes clear in *The Other Wind* that the Split between men and dragons was, beyond the propertarians' greed for material possessions, also caused by their metaphysical individualist greed: the yearning for personal immortality as a soul in afterlife. "Men want to own life, possess it, as if it were a jewel in a box," says the woman-turned-dragon Irian (225). In our world, the monotheistic Churches usually paint the other world as a place of delight for those who deserve it, even quite fleshly in Mohammedanism. None of that in Earthsea. The *verw nadan* contract ensures that all will "deserve" it, but what the fabric of nature allows them to get instead is a worse variant of the European Antiquity's dark underworld – without sunlight or fleshly life, and furthermore bereft of the Hellenic underground rivers. The result of such a truly devilish pact leads to a good approximation of a Hell without devils, but with the possibly greater horror of total and everlasting non-relating to life: sun, water, other people, plants or animals: "To stand empty-eyed, unspeaking, in the shadows of a shadow city" (79) – the exact and full inversion of the glad stanza from the *Creation of*

Éa cited at my beginning. A ghoulish Un-creation. The dragons insist, as do the Kargish people, that the devilish contract (in post-Daoist terms this would be the totally wrong Way) allowed for people "never to die and never to be reborn" in return for learning how to do sorcery, how to "master" nature: "Only their bodies die. The rest of them stays in a dark place and never gets reborn" (125). Inverting monotheist religions, this split of body and soul is the supreme sin. Obversely, the dragons, animals, and the Karg don't go to the "dry land" but "rejoin the greater being of the world. Like the grass, the trees, the animals" (145).[3]

It doesn't matter for my purposes how the happy ending in detail happens, suffice it to say that it does, there is not a harrowing but a taking back of hell: "great multitudes of men and women, who... stepped across [the wall] and were gone: a wisp of dust, a breath that shone an instant in the ever-brightening light." Alder and Lily too "[cross] together into the sunlight" (239).

This is of course an eschatological discourse: changing the mode of death and immortality, making humanity whole, speaking of last things, a kind of lay Day of Judgment. As in every Comedy, it ends in a marriage bond, here of Lebannon and Seserakh, so to speak the Ged and Tenar of the younger, post-magic generation. It is lay, for it is about freedom. It may be encapsulated in the old song remembered by king Lebannen and, on the last page, by Tenar coming home to Ged: "O my joy, be free!" (198 and 246 – the whole latter part of this book is to my mind luminously poetic).

What of this may be receivable for our non-Earthsea world? This is a question about the cognitive status of *Earthsea*, perhaps the best that Fantasy (if it is still that) has to offer us.

6. Of Cognition, and an Inconclusive Ending

I am in a quandary here, as I've been for ever and a day committed to the split between SF and Fantasy (perhaps my own version of *verw nadan*). The reason for it is the presence vs. absence of cognitiveness in these two genres. By cognition I mean a transitive understanding, which the readers can transfer from the pages of fiction to their own personal and collective lives. Reading has other delights of form, but this delight contains them all, and why settle for anything less, especially in these highly endangered times of ours where we badly need the cognitive delight? I believe Le Guin too is committed to learning and understanding, the tacit and spoken light of knowledge, though her farthest dragons are not. As for Fantasy in particular, I argued at length in "Considering" that its general absence of cognitiveness is bound up with denial or repression of key elements of earthly history, what we usually classify as political and economic interpersonal regularities, tendencies or strictures (I don't much believe in laws). If so, "why should men listen to stolen stories unless they concern important things – that is, the doings of men?" (*ER* 7). Thus the question here is: how might the second *Earthsea* trilogy carry historical cognition or understanding? If it does to a significant degree, is this an exception? Or is it not Fantasy? Or should my stance towards Fantasy be "revisioned"?

Let me first mention only two of its key splendid achievements, beyond Le Guin's delight in the revisioning of women and the diversity of humans, totally incompatible with racism and sexism (two matters that she has often spoken about and that are, I hope, implied in my foregoing text). *First*, she has triumphantly managed – like her beloved Tolstoy – to reconcile a supreme collective interest, in this case of the human species, with her memorably vivid personalities (I would have to mention here almost all her characters, from Tenar, Therru, and Ged to Alder and the wonderful princess Seserakh) as well as a Thoreauist conviviality with non-human nature. The love of plant life – grass, bushes, flowers, and most of all trees – may have been encouraged by her readings of Tolkien, but her delight in animals of many sizes and shapes, from the stubborn goats on Gont to Alder's kitten (reminding me of Shevek's startling vision of the donkey in *The Dispossessed*), has few peers in literature – though let us not forget, as she did not, Cordwainer Smith. Their irreducible warm corporeality, short-circuiting life and knowledge outside of human morality (cf. *OW* 52–53), feeds into, and is no small part of the mystery of, the dragons, whom detractor mages call, with exquisite compound wrongness, "merely animals."

Second is her contemptuous refusal of theism, and most pertinently Christian monotheist individualism (the soul). Already in her early SF novels the dominant belief was what the future language called Thurro-Dovism (Thoreau-Daoism, suitably transmogrified by history). As in the original Dao, the transcendental needs here no faces, only a Way, which may be thought of as a wind with the dragons of human imagination frolicking in it. Yet in a way, *Earthsea* is a myth – an unclean term that lends itself to misuse, I explained in *MOSF* – comparable in depth and in power to move to what the Christians claim as Vangels, not only in its meaning of *eu-angelium*, the glad tiding. (It even uses the same supremely effective narrative trick of rewriting the same story in different variants, though – being the product of a limited single human's experience rather than of a revolutionary community – it has not managed the Evangelists' four variants but only two. Think what we might have if Dostoevsky could have rewritten the *Brothers Karamazov* in four equally powerful versions, the last one a bit crazily mystical!) I don't know to which side this parallel might be considered blasphemous, for me to neither. The major difference, of course, is that the *Earthsea* writings are not blueprints for direct belief but overtly fictional parables for indirect cognitive transfer to the readers, where possible.

However, I don't pretend to exhaust the *Earthsea* strengths thereby, but my points Three and on will be here left aside to face the problem of *history*.

How does history – our history, the author's and reader's history – enter *Earthsea*? In it dragons live – at least tendentially, and at the end really – outside history (as the original human-dragons unity did), only humans live in history, bound up both with making things and knowledge of good and evil. But there is no politico-economic history, only magic domination. This usual norm of Fantasy usually means there is very little or no cognition in it, be it (to stop at the classics) Conan's lone machismo pitted against the world or the subterfuges of Leiber's sympathetic thieves in the interstices of the bazaar. I find a very important key for further placing: Le Guin has noted how there obtains a (supple and anamorphic) *parallel between the time or historical moment of the author's world and the historical moment inside Earthsea* – see the "Foreword" to *TfE* cited at the end of Section 1; this allows her to imagine new shapes of destiny in Earthsea. The time, the cosmic juncture, of *The Other Wind* is a historical moment parallel to that of the rise of new wars and new global disarray, the huge sufferings of ever more among "the poor and powerless" (*TfE* 2) of the world under US military hegemony in the later 90s, where the wizards' meddling with the laws of life and death endangers the whole world. A collective decision about magery and mortality, not a single heroic mage, is now absolutely necessary. (I am not sure – but this is a matter of my speculation about historical horizons – that Le Guin has fully gauged the perils of turbocapitalism not only for people but also for nature, or better for vertebrate life. She speaks sometimes as if nature will eventually right itself. Yet we are already seeing the hurricanes, tsunamis, and rising sea-levels. So much the worse for all of us.)

Has Le Guin therefore managed to evade the gravely non-cognitive nature of Fantasy, while paying her dues by the use of magic (however downgraded), True Speech, and by the quite non-cognitive political set-up of medieval feudalism – even if modified by an enlightened king, in some ways farcically fallible? Is this simply condensed, mythical history?

To face this, let me return to the dragons and True Speech, indelible markers of distance from SF. *Dragons* are Le Guin's emblem for wild freedom "of the spirit and of the earth," not owned and dangerous, simultaneously Nietzschean super-animals and the Other of the furthest reaches of human imagination and trans-historic delight. They also embody a modern intellectual's deep irritation at the claims of social morality and politics to set goals and limits to her imagination. Yet beyond ephemeral recipes of the season, any narration is always already political in a deeper (say Aristotle's) sense – as Le Guin full well realizes, though best in gender politics. What does then their frolicking "on the other wind" mean for us? I think it is ambiguous: partly a valid refusal of orthodoxy, partly an understandable but I think vain yearning, as Brecht put it, not to let even just anger make one's (narrative) voice grow hoarse. Yet a slight hoarseness doesn't much matter if your anger remains cognitive, and Le Guin proved it in *The Word for World Is Forest*. The dragons' splendour may hide a not fully articulated or reflected upon split between propertarian and creative reason.

True Speech – and here my distance from Le Guin's envisioning may show – is to my mind also ambiguous. Straining to accommodate it, let me try to translate this into my idiom. What may from where I stand, a disaffected radical from the bourgeois class, be such runes or formulas which have had immediate or long lasting "reifactory" powers, as Le Guin calls the words directly creating things? In the unspeakable carnages of World War 1 for no more than redrawing frontiers of imperial exploitative power, such was Lenin's call to "turn the imperialist into a civil war," that is, to turn the soldiers' arms against their commanders. It worked. More lasting, pertaining to long duration, was Marx's vision of fetishism of commodities as underlying the capitalist maleficent re-enchantment of the world, alienating living labour into capitalist profit and reification.[4] Could True Speech, say the Naming of people, be translated into this key? I don't see how: how does the true name of Medra give us more understanding than Otter (I think it gives less)? Is there a possibility of True Speech in economics and politics? If so, it is absent from *Earthsea*. It seems to me to conflate unduly poetry – a dragon matter – and political economics – a human matter, not explainable simply in the moral terms of greed.

Does this mean *Earthsea* is in any way, even cognitively, automatically "inferior" to SF? Of course it doesn't. My no doubt limited analogies here are twofold. The *first* reposes on a very simple model of two measuring rods, say thermometers with mercury. One thermometer can go from zero to 100 degrees, the other, made for human bodies, only from 30 to 43 degrees centigrade. The bigger one is to me SF, the smaller one Fantasy. But since the huge majority of SF uses very little of the genre's cognitive potentialities, most come only up to, say, 33 degrees: two thirds of what would be possible is wasted. Obversely, a very few Fantasy works (Le Guin) come up to, say, 41 degrees – I'd put Tolkien, in this somewhat ridiculous metaphor, at 37 – and are thus superior to 98% of really existing SF writings. It is not the case that any narration is 100% cognitive in this genre and 0% in that one, and my *MOSF* and "Considering" speak only about an overall tendency and an implicit normative horizon, as befits historical poetics. My *second* model derives from "Liebig's barrel," which I was taught as a chemistry student. The great Justus Liebig wanted to explain the interrelation of chemical elements to fertilizing the soil. He imagined a big vertical barrel with staves of unequal length, so that the lowest stave determines the height of liquid that can remain in the barrel. Staves represent the elements: you can put as much sodium or potassium as you want into your fertilizer, it will do no good if the magnesium stave is short, if the pinch of magnesium is below the critical threshold that makes plants grow.

Furthermore, if these writings are parables or very loose allegories, this does not at all imply the need for instant one-to-one translatability of any one element of Fantasy (as of SF neither). What pointer does Therru's escape into dragonhood supply to a young woman or say a downtrodden immigrant into our metropolises, an activist may well demand? My answer would point to two matters. First, as Le Guin suggested, that the wronged and wounded have a privileged epistemological and political status: our actions should focus on them and not on property, law, order, security, etc. Second, and to my mind secondarily, this points to dragonhood and making whole in general, as a *pars pro toto*, a minor narreme that stands for something paradigmatically important (and is also a whopping good story, that Heinlein could have called "the little seamstress"). Is the burned-away side of her body – hand, eye, beauty – redeemed by her turning into a dragon? I think Le Guin would agree no outrage cannot be fully redeemed. To assume that the hurt flesh and psyche can be subsumed into the frolicking in free imagination would be to fall back into standard religion. Modern allegories, Kafka's, Brecht's or Le Guin's, are not as Yehoshua's rabbinical parables, where he could explain the one-to-one translatability. They are fluid, multivalent, and open: the vehicle doesn't exist only to be incorporated into but also to codetermine the tenor (see more in my "With Sober").

I end with more questions than answers, but I trust posing right questions at least whittles down the possible answers. My provisional conclusion, to be thought about further, is that it seems some (very few) among the most interesting new writings in Fantasy, from Le Guin to Miéville, do not quite fit my parameters. There are, logically, two possible answers to it. Either we have here to do with a not-yet named and thus unrecognised genre of estranged fiction, possibly nearer to Kafka but turned into an epic story after Tolkien, for which new parameters are to be found. Or I was simply wrong and my essay on Fantasy would need to be at least supplied with a further section, if not rethought *ab ovo*. *Chi vivrà vedrà*, as my Italian neighbours say: Who lives long enough, may see the answer. The answer, after all, is historical: and history is rushing on faster than we think.

In the meantime let us rejoice in what the second *Earthsea* trilogy did to the first one, the powerful grace of it. "O my joy, be free!"

Notes

* My thanks for help in writing this essay can be found in the original publication. But it wouldn't have come about but for Ursula Le Guin – and I don't mean simply her writing these brilliant and sweetly fierce books that further life. We are such old friends by now that we can afford to disagree with and even (rarely) be angry at each other. She wrote me in 2001, I believe, that she had sent me an angry letter about my essay on Fantasy in *Extrapolation* a year earlier, and in particular about what I had to say in it on *Earthsea*. The letter I (un?)fortunately have never received. Yet, regardless of a few disagreements with her after the mid-70s, I take Le Guin's writing and wisdom very seriously. So the fact that she had written such a purloined letter was enough to make me pause and ponder. Other signs and portents increased my sense of urgency.

Oh, and she also had sent me a copy of her unavailable talk *Earthsea Revisioned*. I am glad my notes about *Tehanu* were complete by the time I read it, so that my full agreement with it – barring three sentences, one of which shows remnants of her waning Jungian interests, that is 6 lines out of ca. 700, so maybe I'm in a 992 pro mille agreement – came as a most pleasant surprise and confirmation. I have added three or four (acknowledged) nuggets from it to my text, particularly about the mysterious dragons. (This doesn't mean she will agree with me in matters or approaches that go beyond what she was writing in that booklet. But one can always hope.)

1 I am writing this in a situation that enforces a focus only on Le Guin's texts, without the enlightenments that could come from critical literature. The constriction is detrimental to fuller argumentation. But the judo masters tell us your weakness may be turned into strength – if you know how.

2 Le Guin's feminism is akin to Virginia Woolf's, and a significant work could be written about Le Guin's evident interest in her. To mention just one matter, *To the Lighthouse* also focusses on islands (one only, in truth, but itself imaginatively composed of Cornwall and the Hebrides), the end of an epoch, and incidentally has a protagonist named Lily. The main difference may be that it's about a family, which disintegrates into lonely individuals: "We perish each alone," preaches Mr Ramsay. The urge to freedom and against tyranny, against empire and patriarchy, is however the same.

3 This may be well compared to one of the classical formulations of pantheist-cum-atheist mortality, Usbek's Letter 76 in Montesquieu's delightful estrangement (and double vision) of *Persian Letters*: "When my soul shall be separated from my body, will there

be any less order in the universe? Do you believe that any new combination will be less perfect or less dependent upon general laws, or that the universe will have lost something...? Do you think that my body, having become a blade of wheat, a worm or a piece of lawn, would be changed into a work less worthy of nature...? All such ideas... originate in our pride alone." Montesquieu's idea of necessary disloyalty to our local civilisation in order to interact equitably with others is a direct precursor of Estraven the Traitor.

4 Marx's capitalism is often phrased in terms of a whole horror-fantasy repertory, cf. my "Living."

Works Cited

The Le Guin titles are adduced in chronological order. Those named in each section's title are cited only by page number, others by title word or abbreviation plus page number.

Le Guin, Ursula K. *Tehanu*. Bantam, 1991 [orig. Atheneum 1990].

Le Guin, Ursula K. *Earthsea Revisioned*. Children's Literature New England, and Green Bay Publ., 1993 [cited as *ER*].

Le Guin, Ursula K. *Tales from Earthsea*. Orion, 2003 [orig. Harcourt 2001; cited as *TfE*].

Le Guin, Ursula K. "Foreword" to the above, XI-XV, and "A Description of Earthsea" in it, 267–96.

Le Guin, Ursula K. *The Other Wind*. Orion, 2003 [orig. Harcourt 2001; cited as *OW*].

Nancy, Jean-Luc. *Être singulier pluriel*. Galilée, 1996.

Suvin, Darko. "Considering the Sense of 'Fantasy' or 'Fantastic Fiction.'" *Extrapolation* 41.3 (2000): 209–47 [chapter 4 in this book].

Suvin, Darko. "Living Labour and the Labour of Living." *Critical Q* 46.1 (2004): 1–35.

Suvin, Darko. *Metamorphoses of Science Fiction*. Yale UP, 1979.

Suvin, Darko. Afterword. "With Sober, Estranged Eyes," in P. Parrinder ed., *Learning from Other Worlds*. Liverpool UP, 2000, and Duke UP, 2001, 233–71.

12

Poems of Old Age II (2006–10)

NAVIGATOR TO PILOT

I have found us the fertile planet, haven't i? I
Promised, i did it. Now land please, in the strange
Nebula. I have perfect confidence in your steering touch.
The two of us together, i never feared death. Where

You need it, ask, i shall help again: just get me
A good star chart and distance gauge, i beg you.
Plant then our sunny flag deep, let us map in
The grounds. There may be tygers, incompatible monsters

Hidden under the alluring face: the black forests,
The amber-green pools, the quirky contour of the Medi=
Terranean like an unforgettable mouth amidst
This improbable sighting, of course, we do not know.

But the latest omen is good: i have spotted a white
Soarer, perhaps resembling a pelican, it
Fluttered nearer and further again, a delicate
Dance, not afraid. It – he – she looked at me:

Our looks may cross, link, click –
One day, who knows, we might be companions.

584-06

Glossary: Line 8: old maps of unknown continents had the legend "There be tygers here"; a Bradbury story takes its title from there.

COLD COMFORT (INTRUMO)

In a dream a dragon came to me, looked at me,
Splendour of shimmering copper scales
& scarlet thorns, scythe-taloned. I looked
Back, at the amber mist around his huge eyes, above

The fuming nostrils. The red-black smoke from her mouth
Hissed: "Don't despair, short-lived Earthling. Soon
You shall die, soon will expire your kind's cosmic contract.
This muddied globe your Mother is unforgiving as the winds we ride.

But in the new creation the Mother shall whelp, a few shards
May be dug up & deciphered by successor populations,
Hexapods perhaps, stabler far, winged like ourselves:

A few testimonials, like the ones you found of Gilgamesh
& Intrumo, shall show yours was a redeemable kind.
>What a pity!< the unsentimental hexapods will chirrup,

Winging on to their inscrutable business of conviviality".
26806

Glossary: "Intrumo" was the e-mail moniker of U.K. Le Guin

IN THE ICE AGE
(A COUNTER-PROJECT TO XIUNG XI-LING)

All that we feel is the freezing storm
But who is there to grieve for the warmth?
As you're leaving, bequeath this wish:
Everybody should afford happiness!
19408

"I SEEM INSANE TO YOU"

I seem insane to you. I'm not sorry
But tell me your reasons. "Because you go on
About justice, because you were always bewitched
By the Great Goddess." Indeed i do, indeed
I was, i am. This folly, all ye gods
& sea-nymphs, may it never leave me!
14109

TO CARRY OVER

A compliment to John Berger

We exiles are all
Specialists in packing
We know what to leave behind

We take with us
Suitcases that we can lift
We leave behind us
Connections & ways of life

We take with us
Birthdays, marriage anniversaries
The shelters of gestures & jokes
The words for bread & coffee

We know desperately well
Railway stations & airports
We anesthetise this Fate
By crosswords & science fiction

Our luggage is
Anxiety & hope
To survive have friends
To work make sense

Wherever we come, languages shift
To the dismay of lexicographers
The orthography grows unreadable
We build new houses of words

We are carriers
Transported & deported
Thus metaphors
This wine our blood

The poetry of mongrel tomorrows
Will be in our languages
We carry it
Like cattle-cars cattle

The maximum diameter of the universe
Is 240 times 10 to the 24th kilometres
We had no need
For this calculation

It's not so easy
Bridging Milky Ways
We are thirsty
Carrying goods over

London 14509

MY LADY HOPE

To the memory of Anne McLaren, 1948 onward

I dreamt of Lady Hope tonight
She smiled on me so sweetly,
Fair as in days of our keen youth
When she kissed me very sweetly.

"Where did you go, my Lady, my love,
What countries saw your features?
Your flaming gaze, your sunburnt hands,
Your reach to other futures?"

"I've always been here, young man of mine,
Here where the wise can see me,
You grew up & lost your keen eye
& the faint are not able to see me."

"We all must grow up, my Lady, my love,
How can I again see you?"
"Remember how knowledge led you to love,
Hold fast to that, & you'll see me."

"But you're no longer a girl, my love,
Rosy as dawn & eyes shining."
"We all grow up, old man of mine,
I'm a woman now, eyes shining."

4510

13

Literature, Politics, Brecht, Science Fiction vs. Fantasy: Interview with Maria Xilouri (2008)

Note 2020: This interview in Athens at end of 2008 was with a young collaborator of the Left-wing periodical Aristera! who sent me a version with the notes being hers. It was mildly added to from my notes.

Maria Xilouri: Please tell us what you write.

Darko Suvin: The kind of things I write are fairly heavy essays – mainly for academics. I don't try to be heavy, of course; on the other hand, nobody asks a mathematician to be understandable to a first-year student; you must put in some groundwork. I have been very interested in Chinese and Japanese thought – I have written a book about Japan – and I read that Confucius said *I give my pupils one angle of a quadrangle.* Confucius had chosen, private pupils who lived with him, he wasn't a professor at a mass university. But he said *I give them one angle of the quadrangle, the rest they must find.* Which is very difficult. When I was a professor, I said to my class, *I give you three angles. But you really got to find the fourth!* Which is easy, because if you give them three angles the fourth will appear by certain rules you were taught. But you must know these basic rules of the quadrangle.

MX: When you're learning something, you'll always have to find some things yourself, based on your knowledge. Something like inventing.

DS: This is much better pedagogically. Because if you are fed like a bird feeds its young – well, you are not hungry today, but what happens tomorrow?

Politics, Realism, Brecht, Cognition

MX: From my understanding your work focuses on utopia, which is connected with SF, and Bertolt Brecht.

DS: And lately my work is about a third thing which I call political epistemology. About war and immigration and what's been happening to us the last 20 years.

MX: [He says that his essay on immigrants is going to be published in Mr Milios's journal *Thesis*, and asks for criticism and feedback on how this work sounds in Greek. He notices that, as a poet, he tries to write as precisely as he can, but a writer is at the mercy of translators. Mr Suvin writes directly in English; trying to write in his native language would result, he says, in Serbo-Croatian with an English sentence structure. This talk on translation problems gives me a hint to show him a very rough translation of Yiorgos Chouliaras's *Brecht in Greece*, a poem on what's been happening in Greece after Alexandros Andreas Grigoropoulos, age 15, was murdered by a policeman. Something that Mr Suvin is of course aware of.]

Some poets have published poems through a webpage (www.e-poema.gr), about what is happening. This is one of the poems.

DS: [*Instant reaction.*]

MX: And this particular poem refers directly to Brecht. It is called "Brecht in Greece."

[I read a very rough translation of the poem. He then takes a look at my notes, and asks about the final phrase's meaning. The poem goes like this:

Brecht in Greece

He is so famous that they invite him, though he is dead
To direct reality as a reality show
Before the breaking of the screens by stone words that
Primary school children are called to throw.
Luckily, as he is so well known to the grownups,
They will notice that since they themselves don't change
The only thing that remains to be done is to change their children.]

What impressed me most about the poem is the poet's need to come back to Brecht.

DS: He is not fully dead. And a good thing, too! And this is why I came here. I was really thinking, given the situation, should I come? There is a fairly nasty play written by Günter Grass about Brecht, called *The Plebeians Rehearsing for Uprising*. The protagonist is given another name, but he is a theater director in East Berlin at the time of the 1953 uprising of the workers against the economic situation and the work norms in East Berlin.[1] And the famous director is in his theater, rehearsing a play about the revolution, while the revolution happens outside and he doesn't want to have anything to do with that. This is totally unfair, because Brecht was at the time in fact not rehearsing, but out on the streets; that's the historical truth. But Grass was a political enemy, he was in the Social-Democratic Party, and this play gained fame as it was used by ideological enemies of Brecht to show that he is really a careerist interested in his plays and not what he pretends to be. So I thought, are we going to do what Grass falsely attributed to Brecht? Are we really going to sit in

Piraeus, discussing Brecht while the kids are on the streets? And I thought very hard about this – and I decided that if this would help to bring some elements, aspects, understandings out of Brecht, I cannot say no. This wasn't about danger, whether it would be dangerous to come or not.

MX: So you think a writer must not only write about the revolution, but he should also fight for it?

DS: Look, Brecht was a short man with glasses, he couldn't do a lot of fighting. He would have had trouble with a rifle, I think. But he was on the streets to participate as a citizen – a correct thing to do. There is a famous anecdote, I've used it in one of my books as a kind of introduction. It is apocryphal, imaginary. And the anecdote goes, Victor Shklovsky, Russia's most famous formalist critic, said to Trotsky, the Commissar for War: *As a literary or theater critic, I'm not interested in war.* And Trotsky replied, *But the war is interested in you.* So you may say as a poet that you are not interested in the deep malice of society. Yes, but it will come to you!

MX: I'm asking this because a lot of people these days are wondering whether the artists are with them in this crisis or not; they seem to seek for artists' opinion and support on this.

DS: It's a fair question to ask. But I think the artists also have the right to address the same question to the kids. *Where are you at? I know what you don't want. But what do you really want?* In other words, *if you invite me to risk myself, what for*? Or at least *what are you beginning to think about? You haven't had practice in political thinking, but something must be coming to your mind. So what do you want*? Nature opposes a vacuum, we are taught. So if you don't know what you want, maybe somebody else will know – for example, the extreme Right wing. This is what happened after 1929, remember who came? Hitler. Because the Left wasn't up to it; they were fighting each other. Now, if they are fighting each other on matters of principle, that is good. My position is A, B, C, and yours is D, E, F, and I hold to my position and you hold to yours. Let us cooperate on a minimum program, and for the rest let us see if A, B, C is correct or D, E, F. If Left parties don't do this, that's suicidal.

MX: [I'm explaining that this a major problem for the Greek Left; while Greek Left parties are involved in a fight about the uprising, the Far-Right Wing is trying to create a climate of fear among "peaceful" shop-owners and civilians. He notes that this climate is very easy to create and offers some insight on the situation in Germany, derived from a friend's research on the neo-Nazi movement:]

DS: The neo-Nazis have successes in West Germany, they have a food program for the poor, Salvation Army kind of stuff; we give you food and we indoctrinate you. They talk about social justice – national social justice, of course – and their percentages in some parts of Germany rose from 2 or 3% to 10 to 15%. That's five times more. Why?

Because the Left doesn't do that. The Left isn't into this *first we give you food, then we tell you the truth* thing at all. The Left talks about elections, parliaments, and theories. I am in favor of theories – I am among other things also a theoretician – but for heaven's sake, only theories? Of course the analogy between 1929 and today is just an analogy, not an identity, but it is a powerful analogy and one we should learn from. As Brecht learned from it. He lived through this. And all of his work from 1930-31 and on is an answer to Hitlerism really. He would have written totally different things otherwise.

MX: Would you say that an artist's task is to reflect reality? I think that this is a common misunderstanding among people and artists.

DS: "Reflects" is a very loaded word. You remember the debates on Lenin's book about reflecting reality, the *Materialism* book. That is an unfortunate book, which by the way he wrote for political, not philosophical reasons. He wrote it against some people who were trying to lead the Bolshevik party in a way he didn't like. And Lenin wrote some philosophically extremely interesting stuff, such as his comments on Hegel and dialectics in 1916-17. These are totally different from the *Materialism* book, but the former was pronounced by Stalin to be the culmination of the Marxist philosophy about culture, which it wasn't at all. I had to read this in Yugoslavia; it is an interesting book, it is a great political polemic, but not a good philosophical book. And he uses the metaphor of mirroring. It is a dangerous metaphor. First of all, which mirror do you mean? You mean the one to one mirror, the parabolic mirror, or something else? There are all kinds of mirrors. No poet mirrors anything in any precise way. Aristotle's *mimesis* doesn't mean imitation. He says *the dithyramb makes mimesis by means of flutes and lyres*. How can we do a mimesis by way of music? In other words – let me put it as crudely as I can: you hear a donkey on the street doing *Eee-aaah!* and you try to put this sound into the music through an instrument. Is this imitation? No, it is a transposition into what the lyre can do. It's not really one-to-one mirroring.

MX: So what is realism after all? How can we understand realism today?

DS: The word realism comes from the word *res*, thing, meaning material reality, and that sense was invented by the bourgeoisie. Why? Because they said, *Never mind what the church says happens after we die. In this world, can I make a profit or not? So let us be real or realistic. Can I have a factory that produces things*? That, I think, was a great historical advance. The greatest laudation of the bourgeoisie is in the *Communist Manifesto*. But today we must say that there is a price to pay that perhaps Marx did not fully see in 1848, because the price wasn't so high then. Newer investigations in psychology and philosophy, for example Wittgenstein – the later Wittgenstein which in my opinion is totally materialistic – have shown that you cannot see anything without seeing it as X. This [*he turns to the recording machine*] is a recording machine. If you were in a demonstration, you would see it as a brick to throw at somebody. You don't see its essence given by God; you see it in a given situation as X. There is no such thing as *going out and seeing things and then merely describing them*, unless you know what to see them as, which means also what to see them for, which function do they have – this thing's function, is it the function of recording or being thrown at somebody's head? So a writer may go out and say *I notice these details* – like Zola who went out filling notebooks. But then Zola had a theory: in *Les Rougon-Macquart* the whole family has "bad blood" and each novel is about a member of this family[2] – despite this theory, which was wrong, he wrote quite a number of good things because he was a very interesting writer, politically active in the Dreyfus case,[3] and so on… You cannot write a single page without a certain purpose. Which means a certain interest, accompanied by a certain emotion, by certain positions – all of these can be more or less useful to a smaller or bigger group of people. Maybe it's useful only for your bohemian friends, or it's useful for one whole social class or everybody at a certain point – or let's say for a significant majority.

I'm not sure, therefore, whether realism means anything today – I think it is a very tired word. Like a poor donkey, beaten until it collapses. And here people like Brecht give us great examples. Brecht asked *What can you understand about Krupp's Steelworks from a photograph?* You get a good photographer, you get a wonderful lens, you get a photo of the whole factory. What do you understand? Nothing. Sure, you know it is a big factory and a lot of people must work in it. How do you understand it? You must draw a blueprint, you must have a flowchart of its products, you must have economic information, you must have trade union information – then you can use the photograph. In other words: classical realism, Stendhal says, is a mirror by the street side. It catches the people passing by. But this is not enough for Krupp's Steelworks. I think, if I may interpret Brecht, that Krupp's Steelworks, used as everyday economics and as politics, is our equivalent of Greek tragedy's destiny. We don't believe in gods, but there are political and economic powers which determine our lives, it is our destiny. Krupp's Steelworks was the biggest capitalist of the time, so it stood as a metaphor for capitalism as a whole. The real realism is the one that uses a flowchart, either literally or some equivalent of the flowchart. What products come in? What products come out? Who works there? How much are they paid? What are the profits? What are the taxes? Then you understand whence the distribution of working space, the people in them, and so on. And the beating heart of the steelworks is *capital*. So you get a handle on understanding it – as the owners do, but against the owners.

Let us assume you want, say, to write about miners: in a novel like Zola's *Germinal* the miners are structurally not allowed by the novel itself to understand why a mine would open or close. Just as a tragic hero, for example Oedipus, doesn't understand why the gods are subjecting him to horrors, it's simply destiny. Brecht, and the Marxist enterprise in general, says destiny is made by these people, organized in some ways, or some other people, organised or not organised in some other ways, through institutions like the market or the army or the factory or whatever. If the gods make it, we have to shut up and admire – with pity or with sorrow, perhaps, but we cannot do anything else. But if people make it, then people can unmake it. This requires certain techniques of understanding. First of all, as I mentioned, Wittgenstein's – you cannot understand anything except as something. This is a pillow, but I also see it as support to my back, because I have problems with my back, that's why I put it here; I can also see it, if I'm interested in embroidery, as a very interesting piece of embroidery, but since my interest is very different I see it in a very different way. So there is no simple realism of this kind – just *go out and look at the people*. What is your framework when you are doing this? What is your system of presuppositions?

If there is no such thing as writing without a framework, you have a choice of a conscious framework or of an unconscious framework – and I don't mean it in Freudian terms. Your framework is a kind of mosaic of your own prejudices, which you have because you were brought up in a certain way, you lived in a certain way, you read certain things, you fell in love with certain things; it is an unexamined framework. Unless you are a great genius, a Van Gogh or somebody – who by the way was a socialist preacher when he was younger, his is an interesting politico-ideological profile. I have nothing against interpreting him in terms of his psychology, in terms of madness – madness is very important, but again in what context? Is it like a bacterium which you catch and it makes you mad or is there some reason behind it, which is applied personally of course because we are talking about a person, but which is super-personal, which is collective? So if you do not have an explicit framework you will have an implicit framework, and the problem with an implicit framework – unless you are a Van Gogh, one in a million – is that it is uncorrectable, because it is implicit, you don't really know it; if it is explicit, you can see a mistake. If you thought that Stalin was a great hero, you might come across some important experiences that contradict it. So your belief can be readjusted. And then if I come up with different data that prove otherwise, we can argue about this. But if it's implicit we cannot argue, you just say *I feel like this*. I'm not saying that an artist should have an articulate, developed ideology. Some should, some shouldn't, it is a matter of personal backgrounds, orientations – I'm saying that to say *in principle, I do not want frameworks* is not very intelligent. There are people who can write good stuff without being very intelligent, but those are very few. The statistics are against such kind of writing.

Brecht lived through the First World War, he was an orderly in a military hospital, he saw soldiers coming in without legs, with syphilis, with god knows what breakdowns – he saw a little bit, but if you are a poet your antennae are very sensitive, even if you are not an orderly in a military hospital you will understand that what's happening is terrible. And then he saw the collapse of the civil society after the First World War. He saw the collapse of a whole order, the old German bourgeois order, and then the rise of Leninism, which got him very interested, because it was something new on the horizon, promising a way out of this collapse. Then he saw Hitler, and I think he saw Leninism become Stalinism, he saw fascism not being stopped – and as a result of all this and of the fact that he was, after all, German, he became highly interested in theory. Since he was very intelligent, he could make good theories alongside of being a good poet. Not every poet can do this and of course very few theoreticians are good poets. Marx wrote some very bad romantic poetry when he was young. But then Marx is a very good poet, in prose. You see this in the structure of the *Communist Manifesto*.

Brecht rewrote the *Communist Manifesto* in verse. In 1944–45, when the Russians were getting to Germany, Brecht wondered what will the workers read when they are liberated, since Marxism had been destroyed by Hitler. So, he thought, *if I put the*

Communist Manifesto *into verse maybe they will read that*. He worked very hard at this, though most of his friends considered him crazy at the time. But Brecht wrote this anyway and I translated it in English a few years ago. *The Manifesto*, 402 hexameters, on the model of the German translation of Lucretius that he loved. Poetry's relationship with the doctrine is not something new; Milton wrote about politics disguised as cosmology; obviously in Greek tragedy you didn't write simply about personal feelings. Today it seems strange to us that poetry can have a relationship to a doctrine, but historically it is not strange at all. So the question is, what is this relationship? If you are a poet at all, you will not be literally repeating the doctrine, because the doctrine doesn't need you for that, it can be read straight, without the poet. Brecht found out that he couldn't merely repeat the *Manifesto* – also, he was living 100 years after Marx. So the poem begins like this – *Wars are destroying the world. And in the wars a specter is seen, The specter of communism*. Wars. That is not in Marx's writing. And that's because Marx didn't see two World Wars. It seems to me a totally legitimate extrapolation. *What can I say to the German workers of the 1940s? Their country has just been destroyed by a war, so logically I have to talk about the war*. And then he put in some very comical stuff about the blind God of Profit, the worship of this blind God.

You have to be very careful when you are writing poetry, nobody can say *a priori* that he wants to have a doctrine or not. If you, as a poet, feel that you need the doctrine and you think you can handle it, then it's fine. And if not, you can still write great poetry, like Rilke, with the doctrine he absorbed as a child but considers just natural.

In brief: writing realistically for me means writing in a way that makes you understand things better.

MX: Can writing change the world?

DS: Saying that a book can change the world is a metaphor. When you say a book has changed the world, this is to say that a book has changed 5,000 people who have changed 500,000 people and those 500,000 changed the world. Of course a book can't do anything on its own. A book is a kind of condensed experience dissemination. Today we have a mass market capitalist book industry where publishers ask writers to repeat something successful and then call it a series. In Fantasy you must write a trilogy or you are nobody. And our life today is much more complicated than it was in the past. Putting television or the internet aside for the moment and focusing on books, I think there is a legitimate evasion or painkiller function of books. If I'm in an airport, usually a horrible place to be, and my plane is late for some reason, and I have to wait there for six hours, instead of going crazy I can read two silly books. They may be silly love stories or silly detective stories but they function as painkillers. This of course doesn't mean that they are good books or that I would read them if I weren't at the airport or an equivalent situation.

And then there is a cognitive function of books. Traditionally, and I think today too, cognition was not only carried by science but it was carried by everything that helped our understanding – which includes all art, and certainly books. I think that if you understand cognition widely, not simply as scientific or mathematical – which I believe, having studied science for six years, is not the only possible cognition – then there is a cognitive function of books that cannot be in that way found on the TV or in the movies or on the internet. The book is handy, you have it at your hand, it is articulated, it can be contradicted. So it is a bad sign that we have degraded the function of books. I use the internet, I am a film fan, and when I was young I listened to the radio all the time, it was very important to me. I have absolutely nothing against all of them as possibilities, but nothing can replace a book. And yes, some movies' function might be just as cognitive as a book's – for example some films by Jean-Luc Godard, who was deeply influenced by Brecht. On the other hand, in SF all the good stuff is usually in books, most movies are horrible. Lem's book *Solaris* was much better than the movie, even though the director, Tarkovsky, wasn't bad – especially his first films. But he cut out all the cognitive discussions, reducing it to his Christian existentialism – something like *there is this man and this treasure and what's going to happen*? While Lem had invented a non-existent science, this whole history of solaristics, in a kind of mimicry of existing scientific doctrines. Perhaps this was difficult to show in the movie, but then again why not try?

Finally, the use-value of a book is that you both understand more about something and that this understanding is pleasurable. Even if the conclusion is black, you have understood how and at least in part why it is black.

MX: Well, film language is a different kind of language. You can't literally translate a book into film.

DS: Of course, but on the other hand, this gets to be an excuse for many stupid decisions. *Yes, I would like to, but this is a movie and I can't.* Well, if you are a good enough director you can do all kinds of things. Sometimes it happens that from a mediocre book you get a great movie: fair enough. But this is not the case in SF. If you want to know what SF is, you'll have to read the book. Just a month ago, I watched a horrible Japanese *anime* adaptation of Le Guin's *Earthsea*. She was horrified, she wrote this to me years ago. It was the kind of a stupid Fantasy story which Le Guin would never write.

Science Fiction and Fantasy

MX: Why do you stress the difference between SF and Fantasy?

DS: I think that my notion of Science Fiction as appealing to confident social groups, and Fantasy appealing to social groups that see no future, is mostly correct in the statistical sense. On the other hand, there are some interesting developments in Fantasy, which I have understood in part since I wrote that essay, some 6 or 7 years ago, and I have therefore written another essay about Le Guin's second *Earthsea* trilogy. There are six books, the last three looking back at the first and taking them back in a way as macho. A feminist reply to herself! Her hero refuses his function, and goes off in a self-exile, so to speak. I still think I was correct about Tolkien and maybe 98% of Fantasy. There is a 2% for which I should rectify. In other words I should create some category – I am a great believer in categories until they grow stifling – to fit this 2% in.

I see categories as frames. My frame is SF. This book is inside this frame. Outside of this frame, it is not readable. If you don't know the presuppositions, if you haven't read SF you can't understand an opening line like *He landed in the light of the blue sun*. This, if you've never read SF, makes no sense. But what does it mean when framed? Easy: we are in another solar system, and not in ours where the sun is yellow. If you are a fan, you won't wonder. *So there is a blue sun, so what, let's go on*. But if you are not? After five sentences like this, you'll get lost because you don't know which category you are in. Re-categorizing is a deeply philosophical cognitive pursuit. Of course if you don't know how to read, categories won't help you. You must have a feeling for the microstructure of the book. As if in a poem: how do the words function, how does the rhythm go – if you don't have that, then you better not write about literature in this category or that category or any category. You need a collection of interests and qualities to understand SF, one is a normal critical understanding of the words on the page and another is an interest in categories, which we call literary genres. Genres are not prisons. You can break the rule. But then you are breaking this rule and not another rule. And the book can only be understood as "Aha! Up to page 80 he follows the rule and then something else begins." You can of course create your own book from what you have read, which has little or nothing to do with Le Guin or Lem. But usually, since you the reader are not a better writer than Le Guin or Brecht, it's going to be a poor book. If you are a fantastic young girl or boy who has a great imagination, maybe your own book might be better. But you cannot communicate it to anybody, as it is not written, it's in your mind.

MX: What about reading Tolkien?

DS: I cannot say, of course, to someone who takes pleasure from reading Tolkien's work not to read him. There are so few pleasures in life that one should appreciate them. And in my opinion Tolkien is a great writer on paragraph level. Also, he has an interesting love of nature in his work and is, of course, a great linguist: when I studied the Anglo-Saxon poem *Beowulf*, his was the obligatory commentary. But as far as his ideological horizon goes, which in a good writer delimits what s/he writes, one should be careful with his work. It is a conservative program. Let's take Aragorn, for example. What does Aragorn stand for? He is a naturally royal person against the powerful and for the little people, the Disraeli program for British Conservatives. Or the orcs: you'll notice that they have certain characteristics – industrial knowledge, iron, a thirst for blood; so we could say that this is a horror image of the proletariat in arms, evilly ensorceled by a subversive power.

MX: Is there a Fantasy writer whose work you'd recommend in terms of both literature and politics?

DS: I'd suggest China Miéville, especially the *Iron Council*.

MX: And Kafka?

DS: Due to his financial problems, Walter Benjamin, to my mind perhaps the 20th-Century critic that speaks to us most loudly, was invited by Brecht to stay with him in Denmark in the 1930s. Their very interesting discussions on Kafka resulted in two essays written by Benjamin.

Brecht criticized Kafka for introducing mystery for mystery's sake; but in other aspects, he saw him as a quasi-Bolshevik writer, a radical. Benjamin used elements from the Jewish writings to understand Kafka – especially the difference between *halakha*, folk stories and religious but not holy writings, and *haggadah*, the doctrine. In Kafka, the *halakha* is like a lion who crouches at the feet of the *haggadah* but suddenly it raises its mighty paw (against it).

To my mind, we can see that there are hidden rulers at the Castle, in the novel of that name, but no religious doctrine, just pervasive power; Kafka didn't know how to understand this or what to do about it, but he knew perfectly well how life inside it is. In fact, Kafka's "doctrine" was the pain of not having a doctrine (guide, orientation) to live by, a horrible pain. It's as if you've suddenly become another species, like his giant thinking but helpless cockroach, and cannot understand why humans do what they do.

Notes

1 The reference is to the June 1953 uprising in Stalinist East Berlin suppressed by Soviet tanks and the *Volkspolizei*. Brecht refers to this uprising in the poem "The Solution," with the famous ending: "Would it not be easier/ In that case for the government/ To dissolve the people/ And elect another?"

2 The series, consisting of 20 books, examines two branches of a single family: the respectable Rougons and the disreputable Macquarts, for five generations.

3 Alfred Dreyfus was a Jewish artillery captain convicted to life imprisonment after accusations of espionage; Zola, risking his reputation and career, stated in the famous *J'accuse* that the accusations were false and this was a case of obstruction of justice and antisemitism. The Dreyfus case resulted in a deep division between the reactionary army and church and the more liberal commercial society of France.

14

Darwinism, Left and Right: And Some S-F Probes (2010)

Note 2020: *This essay came about during the Darwin Year, when friend Carlo Pagetti organised a meeting in Milan about it. I adapt and condense here some points developed at more length in "SF Parables of Mutation and Cloning," in my book Parables of Freedom and Narrative Logics (2021); however, I am refunctioning them as a test case for the role of Darwinism in SF. See also the more extensive argument about Weinbaum in that book, "We've Met the Aliens and They Are Us," in particular its note 1. The two pieces support each other.*

> *We know only a single science, the science of history. One can look at history from two sides and divide it into the history of nature and the history of men. The two sides are, however, inseparable; the history of nature and the history of men are dependent on each other so long as men exist.*
>
> Friedrich Engels and Karl Marx, draft for *The German Ideology* (1847)

0. Cutting short discussions in legitimately many shelves of books, I'd most briefly understand Darwinism for present purposes to mean what Darwin himself said in *The Origin of Species*. He started in chapter III with Struggle for Existence (or Life) and its bearing on Natural Selection but (unfortunately) immediately adopted as a synonym for it Spencer's "Survival of the Fittest," approving its stress on competition (66–67). He went on to carefully explain and abundantly exemplify that "the fittest" meant for him those best adapted to changing conditions in their environment, including Sexual Selection in transmitting their adaptation to posterity. The "struggle for life" is in Darwin a capacious category, which includes for example the direct or indirect influence of climate and can be even extended in a wide and metaphoric sense to mean any phenomenon of reciprocal dependence of living beings on each other and the environment. As Mayr has argued, Darwin substituted population thinking and incessant changeability for Platonic and Christian essentialism. I would say he denied nominalist essentialism and dogmatic teleology. About the former, he explained: "I look at the term 'species' as one arbitrarily given, for the sake of convenience, to a set of individuals closely resembling each other" (*Origin* 108); in today's language, truth is always historical and concrete. And in lieu of teleology, he established a materialist argument for how organisms necessarily change over time according to the changing

situations. In sum, Darwin introduced a dominant historical, albeit *longue durée*, factor into nature and natural science (cf. Angus, and Bernal 663).

I shall argue that the exotic living beings represented in SF (aliens and androids) are mostly not subject to Darwinism proper, and that perhaps we couldn't expect them to be, but that a Darwinian ecological approach permeates most of them. However, SF was subjected to the strong pressure of the political ideology of "Social Darwinism," so that I must first make a clear distinction between this abuse and cognitive Darwinism. I shall be citing Hofstadter's classical *Social Darwinism in American Thought* (as H) – using the USA as standing in for capitalism writ large (what Wells called, in a glance at his *When the Sleeper Wakes*, "in a state of inflamed distension"), and yet open enough to generate copious public discussion. Hofstadter does not deal with modern developments within Darwinism, though for all their richness and sophistication I do not think the furthest horizons as I discuss them below have radically changed. At any rate, his material is necessary and sufficient for my SF probes.

1. Brief Approach to Darwinism in the Public Mind and in Literary Fiction

1.1. Darwin's public fortune immediately gave rise to two strong tendencies, Social-Darwinists (or Right-wing Darwinists) vs. what I shall call Left-wing Darwinists. Both of these currents could cite many passages in Darwin's writings in their favour. Despite Darwin's care, commentators and the public seized on the very ambiguous and misleading Survival of the Fittest, and even more so on Malthus's Struggle for Existence: as Darwin put it in a perhaps unguarded moment, "let the strongest live and the weakest die" (260). What this meant in practice was well seen by Henry Demarest Lloyd's unjustly forgotten *Wealth against Commonwealth*:

> Our industry is a fight of every man for himself.... The man who should apply in his family or in his citizenship this "survival of the fittest" theory as it is practically professed and operated in business would be a monster, and would be speedily made extinct. (Lloyd, in H 122)

There is no denying that "the Hobbesian... spirit" (Hofstadter 91) in Darwin's writings powerfully contributed to some of the worst deformations in life under capitalism.

The monstrosity of Social Darwinism was especially prevalent in social life of the dark US decades 1860–90 and 1975 until today. It found voice also in imaginative writings, say in the weakest aspect of Jack London. It could be encapsulated in a lyrical flight of fancy by none less than the founder of the Rockefeller dynasty, John D. the First, in his Sunday school address parable of the American Beauty rose:

> The growth of business is merely the survival of the fittest.... The American Beauty rose can be produced in the splendour and fragrance which bring cheer to its beholder only by sacrificing the early buds which grow up around it. This

> is not an evil tendency in business. It is merely the working out of a law of nature and a law of God. (H 45)

Thus, "Darwinism was used to buttress the conservative outlook," meaning "that all attempts to reform social processes were efforts to remedy the irremediable, that they interfered with the wisdom of nature…" (H 6–7). This interpretation became "a kind of secular piety" with an economic ethic "necessary for the disciplining of a labor force and a force of small investors" (H 10):

> It made possible the justification of everything that was going on in the capitalist world, the ruthless exploitation of man by man, the conquest of inferior by superior peoples. Even war itself could be justified by comparison with Nature, "red in tooth and claw." The old excuse for the dominance of classes or races, that they were chosen people or the sons of Gods, had faded, and new excuses were needed to justify their continuation in a rational and scientific world. Darwinism provided it, although this was the last thing Darwin himself wanted. (Bernal 663)

Nonetheless, there developed an able "Left" interpretation – including his admirers Engels and Marx (cf. Angus and Foster), Kropotkin, as well as Millian liberals, socialists, and dissenters like Peirce, Veblen, Dewey or Henry Adams – opposed to the apologists of robber-baron capitalism. Two quotes may encapsulate this confrontation:

> William Graham Sumner: The millionaires are a product of natural selection…. It is because they are thus selected that wealth – both their own and that entrusted to them – aggregates under their hands…. (in H 58)
>
> Lester Ward: …so far as the native capacity, the potential quality… of a higher life are concerned, those swarming, spawning millions, the bottom layer of society, the proletariat, the working class, the "hewers of wood and drawers of water", nay, even the denizens of the slums –… all these are by nature the peers of the boasted "aristocracy of brains" that now dominates society and looks down upon them…. (in H 83)

Theoretically, a dissenting economist concluded, in one critical respect, Darwin's theory "was the exact opposite of Malthusianism. Malthus assumed that man has a definite and unalterable set of attributes; Darwinism holds that man is pliable and circumstances determine his characteristics" (from Simon Patten, H 147). Darwin himself stressed that "Natural selection, also, leads to divergence of character; for the more organic beings diverge in structure, habits, and constitution, by so much the more can a large number be supported on the same area…" (125).[1] For this and other reasons, it is quite misleading to apply Malthusianism to human social life, unless one aims to justify rapacious capitalism. And practically, the best dissenter among economists, Thorstein Veblen, contradicted head on the Rockefellerian thesis that millionaires were the fittest, that their capacity for acquiring possessions was noble and beautiful, and that their character fit their riches. On the contrary, the business class was essentially predatory, and the character of "the ideal pecuniary man" was described by Veblen in terms fitting for moral delinquents (237–38, and see H 152–56).

1.2. Another problem, quite outside strictly scientific discussions – but to my mind not at all outside cognitive discussions – arises when we get to the behaviour and destiny of narrative agents in literary fiction. I'll confine myself to what we may call "biological SF," that is: all SF centrally dealing with *radical difference in cellular bases or other bodily determinants of living beings* (more in Suvin "Science Fiction Parables"). Such non-human yet equally self-reflexive life can, I think, be used in three ways. First, as a gratuitous thrill, a plot gimmick; second, as an awful warning to us humans. The warning was a variegated congeries, often bordering on horror, from the popular uses of *Frankenstein*, through Julian Huxley's "The Tissue-Culture King," to scores of B or C movies passing for SF, and then to incorporating all UK and US chauvinistic fears of weird or poorer strangers, from the ludicrous ones of "Doc" Smith to the cleverly ideological of Niven and Pournelle (see my "Of Starship," chapter 9 in this book). A third use is a narrative discussion of intriguing, perhaps positive, possibilities (for example in Weinbaum's "A Martian Odyssey"), though often the dark and bright horizons got intermingled (for example in Stapledon and Lem).

It has been rightly observed that biological notions function in SF literature centrally as "metaphors applicable to social relationships..." (Stableford 124). Their development into a narrative constitutes in most significant cases a *parable*. In other words, the use of themes based on evolution does not function in SF as any serious extrapolation. I have argued at length elsewhere that scientific extrapolation cannot be the function of SF as fiction. Rather, these themes centrally function as vehicles for a sociopolitical tenor, for developing analogies to possible relationships between people in the author's present. No doubt, what happens to the uses of – say – genetic manipulation or cloning in a novel's rich web of verisimilar relationships may well supply precious public insights about the pros and cons of a given societal experiment; but this is incidental to the thought-experiments of SF. The actual scientific theme or element used is subordinated to its analogical function in the narration.

2. Olaf Stapledon's Utopian Communism and Humanist Mentalism: Mutations in *Last and First Men*

I shall use what one could, in Stapledon's running metaphor from music, call the "biological movement" sandwiched between the sociopolitical and the cosmic movements, and consisting of chapters VII to XII/2 of *Last and First Men* (further LFM, pp. 132–243 in the Penguin 1963 edn.; citations will be to subchapter rather than page). It begins with the Second Men who appear as the result of "an epidemic of biological variations," which brings a much improved physiological organization and maturity at 50, but most importantly a transformed mind. This centrally meant an extension of delight from erotics to an "appreciation of the unique physical and mental forms of all kinds of live things," or "altruism as a passion," tempering the "competitive self-assertion" of the First Men which "cursed [Homo Sapiens] with industrialism and militarism." Passion and energy are invested in a "vision of a world-wide community of persons" and one's function in it, and concomitantly in "the higher kinds of mental activity" and their subtle objects – philosophy, mathematics, and above all music (VII/1).

However, a crisis befalls the Second Men due to their brain outgrowing their cranium and circulatory system – a metaphor against over-intellectualizing. It is resolved by a *deus ex machina* appearance (presumably through mutation) of a new, "more stable variety," a "roomier-skulled and stronger-hearted type," which fortunately "proved to be a dominant Mendelian character" (VII/2). In an almost embarrassingly blatant way, this is a parable for the need of head and heart to be redone if the new type of human relationships is to flourish. After an interlude of Dark Times due to the virus of a mysterious fatigue, the third civilization of the Second Men (this time *not* due to mutation) rose to a culmination made possible by scientific advances securing more energy from the environment for the species, by the gift of mutual sympathy, and by

> their combination of a practical commonsense that was more than British, with a more than Russian immunity from the glamour of wealth, and a passion for the life of the mind that even Greece had never known. (ibidem)

The whole central "biological" movement of LFM is based on Stapledon's revulsion against the bourgeois civilization that culminated in World War 1 and a debate with what seemed the evident successes of the original Soviet experiment in the 1920s. The "Russian" in the above passage is his interpretation of Leninism as a populism of the Tolstoy and Dostoevsky kind, and its high-flown demands need corrections from the "British commonsense" as well as a final yoking to the Hellenic "life of the mind," again a curious, pre-Nietzschean picture of Greeks as Apollonian philosophers. I propose that the Second Men clearly figure forth a kind of utopian communism based on a combination of Idealist (rather than Materialist) philosophy with what one may call a "physiological materialism," the belief that human nature has – literally – to be radically changed in order to achieve such a life. All these ideologemes were, of course, current on the British Left in the first postwar period. And the two prongs of mentalism and materialism could be combined in a Lamarckian rather than Darwinian way, by having for example "spiritual disaster... take effect upon germ-plasm" (IX/3).

The theme of the individual's function within community recurs in the conflict between the Martian group-mind cloudlets and the Second Men. The Martian vibratory droplets, the first real post-Wellsian Aliens of SF – they have "prejudices very unlike those of man" – are a cross "between an extremely well-disciplined army of specialized units, and a body possessed of one mind" (VIII/2). Their "sameness to one another" entails the lack of love and spiritual knowledge, and centrally of the knowledge "what should constitute individuality, and its advancement" (VIII/3). Being fluid, they worship rigidity: the attack on Earth is a crusade to liberate diamonds as well as to capture water for their arid planet! However, during a protracted war a conflict develops between the more realistic "colonial" cloudlets on Earth and the centralized militaristic "Leviathan" back on Mars, which is repeatedly forced to wipe the dissidents out. Finally, the Martians are all destroyed by bacteriological warfare, even though this also wipes out the civilization of the Second Men (IX). A good part of the distance between Stapledon's utopian and Lenin's militant communism is constituted by the atheistic but strongly religious streak of LFM: for example, the inter-Martian conflict is conducted in terms of the "colonial" heresy favouring more life of the mind as against the home-planet orthodoxy of radiation. Having won the war, the Third Men, themselves reborn through a series of mutations, learn to manipulate the foetus and, later, hereditary germ-plasm. After a series of breakdowns, and with help of a Fourth Men species of Great Brains, the Fifth Men are totally redesigned, including "the incorporation of Martian units in the new model of germ cell." Only then can passions be affirmed while socially controlled, self be regarded "chiefly as a social and intellectual being," and a balance struck between "the organized community of all minds" and "love of individual spirits of every kind" (XI/3) under the aegis of art and religion. This must have at the time been a transparent judgment on the role of the communist stance as indispensable, even if not sufficient for a full humanism.

My upshot is: first, Stapledon is writing a co-ordinated series of parables. They differ from the usual ones, which need a dogma to lean on and work for, by his improvising a creed of his own, which for the "biological movement" of LFM I call utopian communism but for the horizons of the book as a whole could be called a humanist and cosmic mentalism. Second, for this tenor the vehicle of mutation is convenient but not decisive, so that it can be dispensed with at will. The signifier or vehicle of mutation is wholly subordinate to the signified, the author's wished-for tenor: utopian communism without wars or industrialism. Just as in the Parables of the Kingdom (Matthew 13), it is secondary whether the vehicle is a mustard seed, good earth furthering the seed, or eradicating an enemy's tares in one's field, so here it could be a mutation, a slow biological evolution without mutation, or simply social changes and/or a change of heart within given conditions. However, in Stapledon some biological mechanism is necessary to validate the physiological change that is consubstantial to the new mentality. His work could have been written without Mendel, but it could not have been written before Darwin and Wells.

3. Brief Conclusion

Returning to Darwinism within SF, Stapledon's Aliens (Terran and Martian) may point to the fact that in some significant cases Natural Selection and the Struggle for Life can be used as justifications within an SF plot, but that this very rarely hinges upon a specifically Darwinian justification. My extensive discussion of Weinbaum's short stories about aliens, mentioned in the introductory note, may show that in them the various species' ways of coping have provided indispensable jumping-off points or vehicles for SF plots; however, the Struggle for Life is then reduced to human intelligence as cosmically superior or inferior, and to a competitive will making for sexual selection (most clearly in "Lotus Eaters"). Should this be confirmed by further, more numerous probes, Darwin's supposed two main laws would be shown as fictionally dispensable with. Nonetheless, Darwin's ecological or population thinking has permeated the best

SF at least as much as Freudianism has permeated its lower reaches. Both Stapledon and Weinbaum use an open parable form within a more or less improvised, impromptu doctrine, which is also a clear semantic topology. Since their stances are rather different, utopian communism and cosmic mentalism in the first case, and dissenting individualist intellectualism on the other, I'd claim that my hypothesis of SF as centrally a parable mode has been much strengthened. The parable's shape and some formal laws are similar to what Lévi-Strauss analyzed as the South American Natives' myths, but its vehicle is adjusted to an age where believability is bound up with sciences, in particular natural ones – such as Darwinist evolution. Yet the tenor is, as (I think) always in culture, some alternative of human stances for living together.

Note

1 See the whole section on divergence of character 105–25, also T.H. Huxley's *Evolution and Ethics*, which points out that under certain conditions low organisms would be the fittest, and argues for an analogy between social policy and horticulture that adjusts life conditions to the plant.

Works Cited

Angus, Ian. "Marx, Engels and Darwin." *International Socialist R* (May–June 2009), www.isreview.org

Bakhtin, M.M. *Rabelais and His Times*. Trans. H. Iswolsky. MIT P, 1968.

Bernal, J.D. *Science in History*, Vol. 2. MIT P, 1981.

Darwin, Charles. *The Origin of Species*. Penguin, 1958, full text at http://darwin-online.org.uk/

Foster, John Bellamy. *Marx's Ecology: Materialism and Nature*. Monthly R P, 2000.

Hofstadter, Richard. *Social Darwinism in American Thought*. Beacon P, 1971.

Huxley, T.H. *Evolution and Ethics. Collected Essays 9*. Appleton, 1903.

Mayr, Ernst. *Animal Species and Evolution*. Belknap P, 1963.

Stableford, Brian. "Biology," in J. Clute and P. Nicholls eds., *The Encyclopedia of Science Fiction*. St. Martin's P, 1993, 122–4.

Stapledon, Olaf. *Last and First Men*. Penguin, 1963 [orig. 1930].

Suvin, Darko. *Metamorphoses of Science Fiction*. Yale UP, 1979.

Suvin, Darko. "Science Fiction Parables of Mutation and Cloning," chapter 32 in *Parables of Freedom and Narrative Logics: Positions and Presuppositions in Science Fiction and Utopianism*. Ed. Eric D. Smith. P. Lang, 2021.

Suvin, Darko, "Utopianism from Orientation to Agency: What Are We Intellectuals under PostFordism to Do?" *DBH*. P. Lang, 2010, 217–68.

Suvin, Darko. "We've Met the Aliens and They Are Us: Weinbaum's Parables of Class," chapter 29 of *Parables of Freedom and Narrative Logics* [see above], 2021.

Veblen, Thorstein. *The Theory of the Leisure Class*. Modern Library, 1934.

[Weinbaum, Stanley G.] *The Best of Stanley G. Weinbaum*. Ballantine, 1974.

15

Ideologies and Criticism: An Interview with Andrés Lomeña (2011)

Andrés Lomeña: I would like to locate your ideological position in literary theory. I suppose that you feel close to Terry Eagleton and Fredric Jameson (even Slavoj Žižek). Moreover, I suppose that you disagree with aesthetic purism (Harold Bloom) or certain relativisms (Stanley Fish and his interpretative communities, poststructuralism and deconstruction). I would like to know your reflections on current literary theory — for instance what about the New Historicism of Stephen Greenblatt?

Darko Suvin: I remember a splendid note of Lenin's in his *Philosophical Notebooks*, where he says that to an intelligent materialist critic, an intelligent idealist critic is nearer than a stupid materialist one. So allow me to begin by doubting, not the existence or importance of, but the exclusive nature of ideological kinships. For example, I've followed step by step almost the whole of Jameson's opus, especially since we collaborated in the journal *Science-Fiction Studies* and other venues, while I have used Eagleton's *Theory of Literature* as the best available introductory survey in my graduate teaching at some point but otherwise not learned too much from him. On the contrary, I've been deeply influenced by and am still writing in the wake of his teacher, my friend Raymond Williams.

I loved some of Bloom's early works, say on Romanticism, but when he became an ideologue pure and simple, he became useless. This is the problem with most postmodernists: while declaiming against absolutisms, their supposed relativism is more absolute than that of most modernists. I do make an exception for some so-called deconstructionists such as most Guattari and the later Derrida (after the *Spectres of Marx*). My criterion is simple: what can I learn and build upon from any critic? A bit from Greenblatt, almost nothing from Fish, a lot from the materialist feminists, how to charm people by bringing together philosophy and pop culture from Žižek (and of course how to fight the prohibition against talking about communism).

AL: *Metamorphoses of Science Fiction* is a masterpiece. I think that the first world edition was in 1977. We have lived through a lot of events since then: the fall of the Berlin Wall, the Dayton agreement, September 11 attacks, war in Iraq and Afghanistan, financial and economic crises, the Wikileaks revelations, and so on. Also literary theory has changed: the rise of feminism (Nancy Armstrong, Elaine Showalter, etc.), the rise of gay, lesbian, and queer theory (Judith Butler), and so forth. What would you change of your book in order to update it? Or perhaps you would prefer not to add or modify anything (I see there is a Croatian version in 2010, maybe that is the answer to my question).

DS: It was published in 1979 but written in the preceding ten years. I don't think the book can be updated: it should remain as it is, branded (as Brecht said, like calves on the ranch) by its historical date: the epoch of hopeful High Modernism. What must and therefore can be updated are some of my views – though NOT my values, I dislike renegades. I have done this, as concerns both my epistemological approach and, in particular, some aspects of the Fantasy genre, in numerous articles of the last 15 years, a longer and kind of summarising one of which is the "Afterword" to the *Festschrift* for me edited by Patrick Parrinder, *Learning from Other Worlds* (2000). It also has a checklist of my publications where interested readers can follow the post-1979 developments.

AL: What do you think about "theory of fictional worlds"? For instance: *Heterocosmica: Fiction and Possible Worlds* by Lubomir Dolezel, or *Fictional Worlds* by Thomas Pavel, even *Postmodernist Fiction* by Brian McHale. I ask you this because there is a strong connection between fictional worlds and SF as a genre; I think that sociologists of literature should study how society creates different fictional worlds (that is, connections between types of societies and ontological properties in fiction stories).

DS: You're quite right about the kinship. If you had looked at my work after 1979, say the four other books on SF, you'd have found me using a variant of Possible Worlds' theory. I knew both Dolezel and Pavel, I had my students read them, not quite casually: we were all immigrants to Canada, with experience of different worlds… McHale is too postmodernist for me, in panic flight from orientation: he refuses ontology (that there is a real world out there) in favour of hermetic epistemology (that we can only live in imaginary worlds, so to speak). While my methodologically most advanced book on SF, *VSF*, is an attempt at a Williamsian "social history of literature," in feedback with a certain class spread in authors and readers.

AL: In your opinion, what will be your legacy? How to follow your enterprise from a Marxist perspective – or post-Marxist, as you prefer – in a world ruled by late capitalism and the end of history (Fukuyama)?

DS: I think Fukuyama has been proved totally wrong, don't you? The present crisis of senile capitalism is proof that history goes on, as murderous class conflict at that. Our alternative is socialism or barbarism (for Rosa's by now, alas, bland formula, maybe we better substitute a "communist direct democracy or savagery").

In that perspective, my legacy is of secondary importance. In one case it will be forgotten as an aberration, in another maybe cherished as a far-off precursor who didn't quite have all the tools but at least identified a field and a stance toward it.

AL: I know that you are not a novelist, you are an accurate thinker. Anyway, I enjoyed your book as a really good novel. By the way, could you tell us three or four books, fiction or non-fiction, that you consider compulsory to read?

DS: You are not quite right, I've published four books of poetry and some short prose. This should be as accurate as any scholarship, only less exclusively notional.

My four books, today (tomorrow some might be rather different): Marx, *Das Kapital;* Brecht, *Saint Joan of the Stockyards;* Saramago, *The Cavern;* Andrić, *The Bridge on the Drina* (but I could name 40 others, only fanatics can exist on less than that, the One Final Book).

AL: Any conclusion?

DS: Early on, I wrote an essay in praise of open endings.

AL: Thanks so much.

16

On Climbing the Mountain of Life (2011)

Let us assume we are in an SF world consisting of one huge, continent-like mountain, but for the rest physically similar to Terra. The fauna and flora are also as on Terra, but all animals, including people, find themselves upon birth at the foot of the mountain, and each day wake an identical bit higher on the mountain. We don't do anything to achieve this, it's just a cosmological given of this world. The mountain has belts of horizontal climate, maybe with pheromones and other substances influencing behaviour, that correspond to our infancy, youth, middle age, elder, and old age. Our freedom consists in what we do, while awake, to each other and to our self-understanding, but whatever we do, we shall wake tomorrow morning another bit higher on the mountain. So too shall all the people around us: the very many who are at the beginning above us, those of our cohort progressing vertically at the same speed, and an initially small but inexorably increasing number of people below us, following us upward. We can all meet during the day as chance and will have it, but next morning our height on the mountain will have changed equally for all of us, however we may have roamed left or right.

At the beginning, the fact we can mingle freely during waking, indeed the very fact of being on Life Mountain, makes us neglect this ascension. There is no other way to ascend anyway, nobody can go up and nobody can go down (unless in fancy and in memory), and of course nobody has ever seen the Top of the World. We all simply live together during the day but wake in the morning in our new higher belt, impregnated by its colours and effluvia. The naturally or artificially sleepless ones fall asleep at a given point before dawn and simply wake up higher. Some of us may suspect the way up the world is arbitrary or indeed unjust, but of course, the mountain shape is the only one possible in any world. We have many sayings by our philosophers roughly meaning "the way of the Mountain is unfair," and I spare you the silly preachments of our priests (mostly Gnostics) on why their benevolent or malevolent gods have made Ascension a law for life.

The only thing that changes for a given height (that is, age) cohort is that our view widens. When we are low, we all look simply around us, at our own height and generation; then we become interested in what those above do, for they rule and teach us. Sexually, for example, higher-up males are much more interesting for girls, and higher women even more so for boys. But until we are in, as we say, the 10 veli-s (that is, after 10,000+ daily ascensions) we don't really look down, except to laugh at the mistakes of the neophytes, very similar to our now forgotten ones; of course, for some this happens much later, or never. However, around the age of 18 veli-s – and given our ever progressing age in this epoch of progress, the average length of life is now about 25 veli-s – when the cohort has begun noticeably thinning, some people begin to look wistfully not only at their memories of the foot of the Mountain but also at the lower cohorts. Indeed, for the sillier among us (usually male), there is a rash of divorces at what is called "the airy eighteen" in order to marry anybody between 6 and 10 veli-s, in a kind of magical belief that prolonged contact with a younger skin shall make you shed many veli-s. This doesn't happen, you inexorably wake up each morning at your given heights of ascension, so the new cohabitations usually don't last too long, but I suppose they can be fun for both sides while they last.

For those philosophically disposed, which means seeking sense, the airy eighteens and perhaps the next five veli-s are a kind of imaginary apex of one's personal metaphorical mountain, pictured as a cut-out your ascension has made on Life Mountain: still in possession of fair health and good sight, yet relatively high enough up the slope, one can begin looking at what one has done, why not more or better, and perhaps remedy the worst ascensional aberrations. This has been happening to me, dear Terran Reader for the last, say, four-and-a-bit veli-s, or to make it more comprehensible to you, dozen or so solar years.

17

Some Grateful Memories of Fred Pohl (2014)

Note 2020: This was a letter I sent to Pohl's widow, Elizabeth Anne Hull, in response to a request of hers after his death about such memories. I was glad to hear that my contribution decided her it was worthwhile to unite such testimonials and publish them, but have no notice of this having been done.

I had known about Fred Pohl from the SF anthologies edited by Groff Conklin and others after World War 2, which had found their way into a small group of assiduous readers among young Zagreb intellectuals. He was then to be extolled (together with Kornbluth) as a paragon, to my mind quite rightly, by Kingsley Amis's *New Maps of Hell* in 1960. However, I first met him at the annual Summer SF Film Festival in Trieste, Italy. From the late 50s to the early 70s, roughly, we were frequenters of that rich and pleasant venue in the old commercial city at the Balkan gates. It is there that participants like Brian Aldiss, Jim Blish, and I saw the first Lunar landing, though I do not remember Fred being there too. Most of us were in two minds about it: of course, we were all enthusiastic about the first step of mankind into the universe and appreciative of the enormous technological achievement, but I also wrote an article after returning to Zagreb pointing out that both in the USA and the USSR case it was high officers of the armed forces who were representing mankind.

In 1965–66 I had a Ford Foundation grant in the USA, and spent a part of that time at Yale University. I then returned to my home in Yugoslavia, but ran into a bad collision at Zagreb University, kind of falling in between the two stools of the official Communist Party and the creeping nationalists, which resulted in my resigning my post and moving to teach at the University of Massachusetts, Amherst, in 1967–68. At this time, Fred was my first entry into the world of SF fans and publishers. I remember well meeting him in the Manhattan office at Ballantine's (I think), probably in 1965. He impressed me no end by briskly whisking through a rotary address-file, which I then saw for the first time, and culling from it half a dozen addresses of publishers and other people I should contact.

Together with contacts at Yale, this eventually resulted in my first book on SF published in English, *Other Worlds, Other Seas*, a commented anthology of SF stories from "Socialist" countries, mostly Russian and Polish (the latter represented by four stories of Stanislaw Lem, thereby discovered for the English-speaking fans). As a good Titoist, I had given it the subtitle of "SF from Warsaw Pact countries," which I still find much more appropriate, but the publishers overrode me. Fred was thus instrumental in my getting a toehold in the weird and wonderful world of US publishing, in which I proceeded to have a career – as one of many such authors that Fred has helped.

At some point soon afterward, he invited me to spend a day with his family in his house of Redbank NJ, an uninspiring place across the river from New York City. But the house was wonderful, from cellar to attic cram-full of SF books and materials, which I could browse at my heart's content, so that, together with our debates, time flew rapidly. I had met already in Trieste his then wife, and in Redbank I met also young Ricky Jr. Fred drew my attention to the first three books of Chip Delany, then in Ace paperbacks, that I MUST read. I did and found an extraordinary talent, a first whiff of the insurgent 1960s streets in US SF.

I find these two episodes characteristic for the generosity whereby Fred put his vast knowledge, I would not hesitate to call it erudition, at a very practical disposal of many friends and acquaintances. He was a most open-minded person, quite immune from the patronising tone not so rarely adopted by colleagues from the USA and UK towards people from smaller countries with smaller armies. In fact, shortly thereafter, he tried to edit for some time a journal called *International SF*, publishing translations, in which I believe I fitfully collaborated. This was in tune with his politics, which I was glad to hear him say included campaigning for Senator McGovern on an anti-Vietnam-War platform. It is clear this was the overarching political critique in his fiction, and he further also wrote on and participated in "practical politics" on the congressional and local level.

Of course, we did not always see eye to eye. At one of our last meetings his latest enthusiasm for a new voice was Larry Niven's first (and to my mind best) book, which left me somewhat perplexed. I remember once faulting Fred for some view that I ascribed to his Christian background, at which he half corrected me with "well, Lutheran." But our debates were open, friendly, and accompanied (I like to think) with mutual respect. Certainly I admired much of his writing, during and after the collaborations with Kornbluth. He was therefore, together with Asimov, Blish, Bradbury, Heinlein, and Lem, the only modern SF writer about whom I managed to smuggle a necessarily brief entry into the *Enciklopedija Leksikografskog zavoda* (Yugoslav General Encyclopedia) in 1969, reprinted in the 3rd edition 1980; the entry was written in 1965–66, I don't remember whether before or – more probably – after my first US stay. However, I found, somewhat to my chagrin, that I could not write criticism about friends whom I partly admired but also in some significant ways disagreed with. Thus I have never written about Aldiss, Blish or Fred Pohl. I regret this a lot, it was "the bitter disposition of the time," as Shakespeare had it.

I did not see Fred often after I moved to Canada, except at some conferences – hurried conversations mostly. I am therefore very glad to contribute to the August 2014 memorial meeting at least these few impressions of an upright, talented, and most creative man with a rich life, whom I had the fortune to meet and befriend for a short while.

Lucca, June 2014.

18

A Note on Ursula K. Le Guin's Declaration of the Arts' Independence from Capitalism (2015)

Ursula K[roeber] Le Guin, born October 21, 1929, is a US author of poetry, essays, and prose fiction, mainly in the genres of science fiction, Fantasy, and children's or "young adult" literature. She has also written remarkable essays and ten collections of her sensitive verse – which have to my mind not received sufficient attention, and which I must slight here in order to speak mainly about what I can do in brief, her work in SF and Fantasy.

Le Guin's work has been strongly interested in alternative worlds with different politics, natural environment, gender, religion, sexuality, and/or ethnography. In SF and Fantasy she belongs to the "warm current," based on anthropological sciences and estranging ruling certainties. One of her critics has characterised it well as "identifying the present dominant socio-political American [that is, US] system as problematic and destructive to the health and life of the natural world, humanity, and their interrelations" (E. McDowell). The best known of her numerous SF works are the novels *The Left Hand of Darkness* (1969), which I'm proud to say I spotted in a review as the best SF text of that remarkable peak year, and *The Dispossessed* (1974), which is – as I argue in a lengthy essay – the culmination and in a way the end of the SF Golden Age 1960–74. Her most complex, and I think her own preferred novel is *Always Coming Home* (1985). She also wrote a number of brilliant short stories, my favourite being "The New Atlantis," which I read as a coded freedom-loving parable of our times; it is the highest praise I can imagine to say that this applies to all her works, no doubt in different ways. Her numerous forays into Fantasy fiction culminate in the *Earthsea* series, six novels that fall into two "trilogies," one published 1968–72 and the other 1991–2001, of which the second uses a womanist point of view to largely take back the earlier one. Characteristically, when asked for her opinion on the Harry Potter novels, she said that she found the first Harry Potter book to be a "lively kid's fantasy crossed with a 'school novel'" but also found it "stylistically ordinary, imaginatively derivative, and ethically rather mean-spirited"; a commentator said that "Rowling can type, but Le Guin can write." See for more bibliographical info https://www.ursulakl eguin.com/bibliography.

Her youth was spent in Berkeley. Her father Alfred L. Kroeber, of German descent, was a famous anthropologist and theoretician of culture and professor of anthropology at the University of California, and her mother, Theodora born Kracaw, was a remarkable writer best known for her books *The Inland Whale*, a retelling of California Indian legends, and *Ishi in Two Worlds*, a biography of the last member of a California Indian tribe. Ursula Kroeber got a B.A. at Radcliffe College (the female wing of Harvard University) in 1951, and M.A. from Columbia University in 1952, in French and Italian literature. On ship in 1953 to study for a Ph.D. in Paris on a Renaissance writer, she met Charles Le Guin, a historian, whom she married. They settled in Portland Oregon in 1958, had three children, and have lived there for over half a century.

For her 80th birthday a book of homage to her, which includes also poems and stories, was edited by Karen Joy Fowler and Debbie Notkin, with 40 contributors, most of them women authors in or around SF. All those of reading age when *The Left Hand of Darkness* was published adduce it as their eye-opener, but there are comments on a number of later novels too. The critical highlight for me was Eleanor Arnason's piece, "Seven Ways of Looking at Ursula K. Le Guin," that asks in which areas would SF be diminished without UKLG. Her persuasive answer is: in feminist SF, in anthropological SF, in anarchism or systematic self-realisation including Taoism, in realism, in description of aging, in style, and "in my own writing." This encompasses a lot of terrain and it could be further developed, but I would certainly apply it to myself. (For just one example, I learned from her splendid *The Word for World Is Forest* how gods – or if you wish divine heroes to be venerated by later generations – are made and usable in human history.)

* * * * * *

Le Guin has won many significant literary awards. The speech which follows was pronounced in 2014, when she was awarded the National Book Foundation Medal for Distinguished Contribution to American Letters; it can and should be heard at https://www.youtube.com/watch?v=s2v7RDyo7os. It was preceded, significantly, by her resignation from the Authors Guild in 2009, to protest its endorsement of Google's book digitisation project: "You decided to deal with the devil," she wrote in her resignation letter. "There are principles involved, above all the whole concept of copyright; and these you have seen fit to abandon to a corporation, on their terms, without a struggle."

I shall try to analyse from my vantage point, no doubt coarsening and making blunter, her brief but rich and enlightening speech at being awarded this prestigious prize, delivered before a full house of writers, editors, and other people dealing with literature. It begins by breaking a lance for her comrades in the genres she is best known for, Fantasy and SF, the "imaginative writers." The reason for this is, first, that we are witnessing the coming about of most difficult times, which means a serious *peril for the freedoms* not only of imagination but also action, and I would say even survival, of millions of people, including prominently the best minds of our generation. Such "visionaries, realists of a greater reality" are desperately needed to counteract a most dangerous society, generating a rising tide of blind panic amid quite destructive technological possibilities: to my mind, a nuclear war (we cannot know how limited or unlimited) is today quite conceivable, while the destruction of planetary ecology by a blind and frenzied capitalism proceeds apace. A second reason why imagination is the beginning of all wisdom is the endangering and erasing even of *the memory* of freedom, the *damnatio memoriae* of all the most rich and multifarious achievement of the age of Lenin and the Keynesian Welfare State, from bread and butter for almost everybody – in some privileged Northern parts of the world at least – to magnificent achievements of arts and science enlightening billions of people. In a way, thus, Le Guin's speech is a call to revive truly liberating liberalism, that of J.S. Mill and Garibaldi for example, as against the fake "neo-liberalism" of today that brings freedom only to profiteers at a huge cost in misery to billions. It is clear that we have to "see through our present society" – that is, see what could be different from and what is hidden by it. (Let me add that all readers of Le Guin know that her cosmic vistas transcend present-day politics: they are shaped by an update of Daoism, and scathing about organised religion.)

Since she is speaking at and about a book award, Ursula Le Guin then focuses on "the difference between commodities for the market and [true, DS] literary activity," or creativity. I shall not comment on each sagacious part of her indictment: let me only say that I read this speech as a radical indictment of capitalism from the privileged option for the arts. If I should be accused of oversimplifying, I shall take leave to ask you what is the central feature, lever, and *movens* of capitalism? Obviously it is profit. And, Le Guin tells us: "often, profit is in conflict with the ultimate ends of art"! Gently, clearly, but inexorably, the finger has been pointed. Furthermore, capitalism is expressly named as a tyrannical force analogous to the divine rights of kings against which the 1776 revolution of Washington, Paine, and Jefferson was fought. At the end of her life, at the age of 85, a prominent intellectual writes as it were her ideological testament. What does she end it with? With the final recompense work can have, beyond (but of course including) nourishing the worker: which is Freedom. As the French revolutionaries said in the Marseillaise: *Liberté, liberté chérie*. This revolutionary liberalism shakes hands across centuries with socialism and anarcho-communism – as you can read at length in Le Guin's masterpiece of *The Dispossessed*.

This, dear Reader, is a concise but precise Declaration of Independence of the Arts from Capitalism.

Lucca, September 2015

19

Cognition Is the Esthetic Measure of Estranged Genres: An Interview with Zorica Đergović-Joksimović (2016)

Note 2020: *Professor Zorica Đergović-Joksimović teaches in the English Dept. of Novi Sad University and has a special interest in utopian studies, about which she has written extensively. She is also a dear friend of my old age, and I particularly enjoy discussing how to write poetry with her little daughter.*

Zorica Đergović-Joksimović: You are among the pioneers of the academic studies of SF and utopia. Decades of devoted work are behind you. Today, when SF is established as a legitimate literary genre studied at universities across the world, can you look back at your beginnings? What obstacles were you facing in the then Socialist Federative Republic of Yugoslavia and in North America, where, among other things, you were a co-founder of the journal *Science-Fiction Studies?*

Darko Suvin: Frankly, I didn't encounter any big obstacles either in SFRY from 1955 until 1966, or in North America afterwards. What's more, I was hired by McGill University in 1968 precisely because the students asked for SF and I was able to teach it, along with drama, literature, and theory. This was a part of what Marcuse called co-optation at that time: You people are asking for some power in the university and for SF? – Very well, you'll get SF. For sure, there were dinosaurs – say at Oxford and Cambridge – who thought that Anglo-American literature studies should end with 1814, and in the UK they succeeded to temporarily hobble SF studies, academically poorly treated in Europe in general (in Germany, it was classified as *Trivialliteratur*). I was simply lucky: today one can see I was surfing the wave of an increasing interest and then, around 1968–1973, of the apex of quality SF: Ursula Le Guin, Philip Dick and some twenty more, the translations of Lem, Čapek, and the Strugatsky brothers. In 1976 I even got a considerable sum of money, no strings attached, to organise a world congress on Wells and SF at McGill, and so on. My spontaneous interest came at the right time. Today we see this was the Golden Age of the Welfare State ca. 1945–73, when the countries of developed capitalism invested huge moneys in production, education, and science, fearing the non-existent communism and the quite really existent Soviet army.

ZĐJ: The turning point in approaching SF was your introduction of the notion of cognitive estrangement, inspired by Shklovsky's *ostranenie* and Brecht's *Verfremdungseffekt*, which were little known and written about in the West. What made you confront the dominant discourse of the time that insisted on extrapolation as a key feature of science fiction?

DS: Just these days I have received notice of a conference in Germany to mark a centennial since the introduction of the term *ostranenie* by the great critic Shklovsky and I am hoping to go there and account for Brecht's epistemologico-political reformulation – a Copernican turn, I should say – of that Formalist device (*priëm*), and then for the more than ever interesting possibilities and necessities of its use today.[1] Namely, the attitude of cognitive estrangement in Brecht emerges from performance texts and written texts and enters into a feedback relation with the reactions of the audience, who should interiorise the attitude by means of the exemplary procedures of art. It is grounded in the belief that no entity or relationship is God-given (even if for God you substitute History or Nature), but is made by people within the conflictual history of human groups, so that it can also be modified by people once they realise the causes and interests which have led to that entity or relationship. Thus, for instance, when Galileo watched a pendulum swinging, he realised its cause is the rotation of the Earth. Or to apply this to today's circumstances: according to Marx, the cause of an economic crisis is the hyper-production of goods that cannot be sold because workers are underpaid; if you want to see this in art, go and see Brecht's perhaps greatest play *Saint Joan of the Stockyards* – itself covering the crisis of 1929–33. Therefore no mega-billions for the banks will change this, it will only increase the number of millionaires. Instead, either the workforce should be better paid (according to Ford and Keynes), or the production of goods for capitalist profit should be replaced with the production of goods for human use managed by the associated producers (according to Lenin and Gramsci).

Extrapolation is something I learned about as a student of technology: it is a procedure or action which presupposes that in a certain situation all factors are stable but one, the consequences of whose changes are then predictable. For instance, in Gay-Lussac's gas equation, the volume depends on the temperature and pressure; if the temperature rises at a constant pressure, the volume will rise proportionately. The extrapolation thus supposes, first, that all factors are known and quantifiable, and second, that all remain stable except for one (for example the ruling class repression). To apply this to human, historical and social, processes is as a rule impossible, since their meaning, including SF, lies in the interpersonal relationships – even if the "psychozoa" or surface agents of a story are, let's say, nautiloids, as in Stapledon, or thinking plants, as in Weinbaum. To extrapolate the extrapolation from physics or biology into "soft" sciences is therefore both scientifically illegitimate and ideologically conservative or rightist, based on the assumption of statics and technocracy. We should recall that the US and UK fans in the 1930s and 1940s largely leaned towards technocracy, an ideology claiming that the development of technology automatically solves social problems. This has proved to be completely false: today we have a very high technology and semi-fascist barbarism growing apace everywhere, from the US Tea Party to Yugo-sphere chauvinisms and Hindutva or similar Asian phenomena… Therefore, the problem no longer lies in the forces of production but in the *relations within the production*, and in politics, in the triumph of unbridled capitalism.

ZĐJ: One of your books on SF published in Serbia was titled *Science Fiction, Cognition, Freedom* (2009). Can you clarify the relationship of these three notions?

DS: On cognition or understanding as a precondition for determining what is and what isn't SF I spoke above. Freedom, however, in the sense of the possibility for individuals and large human groups to make a conscious choice between alternatives – for example the Yugoslav peoples choosing to go or not to go into the antifascist struggle 1941-45 – is important for SF in two ways. As in any art, this begins with a creator's free choice to shape a statement and its meaning with every sentence – brushstroke, chord, etc. But then, it is also a horizon within which the best art is placed, to which it strives, and according to which we can value and assess it. If we lived in better times, we could emphasise other factors as well. But in our dark age, when the freedom of people's normal living is endangered as never before and also shamelessly faked with partial and often illusory group freedoms (nationalistic, racist, gender, etc.), it had better be put in the spotlight. So, my book *Surviving the Flood: Fantasy, Commodification, and Liminal Cognition* (Zagreb, 2012) ends with the discussion of Le Guin's novel *The Dispossessed*, where I prove this on the example of her confronting anarcho-communism with capitalism.

ZĐJ: How do you interpret the fact that, on the one hand, a dystopian vision has prevailed in SF, while on the other hand, today Fantasy is on the offensive (*Lord of the Rings, Harry Potter, Game of Thrones…*)?

DS: I salute the predominance of dystopia as a realistic assessment of the state and mood of writers and readers: we live in growing shit and we should realise it. Only we shouldn't forget (to use a metaphor from physics) that with pressure, as a rule, resistance also grows, or at least the purpose and necessity of resistance.

As regards the predominance of Fantasy, this is a very notable socio-political fact, as is that it pushes back SF. The publication ratio of Fantasy to SF was 15 years ago, in my estimate, 4:1 and today it is probably even more. I find this a regressive phenomenon of "weak thought" in Post-Modernism, although I certainly wouldn't deny that a talented author can write an interesting and to a certain extent useful thing in any genre. However, in principle the cognitive possibilities are much smaller in Fantasy than in SF. In a longer essay considering this genre (chapter 4 of this book), I express it in the image of two thermometers in the following manner: the value and significance of SF goes from 0 to 100, and of Fantasy, let's say, from 0 to 40. This doesn't mean that Le Guin's so-called "second trilogy" of *Earthsea* isn't at 39, while most of SF is at 5 to 20. This means that good SF works are far better than the good works of Fantasy: SF can contribute more and better to the readers' understanding of life in the world. That is to say, according to my core thesis, cognition is the *esthetic* measure of the so-called "estranged" or non-naturalistic genres such as SF, Fantasy, fairy tales, myths, etc.

ZĐJ: It is little known that you were or are acquainted with some of the most important SF authors. Can you share an anecdote with us?

DS: There would be many, although I soon realised that unless a critic has a (nearly) complete sympathy with an author, which in my case happened only in relation to Ursula Le Guin – Brecht had died five years before I, having no foreign currency, could go to East Berlin – then it is better not to force chance acquaintances in any way. And in fact, I never wrote about works by Blish and Pohl, whom I will now talk about, it is uncouth to criticise friends publicly unless huge socio-political reasons demand it.

From the mid-1950s, surely for tourist reasons, every Summer a "Festival of Fantastic Film" took place in Trieste, which was also within reach of our meager travelling allowances. I used to go there regularly, the movies were interesting and from all over the world, and there were also writers from the UK (Aldiss, Blish, Harry Harrison, who lived in Ireland at the time), or some especially interested in international relations, like Pohl, and there was I, straight from my vacationing on the nearby island of Lošinj. Thus, watching the black-and-white TV of the waterfront hotel, we lived to see the first landing on the Moon, that "one small step but also a giant leap," as the astronaut put it, following the script of NASA's propaganda department. However, on my return I wrote an article for the *Telegram* weekly discussing a curious discrepancy between utopia and reality, since it was officers of the armed forces that landed on the Moon… I used to visit these three authors (excluding Harrison, who soon disappeared) in England and New York, when I arrived there.

My mother and I also translated a novel by Jim Blish that I then particularly liked, about miniature people (before emigrating from the USA to the Thames valley, he used to work in the laboratory of some tobacco company, I think, so he was well-acquainted with microscopy). He was a smallish, lean man of quick movements and even quicker brain, with wide interests in very many things, except for the social structure of the USA that he hated to the bone. Therefore, he applied himself sometimes to Catholicism, as can be seen from the novel whose hero is a Jesuit – more out of nostalgia, seeing it as a remnant of the old-fashioned concern for ethics, than out of some religious conviction; and he was also a fervent follower of the great poet Ezra Pound, an admirer of Mussolini's for whom he delivered propaganda speeches on the radio during the war, an anti-capitalist "Left fascist." The US army captured Pound in 1944 and imprisoned him as a traitor in a valley near Pisa – where they still have a huge camp – but after some years, his admirers such as T. S. Eliot, soon-to-be Nobel laureate, managed to get him out of there, transfer him to a hospital as an allegedly mentally ill person (which he wasn't), and finally, set him free. I appreciated Blish's inquisitive openness, so the four of us would walk around the charming little town of Marlowe, where I tried to prove to him that he didn't know the first thing about fascism (and indeed, up until the mid-1960s SF authors wrote about anything imaginable except economic policy), whereas I did know, having experienced it as a victim, and that his idealistic tendencies towards collectivism and justice were misplaced in that false and murderous movement. Nobody managed to convince anybody but we agreed to disagree, and it was through him that in 1969 I got the task to write an overview of SF for the annual anthology of the best SF stories. This is when I became fascinated with Le Guin's *Left Hand of Darkness*.

In my career I think I have written four obituaries: for Blish, Pohl, Lem, and my co-editor in *S-F Studies* and its initiator, Mullen. Fred Pohl welcomed me in his New York office in the center of Manhattan when I arrived there in 1965. At the time, he was working for the publishing house of Ballantine and he made a huge impression on me, an ignorant European, by opening his rotary address book. This was a mass of alphabetised typed cards punched so they could be stacked on a little vertical wheel, which was then quickly rotated to find all the data. From this address "book" he dictated to me whom I should meet from the SF publishing and writers' community: the names, telephone numbers, sometimes idiosyncrasies (you can see something similar in Heinlein's *Double Star*, his political novel that is closest to me). One weekend I was invited to Fred's house in Red Bank, New Jersey, a dismal rusty little town across from New York, about an hour's bus ride, if I remember correctly, but precisely because of this he could afford a small three-story house there, with his wife from back then – they kept changing – and his son Ricky Junior. The house was loaded with SF books that he had collected ever since he was an avid fan in the 1930s, then a literary agent, etc. He showed me his latest discovery, books of the African-American writer "Chip" Delany, whose first trilogy *Fall of the Towers* made a strong impression on me as a transfer of New York street fights into SF; I later met Delany and visited him when he lived in London, and after that in a commune near Columbia University in Manhattan. The very talented Chip was coming from relatively well-off Harlem bourgeoisie; he became a rather strict Post-Modernist nihilist and would pout at me because I didn't share his anarchist, first leftist and then rightist, convictions, both political and sexual (I'm not into sex involving more than two participants). To Fred Pohl I once said, in Trieste, "In fact, the underlying thread of your novels is rather Christian, fall and salvation, or something like that," and he frowned and reluctantly muttered through his teeth, "It's Lutheran." Today I would interpret this as "salvation through both deeds and faith," according to Luther, which I rather like.

My obituary for Lem, for and against him finally, because the best service you can do to a writer is to be truthful, was published in 2007 in Zagreb, so I'd rather here present a disagreeable counter-balance to the above fond memories. Who was it that wrote about me and to the FBI at that? It was P. K. Dick, because in 1975 I was editing a special issue of *S-F Studies* about him – which was his breakthrough from fandom to professional criticism – so I telephoned to California to ask him for an unpublished essay, which he did send. At the time he was exchanging letters with Lem, who considered him an exception in the swamp of the otherwise bad US SF and told him that he had a ton of Polish zlotys from the translations, to be spent only in Poland. He also received a visit from Fred Jameson, Jameson's friend from student days Peter Fitting, a professor in Toronto who wrote about SF and utopia, and Fitting's current blonde girlfriend. Dick was in a deeply paranoid phase, possibly because of the pills he swallowed, and he had convinced himself that Lem was the name of a secret KGB committee because Lem wrote to him mixing different languages, from German to Latin (this custom of Lem's didn't bother me, I would write him back using pig Latin). This committee operated in North America through the Marxists Suvin, Jameson, and Fitting, and its goal was to lure him, Phil Dick, to Poland and then into a Siberian prison with the help of a blond seductress (it's not clear why). When Dick's correspondence was posthumously published, the copies of those letters to the local branch of the FBI in San Francisco, I think, were found, only it is unclear whether he really sent all the originals or threw some in the garbage because he was convinced that the FBI was going through his garbage and would find them there. In my opinion, he wrote those letters to redeem himself in the eyes of the FBI as a former sixty-eighter and opposer of the war in Vietnam, so they wouldn't persecute him, he was really afraid. In any case, the FBI didn't react to these follies. Like the vast majority of Americans, Dick didn't have a clue about how much harm he could do to people with such reports. For example, they could well have forbidden me from entering the USA from Canada and this would have put a serious crimp into my plans.

ZĐJ: At one point you turned to political epistemology at the expense of writing about SF. How and why did it come to that?

DS: I could distinguish two reasons. First, I had said about SF more or less what I could say in the time I had had, and I have added to that only a few weightier things over the past 20 years, for instance on Fantasy or the obviously topical overview "War and Militarism in the US SF" (chapter 9 in this book). Second and more important, after the Yugoslav secession wars, during which I lived mostly in Berlin, I felt that to continue focusing on beauty and literature was becoming a luxury for me. Instead, it was necessary to understand how come we had believed what we had believed, where in all this we had made a mistake, what remained of our beliefs, and even generally, how do people and groups of people happen to believe what they believe – and this is the subject of a branch of philosophy called epistemology. So back to the roots of cognition and cognising, which should be re-examined. Whoever takes a look at my book *Splendour, Misery, and Possibilities: An X-ray of Socialist Yugoslavia*, and then goes to my websites http://darkosuvin.com/ and https://independent.academia.edu/DarkoSuvin/Papers, will find some results of these re-examinations.

ZĐJ: From a young age you have continually written poetry, and you often translate poetry as well. Is there some hidden connection between poetry and SF, perhaps established through a cognitive poetics, that is through metaphor, novum or parable that you wrote about discussing SF?

DS: This is a deep, excellent, and in many ways crucial question, which I broached in the theoretical writings on SF that you mention, as well as in separate essays on metaphor and the like. I am quite convinced that every narrative is founded on a certain metaphorical system – if we want to be precise, on a system of *topoi*, the crown and essence of which is metaphor – to which narration then adds spacetime and agents. If we take metaphor very broadly, considering the root of the word meaning *transfer*, then in fact the whole of imagination would be a metaphor (unless it were *condensation*, as Freud observed in what is, to my mind, his greatest achievement). For example, the very notion of the Possible Worlds, lying at the core of SF, is a macro-metaphor. Each metaphor resembles the old-fashioned model of an atom with a core and a swarm of electrons surrounding it: that is, it has a core dictionary meaning (a denotation) and surrounding it is a thick swarm of secondary meanings that would be discussed in an encyclopedic article on this expression and notion (connotations). For example: when Njegoš in the "Inscription" of *The Mountain Wreath* writes, "'Tis not hard for a lion to come out of a great bush,/ within great nations a genius makes his nest" ("*Iz grmena velikoga lafu izać trudno nije,/ u velikim narodima geniju se gn'jezdo vije*"), the first line is a metaphor, and the second – following the parables of the great teacher Yehoshua, or Jesus if you will – an interpretation: the connotation of the Montenegrin expression *grmen*, meaning thicket or bush, is people, and of the lion is genius, the Romantic term for a great man or hero, here warrior, leader, and liberator of people, as was for Njegoš the leader of the Serbian 1804 insurrection, "Karađorđe, the tyrants' whip." How can a lion denote a man: the transfer is carried out by means of the common denominator of courage (greatness, majesty, etc.), disregarding all other qualities – such as quadrupedism, tail, bloodthirst, etc. The way I see it, this is how every SF story is more or less clearly organised around some assembly of meanings in a Possible World, which can be understood only if we take our "normal" world for its basis and then see how this possible world departs from it – in particulars, the most important of which are the relations between the agents, because they point back to the relations between people from the reader's time and space.

Therefore, a good SF story has essentially qualities very similar to the poetic ones, namely, a condensed clarification of relations, to us still puzzling, between people themselves and people and cosmos via the society.

ZĐJ: You are a cult figure among Serbian researchers and fans of SF. Do you have something to say to them?

DS: First, I hope you're wrong because I don't like cults of anything and anybody. Reverence for teachers is another and a necessary matter, but always with a critical affection, I hope. I'm certainly glad if they read my works and even more if this turns out to be useful for their own thinking, which, what's more, makes agreeing in particulars of quite secondary importance: the readers should think and act further and better than me.

I am personally fond of Serbia, as also of some other parts of ex-Yugoslavia, especially because I have had good friends in Belgrade since 1947 and we often visited each other, I wrote for Belgrade magazines and I published a book on Brecht's theory in the wonderful Nolit series edited by Miloš Stambolić. On two deceased writer friends, Ivan Lalić and Jovan Hristić, I wrote a poem "Inscriptions: Belgrade, 2012" ("Upisivanja: Beograd 2012") when visiting their graves. Closest to me personally and most bitter is the fate of the Serbs in Croatia, since with their expulsion both sides lost a lot, the Serbo-Croatian historical complementing each other got broken. In my opinion one group had what the other one lacked – I'm not saying this completely abstractly, my wife of over half a century is a Serb from Tuzla. And this can be seen at length in my interviews given to the weekly of the Serbian minority in Croatia, *Novosti* in 2010.

Note

1 Note 2020: Alas, the organisers of that conference thought my idea was not interesting enough, so I never wrote this variant – that's pure Slavic studies for you… But I did write something similar, see "Parables and Uses of a Stumbling Stone," *Arcadia* 2017.

20

On Splitting Notions: Communism, Science Fiction (The Blagoevgrad Theses) (2018)*

Note 2020: I was asked to open the conference "Science Fiction and Communism" organised by the American University in Bulgaria, Blagoevgrad, in May 2018. I couldn't attend, but we agreed I should send Theses to be read at the beginning of the final wrap-up discussion, in which I then participated via Skype. For both time and recapitulation-with-renewal reasons, I have used here large chunks of my previous texts. I hope regrouping and bringing them to a new point might result in further insight, and thus still be of help. There was a final part about Utopia and Antiutopia that is developed further in chapters 23 and 24 of this book.

> *[What is necessary] is a theory that thinks the whole in its untruth.*
>
> T.W. Adorno, *Eingriffe*

> *[W]hat these Utopian oppositions allow us to do is by way of negation, to grasp the moment of truth of each term. Put the other way around, the value of each term is differential, it lies not in its own substantive content but as an ideological critique of its opposite number.*
>
> F. Jameson, "Utopia and Actually Existing Being"

> *Nun muss sich alles, alles ändern.*
>
> *[Now all, all has to change]*
>
> Ludwig Uhland, "Frühlingsglaube"
> *["Spring Belief," also* lied *by Schubert]*

0.1. These theses are written in the mode of a hypothetical imperative.

0.2. At the strategic beginning of *Works and Days*, Hesiod puts the allegory of the two Erises or Strifes. The first one makes for pernicious war and discord. The second is the good Strife that urges the mortals to work, for potter vies with potter and a singer with another singer (vv. 11–26). I find this *splitting of notions* into good vs. bad a most useful procedure, for it allows both a conservation of cultural inheritance and its radical renewal. Of course, this binary heuristic has to be believably supplemented in any particular investigation by an analogue spread between two ideal poles.

Group 1 – Good Versus Bad Communism

Premise: We are talking about the relation between the original Marxian project of full social emancipation of people versus the State, of political relationships between people and institutions. We may identify the *two poles* as: *a real plebeian, direct-democracy communism that liberates and empowers people (Communism 1)*, versus *the official State-Party communism, at its beginnings often emancipatory but then as a rule devolving into oligarchy, statics, and repression (Communism 2)*. C1 is the axiological sense of the notion, or Ernst Bloch's "concrete utopia," C2 is its pragmatic embodiment in so-called "really obtaining socialism" of the 20th Century, paradoxically evolving from eutopia to dystopia (cf. my "Reflections") – and finally, in the return to capitalism, to direst antiutopia.

Thesis 1.1: To Rework Marx

When the communist State freed itself from capitalist class rule while preserving, in the best case, a hierarchical top-down organisation of production and bourgeois law and while operating on the world capitalist market, the working people or plebeians were not freed from the "capital relationship," that is, the exploitation of labour and all particular group and personal egotisms that arise from it. This was accompanied by other class alienation factors: the legacy of patriarchal despotism, gender discrimination, city vs. country, intellectual vs. manual labour, and ecological blindness.

Political and legal emancipation through the State is, no doubt, a big step forward. It is the final step of human emancipation possible in the hitherto existing macro-framework of States and classes.

However, when people proclaim themselves socialist/communist *through the medium of the State*, they still remain non-communist (not C1 but C2), because they acknowledge themselves only through an intermediary, as in a lay religion: the State is the intermediary between people and their freedom. Similar to a State which professes religion, the so-called communist State is the imperfect State, and communism is regarded by it as the supplementation and sanctification of its imperfection. Communism thus necessarily becomes a means, and the State – a hypocritical State.

Thesis 1.2: On Party/State Communism

But what are the *limits of applicability* of this argument, adapted as closely as possible from Marx's *On the Jewish Question* (see more in Suvin "15 Theses")?

A central hypothesis for understanding "real socialism," as argued in my book *Splendour* about the Socialist Federal Republic of Yugoslavia (SFRY), is that *the Party/State government was a two-headed Janus* (at its progressive best, ca. 1945–68). It was then not only a factor of alienation, but also the initiator and lever of real liberation – up to a certain limit (the liberation is important and the limit is important). Liberation: banishment of occupiers and collaborators – capitalists, bureaucrats, and mercenaries – hence independence of the country as a prerequisite for all other moves toward self-government (Tito); nationalisation and creation of a unified planned economy (Kidrič); realisation of a bourgeois revolution, with universally accessible education up to and including the university level, in a traditionally patriarchal-comprador and despotic country; first steps toward a communist solidarity (the Welfare State). This opened the doors to a possibility of full freedom or disalienation, its emblem was *policy*. It was a road to C1.

Limit: at the same time, the Party/State government was the custodian of a liberation that increasingly turned towards oppression; in SFRY, the oligarchy grew in the 60s into a consolidated class, mercilessly suppressing the 1968 student revolt in Belgrade. In the Soviet Union, this happened in the most bloody turn to Stalinism after 1928 (cf. my *Lessons*). The Party/State machine closed the doors to Marx's full human emancipation, its emblem was the *police*. C2 was fossilising and fencing in C1.

Gloss: The historian can find overlapping causes for this enclosure: the Stalinist tradition of monolithism and non-transparency (obtaining in all States that did not have a radical bourgeois revolution); the strong economic and ideological pressures of capitalism from outside, and then increasingly from inside as well; the unfavourable turn of capitalist world market after 1973 against smaller and poorer states; and so forth. But the stone does not excuse the fallen.

Thesis 1.3: The Aporia And The Alternative

In revolutionary periods when State power is born violently out of society, when liberation through the State is the form in which people strive towards their liberation, in this time of etatistic self-confidence, the State seeks to suppress its prerequisite, the society of citizens, and to constitute itself as the real human fullness, devoid of contradictions. But the State can achieve this only by contradicting its own presuppositions, by permanent repressive violence, and the drama necessarily ends with a change in the character of the State or a change in the character of the society.

Only when real, individual people re-absorb in themselves the abstract citizen of the State and when individual humans have become in their day-to-day life, work, and relationships integrally human beings, only when people have recognised and organised their own powers as *societal* powers, and, consequently, no longer separate such power from themselves in the shape of *State* power, only then will human emancipation have been accomplished – that is, no human group subsisting on oppression and exploitation will remain.

A real and integral democracy, both political and economical, is communist (C1): in it, people and their associations would be carriers of self-determination and self-awareness restraining and humanising the often necessary State. Official State communism (C2), however, may at best – when it is not simply a lying veil for a police State – dream of and postulate the sovereignty of Humanity as the highest being, but this being is different from "really existing" people, the tangible reality, present material existence.

Gloss: Thus, whenever the State (C2) suppresses plebeian democracy from below (C1) – Stalinism, today the State capitalism in PR China and elsewhere – this is a counter-revolution that annuls the beginnings of disalienation (Enlightenment, Welfare State, attempts at self-government). My metamorphosis of Luxemburg's slogan "socialism or barbarism" in conditions of hegemonic world capitalism with permanent warfare is: "Communism as plebeian democracy (C1) or counter-revolution into savagery" (cf. Suvin "Communism").

Group 2 – Good Versus Bad Science Fiction (Criteria)

Premise: We are talking about the ideal poles of useful vs. harmful in the narrative incarnation of a science-fictional stance of cognitive estrangement and of focus on a novum.

Thesis 2.1: On Estrangement Theory

Estrangement always comports and signals the fact that a semantic shift, putting a dominant stifling norm into doubt, has occurred. It uses pleasurable perception against positivistic illusionism and Kantian *interesselos* (ambiguously "disinterested") esthetics. Yet epistemologically, which today means also politically, estrangement has two poles, *the mythical* and *the critical* one.

Brecht provides one "ideal type" of the critical method. In it plotting proceeds by fits and starts, akin to what Eisenstein called a montage of attractions. The intervals tend to destroy illusion and to paralyse the audience's readiness to empathise. Their purpose is to enable the spectator to adopt a critical attitude both towards the represented behaviour of the play's agents and towards the way in which this behaviour is represented. It is therefore also a permanent self-criticism. This means there is in Brecht's plays very little suspense as to whether and how a goal will be reached, but mainly a convergence towards increased clarification as to the nature and causes of the conditions uncovered and seen afresh; the goal is implicitly presupposed and subtending the events. To the suspense of illusionistic theatre or media this opposes astonishment at many ensuing events and the human condition they delineate, differing from the humanising goal and ideal.

The other pole is best represented in fascist ideologies: Hamsun, Jünger or Pound practiced an estrangement wedded to various proto-fascist myths, rightly identifying liberal ideologies as hypocritical and wrongly arguing for a return to simplified brutality. To take a poetically pertinent example, Ezra Pound's powerful invocation and condemnation of *usura* in the *Pisan Cantos* is a major semantic shift or estrangement of those aspects of capitalism that the "Left" fascists were sincerely (though quite inconsequentially) spurning. However, as all such fixations on a supposed hierarchical *Gemeinschaft*, it is a cognitively sterile – or even actively misleading – estrangement: it does not make for a permanent critique and renewal but leads back to as dogmatic and pernicious certainties as in the most hidebound epochs, in a way worse than the conservative certainties it was rejecting. It spurns self-criticism as bloodless intellectualism: protofascism or full fascism is always dead certain.

Gloss: In short, in today's retrospect, estrangement *(Verfremdung)* is a neutral technical term, akin to Shklovsky's only perceptive – or at best esthetic – *ostranenie* (cf. more in my "Parables"). Brecht then used it for a disalienating politics.

Thesis 2.2: On A Critical Estrangement Practice

I have argued (in my *To Brecht*) that Brecht's *Caucasian Chalk Circle* is to be understood as an open dramaturgy, opposed to predetermined religious as well as Stalinist horizons and embodying a directionally oriented but open, tendentially possible, just, and redemptive history. The historicity of matters shown is retained and encouraged but inserted within a formal process participating of utopian expectation. To apply Auerbach's *Mimesis*, it is a figural allegory "far more indirect, complex, and charged with history than the symbol or the myth" (57), but its use of venerable or legendary matters is "youthful and new-born as a purposive, creative, concrete interpretation of universal history" (58). It uses a lay and earthly pluri-temporality in all its sensory differentiations. Instead of an incarnation of the Word, Brecht and his ilk start from a topological and verbal rationalisation of the flesh and body, where the sensual and the visionary are not sundered. History does not end, so that each point reached is also the starting point for new contradictions and resolutions, subject to new estrangements.

Estrangement is then, at best, a periscope or prism to help us see ourselves in a different light, as the stranger of strangers or Other of the others – and often at that as the powerful Other against the powerless, humiliated, and exploited others (say the "extracommunitarians" of Africa and Asia drowning off European shores, or inside our society together with the native proletarians). It is clearly akin to the utopian slogan "things could be not so but radically different," to the novum, as well as to the shocking recognition of beauty as a kind of estrangement-effect alerting us to aliveness.

True, it is one matter to digest a perceptual-cum-cognitive shock, another to pass from an understanding to effecting change. Logically this may be a small and almost immediate step, practically it is a huge and time-consuming leap with a series of complex mediations against immensely powerful rulers. Thus, this theoretical premise demands in any particular case a properly sociopolitical and historical examination *en situation* of the intended and the real addressee and user of art, poetry or estrangement – the potential plebeian dissident.

Gloss: The practitioner of critical estrangement is thus in the company of poets or philosophers, and an ally – in however roundabout ways – of the ruled and exploited classes, she aims at cognition wherever it may take us, as long as it participates in finding out a radical novum in people's sociohistorical relationships. The practitioner of mythical estrangement is in the company of priests – in precapitalist social formations he often was a priest – and an ally of the rulers and exploiters, he aims at catharsis as a sophisticated reaffirmation of the class status quo, as long as it reveals the hidden transhistorical and cosmic forces.

Thesis 2.3: On Novum Theory – Presuppositions

In *MOSF* (and then in chapter 13 of *DBH*) I defined estrangement as a feedback oscillation that moves now from the author's and implied reader's norm of reality to the narrative Possible World in order to understand the plot-events, and now back from that world to the author's reality, in order to see it afresh from the new perspective gained. It is a cognitive strategy of perception-cum-evaluation based on a radical swerve and desire away from the ruling encyclopedia (Eco). In this intent, the novum is its main diegetic device, and it borrows its method from art, science, and empirical production. I proceeded to doubt its univocal use in 1997 (see chapter 8 *DBH*), much before the analogous doubting of estrangement (see the meticulous account of Moylan, "Look").

Concerning science, what struck me was not only that applied scientific mass production first came about in the Napoleonic Wars, and that the novums of institutionalised science have a huge stake in war, in killing and maiming people. The popular emblem of SF, the large space rocket, was developed and used mainly by competing genocidal armies. Science as institution has grown to be largely a cultural pressure-system legitimating and disciplining the world's cadres or elite, in unholy tandem with the converging pressure-systems disciplining and exploiting the less skilled workforce, usually through sexism and racism. It has been largely subsumed into the economy of overripe capitalism, whose systematic dependence on weapons production as well as on strip-mining human ecology for centuries into the future shapes a productive system efficient in details but on the whole supremely wasteful, irrational, and bearing death for millions of "lower" people. Finally, the elite enthusiasm for bureaucratised and profit-oriented rationalism engendered an understandable (if wrong) mass mistrust and horror, reviving all possible irrationalisms, and incidentally downgrading SF into a nostalgic precursor of a Fantasy mainly complicit with everyday horrors: I therefore proceeded to write quite a bit on the divorce of wisdom and knowledge, Science1 vs. Science2. To base novums on formal innovation as hegemonised by modern science grew quite untenable after its overarching novum became the transformation of Science2 into capital: and clearly so when it was force-fed by much Rightwing money into "hard" SF, the "space cadets" of imperialist warfare (see my "Starship," chapter 9 in this book).

But at a deeper level, a suspicion also grew in my mind that the novum – the surplus or newly created knowledge – was finally anchored in the extortion of surplus or newly created value from the labouring people. To the extent that this may be true, it is poisoned or at least rendered ambiguous at the source.

The plagues bothering us will not be dealt with by old antibiotics: progress, expanding GNP, onwards and upwards, reason identified with the bottom line. We are in between two major bifurcations: the "short twentieth century" ended about 1989; the other, economists whom I think well of speculate, may be expected somewhere around

2040, give or take a decade, and barring an earlier nuclear war. The old, including the old New, is dead, the new has not managed to see the light of the day, and we are not sure whether it will in our lifetimes (surely not in mine). In the meanwhile, a too long while, the old masquerades as the newest; as Gramsci and Brecht concluded, in the half-light monsters rise up. The incantatory use of the novum category as explanation rather than formulation of a problem has to be firmly rejected. Novum is as novum does: it does not supply justification, it demands justification.

Gloss: I could here invoke many critical allies, in the first place Fredric Jameson, but I'll mention only three. First, on the novum in general, see now Wallis "Innovation." For the emblematic example of the US SF films of the 1980s, Vivian Sobchack has persuasively shown that their new depthlessness, ahistoricism, and hysterical tone no longer show the alienation generated by a new economic system, but rather our incorporation of that new system and our absorption by it. Just so in the SF ecosystem, the endless Post-Fordist succession of unbearable 1500-page Tolkienesque or military series subordinate use-value (cognition and estrangement) to the brand-name "event" - eternal recycling, Benjamin's *das Immerwiedegleiche*. Brian Aldiss phrased this as, "The awful victories of *The Lord of the Rings, Star Wars,* and *Star Trek* have brought - well, not actually respectability, but Instant Whip formulas to SF. The product is blander. It has to be immediately acceptable to many palates, most of them prepubertal" (108–09).

Thesis 2.4: On Novum Theory – Positions

In brief, innovation has deliquesced into a stream of sensationalist effects largely put into service of outdating and replacing existing commodities for faster circulation and profit. David Harvey has even suggested, after Debord, that spectacles and their practically instant turnover time, that is, the production of events rather than of goods, provide the ideal Post-Fordist model: just as oil, steel or electricity companies can only look with envy at the model monopolisation in book publishing. In the USA already in the 1980s 2% of the publishers controlled 75% of the books published; three distributors handled 95% of all SF and Fantasy. The lay of the land for the novum has changed from Baudelaire and Rimbaud to investment of billions, to science and technology as the racing bloodstream of corporate capitalism, where innovation is divorced from making our lives more pleasurable, beautiful, and easeful. Entire industries are based on "perpetually accelerating obsolescence," most clearly the computer one (Wallis, *Red-Green* 82). Novum's "semantic impertinence" (Ricoeur 50) is in a great majority of cases abused for salesman touting. In sum, I strongly suspect we are already at the beginning of the Deluge. Is the proper position of a provisional survivor that if there's no dry land left – no guiding values – and if God and Communism are dead, then everything is permitted? Or is it rather, how many arks of what kind do we need, who could build them how, and in which direction may the dove look for shores?

Therefore, *we need radically liberating novums only*. By "radically liberating" I mean not only a new quality as opposed to simple marketing difference: I mean a novelty that is also *in critical opposition to degrading relationships between people* as well as to the commodification of human and surrounding nature, and in fertile relation to memories of a humanised past (Bloch's *Antiquum*). I mean further a novelty enabling us to understand whence comes the rising tide of racism and fascism 2.0, and crucially that it is fed by central commandment of capitalism: profit now, more and more profit, and let the straggling hundreds of millions be eaten by wolves (cf. my "To Explain"). A textbook example: Heinlein's super-racist united humanity of egalitarian super-militarists in *Starship Troopers*, with genocidal discrimination transferred to non-humans – read: the dangerous classes or communists – and economics suppressed (see the final GRAPH SEQUENCE OF NOVUMS below).

Further, perhaps a labour-saving and nature-saving eutopian society would also need novums, but just how many? Might we not rather wish, as William Morris did, for the true novum of "an epoch of rest"? Philosophically speaking, should we not take another look at the despised Aristotelian final cause? Politically speaking, what if science is a more and more powerful engine in the irrational system of cars and highways with capitalism in the driving seat heading for a crash with all of us unwilling passengers – what are then the novums in car power and design? How can we focus on anti-gravity, or at least rolling roads, or at the very least electrical and communally shared cars – which could have existed in 1918 if the patents had not been bought up and suppressed by the automotive industry? How can we constitute a power system able to decide that there can be no freedom for suppressing people's freedom?

For, as in Brecht-Weill's *Alabama Song*, if we don't find a way out from the genosuicidal mastery that rules us, then "I tell you, I tell you, I tell you we must die." But then, as I concluded in "News from the Novum," we need a new reasonableness: a rationality that incorporates much refurbished science but also permanent self-estrangement and self-criticism under the eyes of plebeian salvation, including practices not reducible to clear-cut concepts yet articulated in topological propositions – for example, those usually called emotions and approached in pioneering ways by some Feminist theoreticians (see my "Cognitive"). Already Nietzsche had surmised that we have to "look at science in the light of art, but at art in the light of life" (19).

Gloss: As can be seen in the best works of SF in or following the generation that for me culminated in much Le Guin and Lem and perhaps half of P.K. Dick, say by Marge Piercy or Octavia Butler or Pat Cadigan or Stan Robinson or C.J. Cherryh or Ken MacLeod.

Appendix (To Thesis 2.4): The Cascade Sequence Of Novums

1. Graph: Stimulated by Badiou, *Logique des mondes*, without his ontology; TRUE NOVUM + POINT-LIKE NOVELTY as defined by Suvin in earlier writings; SINGULARITY and EVENT taken over from Badiou with thanks and anchored in Possible World theory.

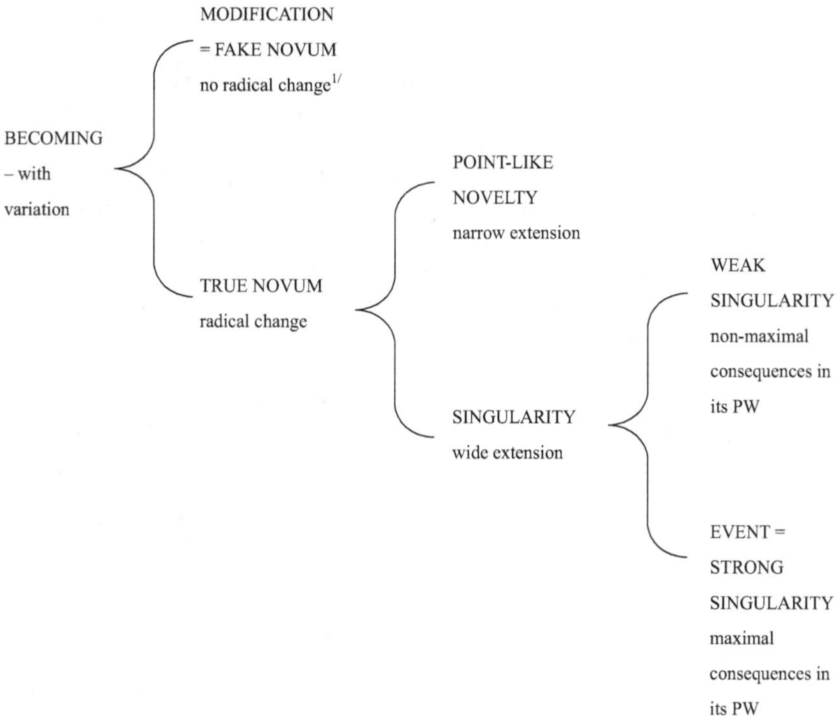

2. Discussion of the Graph (with examples)

- Fake Novum Easy: more powerful and faster machines to kill and maim people – as all military technology – or to destroy nature; all private cars even if they have AI. Or the capitalist *Das Immerwiedergleiche* (Benjamin), though always with glitzy surface variations simulating novelty – such as chrome tailfins on cars in the 1950s or NGOs pushing civil society in Eastern Europe of the 1990s.
- True Novum Collective means of transport with minimum possible destruction of nature: armies without weapons to destroy people and nature but intervening usefully into relationships between people and with nature, as explained by Fourier and Jameson.
- Point-Like Novelty Truly useful but only for a relatively limited purpose – find your own examples.
- Weak Singularity A true and widely applicable novum but with limited consequences for its world (PW) concerning only some sectors, trades or groups – say, nylon. This is probably connected with compromise formations, such as Obama's initial healthcare proposals (anyway torpedoed because too near to a True Novum).
- Strong Singularity, Badiou's Event All true novums as inventions significantly benefitting potentially everybody and/ or the human habitat as a whole – or at

least a strategically large and growing part of either – and having no major negative consequences: say, invention of printing or of vaccines.

Two mega-events belong here: *1st*, the invention of *human solidarity for all working people*, as suggested early on by rabbi Yehoshuah's solidarity within his communism of love and then by the French and Bolshevik revolutions (but soon squelched in their aftermath); and to ensure it, the institutionalization of Power going from such people below towards the momentary government in all plebeian revolutions, called Soviets in Russian, Räte in German, and I'm not sure what by the ELZ in Chiapas. 2nd, *electricity*, popularly also rightly called *light*: without light, no Enlightenment. The two were fused in Lenin's formula for introducing communism to backward 1920s' Russia: "Soviet Power and Electrification of whole country" (cf. more in my *Lessons*). For the mega-event of Communism in Marx's sense of abolition of power and exploitation by classes of rulers over everybody else – that is to my mind the only possible emergence from our Deluge – we'd today have to add, say, three more factors to Lenin's.

Note

* Theses do not suffer notes gladly. But I must thank the kind colleagues at Blagoevgrad, Dr. Emilia Karaboeva, Ralitsa Konstantinova, and Prof. Emilia Zankina, and the responses and encouragement of Antonis Balasopulos, Rich D. Erlich, Fredric Jameson, Nenad Jovanović, Aleksandar Matković, and Tom Moylan.

Works Referred To

My argument would have gotten nowhere without Hesiod and Marx, and then Benjamin, Bloch, Brecht, Gramsci, Luxemburg, the SF writers and critics named, and especially Jameson. I list here first my works (chronologically), in which the arguments treated here were developed at length and where large bibliographies may be found, and then the other works cited (alphabetically).

1. By D. Suvin

Metamorphoses of Science Fiction: On the Poetics and History of a Literary Genre. Yale UP, 1979; augmented edn., ed. G. Canavan. P. Lang, 2016.

To Brecht and Beyond: Soundings in Modern Dramaturgy. Harvester P, and Barnes & Noble, 1984, available at http://monoskop.org/log/?p=9663

"On Cognitive Emotions and Topological Imagination." *Versus* no. 68–69 (1994): 165–201.

"Reflections on What Remains of Zamyatin's *We* after the Change of Leviathans: Must Collectivism Be Against People?" in M. Barr ed., *Envisioning the Future: Science Fiction and the Next Millennium*. Wesleyan UP, 2003, 51–81 [augmented rpt. *Contemporanea* no. 1 (2003): 71–89].

"Of Starship Troopers and Refuseniks: War and Militarism in US Science Fiction," in D. Suvin ed., annual *Fictions* no. 3, special issue on *US Science Fiction and War/Militarism*. [Pisa & Roma] IEPI, 2005, 107–54 [chapter 9 in this book].

Defined by a Hollow: Essays on Utopia, Science Fiction, and Political Epistemology. P. Lang, 2010.

"15 Theses about Communism and Yugoslavia, or The Two-Headed Janus of Emancipation through the State." *Critical Q* 57. 2 (2015): 90–110 [now ch. 5 of *Splendour* below].

Splendour, Misery, and Possibilities: An X-ray of Socialist Yugoslavia. Foreword F. Jameson. Brill, 2016, and Haymarket P, 2017.

"Communism Can Only Be Radical Plebeian Democracy: Remarks on the Experience of S. F. R. Yugoslavia and on Civil Society." *International Critical Thought* 6.2 (2016): 165–89, www.tandfonline.com/doi/full/10.1080/21598282.2016.1172695.

"To Explain Fascism Today." *Critique* [Glasgow] 45.3 (2017): 259–302.

Lessons from the Russian Revolution and Its Fallout: An Epistemological Approach. Rosa Luxemburg Foundation Southeast Europe, 2017, www.rosalux.rs/en/lessons-russian-revolution-and-its-fallout

"Parables and Uses of a Stumbling Stone." *Arcadia* 5.2 (2017): 271–300.

"How To Go On: Political Epistemology for Pandemy Times." *Socialism & Democracy* no. 83 (July 2020): www.tandfonline.com/doi/full/10.1080/08854300.2020.1821338?src=.

2. By Other Authors

Aldiss, Brian W. *The Pale Shadow of Science*. [Seattle] Serconia P, 1985.

Auerbach, Erich. *Mimesis*. Doubleday, 1957.

Bloch, Ernst. *Das Prinzip Hoffnung*, 2 vols. Suhrkamp, 1959.

Eco, Umberto. "Dictionary vs. Encyclopedia," in his *Semiotics and the Philosophy of Language*. Indiana UP, 1986, 46–86.

Hesiod. *Erga kai hemerai*/ Esiodo. *Le opere e i giorni* [bilingual edn.]. Rizzoli, 1998.

Moylan, Tom. "'Look into the dark': On Dystopia and the Novum," in P. Parrinder ed., *Learning from Other Worlds*. Duke UP, 2001, 51–71.

Nietzsche, Friedrich. *Birth of Tragedy*. Trans. W. Kaufmann. Vintage, 1967.

Ricoeur, Paul. *Interpretation Theory: Discourse and the Surplus of Meaning*. Texas Christian UP, 1976.

Sobchack, Vivian. *Screening Space*. Ungar, 1987.

Wallis, Victor. "Innovation." *Historical Materialism* 16.3 (2008): 227–32.

Wallis, Victor. *Red-Green Revolution: The Politics and Technology of Ecosocialism*. Political Animal P, 2018.

21

Poems of Old Age III (2014–20)

UPON THE DISCOVERY OF PHARAOH WOSERIBRE SENEBKAY (SECOND INTERMEDIARY PERIOD)

So there's some hope for us still – four thousand
Years later, an archeologist of the Final Darkness
Will find a written trace & say: "Mirlenien
Reigned here, son of Ka, adoring the Goddess Nut
& the comradely people in arms, in order
To afford happiness. His tomb
In exquisite pink marble is alas much
Destroyed in the Age of Plunder, the magnificent
Paintings only in part preserved. His skeleton shows
A height much above normal. A totally forgotten
Page of history looms hereby
Darkly up."

17214

Glossary: The pharaoh is real, I read it in an archeology journal

A LIMERICK FOR 2015

There is a creature called God
Whose creation is often quite odd
A world ruled by banks
Killing drones & tanks
Does no credit to a creator God.

7415

ON THE DEATH OF A WRITER FRIEND

With thanks to Syl & Bülent

I sit down at my PC
The day is gloomy

Ursula Le Guin is dead
No more verses in e-mail
No more velvet prose steely glance
A glance at this strange world of ours going to pot
An unfolding of strange other worlds of warning & joy
We are orphaned indeed the shock is strong

I sit down at my PC
I go on writing
In the dead of the Winter
What was our yield from Ursula?
We'll need writers who can remember freedom
Poets – realists of a larger reality
Even better: *O my joy, be free!*
Orphans must become parents

But things won't be the same as with her
I bitterly wish this cup had passed me by
Clouds lour rain won't come
The universe is unfair

Farther South than South
Where U went (i like to think)
You're dancing quizzical dragon dear
In a warmer wind

29-30118

Note:
The final quatrain riffs on UKLG's poem on Ea and in general on her *Earthsea* series (where some female characters turn powerful dragons)

- in our e-mails i usually addressed UKLG as "dear U"
- "to go South" is idiomatic for "to die," from Native American belief that the soul journeys south after death, prominently used in places by UKLG

MEHR LICHT

So go now *canzonetta mia*, into
This cruel world where you lack common
Sense, be non-profit but profitable, non-sentimental
Always sympathetic to the suffering & exploited
Courageously try to bring some more light
Air for smogless breathing, food
For starving stomachs & ganglia.
Be

Common, communist, for the commons, earthy
Be of the part of writers & readers, the bombed &
The starved, the Four Whales that hold up
The world: women, workers, lovers, liberators.

Your dress may be tattered but smile upon them
Ironically & cheerfully   announcing & denouncing
Exclaiming & proclaiming WHOA:
We have
Our alternative.

281018

Glossary: *Mehr licht* = "more light" – reputed dying words by Goethe
canzonetta mia = my little song, Dante's phrase

READING CECCO'S *S'i' fosse…*

To Kasia

If i had the power of fire, i'd blow up explosives
If that of water, I'd drown the makers of sorrow,
If the high one of wind, from people's brains
I'd blow cobwebs away – open your eyes, fools,

You can't take it with you, why strut & fret?
Omnipotent, maybe destroy this stupid
Species, for a cleaner to come from fireflies,
Electric eels or hexapods divisible

In two & three. As i'm but Darko, unreconciled
I praise women, learners, lovers, workers,
The insurgent four whales that bear the world,
With robust love may turn it upside down.

1-28019

A FOSCOLIAN SONNET

Che stai? già il secol . . .
questo di tanta speme oggi mi resta!
Ugo F.

What are you waiting for? Incapable of cleanly
Living or ending swiftly, forbidden and forbidding,
Horrific another decade imposes its bidding,
A devolving society hurries, dying meanly.

Once life was adventure, knowledge, glory,
Now it's anxiety, a wandering recollection,

Disappointment, protest and reflection,
Memory of great ancestors that in the story

Shook the earth and stormed heaven. Legacy
Here may be exemplary, a widowed wife:
By irreality find potential reality out, see

By past errors where hypothesis waging
Flowers into theory, and the tight straits of life
Can host the oblivion of disengaging.

28-29120

A STRESS ON SUNSET: À LA LIPSKA

For Ewa Lipska and Marina Ciccarini

> I frequent some prophets on whom i count. As you know, all that is possible suits life.
> . . .
> This is nowhere written yet, tho the words are on their way already.
>
> Ewa Lipska, *Love, Dear Mrs. Schubert*

Dear Ladies, my constant companions, whom I continually
Eye with pleasures from bygone years, still do you remember
The USSR? Anti-fascism? Or a dozen winged cognates, no
Longer actual or possible: student life? Honesty? A freedom
For one and all, from one and all? Forsooth, to share
My gnawing grief with all? A minimally
Survivable winding way of life, track path course ford
Pontoon ferry tunnel subway tube passage – even gateway?
Door – avenue – entrance? Anyhow, somehow or other? An America
To dream of, a rich Indies carnally delightful? Can the fires
Burning the world down still also forge? Our crimes have grown
Up, they are self-sufficient and smirk at the elders. Can we posit
A world beyond evil shockwaves of stupid rulers? Averting
My eyes, i name them: big banks, Big Pharma, agri-
Business, weird commanders-in-chief of mass capital
Murders. Never sated, sleepless the eagle picks at our innards.
And yet there whoosh strange undaunted
Loves still down the Highway toward the Sun, spurning
Diminution, and despite the ongoing tick-tock of the grandfather clock,
Reaping, i keep all revolts burnished, hug them closely to me.
Snowstorms of memory coalesce in a monument not set into stone, for
It is still too soon to be too late.

8-920

22

Orwell and *1984* Today: Genius and Tunnel Vision (2019)

– To the great shade of my friend and teacher Raymond Williams

[W]e look at this display of passions, and the consequences of their violence; the Unreason which is associated not only with them, but even (rather we might say especially) with good designs and righteous aims.... [A] simply truthful combination of the miseries that have overwhelmed the noblest of nations and polities, and the finest exemplars of private virtue, forms a picture of most fearful aspect and excites emotions of the profoundest and most hopeless sadness, counterbalanced by no consolatory result.

G.W.F. Hegel, *Lectures on the Philosophy of History* [1822–1830]

There is, I think no more pressing task for progressive people in the First World than tirelessly to analyze and diagnose the fear and anxiety before Utopia itself...

F. Jameson, *The Seeds of Time* [1994]

1. Introductory

In the first week of the Trump administration, sales of George Orwell's *1984* (further NEF) increased 95-fold, catapulting this title to the top of global bestseller charts. *The New Yorker*'s pundit blithely announced this June: "The postwar Sovietization of Eastern Europe produced societies right out of Orwell's pages, but American readers responded to *1984* as a book about loyalty oaths and McCarthyism. In the nineteen-seventies, it was used to comment on Nixon and Watergate" (Menand). One internet commentator wrote, "As [Trump's spokeswoman] recast White House lies as 'alternative facts,' Orwell's tale of doublespeak read like a manual" (Silcox). This powerful book still interpellates us.

"Practice without theory is blind," said Kant and repeated Marx. And it may be exhilarating to have new theories in our profession – *theoria* after all means vision – but pure ideation needs the feedback from some kind of verification, of which texts are the kind I can best cope with. How is one then to look at NEF in terms of genre and its formal-cum-value systems (see chapter 1 in this book) – not for purposes of pedantic classification but for understanding how may a reader approach it?

What strikes most commentators is that Orwell was always an "occasional" writer, impelled to write in his criticism and fiction, positively or more often negatively, about a concrete collective situation present in time and space: "a particularly interesting experience, or an argument or fear nagging in his mind" (Woodcock, in W-CE 163). Goethe held that the occasional poem, when properly done, is the highest kind, no doubt because vividly felt. It arises as a quintessentially bourgeois democratic form, thisworldly, concrete, and particular, often embattled or pungent; the line of "occasionalists" would in Anglophone literature – the only one that Orwell was ever seriously interested in – run at least from Milton and Swift through the major Romantics to much Dickens and the later Naturalists such as Gissing, names that were also Orwell's main favourites (while Shakespeare and other writers for theatre are obviously always occasionalists). These situations are, Orwell maintains, "in front of your nose," but since perception as well as independent reflection are for a great majority of people deadened by poverty and then by enforced hurry, class prejudice, and hegemonic "common sense," the situations need to be RE-presented by a writer both keen of eye and firm of courage as if seen anew. This *estranging view*,[1] comic and/or elegiac, was both an age-old current in literature and a specifically modernist approach to overload in huge and massified metropolitan cities, theorised by the Russian Formalists and Benjamin, practiced, say, by Joyce and Eliot, with Brecht uniting practice and theory (see more in Suvin "Parables"). In bad times, as Orwell rightly felt his were, it easily turns parodic and satirical.

How can such occasionalistic particularity be reconciled with a general horizon and validity? Matthew Arnold praised, with Victorian certainty, the exemplary writer who could "[see] life steadily, and [see] it whole" (poem "To a Friend"). Orwell certainly saw it very steadily but it is dubious he saw it "whole" – not in the sense of thematically encompassing all, impossible even for Balzac, Whitman or Tolstoy, but in the sense of facing the hugely mounting contradictions by incorporating enriching objections to his steady estranging gaze. Orwell neither wished nor could do this. Even thematically and agentially, he had two *almost* unbreakable limits: his stance toward foreigners and women (though the stance towards manual workers was also rather troubled and finally resulted in their marginalisation in NEF). As to the first, Orwell was in some ways a "Little Englander" – some depictions of the Burmese in his first book are little short of disgraceful.[2] True, he indignantly spurned "the habit of assuming that human beings can be classified like insects and that whole blocks of millions or tens of millions of people can be confidently labelled 'good' or 'bad'" (CEJL 3: 362), and his love for Catalonian workers at the peak of his and their revolutionary socialism remains a shining example of widening horizons. However, he understood as few people did, though as usual one-sidedly, that "the high standard of life … depends upon our keeping a tight hold on the Empire…. The alternative is … to reduce England to a cold and unimportant little island where we should all have to work very hard and live mainly on herrings and potatoes" (*Road* 144) – a step toward Airstrip One of Oceania. Second, all of his naturalistic protagonists bar one are middle-class males trying, and mostly failing, to be intellectuals who should understand not only *how* but also *why*, as Winston Smith puts it. Orwell is imaginatively unable to focus on "rounded" female characters. His only, not too bright, female protagonist, Dorothy in *A Clergyman's Daughter*, obligingly suffers amnesia right near the beginning and becomes a blank slate on which wandering through unconventional societal spaces can be inscribed. I shall return to women and proles in NEF.

"Almost unbreakable": for there is a shining exception in, to my mind, Orwell's best book, *Animal Farm*. It is probably the only fully successful version of his propensity for generic intermixture: an animal fable as political satire. In its allegorical air, ethnicity and gender became irrelevant, and the author's loves, hates, and descriptive strengths stood out cleanly and starkly. Finally in this book, Raymond Williams notes, a class revolt replaces Orwell's stock isolated and protesting would-be mediator: the taboo on the proletarian revolution is broken by the stark simplification of animal workers vs. overlords. Though the revolted animal class is in the end defeated, this is accompanied "in many places [by] a strong and liberating intelligence [that] transforms a bitter perception into an active and stimulating critique" (W-O 74). I wish I could analyse it as it deserves but I cannot do it here.

The world success of NEF, aided by much pushing from the pro-NATO forces and CIA financing, especially of its TV and movie versions (see Thompson in W-CE 80–81, Saunders on CIA, and the useful, if uncritically celebratory, encyclopedic net cast by Rodden in *Politics*), can be gauged by the fact that by the early 1970s *Animal Farm* and NEF were selling a million copies a year in the UK and the USA. Thus, Orwell's work was massively commented upon and fought over, deified and demonised. I shall here briefly summarise one of the weightiest accusations levied at NEF, by Isaac Deutscher, an intelligent anti-Stalinist to be taken seriously even where he exaggerates. He rightly took Orwell's political impact very seriously, since NEF became "a sort of an ideological super-weapon in the Cold War" (W-CE 119, and see the whole 119–32). Deutscher allowed that the text had "subtler" aspects, such as pity for the oppressed characters and "satire on the society of his own days," but these were overshadowed by "stunning the political mind [rather than fertilising and enriching it from the inside]" (120). This stems from an "honourable obsession" with seamlessly oppressive rule, as seen in Stalinism and Nazism but also with significant roots in English smells, sights, and relationships. However, Orwell did not know how to explain this oppression in "the terms of empirical common sense," so that he succumbed – probably in part also because of his sickness and approaching death – to "a quasi-mystical pessimism" (128 and passim). It made for an "extraordinary gloomy intensity of his vision and language and [its] almost physical immediacy," yet "the warning defeats itself because of the boundless despair." History is in NEF brought to a standstill, oppression is invincible, and Deutscher ends by not only citing the famous phrase: "If you want a picture of the future, imagine a boot stamping on the human face – for ever," yet also objecting to it: "*1984* has taught millions to look at the conflict between East and West in terms of black and white, and it has shown them … a monster scapegoat [that is, totalitarianism, DS] for the ills that plague mankind" (131–32).

Some of Deutscher's central arguments I find correct, but his essay does not have the balance I would want today. He was mainly a political historian and theorist, and he fought off a politically incompatible Cold War stance. I think that Williams hit the mark when he concluded half a generation later, "Orwell was neither traitor nor liberator, neither truth-teller nor slanderer. Rather, very deep in his work were *contradictions and paradoxes* – including truth and falsehood, humanity and inhumanity – that he had both articulated and been limited by, … in his remarkable development" (W-CE 4). Williams's booklet *Orwell* remains permanently valuable as path-breaker, and I am in full sympathy with its horizon. Still, this indispensable sketch is today insufficient: it not only demands notional filling in, it demands to be confronted with a "thick" analysis of the text itself.

My hypothesis for Orwell's contradictions and paradoxes is that he was a representatively typical class fraction composed of one person, a view which does not prescind from but rather draws strength from his personal history and idiosyncrasies. This is the type of analysis he himself practiced, most clearly in the essay on Dickens, to which I add only Williams's "class fraction" concept (see his "Bloomsbury") and a few other terms. Eric Blair was born into a lower, professional service fraction of the English and imperial ruling class (the professions were army, administration, and clergy); his father, stemming from a very junior branch of landowning upper class, was employed in the Indian (that is, imperial) civil service. This fraction was "*simultaneously dominator and dominated* [, from which] an at once powerful and disturbed [double vision issues]" (W-O 19, emphasis DS). Yet the fraction's status was sinking, "pushed down by the growth of centralised bureaucracy and by the monopoly trading companies" (W-O 25) – exactly by that combination of the State and monopoly power which was Orwell's major nightmare and enemy.

In the post-Lenin world swept by winds of revolt, this position was for Orwell becoming politically and existentially unbearable. Politically, he found that the real ruling class in position of wealth and power, "half a million people, the people in the country houses" out of 46 million in 1940, was sharply decaying in ability (CEJL 2: 70 and 69); existentially, after five years as policeman in Burma, he rejected the servile component of his class position utterly: "I felt I had got to escape not merely from imperialism but from every form of man's domination over man" (*Road* 134). His embattled horizon was as of the Spanish Civil War in 1936 a revolutionary socialism firmly committed to freedom and equality, and therefore opposed both to Labourite social-democracy, which he thought of (wrongly) as represented mainly by weak-kneed bourgeois intellectuals, and to Stalinist – Orwell used this term! – pseudo-communism (cf. W-O 13 and 55–58). In 1940, he searched for a way of "both defeating fascism and finishing capitalism" (cited in W-O 26), defining it as "a third alternative, a movement which is genuinely revolutionary, that is, willing to make drastic changes and use violence if necessary, but which does not lose touch, as Communism and Fascism have done, with the essential values of democracy" (CEJL 1: 350); this third way between the USA and the USSR was then widely shared in Britain. Therefore, "his account of the Spanish struggle is very similar to later accounts of the struggles in Budapest [1956] or Paris [1968]: bitterly hostile at once to the capitalist order and to orthodox [Stalinist, DS] communism" (W-O 60). But finally, Orwell's lifelong struggle to understand socialism oscillated between reducing it to State ownership of means of production with top-down State planning and a lucid acknowledgement this had to be supplemented by "approximate equality of incomes… [and] political democracy" (CEJL 2: 80).

I shall further concentrate for our purposes on NEF, though I go along with the majority opinion that Orwell's best works are the small gem-like flames of *Homage to Catalonia* and *Animal Farm*, together with a handful of brilliant essays on English culture, highbrow and lowbrow – say, on Dickens, Boys' Weeklies, McGill's grotesque postcards, crime stories… – which he found both inevitably complicit with and yet "to some extent against the existing order" (W-O 23). Pithily, the *Animal Farm* slogan "all animals are equal … but some are more equal than others" remains a terrible warning against mealy-mouthed and lying collective oligarchies that we saw ruling everywhere after the antifascist moment passed – as I argue for Yugoslavia (in *Splendour*), for the Soviet Union (in *Lessons*), and for the "1968 moment" of France and Japan (in *Words and Lesions*). That is why to my mind these writings of Orwell's remain, for all their limits, our Great Ancestors today: as opposed – for all the strong aspects of NEF – to its finally harmful dead end and defeatism, to which I now come.

2. *Nineteen Eighty-Four*

2.0. Approaches

2.01. Allow me to present first my ideological credentials. The first thing I ever wrote about utopia was as the associate editor of the Zagreb student union weekly *Studentski list* at the end of 1955 after my return from study in England (I had, if memory serves, at my first 1951 visit read there NEF, as well as *The God That Failed*). So I wrote a brief note titled "First of All, Analyse," objecting to the attack on NEF by a Zagreb publisher, well-known as a kind of old-fashioned fellow traveller of the Communist party (of which I was an enthusiastic young member). I argued that Orwell's book may well be wrong but that since it is an awful warning against Stalinism, we need it, so that its lessons should be carefully analysed and only then weighed as pros or cons. Two thirds of a century later I'm getting to this.

For the record, I recurred to NEF twice in the interval. First, it was a poem at end of 1983 titled "Eightie-Foure Is Icummen In: Lhude Sing Goddam!; Or: 1948–1984–2048," addressed to "Poor Eric … fashioning/ Out of his pain, rage and dead despair a finally – we must admit –/ Bad book, more important than a score of Jameses on ladies// (Or flower–girls) leaving the shopping mall at five"; and second, in a lost lecture of the inescapable year 1984.[3]

A reminder about method: analysing even an openly and programmatically political utopian SF novel must start from understanding how fiction is always already embedded in the reader's world. A work of fiction is neither a prophecy nor a pain-killer, though neither prophets nor pain-killers are to be sneezed or sneered at. Instead, it is, as the great narratologist Iurii Lotman formulated it, "a particular model of the universe." Thus, it can have no meaning for a reader that would try "to deal with the text totally apart from all its extra-textual relation," and I would add it can have only some authorially unintended meaning for a reader who takes into account only those extra-textual relations admitted in her or his normative ideology. All the presuppositions and conventions that make a text meaningful are supplied by the extra-textual bonds "between the set of elements fixed in the text and the set of elements from which any given element in the text is selected" (Lotman 50). In the terms of Hayden White, both historical and fictional writings need internal coherence and outgoing correspondence (22). This finally means "that the definition of an artistic [or in fact of any, DS] text cannot be complete without ... [taking] the addressor and addressee into consideration" (Lotman 55). Mikhail Bakhtin and Paulo Freire phrased this in terms of dialogical polyphony vs. the monophony. For polyphony we need clear horizons and flexibly responsive positions. Monophony is characteristic of simple illustrations and repetitions of authorial ideology, as in a newspaper article or in the never-ending *muzak* rumour of what I have called disneyfication drowning out thought. Was NEF dialogical or monological or a collage of both? I shall attempt to answer this in my conclusion.

One final double caveat, reposing on an as strict as possible distinction between analysis and further use or indeed reworking of a text (cf. Eco, both titles, and Ricoeur). In my youth literary studies totally forbade using an author's biography to explain a text. The text was undoubtedly there, on the page, and whatever the author privately meant but did not write – including notes or variants previous to the text one was analysing – was irrelevant; the "extra-textual bonds" were either vaguely collective, just "human," or dross and often misleading. When writing my dissertation, I found this was unduly constricting if (and only if) one could find in the actual text on the page a sufficiently firm "bond" to social, including personal, extra-textuality. Thus, when I say "NEF," I am analysing the text cited in my bibliography and no other. However, it would be of course inhuman to disallow a use of the text for biographical, political, or any other purpose, while keeping in mind that such a use is tricky for it necessarily relies on fragments or aspects sundered from the text as totality, and that the critic's purpose or interests have themselves to be evaluated. For this, previous textual analysis and much tact are needed.

2.02. There is a terrible sentence about Orwell's text by the early critic Jenni Calder, attempting to justify the info-dump of extracts from "Goldstein's" book about the Oceania world: "This serves to explain a situation that for most of the novel has been more emotionally real than intellectually probable" (W-CE 145–46). This seems to imply NEF feeds its readers on emotional shocks that are notionally, logically, or realistically untenable – a procedure that would be halfway between an admass horror melodrama and outright fascist obfuscation, thus on the level of Ayn Rand's novels (that symmetrically invert horror into statuesque exemplarity). Calder did not really mean this, for she was an admirer of Orwell, and quickly shifts to his prophetic perspicacity in concocting the tripartite global politics in NEF, but her sentence indicates, somewhat lamely, a real irresolvable internal contradiction – not so much in the stale and untenable terms of emotion vs. reason (cf. Suvin "Emotion") but in terms of textual composition and structure. Let us face it.

This aporia was first identified by Williams, who noted that Orwell developed as person and writer in the years of the Great Depression and advent of fascism, and with relentless courage exposed himself to the "lower depths" in England and Paris: he was unemployed, penniless, later a fighter in Spain. This was the fate of millions at the time, though of few writers. Yet there were serious gaps in and limits to his stance, which was upon return from the imperial colonies that of "a foreign observer, new to England" (W-O 27), looking for analogies between the oppressed natives and the working class and finding them only on the level of existential squalor and impotence. Agentially, "almost all Orwell's important writing is about someone who [tries to get] away from an oppressive normality… but fails… in the end" (W-O 39); this is brought to an emphatically clear point in NEF. Let me therefore analyse this novel as to its agential system, its spacetime descriptions, and its composition.

2.1. Paradigmatic Analysis

2.11. Agential System

Back to Williams: Orwell's central agent is "the figure of the intermediary … who goes around and to whom things happen," not to be simplistically identified with Orwell the author and citizen (W-O 47 and 48). What does his activity amount to? "[T]he deep Orwell pattern [is]: the man who tries to break away from the standards of his group but who is drawn back into it and [as a rule] destroyed" (W-O 46). The reader's entire libido is necessarily invested into this central figure of failed dissident as guide to hell, since it is at the center of the writing all of the time and we see the textual world only through its positions. Yet surely this perennial protagonist and focus is the marker and allegorical personification of Orwell's societal position and stance of the defeated intermediary. The revolutionary war to bring down capitalism of which he dreamed in early 1940s – an abstract but close parallel to Lenin's stance in the First World War![4] – has not happened, and Orwell realistically does not see it happening in "Oceania" in any foreseeable future; rather, faced with the armies of Hitler and Stalin he suddenly veered toward the USA as the least evil.[5] "[O]bservation through a limited intermediary," Williams concludes, "[uses] the limit as the basis for a deeper pattern: a self-proving both of the need and the impossibility of a sustained break…." (my longer analysis below arrives, alas, at the same conclusion). For Williams, a politically valid "active intervention dwindles to a temporary protest of self-assertion" (W-O 49).

A while after Williams's pithy formulation of "simultaneously dominator and dominated," Pierre Bourdieu was defining intellectuals and artists as being the key part of the dominated fraction of the dominant class (cf. his *Pascalian*). It is not necessary to remember this in order to see that Orwell's mediating observer and sufferer is *an intellectual*, however grotesquely failed. Thus Winston Smith, the English Everyman as oppressed intellectual, is – like Brecht's Galileo – obsessed with an urge to understand precisely the deeper structures of society: "I understand HOW. I do not understand WHY" (NEF 91). Brecht's Galileo fails through political miscalculation, but the play brings at the end a cognitive yield transmittable to future generations both in Galileo's dialogue with a parting pupil and the hidden scientific manuscript he confides to him for smuggling into a freer country. In Oceania there is no freer outside at all, the diary manuscript seems known to the secret police from the outset, all horizons are hermetically sealed, and the only bleak future is more of the present, "a boot stamping on a human face – for ever" plus terror-induced brainwashing: "He loved Big Brother" (NEF 307 and 342).

Except for our representative suffering delegate in the text, Winston, all other agents are seen only from the outside – that is, as types rather than supposedly rounded characters. This permanent weakness of Orwell's (cf. Woodcock, W-CE 167–69) is as a rule perfectly sufficient for satire and for utopian and science fiction, which uses the model of the Yahoos vs. Houyhnhnms and Gulliver rather than mariners out of Joseph Conrad (cf. the pioneering Amis), but it leads to problems in the two main interlocutors, O'Brien and Julia. The shadowy Inner Party can well remain "embodiments of the power principle" (Greenblatt in W-CE 116), and the Outer Party members believing clerics in a vile mixture of Catholicism and Puritanism. But already O'Brien is both described convincingly enough and too much invested or cathexed into as a father principle for the sudden mutation into a sadistic torturer to be believable,[6] while functioning well as another in the powerful series of horrific shocks with which the text closes.

And the vision of Julia is much more seriously flawed. Not only is she pointedly identified as rather mindless, though very adept at living in the moment, her only independent activity is a pursuit of pleasure as revenge against the rulers. Thus she alternates as, first, personification of sexual pleasure and private sabotage in drab Oceania, and second as guide to, and almost nymph of, nature outside political control. Woodcock's characterisation of this love affair as a lugubrious travesty may be overdone but it points in the right direction (W-CE 169). Why did Orwell, as I mentioned, never envisage a strong female agent but rather tended to occasional "run-of-the-mill misogyny" in a fairly stock "*combinatoire* of patriarchal assumptions"?[7] An indispensable part of the answer is that in NEF women, including Winston's saintly mother, are the private underclass analogous to the public proles; indicative for the fusion of roles is the superb because overblown prole washerwoman and songstress whom then Winston sees as "she had no mind, she had only strong arms, a warm heart, and a fertile belly" (NEF 251). (By the way though not marginally, the occlusion of male workers is the most significant agential absence in NEF.) For Winston <u>*and*</u> for the narrating stance women and proles are equally identified as, on the one hand, an ideal image of potential energies – private and public, personal or political – that the lonely intellectual dreams of, but on the other hand "[both] are treated as if they were only bodies" (Wegner, *Imaginary* 217 and see 284; cf. also Beatrix Campbell in Norris ed. 133–34). Therefore, the bodies have to be decoded, notes McManus (17, n. 26), by our privileged interpreter, Winston. The advantage of the "private" Julia, herself a low clerical worker, is that she can briefly and marginally, but for him most pleasantly, rebel "from the waist downwards" (NEF 179).

In sum, the <u>*agential constellation*</u> in NEF is one of a petty bourgeois nuclear family: O'Brien as the imposing but finally deceiving and violent father-figure, faint but recurring nostalgic echoes of a soon lost sweet and protective mother, and the lone, so to speak orphaned prodigal son breaking out and transgressing behaviour norms, the "hero-victim" (W-A 96 and passim). Beside this unholy family there are Julia, the mindless masses of fellow-travellers (the Outer Party), for example in the Two Minutes Hate, the warm but stolid and easily contented proles, and the omnipresent power structure of Inner Party oligarchy and Thought Police. Yet behind such a suggested family triangle there looms a kind of Holy Family, with O'Brien as God the Father (supplemented by Big Brother as the all-seeing "Saviour," NEF 19, though O'Brien too is masochistically seen partly as a saviour), Winston as a failed but suffering Christ figure – all seen through a Manichean disgust – and Winston's mother remembered as a distant Madonna-like figure of suffering and protective kindness (cf. Greenblatt in W-CE 116–17). Most important, Winston is the narrative's fulcrum, camera eye, protagonist, and (limited) interpreter, oscillating between estheticizing the proles and confiding into a better variant of Inner Party, in the precise structural position of a shilly-shallying individualist in the middle, his wavering only rendered palatable by the suffering that presents him as more sinned against than sinning.

2.12. *The Chronotope*

The spacetime of NEF has curiously shrunk to space description only, always Orwell's forte that renders all of his fiction interestingly semi-essayistic (cf. Crick 19), that is, reaching for immediately applicable insights. There is a remnant of narrative time encompassing Winston's brief rebellion and downfall, but it is from the outset insistently marked as a lost cause and results in little narrative tension except for how badly shall our loving couple fare when discovered (the answer is very). The time is shown as fully under the oligarchy's dominion, which falsifies the past and puts paid to any different future, so that only a perpetual, shrunken and grim, present remains. It is a time oppressively collectivised both intensionally and extensionally, bolstered by and in fact consubstantial with permanent warfare and missile bombings affecting civilians, brooking no private time beside itself except as deceit and snare – a nightmare stasis without beginning and end, a kind of Satanic frozen and disgusting eternity. I shall return to this in my conclusion on NEF.

The more remarkable is the rich variety of spaces, ranging from repulsive drabness of daily life in Oceania (and one supposes everywhere else on the globe too, unless even worse on the actual frontlines) to a little Arcadian island of privacy and sex for the erotic couple, in two masterly variants: the original country variant of a small forest clearing (NEF 136–45) and the city variant of the room above the old antiquity shop. Both turn out to be no alternative, and doubly so: first, because the secluded *locus amoenus* (cf. Curtius 183ff.) is here deeply shaped by an ugly streak of hyperbolic hate against the hyperbolically drawn oligarchy, which indeed provides a main element for Winston's attraction for sinful Julia as rebel; and second, because they are apparently delightful but in fact treacherous oases, sinister corrupted doubles of the ancient Arcadian escape and the blessed or at least magically sexualised island, if not Earthly Paradise, from Homer to Shakespeare.

The forest glade is a wonderful episode of NEF, but it seems to me history has proved its motivating political point – that political repression needs also sexual repression – to be wrong, a better fit for Orwell's hated Catholic rule, or indeed for a Puritan one, than for capillary capitalism violently insinuating profit into every manifestation of life. To my mind, Aldous Huxley's sex orgies fostered by the Fordist corporative rulers of *Brave New World* are a better choice for the set of elements to be picked out from reality and fixed in the text. However, Orwell's love episodes, and then the final anti-Arcadia of the horrorific torture rooms, draw on two of his firmest convictions. The first one is that "decency" between people is indispensable for any tolerable societal system; I agree with this bourgeois democratic principle, while pointing out a/ that it was often used for enforcing bigoted orthodoxy, and b/ that this would be only the first modest item of half a dozen virtues that a more encompassing plebeian democracy would adopt (such as solidarity). Orwell's corollary conviction was then that decency – beginning with respect for human life, obviously violated in mass State murders and tortures – decayed in England and the world after World War 1. Again I agree: any possible advance towards plebeian or communist democracy must surely incorporate a full undoing of the savagery of ruthless capitalist competition unleashed in the unceasing World Wars, now into their second Hundred Years. True, this orientation of Orwell's was also a very idealised nostalgia for his childhood Edwardian days (he was eleven when World War 1 broke out) that included a reasonable respect for intellect and access to mostly unsullied nature for the middle class of a society pacified by the economic spoils of empire – except for the up to 30% of population "in dire poverty" whose massive wave of strikes was only interrupted by the World War (Rose 30). The breakdown of the empire and decency was a central component for Orwell's internally contradictory stance, which can be glimpsed in his marvellous designation of Swift as a "Tory anarchist" (CEJL 4: 216). I shall return to this in a separate subsection.

2.13. In sum, NEF's paradigm has three main, well integrated conceptual or propositional strands (see W-A 99–100): division of world into three perpetually warring States (prophetic of today even where much too monolithic); seamless internal tyranny of each ruled by oligarchies beyond capitalism or socialism (effective but the easiest to falsify in retrospect); assumption of brainwashing thought control by propaganda communications systems raised to a central mode of domination alongside secret police and torture (much the strongest strand, and the one that has best survived).[8]

2.2. Syntagmatic Analysis: The Composition as Equivalent of Limited Vision

Orwell's standard procedure in fiction is empiricist. He starts by presenting one or a series of experiences and then argues from them – in his terms, first how and then why. This seems inductive but it is nothing of the kind, for the choice of both what and how to present is predominantly shaped by the authorial stance, its insights and blind spots, in fruitful cases well integrated with verisimilar observation but in sterile cases pure ideology. In macro-compositional terms, the description and the explanation are very often not well integrated: even in *Homage to Catalonia* the biographical experiences on the Aragon Front include a central chapter arguing about that war's politics, and then segue into his return to Barcelona where the truth of such politics will come out, integrating the two strands. This "undulant" procedure (cf. Woodcock in W-CE 164–67) is found in a spread between two poles: one in which the use of two text registers is unsure or slapdash and one in which they reinforce each other. Furthermore, pure description will only go so far in a text, and "while Orwell is always anxious ... to provide an opening that will immediately involve the reader, he is so little concerned about his endings that more often than not he goes out with an anticlimax" (idem 166), avoided only in *Catalonia* and *Animal Farm*. His friend Woodcock's verdict is, a bit harshly, one of "the failures of general structure in his books" (idem 169). The author himself acknowledged unspecified flaws in NEF, calling it "a good idea ruined," and even "I ballsed it up rather, partly owing to being so ill while I was writing it..." (Crick, *George* 551 – my dictionary says this slang expression means "to do something badly, making a lot of mistakes"). A "general failure" would apply to NEF if it were a novel aiming for "round" characters, but for all the wealth of acute observation it is not such, nor would Orwell have been capable of one. It does have an unwieldy and kind of broken-backed compositional structure, and the open question is to my mind how far this flaw is compensated for, first, by poetic clamps, and second, by what he got right within the generic expectation of the estranging utopian genre. My thesis is: it is compensated in good part, but not fully – in part because of his illness and haste, but in a major way because of ideological blindness.

NEF consists of a naturalistic sequence of descriptive-cum-explanatory events that could be called "the Winston story" (1) and a second type of texts, itself divided into two, the fully explanatory "Goldstein excerpts" (2a) and the Appendix "Principles of Newspeak" plus a footnote announcing it (2b). In SF criticism, the two non-diegetic texts would both be called huge info-dumps. An info dump is where an estranged story must, in order to be understood, explain its world, agents, and the reasons for their actions in ways not fully or not at all fitting into the standard realistic plot of events and discussions between the narrative agents, often as extracts from a future Galactic Encyclopedia, "Captain's Log" of *Star Trek* or similar. The use of two different text registers, of a broken-backed composition, and of info dumps was pioneered by More's *Utopia*, for it faced the same narrative problems as later SF: to reconcile diegetic travel through a fully alternate world with readers' understanding of it. Both the "realistic" justification and the presumed authorship of Orwell's two non-diegetic texts are rather complex.

The Goldstein excerpts are cleverly justified as an Inner Party fabrication, possibly in part by O'Brien, but they function primarily as an indispensable stop-gap compensation for the authorial failure to discuss the "why" of Oceania, and remain weighty as the text's only available explanation. Though in Oceania banned as oppositional, they are deeply complicit with the ruling system, arguing for its possibility and ineluctability. They are at some points perfunctorily interrupted by Winston's brief discussion of them with a bored Julia; I got the impression this was a kind of apotropaic warding off so that the average reader would not get bored too. For their exactitude is exacting in its cyclical and cynical Hobbesian vision, the dry dreariness of history simply as power struggle where the rulers might have changed (but no longer do), yet the ruled necessarily lose.

As for the Newspeak appendix, perhaps as important as the rest of the book, no author or authors are specified – no wonder, it is realistically incompatible with the atmosphere and set-up of Oceania. It is announced by a strange little footnote at the book's beginning, saying "Newspeak is the official language of Oceania," and then referring to the Appendix. Their common narrative point of view is not the same as in the Winston story for it is, as in the Goldstein strand, "conscious of its audience," uses the past tense (Sanderson 588, whose lucid argument I accept), and positions itself somewhere between 1984 and 2050; yet it is to my mind indefensible to assume some deep plot by Orwell that this should add a totally different perspective to the Winston story by situating a collective happy ending in its future. True, Orwell saw such a procedure in London's *Iron Heel* and may or may not have entertained some such idea at the outset. But within his decision for integral gloom and doom, the Newspeak strand seems rather a parallel brilliant, if flawed and compositionally displaced effort that could well have been a separate satirical essay. It was written out of the same well of indignation but only joined to the plotted strand "at the waist," as a separate Siamese twin, whenever language politics come in or (once) when Winston is mentioned by name. The Newspeak strand has a powerful central perception of the political use of language forms, crystallising mainly in the neologistic portmanteau words. It is also internally inconsistent; as Williams notes (W-A 98), it shuttles in perhaps momentarily effective but illogical ways between the time stance of the Olympian historian similar to Goldstein ("It is with the final perfected version … that we are concerned here") and of the indignant author ("… many Newspeak sentences … would be barely intelligible to an English speaker *of our own day*" – emphasis DS). Furthermore, it is based on and suffused by conservative nostalgia: once upon a time, it seems (in Orwell's childhood?), language was "without any silences or erasures of its own, without any historicity at all before being so degraded; and 'doublethink' describes the same process in the sphere of … a mode of thinking which must once also have been outside history…" (McManus 14). However, this is not to deny the brilliant insights, for example in the three politico-ontological slogans of "A is B" form. These have proved durable.

The other two texts, "Winston's" mainly descriptive and "Goldstein's" argumentative strand, are united by the believable *realistic tone*, rebellious, more or less weary, yet precisely aimed. It is the tone of a directly involved and expert protagonist. Winston is an outraged sufferer, the aggrieved *homme moyen sensuel* yearning for some peace and modest comfort, while Goldstein is Orwell's broken-off attempt at indignant overview; both are in Bakhtin's sense monological, just as the agents in both are opaque monads to each other, relating only on a power scale (though the sex subplot might be a Benthamite felicific calculus). I would call the tone a neo-Swiftian one translated into the high journalism of early 20th Century; it is necessarily more variegated than Swift's in a much larger and more complicated world, but has the same type of inventive and controlled disgust discharging itself in limpid and sharp observation of a lived-in semantic (or should one say a-semantic?) world. This tone is the only common element of the three texts of NEF. However, Orwell knows no longer quite where his reader stands so that the disgust often dissolves into Winston's gloom and doom, or is disguised as a string of mini-facts, or is conservative nostalgia (of which even the Newspeak essay is not free).

The Winston story, our plot backbone, undulates in and out of different interactions: first with his diary, an *alter ego* often as third-person eyewitness, then with Julia, and finally with O'Brien, the traitorous father figure (cf. McManus 13–14). It proceeds through and by means of two emotionally drenched and contagious components, *passive disgust* and *sense of doom*. It has a plangent dirge-like undercurrent announcing absolutely inevitable doom for Winston – and Julia, though we do not see her doom – but also for all humanistic efforts at understanding and decency; in this sense Winston is for a sarcastic O'Brien "the last man" (NEF 309–10). The main poetic clamp or brace of this strand is the repetition with incrementation of the "Oranges and Lemons" ditty, while passive existential disgust oozes from all we see through Winston, including his low self-esteem. The proceeding or device (*priëm*) of sophisticated recurrences of foreboding building up to a climax stems from lyrical poetry, of which Orwell was a good connoisseur and reasonably good practitioner right down to his appreciation of a young Dylan Thomas (though ideological obstinacy made him blind to young Auden). For all their naturalistic gloom, these powerful elements in NEF establish a distance both to a realistic novel and to an old-fashioned utopian story that makes *one* big solid point – say More's communism and no gold. This is part of a larger modernist sea-change, best put perhaps by John Berger's great novel *G.* as "Never again shall a single story be told as though it were the only one" (133), but signalled already by the recomplications of narrative voices and spaces in Wells's *A Modern Utopia* and Zamyatin's *We*, and issuing in Le Guin's "ambiguous utopia" as well as Moylan's "critical utopia" and then "critical dystopia" (in his *Demand* and *Scraps*). On the other hand, dystopia is here immeasurably strengthened by nitty-gritty realistic believability, which might be Orwell's main contribution to this genre and had a major influence in the 1950s–60s.

Thus the composition of NEF is multiply split, with complex interactions between the strands, reminiscent of the rather clearer Great Ancestor *Utopia*.

2.3. Making Sense of NEF

2.3.1. "Tory Anarchism" as Fertile but Limited Vision

What is Tory anarchism? Discussing Swift, Orwell found it meant "despising authority while disbelieving in liberty and preserving the aristocratic outlook while seeing clearly that the existing aristocracy is degenerate and contemptible …, [and being unable] to believe that life ... could be made worth living" (CEJL 4: 216–17). In spite of the strong love/hate involved here, Orwell claimed this appellation for himself early on (Crick, *George* 174, 205, 211, and passim), and I believe it was a lasting, though not the only, stance of his.[9] It meant for Orwell positively a fierce and unremitting opposition to ruling ideas and practices in the name of conserving past values, such as confidence in personal experience – whence his admiration for Joyce and Henry Miller – often inflated as a pure model beyond what was in the past actually available to most people and at most times. Negatively, it is an inability to see how the putative past values could be integrated in a realistic societal future, since the present ruling class of the UK is degenerate and no radical alternative (for which Orwell was in desperate search from the late 1930s on) has proved viable but only the threat of new oligarchies. Its ground bass – what NEF got absolutely right, miles ahead of anybody else I can think of in Anglophone prose – is the misery and wretchedness of the poor under a regime of perpetual warfare. Orwell in some of Burnham/Trotsky's clothing put it splendidly in Goldstein's chapter "War Is Peace":

> The problem was how to keep the wheels of industry turning without increasing the real wealth of the world. Goods must be produced, but they must not be distributed. And in practice the only way of achieving this was by continuous warfare.
>
> The essential act of war is destruction, not necessarily of human lives, but of the products of human labour. War is a way of shattering to pieces, or pouring into the stratosphere, or sinking in the depths of the sea, materials which might otherwise be used to make the masses too comfortable, and hence, in the long run, too intelligent…. (NEF 220)

In brief, as Rousseau and Madison well knew, war is being waged to dominate one's own people as well as, if not rather than, enemy territories.

Of course, Goldstein's central thesis, that there could be three "self-contained economies" on this globe not needing wars for markets and raw materials, is plain wrong, which invalidates the whole NEF system. And today, the "War Is Peace" thesis is repeated assiduously by the US government and all the aligned media from the 1990s on – though, as the present set-up is not yet seamlessly fascist, this is usually put in reverse, "Peace Is War." Therefore we must have, as in NEF, a threatening enemy – after Soviet so-called communism, it would be first drugs then terrorism, and secondarily Russia, China or Iran.

The blind spots in NEF, whether we describe its author as Tory anarchist or not, concern to my mind two quite central matters. The first is, as I suggested about the love affair, a blinkered and stunted view of women and femininity, if you wish of the female yin to Orwell's strong but rather limited macho yang. This of course obtains not simply in the complementarity of male and female (as in the sexual coupling of NEF) but also in all human – and for Daoism even in natural – relationships such as Winter and shade vs. Summer and brightness, or left vs. right, or disorder and order in sociopolitics. This last couple seems what Orwell was interestingly getting at in Tory anarchism, but he never managed to make stubborn Swiftian disgust and resistance into a consistent and liberating horizon. He could mimic James Burnham's or Andrés Nin's texture (cf. Crick, *George* 365), and he knew well what he hated and rejected in detail – as in the famous list from "Inside the Whale" ranging from concentration camps to Hollywood movies and tinned food. However, his "Goldsteinian" attempt at theoretical overview starts with a sound what – which is more than a huge majority did in his time – yet ends in an improvised and unbelievable why: it is not only the Thought Police that prevent Winston from reading the upshot of Goldstein, it is Orwell himself who defaults here.

The second blind spot or hole in NEF, caused by hope-denying conservative anarchism, is a tenable view of ruling class power. The split textual strands are symptoms of what Williams found was a deeper double vision, which might be identified as *being revolted against the rulers but not believing the revolt can succeed*. To begin with, Orwell follows his fellow radical socialist and Little Englander William Morris in disliking both economics and mass production: they are in Goldstein simply supposed to exist somewhere, perhaps in *News from Nowhere*'s underground caverns.[10] At the very beginning of the Goldstein text, a specifically anti-Marxist view of history is introduced: where the *Communist Manifesto* begins (together with Engels's footnote, present in all of its editions since 1888) with "all written history [of] … hitherto existing society is the history of class struggles" (Marx and Engels 14), which is elsewhere explained as a binary one, on the model of "bourgeois vs. proletarian," Orwell begins with a deviant counter-project: "Throughout recorded time … there have been three kinds of people in the world, the High, the Middle and the Low" (NEF 213). But his text then refuses any active status to the mindless Low, and the rich Marxist dichotomy of oppressor vs. oppressed is reduced to the new one of the Middle against the High, or intellect and impotence vs. cynical power. As he formulated it à propos of Ernest Bramah's dystopia *The Secret of the League*: "the middle class… wrongly imagined that they were menaced from below and not from above" (CEJL 2: 32).

No economics entails in NEF no fusion of class with economic interest and no class struggle. As I mentioned in 2.11, male workers are glaringly absent from NEF; this literal blind spot extends to capitalism on the level of conceptual explanation.

Here an insoluble problem arises out of lack of solidarity between the intellectual and the labour of "millions of coolies" on which – as Orwell often reiterated – his up to a point privileged status depends. His talent has an aggrieved, dominated-class "anti" edge, but as he precisely put it, it is a view from "the lower-upper-middle class ... the [shabby-genteel] layer of society [not far from the bottom income of] £300 a year" (*Road* 112). In NEF, this view forgets there is beneath it another, even lower class that it does not want to see – even in the above quote about Bramah those "below" are faceless! – the proles[11]. This view uses naturalistic events of the Dickens-to-Wells-and-Gissing school "in sharp detail, and the sense of a climate, an atmosphere, is memorably created…. Class … is described mainly in terms of differences and snobberies in accent, clothes, tastes, furnishing, food" (W-O 23). But class is never seen in terms of exploitation of labour: only its empirical manifestations and then its transcendental and transhistorical power are noticed. The Winston story is entirely built on *hugely unequal binary conflict* of a puny sick loner against a total State:

> …on one side the regime, its success, on the other, the man, just him, his rage and pain and despair. There is nothing outside of him which can be figured in any positive way…. The novel has no content to give to his rebellion except the sheer fact of it. (McManus 31)[12]

It follows that *power, as the constitutive and all-pervasive adversary of a rational but impotent intellectual, must be (first) irrational and (second) invincible*. Flying in face of all recorded history, the reason for power becomes power. It is not a sociopolitical reason, it is in NEF the reason of power-hunger and sadism (that Orwell blamed *Brave New World* for leaving out), an eternal or "natural" psychology.[13] This is quite untenable as an either Weberian or Marxist explanation of a ruling class, and no sustainable class psychology either.

Lévi-Straussian Table of Oppositions

OUTCOME/QUALITIES	QUASI-CLASS	VALUE HORIZON
SUCCESS – WINNING	Inner Party (the oppressors)	Irrational Power
FAILURE – LOSING	Winston (the oppressed)	Intellect (how & why)

The immediate predecessor from which Orwell drew much about power was the discussion in the Philomath club of London's *Iron Heel*, where the main capitalist spokesman declares: "We are in power.... It is the king of words – Power. Not God, not Mammon, but Power" (384). This reach-me-down Nietzscheanism was bolstered by Orwell's readings of Borkenau and Burnham. Thence O'Brien's final truth about the Inner Party in his torture diatribe, directed equally against Marx and Jefferson: "Not wealth or luxury or long life or happiness: only power, pure power.... The object of power is power" (NEF 302). This "inevitability of the will-to-power in every political intellectual" fed directly into stamping out of efforts at dissidence in the USA and other NATO countries, and indicates the deep kinship of antiutopia with reactionary anti-intellectualism (Wegner, *Imaginary* 227, and see Jameson, *Archaeologies* 171).

True, Orwell oscillated for years whether the total darkness is going to come about: "Some days I know it's impossible, other days I know it's inevitable" (*Coming Up for Air* 160, cited by Crick, *George* 371, and cf. 370–86). What matters is that when writing NEF, he plumped for inevitability, for a fully "occluded future" (Wegner, *Imaginary* 124 and 255). The suffering in the name of urges for decency and knowledge remains, but is left bombinating in a societal vacuum. As he himself best phrased it against Burnham, "*Power worship blurs political judgment because it leads, almost unavoidably, to the belief that present trends will continue*" (CEJL 4: 174, emphasis DS – see Orwell's other excellent objections on 164–81). NEF, where he forgot it, must be judged by this insight.

In sum, Orwell is weak and quite erratic on the synoptic view from above, what Brecht called the events behind the events – and therefore on structure. What is more, the affinity to Swift extends to Orwell's frequent impulse toward extremes and employment of hyperbole: "all or nothing" (Rees 103–04)! His binary oscillations between extremes can lead to a mutual neutralisation or a forked tongue. Neutralisation and stalemate: the rebelling talent makes for revolt, the hyperbolic and anarchoid predilection makes for the revolt's absolutely unavoidable failure. Or: on the one hand his ideal of democratic socialism means "[a] complete abandonment of the upper-class and middle-class attitude to life" (*Road* 146), on the other hand the narrative logic of NEF is built on the impossibility of its coming about (cf. Wegner, *Imaginary* 190–91), while the system is most infelicitously called Ingsoc (English socialism – Orwell at moments believed no less than that "National Socialism *is* a form of Socialism," CEJL 2: 25).[14] Forked tongue: as Jameson has pinpointed, in NEF "the premise – that no science or real thinking is possible – is contradicted by the sheerly scientific perfection of the antiutopian machinery of state surveillance that is then pressed into service as a causal explanation for just that … state of affairs in which no science is possible" (*Seeds* 58). Or: in tandem with often well-motivated horror, Orwell had a tendency after 1936 toward flight into the symmetrically extreme and quite daft belief into immediate socialist revolution as, for one example out of many, his May 1942 prophecy of imminent "revolution or disaster" in UK (CEJL 2: 214), which underlined his being frankly out of his depth.

Unfortunately in the extant text of NEF the disaster alternative, helped by his illness, totally dominated him. It is a far cry from the crystal clarity of Zamyatin, who deploys an equally vigorous, indeed more coherent, narration to prove there can never be a "final" revolution – nor, *a fortiori*, a final counter-revolution (cf. Suvin, *MOSF* 283–87).

No doubt, there remain in NEF great strengths: first, its force lies in the disgust, accompanied by the nostalgia for what has been lost: "the elegiac sense of the loss of the past, and the uncertainty of memory" (Jameson, *Archaeologies* 200). Second, where his thematics were very limited, his textural skill was penetrating. The best encapsulation I know is by Woodcock:

> His descriptions are magnificent; his polemical arguments, even when they occur in the wrong places, are always intensely readable; every one of his books contains episodes which most writers would give years of their life to have written; his style in the narrower sense, his way with words, is inimitable (W-CE 172).

NEF was written in order to stun; it still stuns.

However, Orwell may today, after all, have a Parthian shot. There is an important secondary, though not a full, excuse for Orwell's error: *the long duration rise of fascism*. He noticed very well that and how new amoral power-holders of the World Wars epoch had dispensed with the traditional religious props and adopted a monophonic neo-Nietzscheanism. Such Will To Power is fully present in fascist Master Race theory, while Stalinism had to don a mask featuring the original Leninist idea of doing it for the benefit of the world masses it leads (in the final dialogue, O'Brien sneeringly refutes the Stalinist option and affirms the Nazi one). A significant example, valid again today: "the re-institution of slavery.… The forced-labour camps all over Europe and North Africa … are simple chattel-slavery… [with] conditions probably worse than they were on the American cotton plantations" (CEJL 2: 259 – Orwell had not yet gotten to debt-slavery). The devolution of capitalist politics toward fascism is, no doubt, a quite essential event of Orwell's and then of our post-1990 time, and he was one of the first to draw consequences from it; unfortunately, without integrating into power politics a critique of political economy, they were generously concerned but half-baked and therefore wrong consequences. How the Nazis achieved a comfortable symbiosis with big capital or how the Stalinists replaced it by a growing apparatus of State "capital" never was of interest to him. His vision is of a world ruled by the Manicheans' Satan, and we are lost. The independent lower middle class intellectual cannot win against the big mass apparati.

2.3.2. The Totalitarianism Snare

Autobiography again: the second thing I wrote in our field was a brief 1958 survey of SF and utopias with the title from my recently discovered Zamyatin, "A Sailor on the Mast." Following him, I argued that what the Stalinist censors classified as "harmful" literature, because it was breaking new and heretofore unknown ground, is indispensable to socialism because it challenges "calcification, sclerosis, crust, moss, quiescence" (Zamyatin 109). A dozen years later I spelled this fully out in pages devoted to him, first in an article and then in my *MOSF*, which argued his was not an anti-Soviet antiutopia but mainly a dystopian awful warning by a revolutionary who believed he was going the Bolsheviks one better, against the loss of freedom both in western and eastern Europe. This quite Marxian stance also subtends my book on SFR Yugoslavia (see Suvin, "15 Theses").

In that vein I am arguing now that the central model for the totally controlled and militarised society of NEF is an uneasy and inconsistent amalgam between the Nazi set-up and what Orwell perceived as Stalinist Russia, with odd bits of Catholic Inquisition times (the proles are not mobilised but flooded with propaganda) and other spacetimes thrown in. The Nazi strand accounts for the central features both of power for its own sake (no doubt in Germany papered over by the fake, nationalist science of racism in which Orwell was curiously disinterested) and of there being no way out, the Stalinist one is obvious in the Big Brother vs. Goldstein – the Stalin-Trotsky – relation as well as many minor details. The image of "a boot crashing down on a human face," used to great effect in NEF, characterised the Nazi goose-step in Orwell's *The Lion and the Unicorn* (cited in Crick, *George* 404). From a text of Orwell's about the Nazis (CEJL 2: 259) stems also the "nightmare world in which the Leader, or some ruling clique, controls not only the future but the past. If the Leader says of such and such an event, 'It never happened' – well, it never happened. If he says two and two are five – well, two and two are five"; but then he also read Eugene Lyons's eyewitness report of Moscow being awash in lights proclaiming "2+2 = 5," which actually meant a quite different thing, that is, the Five-year plan will be accomplished in only four. The fusion of the two into "totalitarianism" was powerfully buttressed and validated by localising it into an impoverished England drenched in the shabby, run-down sense perceptions from Orwell's novels and articles after 1929. Cold War blinkers have occulted the fact that Oceania is descriptively mainly a nightmare England of the Great Depression "lower depths," composed mostly of "all that he hated and disliked in his own surroundings" – the filth, drabness, and monotony of the English industrial suburb, the food rationing and government control in World War Britain, the rubbishy newspapers, the government's heavy black-and-white propaganda, etc. (see Deutscher in W-CE 126; the Ministry of Truth is a hyperbolic BBC plus Ministry of Food where Orwell's wife worked – see Crick, *George* 434). This was refunctioned as an inescapably closed horizon ruled by a crude mix of British colonial, Nazi, and Stalinist violence but with the persuasiveness of medieval Catholic plus US admass brainwashing (for the former cf. Wegner, *Imaginary* 201).

Nonetheless, the determining horizon of NEF is arrived at by "the substitution of communism [of the Stalinist stripe, DS] for fascism as the totalitarian threat" within a postwar choice for the USA – about which Orwell knew precious little – as against the USSR (W-O 67).[15] Jameson's summary distinguishes three levels of NEF: first, an articulation of what Orwell knew or assumed about the contingent history of Stalinism; second, "its ahistorical universalization into a baleful vision of human nature as an insatiable and lucid hunger for power and its exercise, and finally the truly pathological and obsessive fixation on this conjuncture … in conversion into a life passion" (*Archaeologies* 200). All of this went had in hand with a total loss of confidence in the survival of freedom: as Orwell wrote after the atomic bomb, "political behaviour is largely non-rational… [T]he world /sic!/ suffers from some kind of mental disease which must be diagnosed before it can be cured" (CEJL 4: 249; Williams rightly calls it "the conclusion that matters… in understanding his last work" W-O 67).

All of this amounts to Cold War tactics promoted to the only possible strategy and fatal horizon. We could debate whether the tactics were correct for the exasperated sabre-rattling years of 1946–51, say after Churchill's "Iron Curtain" speech that stressed "compact oligarchies operating through a privileged party and a political police," with accompanying anti-communist purges in US media, soon to become full-fledged Maccarthyism. "Oceania" or NATO was at that point of High Stalinism facing a USSR much weakened by the war's horrendous bloodletting and devastation yet militarily powerful, mainly defensive yet given to sudden bouts of military flights-forward such as the blockade of West Berlin in 1948–49. I well remember coming in Fall 1948 to the first year of my studies in knee britches and boots, preparing for immediate draft in case of a Soviet invasion of Yugoslavia – the distance of the Soviet armoured corps in Hungary from Zagreb being 95 km, that is ca. 3 hours. Indeed, in the Khrushchev reconciliation years, Zhukov told Tito that Stalin had him prepare two invasion plans for Yugoslavia around 1951; but then the tension got channelled into the Korean War. Now this may show why the anti-Russian tactics could be necessary in a topical newspaper article, but it does not at all speak to the fated destiny of England or the globe for a whole historical epoch – in Orwell's hyperbole, to smashing the human face forever.

In the essay on Swift, Orwell accused him and his Houyhnhnms of lacking any notion "that life here and now is worth living, or that it could be made worth living, or that it must be sacrificed for some future good…." He also judged that in his "permanently… depressed mood" that harps on disease and dirt, "Swift is not actually inventing anything, he is merely /sic!/ leaving something out. Human behaviour, too, especially in politics, is as he describes it, although it contains other more important factors which he refuses to admit" (CEJL 4: 219 and 222). Surely Orwell knew Horace's tag "Change the name, and the story is told of thee."

3. Some Radiations from *Nineteen Eighty-Four*

3.1. Let me here refer back to Hegel's gloomy conclusion with which I opened this essay, mainly a retrospect on the French Revolution from a distance equivalent to our distance from the Russian Revolution between the 1950s and the 1990s. The gloom at the failure is expressed in a rather different language but it is of the same kind as Orwell's in NEF. Hegel's overarching answer was the voyage of the World Spirit, just as misleading as Orwell's totalitarianism (which is a kind of demonic new World Spirit).

I would concede that Orwell's may well be the best concoctable propaganda image of "totalitarianism," where the common denominator of what follows competitive capitalism is the squalor of dominated mass life and the suffering of the dominated intellectual – a view from the victims, much superior to the Burnham-Arendt-Popper theorisations. But the concept itself fuses partly compatible but then also partly and probably wholly incompatible aspects, obvious in the fact that Nazism and (even Stalinist) Communism were mortal enemies. Therefore, even NEF's most impressive, so to speak humanistic image will necessarily be narratively deficient: it can explain neither whence the urge or lust for absolute power – the aspect of Nietzsche leading to Nazism – nor the seamless victory of the bearers of the urge, the new ruling class. It can only persuasively present its awful toll in misery and suffering. A book written in order to persuade by stunning means a dubious choice where the medium threatens the message, but it worked exceedingly well for the "common reader."

I need to put here a disambiguation for the meaning of Communism, though I cannot go into anything approximating its analysis; I have done it at length elsewhere ("15 Theses") and will baldly simplify them. I find the term split between two opposed poles, well exemplified by the kibbutzim as well as by Lenin's *State and Revolution* vision of integral plebeian democracy vs. the KGB's concentration camp hells. If what is meant by it is "really obtaining Stalinism" in USSR after the end of the 1920s and then in eastern Europe after 1944, I recognise that it brought not only unavoidable centralisation and cruelties of two wars and accelerated industrialisation to prepare for a following one, but also a huge amount of avoidable oppression and a finally inefficient leaden oligarchy, ruling without clear input from below. If you allow me more autobiography, I was as a young activist on a KGB blacklist of enemies, presumably to be liquidated if Yugoslavia were occupied. Thus I have no problem at all appreciating not only the bleak wit, spare writing, and satirical edge but also the political horizon of *Animal Farm*: it is fair comment. But Communism also meant the horizon of Marx, Luxemburg, Lenin, Gramsci, Brecht, many great poets and artists and hundreds of thousands of people sincerely devoted to freedom and equality; and it brought immediately after revolutionary accession to power in the USSR, Yugoslavia, China, Cuba, and some other countries great disalienating advances: agrarian reform, universally accessible schooling up to and including the university, universal health service, a move of tens of million from village hovels to cities, development of industry and a large professional class, etc.

To conclude on the conflation of Stalinism and Nazism: this is by now old hat, and totalitarianism as a term and concept has been much doubted in scholarship, though it reigns unabated in the media. None of this should ever deny, as Ian Kershaw and Moshe Lewin summarise their book's findings, that the nature of both Nazi and Stalinist oppressions was most hateful, and the extent of inhumanity and suffering the two brought is comparable to each other – as well as to wild capitalism (now returning)

– and resulted in "unprecedented levels of repression and of attempted indoctrination, manipulation, and mobilisation.... But ... the term 'totalitarianism'... has little or no explanatory power" (Kershaw, in idem and Lewin eds. 89). I would not go to the extreme of denying much similarity between Nazism and Stalinism (as for example Geyer and Fitzpatrick do, 3–21), but if we reject Cold War propaganda, the differences, in part based on systematic Nazi racism, are at least as large, probably larger (Kershaw and Lewin 3–5, and cf. more in Kershaw "Totalitarianism"). And then, communism as a historical phenomenon, rather than the Stalinist perversion, has little to do with this comparison: I contend it has a Janus nature, one face young and eutopian and the other old and antiutopian, that precludes a simplistic endorsement or condemnation in general or forever (Orwell did so in the heat of battle). Each phase of that movement in each country must be judged in its context and on its merits. To my mind, total refusal of a contradictorily rich historical experience is both epistemologically and morally equal to total endorsement: unrealistic and dehumanising.

Finally, my narratological unease at NEF is coupled with and culminates in Ernst Bloch's general position on the horizon of utopias, in a section where he also first introduces the concept of Novum (PH E, I: 222–23):

> To stick to things, to sail over them, both are wrong..... Everything living... has a horizon. An inner horizon, extending vertically as it were, in the self-dark, an external one of great breadth, in the world-light.... Where the prospective horizon is omitted, reality only appears as become, as dead.... Where [it] is continuously included in the reckoning, the real appears ... as the path-network of dialectical processes which occur in an unfinished world [emphasis DS]....[16]

The fully closed, no-exit horizon of NEF excludes the possibility of a utopian correlate, both as eutopian project of freedom and happiness and dystopian awful warning, as well as a real liberating novum.

Factoring this too into the total closure of NEF leads to the conclusion it presents no diagnosis, only an at times masochistic recognition of a class blind alley transmogrified into humanity's horrorific utter and final defeat. I agree with Jameson that what is dominant in NEF is antiutopia in the sense of "a central passion to denounce and to warn against Utopian programs in the political realm" (*Archaeologies* 198–99). Lyman T. Sargent classified early estranged utopianism as "utopias of sensual gratification or body utopias," exemplified by the Cockayne folk story, and "utopia of human contrivance or the city utopia," exemplified by Plato's *Laws* and then More's *Utopia* ("Three" 10–11). To this, Orwell's NEF furnishes a perfect undialectical rebuttal: an antiutopia of utter bodily discomfort caused by human contrivance in the mega-city (O'Brien explicitly tells Winston this). This has serious overall consequences.

There is, however, a potential justification at hand which might almost wipe out objections to Orwell's stance and horizon, if it were true. If NEF were a satire, it would necessarily carry an implicit utopian charge in its generic pact with the reader to call up the obverse of the textual situation, imaginable on the basis of the values present in the text that established a right to satirise. It would then be a very muddled satire – but

I disagree that overall it is one (*pace* Bernard Crick, "NEF" 147–48, repeated in several publications), the differences to *Animal Farm* are deep and decisive. I would propose NEF is a very impure generic mixture of dystopia and antiutopia with some effective moments or aspects of sardonic satire, such as the quite perfect Two Hour Hate or the rewriting of the past. This is why I have attempted elsewhere (see chapters 23 and 24 in this book) a discussion of the nature of eutopia, dystopia, and antiutopia, that is, of the contract with the reader these literary subgenres establish as necessary for their intelligibility and effect. My hypothesis is that the particular genre mixture of NEF, where the awful warning of dystopia is dominant in the description of daily life in Ingsoc and antiutopia in the whole ending, finally tells the reader that nothing can be done about the picture presented.

3.2. Thus, the best brief label for NEF might be a term Orwell took from Chesterton in the article "Good Bad Books" (CEJL 4: 19–22). He is evidently in search of a definition to which he does not quite get, but suggests it vaguely: books that "[remain] readable when more serious productions have perished," his examples being "escape literature," such as the Sherlock Holmes stories, *Dracula* or *King Solomon's Mines*; or books which are not "'good' by any strictly literary standard" but are sincere and tell a good story with characters a reader can feel sympathy with. His main point is "that one can be amused or excited or even moved by a book that one's intellect refuses to take seriously": thus as different from Carlyle, Trollope remains readable though less intelligent than the former. Orwell's supreme example is *Uncle Tom's Cabin*: "unintentionally ludicrous…, full of preposterous melodramatic incidents … also deeply moving and essentially true…." NEF would not quite fall into any of his categories; however, I propose it is a "good bad book" because its premise and conclusion are untenable, but not only is it moving but its strength and limitations give rise to serious thinking about essential matters of political survival in his time – and ours too. Example: as I conclude in 2.13, Orwell's picture included a prescient, if hyperbolically monolithic and causally deficient, vision of the world divided between three mega-centres of power in perpetual warfare with each other.

Centrally, Orwell's strength as well as limitation lies in "a steady insistence in the value of thinking for oneself and of refusing the official simplifications which all ruling groups employ" (W-A 119–20); for NEF, this results in a steady, quite indignant sympathy and compassion for the downtrodden "little man." His major mistakes are well put by Williams: first, perhaps less important, the conflation of a basically World War 2 warfare on the heels of a ludicrously miscalculated impact of the supposed atomic war that then explains the poverty of Ingsoc; his denial of both traditionalist and new forces of resistance to tyranny; and the quite central blind spot about political economics (see 2.31 above), evident from the real history of, say, Germany and Japan within our much more polycentric tripartition of the world. The two last factors logically lead to the theory of "power for power's sake," as well as to his disbelief in the huge powers of recuperation within capitalism, splitting the world today into the still privileged North as against the starving South (W-A 106–12 and 116–17). Thence NEF's finally predestined doom and gloom. In brief, he suffered from a strange alloy of true clairvoyance for some matters (those within his class experience and structure of feeling) and tunnel vision.[17] As I have been trying to present it here.

3.3. In conclusion: while I find NEF to be a concerned, appealing, and in some ways useful text, it *lacks wisdom*. As Wegner perspicaciously noted, it "attempts to create a 'counter-utopia' to the historical vision of utopia as such" (*Imaginary* 197). It stimulates both resignation and a belief that bad as capitalism is, the alternative is even worse. It outlaws hope – Winston thinks "if there is hope it lies in the proles," but the text decrees these are forever quiescent. Hope belonged to the communist, and possibly Nazi, totemic field, and must be denied (cf. Thompson in W-CE 83).

Thus, Orwell's aberrant fictional horizon and validation of antiutopia, certainly striving for and gaining strong political influence but finally one that readers can share or reject, has been logically enlisted into the drive for our present totalising and inescapable extra-literary or existential antiutopia. Antiutopia is not good to think with all other varieties of utopia, it is a preachment to the willy-nilly converted or kept at bay. What it amounts to, behind elaborate smokescreens shaming the puny Wizard of Oz, is a world where all, and primarily all people and human possibilities, exists only as adjunct capitals for profit – unless also as mercenary servants (see more in chapter 23 of this book). Overtly or covertly, this is the dominant horizon of "post-communism."

Notes

1 Rai notes it well for *Road to Wigan Pier*: "He approaches the afflicted areas with all the clear-eyed ignorance of … a Martian" (69).

My warm thanks for much help in bibliographic matters and materials sent go to Lyman T. Sargent and Tom Moylan, for clarifying discussions and sending me their works first of all to Fredric Jameson, also to Patrick Parrinder, Daphne Patai, Darren Webb, and Phil Wegner. Special thanks for Patricia McManus's close reading of my essay and the kind loan of her own draft paper on NEF (cited), that between them allowed me to make a dozen important clarifications, and for a comradely afternoon of discussion. I couldn't have written this essay without the kind and efficient help of the Clare Hall College staff and the Cambridge University Library, also of Jake Culank from Cambridge.

2 Cf. W-CE 159–60, and see the excellent contextualisation for Burma in Rai 57–67 and 174–75.

3 I judged mine to be a bad good poem, that is, not very poetic though notionally right, and didn't publish it in my Canadian collection of 1984, *The Long March*, but it appeared in the *Foundation* journal. Today I'd say I was almost as unfair to him as he was to his ideals in NEF. The lecture was at the University of Lausanne and approached NEF too as a good bad book.

4 The curious evocation of "St. Petersburg 1916" in his diaries (CEJL 2: 374) could suggest he was quite conscious of this revolutionary parallel. I have found no discussion of Orwell's relations to Marx and Lenin. He was certainly not indifferent to the former – I point out below that he must have read *The Communist Manifesto* – but little interested in the latter, and one gets the impression he read little of both at first

hand. Within Orwell's usual adversariness, his opinions about both of them, and of communism, were largely "prejudices [as] angry, antagonistic responses to the ruling left orthodoxy… and in this he anticipated the wholesale rejection of Communism which became a central feature in Natopolitan ideology. And this failure …. denied the possibility of *hope* within the pattern of social change wherever Communist influence could be detected" (Thompson in W-CE 82–83).

5 I ought to record I shared this stance between ca. 1948 and 1954.

6 Calder pointed perspicaciously out that this duality or double vision is of a piece with Orwell's attitude to Hitler, whose projected figure he – rather unbelievably – found both hateful and appealing as a Christ-like sufferer (CEJL 2: 12–14). On the other hand, Big Brother's Q&A speech style (NEF 54) is pure Stalin – shades of an Orthodox theological seminary (cf. Suvin, "Archeology" and *Lessons*).

7 First quote Patai, "Third" cf. also her *Orwell*, which may bend the bough a bit; when I wrote her this, in an e-mail of May 2019, she agreed and answered she would today rather stand by her partial correction in "Third," which she kindly sent me (unpaginated). Second quote Wegner, *Imaginary* 218.

8 Williams commented in 1984: "There have been changes of style and technology but certain basic methods of the oligarchy – endlessly repeated slogans, displacement of one kind of news by another, the regular institution of hate-figures – are still clearly recognisable" (W-A 120). In other words, Orwell knew from the inside how capitalist and bureaucratic thought-control machines work.

9 To begin with, Orwell attributes to Swift many of his most important stances (and blames him for not having some of his), so that the essay's formulations can often be used as involuntary but precise auto-biography. Just exchange the names in these three quotes and see, the tale is told of thee: "Swift was one of those people who are driven into a perverse sort of Toryism by the follies of the progressive party of the moment"; Swift has strong "strands" of reaction plus misanthropy as well as of progress, with the specious excuse that "[t]o be occasionally inconsistent is almost a mark of vitality in Utopia books"; in the Yahoos "Swift has overreached himself in his fury and his shouting at his fellow creatures. 'You are filthier than you are!'" (CEJL 4: 207, 212, and 218). Conversely, Orwell hates the Houyhnhnms and sees them as, so to speak, totalitarians with a fully accomplished Newspeak.

10 Orwell knew quite well what he was leaving out. In the earliest 1943 outline he noted among "To be brought in" the item, "Interrelation between the party & the Trusts" (Crick, *George* 583). By 1948, he had left economics out.

11 "[T]he sociology of the proles, considering their importance as the sole vehicle of hope, is sketchy and, as it stands, implausible," notes the regretful Crick (*George* 551). It is curious how this marginalisation of workers, especially industrial ones, is a besetting sin of most "middle-class" – however ideologically "Left" – utopias and SF, in Twain, Bellamy, Wells, Bogdanov, even Morris and Zamyatin…

12 This is nicely subverted in Dalos's *1985*, where in order to bring down "really obtaining socialism" Winston is (unbelievably) made into a Wałęsa or Havel-like leader of opposition. My thanks to Professor Sarah Brown of Anglia Ruskin University for giving me a copy of the book.

13 There are few, and to my mind no conclusive, approaches to Orwell and NEF based on psychological theory. In Freudian terms, it is not difficult to find both sadomasochism and narcissism in the author and his writings. The real yield would come if this could be integrated with other types of analysis.

14 The Cold War use, latching on to the "Ingsoc" name, of pointing to the Soviet system was quite athwart Orwell's conscious purpose to "[lay the scene] of the book in Britain in order to emphasise that … totalitarianism, if not fought against, could triumph anywhere" (CEJL 4: 502). Williams is quite right: "[T]here is the really savage irony that a citizen of Oceania [that is USA and UK, note DS], in 1984, is thinking as he has been programmed to think, but with the reassurance of the book to tell him that he is free and that only those others are propagandised and brainwashed" (W-A 101).

15 It might be relevant that the "totalitarianism" concept was excogitated in the 1930s by committed ex-communists Ignazio Silone, Franz Borkenau, and Arthur Koestler, and communist sympathisers for a time André Malraux and George Orwell. Borkenau and Koestler had some direct experience of Nazism, the others did not, and none of them could know of its inner workings; most of them hated it without much emotional involvement.

16 I cannot forbear transcribing the beautiful key title of this section of Bloch's – Part II.17, Vol.1: 222–23: "The World in which Utopian Imagination has a Correlate; Real Possibility, The Categories Front, Novum, Ultimum, and the Horizon."

17 An example of Orwell's strategic political clairvoyance coupled with a self-imposed *Denkverbot* to think political economy: "The real question is not whether the people who wipe their boots on us during the next 50 years are to be called managers, bureaucrats or politicians: the question is whether capitalism, now obviously doomed, is to give way to oligarchy or to true democracy" (CEJL 4: 165).

Works Cited

Only the first occurrence will be listed, that is, all Sections after Section 1 may also contain its titles, and so on.

Section 1

Menand, Louis. "*1984* at Seventy." *The New Yorker* June 9, 2019. www.newyorker.com/news/daily-comment/1984-at-seventy-why-we-still-read-orwells-book-of-prophecy.

Orwell, George. *Road to Wigan Pier*. https://libcom.org/files/wiganpier.pdf.

Orwell, Sonia, and Ian Angus eds. *Collected Essays, Journalism and Letters of George Orwell*, 4 Vols., 1968 [further CEJL with volume number: page number].

Rai, Alok. *Orwell and the Politics of Despair*. Cambridge UP, 1990.

Rodden, John. *The Politics of Literary Reputation*. Oxford UP, 1989.

Saunders, Frances Stonor. *The Cultural Cold War: The CIA and the World of Arts and Letters*. New P, 2000.

[Silcox, Beejay.] www.australianbookreview.com.au/abr-online/current-issue/249-may-2019-no-411/5438-this-is-the-way-the-world-ends-by-beejay-silcox.

Suvin, Darko. *Lessons from the Russian Revolution and Its Fallout*. Rosa Luxemburg Foundation Southeast Europe, 2017, www.rosalux.rs/en/lessons-russian-revolution-and-its-fallout.

Suvin, Darko. "Parables and Uses of a Stumbling Stone." *Arcadia* 5.2 (2017): 271–300.

Suvin, Darko. *Splendour, Misery, and Possibilities: An X-ray of Socialist Yugoslavia*. Brill, 2016, and Haymarket P, 2017.

Suvin, Darko. "Words and Lesions: Epistemological Reflections on Violence, the 1968 Moment, and Revolution (with Particular Reference to Japan)." *Critical Q* 62.1 (2020): 83–122.

Williams, Raymond. "The Bloomsbury Fraction," in his *Problems in Materialism and Culture*. Verso, 1980, 148–69.

Williams, Raymond. *Orwell*. Fontana, 1971 [further W-O with page number].

Williams, Raymond, ed. *George Orwell: A Collection of Critical Essays*. Prentice-Hall, 1974. [further W-CE with page number].

Section 2

Amis, Kingsley. *New Maps of Hell*. Harcourt, Brace, 1975 [original 1960].

Berger, John. *G*. Weidenfeld & Nicolson, 1972.

Bourdieu, Pierre. *Pascalian Meditations*. Trans. R. Nice. Stanford UP, 2000.

Churchill, Winston. *The "Iron Curtain" Speech*. www.cia.gov/library/readingroom/docs/1946-03-05.pdf.

Crick, Bernard. *George Orwell: A Life*. Penguin, 1982.

Curtius, E. R. *European Literature and the Latin Middle Ages*. Trans. W.R. Trask. Harper & Row, 1953.

Dalos, György. *1985: What Happens after Big Brother Dies*. Trans. S. Hood and E. Schmid. Pantheon, 1983.

Eco, Umberto. "Dictionary vs. Encyclopedia," in his *Semiotics and the Philosophy of Language*. Indiana UP, 1986, 46–86.

Eco, Umberto. *The Role of the Reader*. Indiana UP, 1979.

Jameson, Fredric. *Archaeologies of the Future*. Verso, 2005.

Jameson, Fredric. *The Seeds of Time*. Columbia UP, 1994.

London, Jack. *The Iron Heel*. Macmillan, 1908.

Lotman, Jurij M. *The Structure of the Artistic Text*. Michigan Slavic Contributions, 1977.

Marx, Karl, and Frederick Engels. *Manifesto of the Communist Party*, www.marxists.org/archive/marx/works/download/pdf/Manifesto.pdf.

McManus, Patricia. "Anti-utopia in Search of Hope." manuscript.

Moylan, Tom. *Demand the Impossible*. Methuen, 1986.

Moylan, Tom. *Scraps of the Untainted Sky*. Westview P, 2000.

Norris, Christopher ed. *Inside the Myth – Orwell: Views from the Left*. Lawrence & Wishart, 1984.

Orwell, George. *Nineteen Eighty-Four*. Introduction by T. Pynchon. Penguin, 2003.

Patai, Daphne. *The Orwell Mystique*. U of Massachusetts P, 1984.

Patai, Daphne. "Third Thoughts about Orwell," in her *What Price Utopia?* Rowman & Littlefield, 2008.

Rees, Richard. *George Orwell: Fugitive from the Camp of Victory*. S. Illinois UP, 1961.

Ricoeur, Paul. *Interpretation Theory: Discourse and the Surplus of Meaning*. Texas Christian UP, 1976.

Rose, Jonathan. "Englands His Englands," in J. Rodden ed., *The Cambridge Companion to George Orwell*. Cambridge UP, 2007, 28–42.

Sanderson, Richard K. "The Two Narrators and Happy Ending of *Nineteen Eighty-Four*." *Modern Fiction Studies* 34.4 (1988): 587–95.

Suvin, Darko. "From the Archeology of Marxism and Communism: Two Essays in Political Epistemology." *Debatte* 21.2–3 (2013): 279–311 [see in particular "Stalinism," pp. 299–303].

Suvin, Darko. "Emotion, Brecht, Empathy vs. Sympathy." *The Brecht Yearbook* 33 (2008): 53–67.

Suvin, Darko. *Metamorphoses of Science Fiction*. Yale UP, 1979.

Wegner, Phillip E. *Imaginary Communities*. U of California P, 2002.

White, Hayden. "The Fictions of Factual Representation," in A. Fletcher ed., *The Literature of Fact*. Columbia UP, 1976, 21–44.

Williams, Raymond. "Afterword: *Nineteen Eighty-Four* in 1984," in his *Orwell*. Fontana, 1984, 95–126 [further W-A with page number].

[Zamyatin, Yevgeny.] "On Literature, Revolution, Entropy & Other Matters," in M. Ginsburg ed. & trans., *A Soviet Heretic: Essays by Y.Z.* U of Chicago P, 1971, 107–12.

Section 3

Bloch, Ernst. *Das Prinzip Hoffnung*, 2 Vols. Suhrkamp, 1959.

Crick, Bernard. "*Nineteen Eighty Four*: Context and Controversy," in J. Rodden ed. [see under Rose in Section 2], 160–78.

Geyer, Michael, and Sheila Fitzpatrick eds. *Beyond Totalitarianism: Stalinism and Nazism Compared*. Cambridge UP, 2009.

Kershaw, Ian. "Totalitarianism Revisited." *Tel Aviver Jahrbuch für deutsche Geschichte* 23 (1994): 23–40.

Kershaw, Ian, and Moshe Lewin eds. *Stalinism and Nazism: Dictatorships in Comparison*. Cambridge UP, 1997.

Sargent, Lyman T. "The Three Faces of Utopianism Revisited." *Utopian Studies* 5.1 (1994): 1–37.

Suvin, Darko. "15 Theses about Communism and Yugoslavia, or The Two-Headed Janus of Emancipation through the State." *Critical Q* 57.2 (2015): 90–110 [rpt. as ch. 5 of his *Splendour, Misery, and Possibilities: An X-ray of Socialist Yugoslavia*. Brill, 2016].

23

Utopia or Bust: Capitalocene and Our Existential Antiutopia (2019)*

Note 2020: *This article was part of my keynote speech at the Utopian Studies Society (Europe) annual meeting in Prato 2019. It was published in Utopian Studies 32.1 (2021) after a long and excruciating series of discussions with the editor, in a final form that I'm not responsible for.*

> *As a classical philologist… I do not know what meaning classical philology would have for our age if not to have an untimely effect within philology, that is, to act against the age and so have an effect on the age to the advantage, it is to be hoped, of a coming age. … But then let this explanation, which I offer with some doubt to be sure, be replaced by better explanations.…*
>
> Nietzsche, *On the Advantage and Disadvantage of History for Life*

Part 1: Where Are We in Today's Capitalocene

> *Take heed therefore how ye walk circumspectly, not as unwise but as wise, Redeeming the time, because the days are evil.*
>
> Paul of Tarsus, *Ephesians* 5.15-16

In the introduction to the 2015 reprint of her classical *Partial Visions*, Angelika Bammer cites the pithy injunction of the American poet and feminist thinker, Adrienne Rich:

> We need to imagine a world in which every woman is the presiding genius of her own body. In such a world women will truly create new life, bringing forth […] the visions, and the thinking, necessary to sustain, console, and alter human existence […]. Sexuality, politics, intelligence, power, motherhood, work, community, intimacy will develop new meaning; thinking itself will be transformed. (Bammer xx – emphasis added by AB)

Bammer goes on a bit later to cite Rich's early and thus optimistic "[W]e stream into the unfinished the unbegun the possible." To these two quotes I can only add "every male" plus whatever other inter-genders you care to add.

Based on sustaining, consoling, and radically altering the present dire state of human existence, I am led to two sets of quite initial arguments: Where Are We in general, and What Are We here at the conference of Utopian Studies Society (Europe), in particular, Doing Wrong. You will, I trust, kindly realise that nobody can in 50 minutes even approach a full listing of either the general or the particular problems I see facing us. What I can give are samples, perhaps representative beyond themselves.

1.1. Where Are We: The Capitalocene

"What may I hope?" was Kant's famous third question in the *Critique of Pure Reason*, after asking "What can I know?" and "What should I do?" Indeed, what can we know and what may we hope in the capitalocene, this overwhelming antiutopian tsunami we are drowning in, swimming desperately each and every moment in order to take hold of a bit of sustaining jetsam and flotsam or even to come within sight of an island – which, as John Donne told us, is "a piece of the continent,/ A part of the main./ ... For I am involved in mankind."

Thus, to begin with, let us cognise. What is the geologically effective age of capitalocene whose bitter taste batters our days and invades our nights?[1] Historically, capitalist corporations engaged as of the mid-1970s in a large-scale offensive to depress wages per unit of production and boost profits from huge to monstrous. Using the fake slogans of free trade and globalisation, the rich organised bundles of radical interventions by major States and the roof organisations of international capitalism (GATT, WTO, IMF, and World Bank) to make themselves vastly richer, while multiplying the poor in their nations, eviscerating the middle class prosperity based on stable employment, and upping the income gap between rich and poor countries from 10:1 to 90:1. We are now in the epoch of huge and extreme plutocracy, where 1% of the world population appropriated 70% of the riches created in 2017, enforcing it by high-tech mass murders and fear-mongering ideologies of *divide et impera* to keep the 97% of losers at bay: NATO's military budget for 2019 is planned at US$1,400 billion, that is, $4 billion per day! A large class of chronically poor was created, and politically neutralised by creating racist fears of even poorer immigrants. In this class warfare from above, ca. 2.5 billion people, the "global reserve army of unemployed, vulnerably employed, and economically inactive" (Foster "New"), struggle today to survive, failing fast, while more than half of them live in the most abject poverty, more or less quickly dying of hunger and attendant diseases (cf. Pogge); so that the hundred million dead and several hundred million other casualties of warfare in the 20th century seem puny in comparison – though their terror and suffering is not. If we add hydra-headed marginalisation and bureaucratic exclusion, in turn causing violent individual and collective retaliations, as well as the "slow" structural violence caused by destruction of the environment and the aftermath of war (cf. Nixon) this impacts a large majority of people in the world. Economic "growth" benefits only the rich, at the expense of everybody else, especially the poor and the powerless in this generation and future ones (for other sources on war see Suvin, *Leviathan* essay 9).

The capitalist economy is globally pursuing a cheap-labour economy on the one hand and the search for new consumer markets on the other; the former undermines the latter. It does not work for the great majority of people, us workers who live from their physical and intellectual work. Capitalism jettisons humanity in all its senses: civilised behaviour, interest of people, and even their bodies. I shall here insist only on two foci of the perfectly sinful capitalocene: war and ecocide.

- War: the Keynesian Welfare State of blessed memory finally succeeded only in tandem with "military Keynesianism" – the heavy rearmament that in the 1930s-40s primed the pump of business upswing and remained the precondition of a relative affluence – and its price was the Nazi regime, High Stalinism, and the 2nd World War. Under the Bush Jr. administration war expenses were 1,000 million dollars per year (Custers, Johnson). Imperialism is today healthy and thriving, with an important US embedded intellectual calling for a "thirty-years' war" (cf. the two titles by Foster). As for fascism, it is doing very well almost everywhere, thank you. If radically anti-capitalist and anti-authoritarian perspectives of exiting from this predicament are not found, we shall have more ongoing wars in the South – including Northern ghettos – plus more refurbished 2.0 fascism in the North.

Clearly, war plays a structurally essential role in all monopoly capitalism (cf. Marcos 51 and 101). I have defined war as a coherent sequence of conflicts, involving physical combats between large organised groups of people that include the armed forces of at least one state, with the aim of political and economic control over a given (see chapter 1 in my *Communism* and chapter 9 in this book). Other aims may be securing advantages for coming conflicts – for example dominion over air, sea or oil resources – the destruction of commodities and people, and evading inner class tension. The ratio of military to civilian casualties in wars during the 20th century has "progressed" from 8:1 to 1:8 (eight civilians killed for each combatant), and the fighters diversified from regular armies into paramilitary groups, police forces, mercenaries, local warlords, and purely criminal gangs. The mass casualties have been mainly people marginal to "White" patriarchal capitalism: the poor, the women, the uppity "middle" States, the people of "colour."

War is securely based in the central forces of antagonistic competition, the "essential locomotive force" of bourgeois economy and "generally the mode in which capital secures the victory of its mode of production" (Marx, *Grundrisse* 476 and 649); it is the surest way to realise capitalism's GOD imperative (Harvey, "Grow or Die"). Continuous warfare has *never* ceased under capitalism: around 160 wars have raged between 1945 and 1993 killing more people than in World War 2; we know what has continued into this century. Capitalism came about in plunder wars; war financing set up its modern bureaucracy and central national banks; and there is no evidence it could climb out of economic depressions without huge military spending, a war mega-dividend. The political fallout is the spread of military rule that subordinates the civil society to its barbarity even in times of official peace – as today.

Armaments commodities are since World War 2 not only the source of greatest extra-profit but a system-pillar of capitalism. The yearly money value of the international armament trade oscillated in the last 40 years, according to the available faulty statistics, between 20 and over 30 billion dollars, and today it is more. The capitalist market systematically favours armaments commodities because of their uniquely high value-added price, their especially rapid rate of obsolescence and turnover, the monopoly or semi-monopoly position of their manufacturers, and the large-scale and secure financing of military research, production and of massive cost overruns – all taken from public taxation. By the time of the First Gulf War, world spending for military purposes was nearly a trillion US$ annually or *between 2 and 2.5 billion dollars daily*, more than half of it attributable to the USA; and today it is way past this. This most profitable part of global trade is the strongest factor of both international violence and the colonisation of life-worlds and eco-systems by commodity economy. The tens of millions of dead in the two World Wars brought about tens of trillions of profitable investments in the huge reconstructions of destroyed homes and industries and ongoing rearmament: *a million dollars or more per dead body*. No capitalism without increasingly destructive weapons and wars which might still destroy the world: the marvellous technoscientific progress means that one nuclear submarine can destroy the peoples of an entire continent, yet eight new US nuclear submarines have been made since the fall of the USSR. One-quarter of the public monies which are expended on weapons commodities would eradicate poverty, homelessness and illiteracy, as well as pay for the cleanup of all our major environmental pollution... (beside Marx, Luxemburg, and Lenin, cf. other sources up to 2003 in Suvin, *Leviathan* essay 3, where my definition also comes from).

Eric Olin Wright's verdict in 2004 (1–3 and 14), when worse was yet to come, was that capitalist class relations perpetuate eliminable forms of human suffering as well as deficits in human freedom and autonomy, largely based on domination of work and large inequalities of wealth; capitalism violated liberal egalitarian principles of social justice and (here I go beyond Wright) it is not only indifferent to mass middle-class democracy but mostly inimical to mass plebeian democracy, where people – a Gramscian civil society – control the State.

I could and should go on about migrants and social justice but must leave this to your imagination and another occasion. However, since the theme of this conference is about "climate change," I shall continue with ecology.

- *Ecocide*: The capitalocene does not work for our ecological balance, sorely upset by over-consumption of energy; to the contrary, to prevent collapse we need a steady-state economy, with growth resulting from efficiency (cf. Chossudovsky, Daly, Daly and Farley). Capital uses nature as dead matter to make more dead matter, rather than as Spinoza's *natura naturans*, a permanently active ensemble of new potencies and potentialities.

A UN *Summary for policymakers of the global assessment report on biodiversity and ecosystem services* was just published on May 6.[2] It was compiled by 145 experts from 50 countries, with input from another 310 researchers and authors, it draws on over 15,000 scientific and governmental sources and it incorporates the wisdom of indigenous knowledge. It should be taken seriously. It found 3/4 of the terrestrial environment has been "severely altered," more than 40% of amphibian species and 680 vertebrate species have been driven to extinction; in the oceans, almost 1/3 of the reef-forming corals and more 1/3 of marine mammals are on the edge of extinction. In sum: *one million* animal and plant species are now threatened with extinction, many within decades.

The report identifies two main and related reasons for this catastrophe: the "current limited paradigm of economic growth" and "climate change"; its language is cautiously non-political but the first syntagm means corporate capitalism, a system premised on private property and profit as the only reason and horizon for existence. Its reliance upon fossil fuel emissions to power its engines is what has ruined the climate and mainly led to global warming.

Also, in August 2018 six Finnish academics released their background paper for the chapter on *Transformation: The Economy* in the UN Global Sustainable Development Report, which will be released later this year.[3] They find that "the era of cheap energy is coming to an end," and all potential replacements for fossil fuels are far less energy-efficient and will be far more expensive. Massive changes are needed in the very design of our societies to reduce global greenhouse gas emissions to zero by 2050: "Market-based action will not suffice even with a high carbon price." In other words, capitalism cannot solve the mass extinction of species and climate change, with ocean levels rising by meters or possibly dozens of meters soon (see K.S. Robinson's still optimistic SF novel *New York 2140*), the greatest rise since the dinosaurs. Quite different ways to manage life on the planet must be adopted and enforced. Transportation and housing need to rely upon public transport and co-housing. Current food distribution systems waste 1/3 of all food harvested. Resources for all this are available even if politically tabooed: tens of billions of dollars in subsidies given to fossil fuel firms and agribusinesses that lead humanity toward annihilation, tens of trillions of dollars in tax havens. If this could be tapped, it would be sufficient to reconfigure energy, transport, housing, and food systems. "Economic activity will gain meaning not by achieving economic growth," write the Finnish academics, "but by rebuilding infrastructure and practices towards a post-fossil fuel world with a radically smaller burden on natural eco-systems." And the summary of the UN report notes that the transition would "entail a shift beyond standard economic indicators such as gross domestic product to include those able to capture more holistic, long-term views of economics and quality of life."

Both the UN reports are, of course, "professionally" forbidden to totalise and name, and I shall return to these categories. But the only possible conclusion is that *capitalocene is a structured whole*: not only proudly global, but also instantaneous and capillary. The bind has however a name: Rosa Luxemburg's "socialism or barbarism" (with apologies to barbarians). Alas, now this choice will be much more painful than when she wrote it, in the horrible but hopeful year of 1916. Thus we need to insist on an equally totalising eco-utopian thought, as persuasively addressed yesterday at this conference by the speech of Lisa Garforth.

1.2. What Are We Doing Wrong

To narrow the focus to our professional affairs, yet keeping very much in mind the above general context that shapes us all, I have three main beefs against what appears a successful tendency in much popular utopology of the last decade or two. I begin with an incident that shocked me and go on with a plea flowing from a Yiddish anecdote.

Of course there is no god's eye view on any textual (or other) event or existent; any understanding or evaluation is historically delimited, "right" for a given social class, nation, epoch, and so on. Nonetheless, if it is difficult to say what is right, we can from collective experience often say what is wrong. While I remain persuaded that without formal analysis we are bound to be wrong, I am now increasingly concerned by any stance that hides its always already presupposed value-judgments. It seems clear there are no utopian studies without values: these can only be open or hidden, right or wrong. My example stems from a large exhibition called "Utopia: The Search for the Ideal Society in the Western World" at the New York Public Library and the Paris Bibliothèque Nationale, 2000–2001, for which some of us were asked to supply a short text online. I did so too – though I was unhappy at the NYPL questions, mainly interested in internet as utopia (see chapter 5 in this book). I have recently been alerted by several sources, the main written one being Jacoby's book cited (x), to the fact that the visitors could find *in the same room* photographs, documents, audio-tapes, and other artifacts from the Israeli collective farms (kibbutzim), from Martin Luther King and the US Civil Rights Movement, and from Nazi propaganda; I checked this also with the relevant pages of the exhibition catalogue, and it was confirmed by an e-mail to me by Professor Lyman T. Sargent after the SUS conference.[4] I gather that the exhibition also presented photographs from the Auschwitz liquidation camp but I do not know in which room. No information pointing out that any of these were included as contrary to utopia or utopianism seems to have been included, or Jacoby and Sargent would surely have mentioned it. I must therefore rue even my marginal participation on the fringe of the exhibition. As we ought to know, the kibbutzim, where a number of my friends lived for a brief time or permanently, were a sterling example of egalitarian and non-State communism, and were logically stifled by the surge of capitalism and militarism in Israel. To couple them as well as the Black movement against racism with Nazism is an example of the deep wrongness of the totalitarianism concept that I discussed in chapter 22 and to which I shall return.

Thus, how is one to understand that room? My question is simple: *Why put Nazism into a* Utopia *exhibition at all?* Why in the name of all that is holy (including scholarship) put propaganda of the Nazi stance, which notoriously enabled Nazi practices of mass civilian murder and war crimes, into an exhibition called "Utopia"? Is a perverse permissiveness in order that draws no limit to what is Utopia as long as a group believes it is searching for its "ideal society"? Or is it not rather that, as the Bible told us, "by their fruits ye shall know them"? First of all, this is hardly a "search," but usually a strongly held certainty. Second, *can you call utopia the violent infliction of torture and murder on huge masses of people* (possibly even on one single person)? I believe you can NOT: *direct or indirect mass murderings are always antiutopian*. If indeed, as even the great Ernst Bloch is guilty of sometimes inferring, utopia is equivalent to all dreams of any heart's content, then we do not need the term of utopia because we have imagination or dreams or search, and you and I in the Utopian Studies are out of business.

To the contrary: we ought to think seriously about polar incompatibilities of horizon, stance, and value within utopia/nism, updating and sublating the dated dichotomies of Karl Mannheim into ideology vs. utopia as well as of Ernst Bloch into abstract vs. concrete utopia, yet retaining their razor edge (quite compatible with Occam's). While I cannot do this here, a tentative approximation to these decisive incompatibilies informs this essay and speech.

Since I was as a child told I was Jewish, though this didn't mean much to me – but it meant a lot to Hitler who wanted me dead at age 11, and was foiled by my very clever mother and the help of a sterling communist called Tito – I'll introduce my focus with the Yiddish anecdote of *Rabbi Sean Fergusson*:

> A new rabbi arrived to a mid-West US community. After the first celebration of *shabbes*, an excited community member approaches him: "Rabbi, how wonderfully you led this celebration and how happy are we that you came to us! But tell me, how come your name is Sean Fergusson?" The answer: "Well, when my family landed at Ellis Island, we had to be vetted singly, so my parents told me 'Now don't forget your name is Yitzhak Katzenellenbogen!' But our wait was long and hot, and when I came to have my name inscribed, tears running down my four-year-old face and trying valiantly not to sob, I said: '*Schon vergessen* (I have already forgotten it)'. And he wrote down Sean Fergusson."

So here is what my beefs are against – *lest we forget*:

1.21. *The pseudo-professional censorship or* Denkverbot *against "total" and "totality"* crudely identified with the Cold-War notion of totalitarianism, anyway outdated and abandoned by most scholarship. We cannot analyse anything unless it's understood as a unit/y, a *provisionally closed structure for given purposes*. In language semantics this is what Barthes called a mega-text, which could for example be all the rhymed distichs in Shakespeare's plays or, as I tried out once, the endings of half a dozen famous SF novels as the place where truth will out.

No doubt, the suffering and degradation of millions, from world wars and economic "depressions" through Dachau, Kolyma, and Abu Ghraib to those bombed out today all over West Asia, remains and must be taken most seriously as our measuring rods. I myself, whose grandfather and grandmother plus dozens of further relatives were butchered at Auschwitz and Jasenovac, have taken antifascist prevention of such suffering and bestiality as the ground bass for my life's work. But we can for no cause abdicate from the disalienating dialectics of weighing the pros and cons, for we would degrade both our memories and ourselves should we replicate the butchers' horizons. Surely we should backstage, say, fascist rants against liberty equality and the pursuit of both individual and collective happiness for everybody, but even there one should be guarded: I would not like to be without some passages from Pound's *Pisan Cantos* or (to return to utopias) from Jünger's *On Marble Cliffs*, and even the violent and genocidal racism of Heinlein's *Farnham's Freehold* and *Starship Troopers* must be weighed in the balance with his brilliant New Deal beginnings. There I would be near to Orwell who utterly condemned Ezra Pound "as a Fascist, a war criminal and a most foul anti-Semite and racialist" (Crick 20), while still affirming his poetry merits a prize.

And when we consider the great Leninian season of Russia and many other places beginning in, say, 1917–28, and ranging from Blok, Zamyatin, Mayakovsky, Pasternak, and Platonov to Brecht – or should I mention Miroslav Krleža, Pablo Neruda, Nazim Hikmet, Hugh MacDiarmid, and a dozen other great opuses from the US to China? – <u>then</u> what Bakhtin called monophonic and I would call pseudo-liberal mutilation of the contradictorily rich and stunted communist polyphony of those times is quite untenable. As Darren Webb reminded us: "Anyone reading the utopian writings of Charles Fourier, William Morris or Ursula Le Guin will agree … that 'the good can accommodate difference'" (the internal quote is from the Mark Olssen essay "Totalitarianism and the Repressed Utopia of the Present: Moving beyond Hayek, Popper and Foucault"). The three colleagues met in flesh whom I would claim as my informal teachers, Lucien Goldmann, Raymond Williams, and Fredric Jameson, certainly recognised this. Conclusion: <u>*it's better to refute than to ignore, for this means articulating your own presuppositions*</u>.

The Webb quote leads into our particular utopological concerns – already present in the distinguished Russian and other names above – pinpointed by Phillip Wegner's review of Jameson's *Archaeologies:* "It is the 'passion for totality' … which distinguishes the radically original invention that occurs in Book Two of More's text from the more tentative sketches we find in Book One…. And finally, it is the passion for totality that accounts for the great fear of Utopia expressed in the anti-Utopia" (Jameson 202). I shall return at length to the antiutopia.

<u>1.22.</u> <u>*The split between narratology and ideology*</u>: On the one hand, I've written enough about narrative and poetic form to be perhaps forgiven if I say it is by itself never enough to centrally characterise a piece of writing without taking into account the reader's normative presuppositions from the current societal encyclopedia. A famous example from SF is "They landed in the light of the blue Sun," which when filled out by the presupposition that our Sun is yellow, means "They landed in another solar system." No amount of formal inquiry can establish this. I am reminded of a disciple of Leo Spitzer in analysis of poetry who in my youth found a famous poem's metrics to reproduce heartbeats. While this is in itself a logical fallacy, confusing the particular heartbeat with the general possibility of rhythmic beating which could arise out of a dozen other sources, the main problem for me is: given the how, <u>*whose*</u> heart beats <u>*for whom or what*</u>? – which rhythm analysis can never tell you.

On the other hand, ideology in the wide and nobler sense of stance toward human existence and its determinants is our daily bread without which we would starve; yet if it is simply the critić's opinion, without feedback and probably complicated modification from texts and their contexts, then it is authoritarian propaganda – in which case it is impossible to decide whether its effects are worse when done consciously or unconsciously.

I arrive at this from my basis in literary-cum-theatre studies and should face the objection that utopian philosophies and colonies are different animals. I would answer yes and no: of course there are serious differences, primarily in how you establish your mega-text and whether it won't have to deal with semiotic systems other than language, but in all cases you willy-nilly must have a text to analyse, be it document and reports about colonies, or even more clearly the rhetoric of utopianism as a concatenation of concepts or notions. We have sufficiently brilliant analyses of, say, the form of Darwin's *Origin of the Species* to know that without the highly metaphorical "tangled bank" and "survival of the fittest" passages it would not be understandable as the readers have understood it. Conclusion: *a plague on the split between formal and ideational analysis of any such narratives, don't use one without the other!* For then you do not isolate the text from its inly informing context – people, society, and ongoing life.

1.23. *A denial and foreclosure of – or more hypocritically and insidiously, a domesticating lip-service only* (see Webb) *to* – *Great Ancestors in philosophy*, which to my mind asks what are we and how are we to live, *and particularly in epistemology*, which asks how do we know what we think we know. Of course in a way the more the merrier, and I really should but cannot here go back to the greatest of our Ancestors: Marx, Diderot, Rousseau, Aristotle… However, to sideline for example Ernst Bloch, Fredric Jameson or Raymond Williams will much help the desertification of utopian studies into a wasteland of unargued presupposition plus empirical data (as has in the last 20 years been the case with some of its eminent European representatives). This also means castrating Thomas More's great invention – at the same time as Machiavelli – of conceiving society as a holistic system, not to speak of his applying communism for the first time to a whole population instead of a ruling elite (cf. Strier 143 and 145–46). Conclusion: as several famous people have said, *whoever does not want to learn from history is condemned to relive it* – and in our days this is the clearly open path to racist and macho Fascism 2.0 (see Suvin "To Explain").

With this in mind, I shall devote Part 2 of this keynote to a main focus on antiutopia, which has lately persuaded me to abandon some cherished beliefs about utopias and utopianism, so that I'm much in need of feedback from colleagues like you. It was arrived at jointly with an analysis of Orwell's *Nineteen Eighty-Four* (chapter 22 in this book).

Part 2. What Existential Antiutopia Means for Us

God has chosen things which are not (tà mè ónta) *to abolish those which are.*

Paul of Tarsus, *Corinthians* I.17

2.1. On Theory of Utopia and the Event of a Mega-Novum: The What

2.1.1. History: Advent of Alternative Totality

I agree with Ruth Levitas: "Utopia is born out of a conviction and two questions. The conviction is 'it doesn't have to be like this.' The questions are 'how then should we live?' and 'how can that be?'" (48).

It is of utmost significance that in the Renaissance utopianism underwent a sea change or metamorphosis from Platonic philosophical argument and blueprint, and then Augustinian theological devaluation of mundane existence, to a *narrative genre*. Within the belly of the new, increasingly totalising and dynamic Leviathan, bourgeois democratic and if you wish capitalist storytelling – that is, the imagination of alternative actions by agents in an alternative Possible World – developed a key novum with two aspects:

- The first aspect was *the freedom inherent in relatively wide* – eventually mass – *reading*, from the very beginning structured as a more or less free market competition for the readers' attention and choice. This was accompanied by a rise of published utopian items in a faster and somewhat more literate society. On the down side this was always *for books* countered by illiteracy, misery, and repression of publishing and circulation, down to Nazi book burning, Stalinist censorship, and post-1989 neoliberal book destructions (the State-ordered mass book destruction in Croatia happens to be documented in Lešaja, but it is surely one among many); and *for mass media* it is countered by high costs, oligopoly, and severe top-down controls in TV and movies.
- The second aspect was a flexible use of narrative as cognitive means to convey a "thicker" overview of life and its experiences with, against, and in lieu of Leviathan. Such narrative amalgamated notionality and sensual evidence centered on deputised protagonists moving and learning in realistic spacetime. From More on, all utopianism reposes on two central, cognate and imbricated imaginative activities and formal procedures: *map-making* and nomination or *naming*. Utopianism is a space-creating machine, inconceivable before the space-eating inventions of economic enclosure of lands and transoceanic ships, and in some ways a desperate attempt to use these huge weapons of domination for freedom (as can be clearly seen in some first stirrings of air travel notions). Consubstantially, space becomes a sense-making machine by means of nomination, turning imperial conquest and colonisation into a possibility of humanising power relationships. There might be additional general procedures or devices, such as a deviant listing or categorising of main human relationships under power (the full survey that L.T. Sargent insists upon in "Utopia" 140–41), but I think these too function by way of the first two. For one example, Morris's taking over in *News from Nowhere* the names and map first of London city and then of the Thames valley serves his purpose of palingenesis, the rebirth of human simplicity and esthetic joy in classless society, but it also marks his proximity to Earthly Paradise rather than to utopia proper, that needs a strategically believable politico-economical overview.

Thus utopian texts – and following them, all utopianism including attempts at philosophy and colonies – were born as political animals wedded to a possibility of freedom, to be negotiated between the individuals and various power currents in the collectivity. At times, "utopia is a matter of innermost urgency, something we are pushed into as a matter of survival, when it is no longer possible to go on within the parameters of the 'possible'" (Žižek, cited in Sargisson 32). True, there were authoritarian utopias galore, most significantly the early ones by Bacon and Campanella, and even More oscillated between democracy and patriarchy, but these were particular choices within an epistemologically open horizon: if America exists, all is possible! – all kinds of freedom and even a new elite authoritarianism. I have been insisting now for almost half a century that "Though formally closed, significant utopia is thematically open: its pointings reflect back on the reader's topia" ("Locus," in Suvin, *DBH* 120), and I cited Barthes to the effect that the utopian *écriture* must mobilise at the same time an image and its contrary (*MOSF* 51).

It is also to my mind incontrovertible that all such Possible Counter-Worlds are modelled upon our everyday Possible World as a totality, a however provisional and experimental world: despite modest early avatars as an island or colony, the space and its meaning is always an exemplary and radical counter-project aiming at a different way of human existing. Near the beginning of the best modern survey, Jameson's *Archaeologies*, he writes that "Totality is then precisely this combination of closure and system .... that presides over the forms of Utopian realisation: the Utopian city, the Utopian revolution, the Utopian commune or village, and of course the Utopian text itself" (5). By means of the "passion for totality" the utopian impulse blossoms into the utopian alternative project (cf. Moylan, "Transgressive" 312), sprung forth full-blown from the pen of Thomas More, as Athena from the brain of Zeus. The paradigm can be grasped, Jameson argues, in the qualitative jump from the preliminary sketches of strange countries in Book One of *Utopia* to the radically original, totalising invention of Book Two: "The [countries in Book One are] … imagined as enclaves within our existent world; whereas, despite the positioning and the supplementary explanations, Utopia is somehow felt to replace our world altogether" (38).

Amid our age of "weak thought," let me disambiguate: here total does NOT mean all-exhaustive (though it is a temptation some utopographers succumb to, witness Campanella – as well as some pernicious bureaucratic meddlers in many capitalist or pseudo-socialist agencies); nor does it mean that everything is planned from above and violently enforced, as in Mussolini's favourite adjective of "totalitarian." Rather it entails a radically different Possible World – that is, a notional totality that for the cognitive purposes of feedback resembles our encyclopedic idea of our world. No image or notion is graspable except as a (provisional) totality. Yet finally, many major utopian writings are in curious and ingenious ways open-ended totalities, from More's final sentence and Bacon's unfinished fragment to, say, the multiplicities of choice in K.S. Robinson's Mars trilogy (cf. Wegner, *Imaginary* 54); and I have been worrying at open-endedness since reading Bloch, who tied his "concrete utopia" to an open system (say in my "Brecht vs. Ibsen").

2.1.2. Modern Times: The Politics of Generic Forms

On top of the two aspects broached above, the strategic factor for grasping the readability of modern utopias is their division into subgenres, beginning with the mega-split between eutopia and dystopia. This came about under the existential pressure of the division in and after the three main bourgeois revolutions – in England, America, and France – between the eutopian *citoyen* face and the dystopian bourgeois face of the new rulers. After the additional shocks of the Russian Revolution and fascism were digested, and amid the youth and New Left revolt of the 1960s–70s, this division was recognised by a group of scholars, astraddle between humanities and sociology, within a theory of literary genres (cf. chapter 1 in this book) – most notably by Lyman T. Sargent, Fredric Jameson, and Tom Moylan (see also Suvin, for example in "Tractate," and from the sociological side Bauman and Levitas); it is by now an accepted presupposition. The good meaning of eutopianism is a presentation, orientation, and striving toward the horizon of radically better forms of relationships among people, an affirmation and annunciation. The bad meaning or dystopianism is a presentation of radically worse forms of relationships among people, a negation and denunciation. I defined eutopia as the construction of a particular community where sociopolitical institutions, norms, and relationships between people are organised according to a more perfect principle than in the author's community, and symmetrically, for dystopia "more perfect" is to be changed into "less perfect." In both cases, what is radically better or worse is judged from the point of view and within the value-system of a suffering and discontented social group or fraction, as refracted through the writer (if you are content, you enjoy or rhapsodise).[5] This duo of eutopia plus dystopia, which was up to the last decades the factually and axiologically main body of utopian writings and horizons, is on the whole Jeffersonian: an affirmation of life, liberty, and the pursuit of happiness – but it had small but sometimes significant wings to the right and left of such bourgeois democracy.

The dystopian Possible Worlds show and show up the horrors of human relationships becoming more repressive, exploitative, and alienating; in Hegelian language, dystopia as an ideal type is a denunciation and negation of *negating* eutopian orientation and strivings. If we follow Sargent, as I do, then *antiutopia as an ideal type is* precisely the opposite: *a denunciation and negation of* affirming *eutopian orientation and strivings*. It is of two kinds, rosy and black, both of which share a switch from politics or history to ontology or "nature." I shall develop this at length later.

No doubt, dystopia, so powerful from Zamyatin, Čapek, Pohl-Kornbluth, and early Heinlein to Piercy or K.S. Robinson and still alive, needs more discussion. I have a feeling Jameson is on the right track when he pleads for a sub-genre of apocalyptic fiction (*Archaeologies* 199 – whatever we might then call it): however uncouth and internally contradictory, its huge popularity in fiction and all media demands to be taken seriously. However, what I am now concerned with is to disentangle the generic model of dystopia from that of antiutopia: for while dystopia is an unruly or boomerang-flight brother of eutopia, antiutopia is the enemy or family wrecker.[6] What is literary antiutopia? As above, it is a significantly different locus explicitly designed to refute a currently proposed eutopia. It is a polemic nightmare that proposes to reveal how an eutopia pretended to a more perfect organisation than any thinkable alternative, while our narrative "camera eye" and value-monger finds out it is significantly less perfect. It was written to warn against utopias, not – as dystopias do – against the existing status quo, and in fiction perhaps culminated, if that's the word, in Ayn Rand's *Anthem*. As Tom Moylan discussed at length (*Scraps* 194–96 and passim), dystopia's mobilising pessimism entails that the reader should do something about it; while now antiutopia's demobilising pessimism entails that nothing could or should be done.

The pedigree of antiutopianism has been little explored, but my hypothesis would be that, except for possible precursors like Aristophanes' *Women in Parliament* (cf. Sargent, *Utopianism* 25), it began in ideological horror at the French and similar revolutions, in England by Burke and the conservative romantics.[7] Such reactions in part rightly sensed the dangers of State-worship among both capitalists and communists, but then used it to oppose the horizon of human disalienation and radical democracy in the 19th Century. This became neuralgic especially after the 1917 Russian Revolution and its direct or indirect fallout, within which utopianism was often wedded to communism or socialism: the Welfare State.

In terms of literary history and narration, antiutopia was mainly confined to two reactionary clusters, the anti-Bellamy one in the 1890s and the anti-Leninist one in the 1920s–30s, reprised from the 1950s on. As a rule, it was poor. The writer and style were less important; absent were all the usual qualities by which, first, not only the great ancestors, from More to Percy Shelley, but also Wells or Zamiatin or Lem or Le Guin or the Strugatsky Brothers were great writers *tout court*. But second, those qualities also characterised a thick supporting substratum of what I'd call a "2a class" of considerable writers supplying stimulating ideas, alternatives, and plots – from Jack London, A.T. Wright, Olaf Stapledon, Stanley Weinbaum, Aldous Huxley, the US 1940s–50s "new maps of hell," and Orwell to (say) Brunner, Russ, Mitchison, Callenbach, Piercy, Dick, Atwood, MacLeod, and a dozen other SF writers. Antiutopia gets its force from outside fiction, from obsessive inculcation of its ideological points in all aligned media and think-tanks and from the whip of obscurity and hunger (where not drone liquidation) for dissenters. However, I am concerned with its existential embodiment rather than its narrative form here.[8]

2.1.3. The Event of Existential Antiutopia

Politically and ideologically, antiutopianism is an embattled adoption of the point of view and value-system of globally ruling capitalism and the class – or classes – bearing it. *Antiutopia is a targeted ideologico-political use of a closed horizon not simply to refute or ridicule, but to* render unthinkable *both the eutopia of a better possible world and the dystopia as awful warning about the writer's and readers' present tendencies*, thus to stifle the right to dissent and to strive for radical novelty, to dismantle any possibility of plebeian democracy. It is always "a political reply to the political project of realizing utopia" (Jacoby 81). The intertext of antiutopia has historically been anti-socialism and anti-communism, as this was the strongest "currently proposed" eutopia after ca. 1915–75. It is no longer, as heretofore, consubstantial with radical criticism of the intended reader's present but celebratory of it, so that any criticism is only perfective and marginal – though often touted as "revolutionary" – amounting to: how can we or I profit more?

My central socioformalist and historical thesis is that a world-historical novum or Badiouan mega-event hit humanity after the end of the Cold War, like the Yucatan comet that extinguished the age of dinosaurs: in a ruse of history, the ideologico-political development of capitalism (that had all along produced fake novums galore) morphed into an encompassing monster – *the existential antiutopia*. This is in our scholarship a scandal, in the original Biblical sense of a stumbling stone to be disbelieved into (cf. Suvin "Parables"), for any theory of utopia/nism worth its oats after ca. 1968 made it crystal clear that utopia is an epistemological and not ontological beast. The argument that an approximation to eutopia (or even dystopia) may be found or constructed in reality, as in blueprints or colonies, disregarded why they all necessarily fail – as Marx told Cabet when the latter was founding his US colony. We all concluded utopia cannot be realised or not realised; it can be only imagined as a contrast and/or yardstick, a Fata Morgana in the desert of the oppressively real, a memento for the downtrodden or a stick for beating one's ideological opponents.[9] But history is slyer than any theory yet invented by poor human singletons, and in our stress on values we should have remembered that axiology also entails finality (*telos*), so it spills over from epistemology to ontology. We were right to oppose Stalinist and right-wing simplifications by insisting that meaning is conveyed only through forms, yet I have to acknowledge we were finally wrong that utopia/nism cannot have a political embodiment. A powerful approximation to antiutopia, armed to the teeth, can and is being globally realised by present-day capitalism, its banks, States, and ideologies. This unprecedented emergency, whereby we are living in and being existentially shaped by this most corrupt or perfectly sinful in a Fichtean sense form of utopia/nism, must be considered and articulated.

Given the very small role and poor quality of antiutopia in literature, I earlier thought it was a weird variety of the "black" utopia, but this turns out to be wrong. All of us now live within a leaden existential global closure where we are threatened by antiutopia as Destiny of subjection within a long-duration collapse of capitalist structures of accumulation – Lehman Brothers, Trump or Brexit, anyone? This introduces a radical reversal, or more precisely eversion, from a situation in which interested readers looked *from outside* at utopia/nism as a choice of freedom, an exhilarating Possible World, to a situation whereby all of us are willy-nilly *inside* antiutopia in our empirical, more and more decaying Zero World. This antiutopian world functions rather like the mathematised models in capitalist financial speculation designed to make the modelled state of affairs more like the model. In it, imaginative understanding is being pre-empted by myopic and malevolent doing, while our choices are diverted from root – that is, radical – problems to fickle fashion. We are being forcefully and often forcibly lived by antiutopia, a growing restriction of possibilities to work for life-enhancing change. This is physically obvious when entire parts of the world are being thrust into destruction by capitalist and/or its complementary nationalist armies, and even for the richer enclaves (just so nobody should be spared) in the capitalocene climate change. *This changes all* – including utopia/nism, its theory and practice. And our analytic tools have to be adjusted to this victory of ideology over utopia. One guideline: this cannot be done unless accompanied by thorough and explicit analysis speaking against the central features of antiutopia – that is, today's capitalism sliding into more or less fascism: sexism, racism, terror, ecocide, and perpetual mega-warfare. To use critical dystopias and eutopias in order to roll back antiutopia is a matter of life and death for most of us, possibly for humanity as a whole.

2.2. On Antiutopia as Ptolemeian Counterrevolution: The How and the Why

So what happens when, in a most radically bad novum, all of us find ourselves thrust inside antiutopia, a kind of demented *Tron* or *Matrix* movie we cannot get out of, increasingly more bitter if not impossible to live in? If we are to think about getting out, what are the events behind the events (Brecht) or some approximation to deep causes? Whence the rise of antiutopia as closed horizon to politico-existential dominance or hegemony, beginning with the breakthrough of Thatcher and Reagan and fully affirmed by the 1990s?

As suggested above, there is a central existential difference between *a life-world one is necessarily inside of* and *a Tolkienian secondary creation one is as a rule outside of*. In any really existing situation people willy-nilly live, work, die, and (often) get children: their body and psychophysical interest is fully engaged in their location. To the contrary, a piece of utopian fiction, a Fourierist blueprint or even a Disney World does not fully enclose a person: one may visit it, but not live in it, one may dwell on but not in it, one is never completely inside. Utopian colonies attempting to span this abyss regularly cracked up. The Book of Nature is not really a book, whatever hieroglyphs it may contain; the Theatre of the World (or of Society) is not really a theatre, whatever plays or games may come and go on it, for we are not an audience but on stage. The relationships and traffic between virtual and actual reality, between the Life World and secondary virtual creations or Possible Worlds are multiple and complex, since all of them partake of human imagination in differing ways, but most of the time the entities themselves remain distinct; as Freud noted: "nobody can be killed *in absentia* or *in effigie*" ("Transference" 107, translation amended). Traffic piles up unless it proceeds between two distinct places.

I would argue that every significant work of art is a kind of – non-notional – truth that opens up both its own possibility and "the formal possibility of *other* possibilities, ones as yet unsuspected by us" (Badiou 12). Both egalitarianism and possibility are thematised and foregrounded in utopia/nism's overt appeal to critical reason. Antiutopia pre-empts and enforces denial of these contracts. It denies and occults what Jameson rightly saw as the "stereoptic" quality of the utopian imagination that "places the utopian fantasist in two distinct worlds at the same time and generates a unique kind of discomfort by the seemingly irreconcilable demands it makes to disengage absolutely from what is at the same time that one cleaves absolutely to the being of the world as some ultimate limit" (*Seeds* 161; I would read the final mention of "the world" as what I call a Possible World). Antiutopia effects as it were a counterrevolution within the utopian revolution by flattening all possibilities of radical alterity or novum into the dominant "one-eyed" capitalocene hegemony that absolutely takes the structure of what is as the ultimate limit.

However, there are two ideological variants of this antiutopianism, both violent. The cheery one is peddled by think-tanks and governments supported by billionaires and most of their world media; it is as a rule gung-ho, pretending we live in Social-Darwinist eutopia. It says "we live in the best of all possible worlds, you just gotta be competitive!" However, among intellectuals that usually hate eutopia and dystopia, one often finds the gloomy one; it says "life is hell and nothing can be done, we live in the best of all possible BAD worlds" (cf. Baggesen); this too is frequent today in movies or TV serials – *Game of Thrones* anyone? The black horizon can often pose as opposition to the idiot smile of the first one, but they are Siamese twins inasmuch as both propagate acquiescence in what obtains. In practice a number of "black" texts meld critical dystopia and various kinds of unsurmountable antiutopia, to my mind at the expense of their quality, most prominently Orwell's *1984*.

In grim Post-Fordism, where compromise with the ruled by means of co-opted consumerism is no longer very necessary, the welfare measures – developing public health, education, housing, and other services for the people as well as controlling savage capitalism – are replaced by measures to monitor, penalise, and sequester the poor (cf. Wacquant, also Brown). The Ayn Rand supermen operate by means of either direct physical killing or total precarisation with a permanent threat of hunger and destitution. The totalised control as well as the intensification and celebration of being commodified is extended over the whole globe, a new Borgesian map identical to the territory. As in the "American Dream" picket fence appearance of *The Truman Show* movie and in similar fakely ideal sets in a number of SF stories by Philip K. Dick, antiutopia can only be maintained if the inhabitants are persuaded it is the only reality. The utopia of personal-cum-collective freedom, as ideal or protest, is simply made unintelligible. As Debord told us, "Modern economic production extends its dictatorship extensively and intensively" (Debord, point 42; see also Foucault in section 3): there is no different present or future, time duration has for almost all of us shrunk to the next financial deadline for survival.

Most briefly, this is my hypothesis: *Capitalism has by now grown fully parasitic* – profit is no longer accompanied by rising accumulation or productivity, it comes increasingly from political manipulation of "rents" rather than from production (except in China). The system survives only by continuously increased extortion of surplus labour from the 95% of lower classes and nations to the rulers. It is by far the biggest manmade threat to liberty, cognising, and creativity invented by our species. Or simply to survival.

The existential antiutopia was historically brought about as a global ruling-class counter-project to the post-1917 Welfare-and-Warfare State, which first lost its welfare wing and was as of the 1970s rapidly devolved to Warfare-and-Bamboozlery State. Warfare was exported outside the State-system of the metropolitan (capitalist, patriarchal) North, represented at the end of 20th Century by the "trilateral" group of North America, west-central Europe and Japan plus a smattering of their outcrops – the "little tigers" of East Asia, the "White dominions" of ex-British Empire. And warfare grew into a new norm in strict parallel to the dismantling of the (sometimes spotty or unwieldy) solidarity and justice that had brought about and sustained the Welfare State in its Leninist as well as – reactively – in its Keynesian wing; thus violence as war abroad also meant increasing violence as repression within, needed to quell the rising despair over, and possibly protests against, the sabotage of public health, education, housing, and all other services for people and controls over savage capitalism without a human face, spearheaded by the rising exploitation of immigrant workers without civic rights.

Beside warfare, the new supertechnological capitalism is centrally developing through an in-depth *attack on life*. The pulsating heart of capitalism was always the unequal exchange of life (people's time and labour-power) for money, well compressed by Ben Franklin 250 years ago as "Time Is Money." Now private property, having exhausted things, annexes also relationships – prominently including vital relations between things, to which people are reduced (reified) as equally strip-mined "human resources." A strategic link is private property on knowledge that exploded with the right to patent living matter for profit, from genes to species, as decided by the US Supreme Court in 1980; it is estimated there are by now more than 100,000 such patents. The true owners of life today are, besides the armed forces, the pharmaceutic companies, agrochemical monsters, and information profiteers, all connected through international mega-banks.

In sum, the specter haunting us today is the Police State or indeed a reborn Fascism 2.0, where bamboozling is replaced by outright Social-Darwinist cynicism – the Warfare and Repression State. As a rule these repressions returned from US-organised dictatorships around the world to roost in the native soil, first hypocritically and then openly as of the Bush Jr. administration "war on terror"; the old imperialist nostalgias of France and UK, and then the rising State capitalist power of China and the somewhat reconstituted Russia follow the same oppressive pattern, while providing some opportunities to maneuvering for smaller States and groups. Each listener can fill in the list of moral and political reasons for our indignation at such a huge impoverishment and militarisation of our lives.

This poses an epistemological problem. Since I do not believe in Original Sin, and especially not that the Devil rules on Earth, I have to – all of us have to – explain this slide from epistemology to ontology, from a thirst for understanding to a fetishism of the oppressively existing. At stake is after all what Ernst Bloch called "the principle of hope."

2.3. Antiutopia as Constituted Absence: The Deeper Why

As to our theory of utopia/nism, we could salvage it by assuming *eutopia is in antiutopia latently present as a constituted absence*: the sinister hollow is defined by a possible threatening plenitude – as in the superordinate constitutive relation between death and life.[10] This calculated though mostly unacknowledged absence is all-pervasive, it determines all defining traits of antiutopia: not only the usual fake novums foreclosing radical ones, but also quantity instead of quality, closure instead of openness, fake ontology instead of modest epistemology, point-like inescapability instead of fertile traffic between past present and future, monologism instead of contradictions, impotent horror instead of intervening hope and indignation, cynicism instead of belief, vertical leadership and horizontal identities instead of polymorphic diversity enforced by recall democracy: Mussolini, Carl Schmitt, and von Mises as Great Ancestors instead of Rousseau, J.S. Mill, and Marx. Such traits culminate in the subsumptive unholy trinity of antiutopia – *hatred of plebeian creativity and roaming intelligence* (Denkverbot), *the State as repressive violence instead as public power*, and *annihilating warfare instead of creative emulation*. These traits amount to an antiutopian "mythological machine" (Jesi), blending degraded numinosity, power, and commodity esthetics. It does not aim for truth – indeed truth is repressed and left in obscurity, somewhere far behind – but for performativity, a fascistoid effect on corruptible masses. In relation to the light of a disalienated humanity, it is, to cite Milton, "No light, but rather darkness visible" (*Paradise Lost* I: 63). Sociologically, it is an imperious reality concretised as capitalist mass media shaping mass opinion, with economic whips and militarised violence enforcing it. It entails a thoroughgoing abolition of free choice, on which any worthwhile culture, and within it the system of literature and its genres, reposes – quite analogous to the lack of meaningful choice in elections for the US Presidency or the Council of Europe or the Chinese Communist Party Central Committee, or in the fate of bombed out millions. Its ultimate horizon is not freedom but a Police State, kept up by what cannot be thought of (Figure 1):

As Foucault, despite some central waffling on neo-liberalism, never tired to argue, governing in his time comports "a formidable extension of the control and coercion procedures.... [of] the major disciplinary techniques that take in and take care of (*reprendre en charge*) the individuals' everyday behaviour up to the smallest detail" (98). The pretense at inclusion of people into power and meaning is in fact a most frustrating exclusion, where the body or "naked life" is the final and often only "capital" left. The brunt of denial is aimed at the category of revolution and any claim to fertile universality or open-ended totalisation (Wegner, *Imaginary* 121–28).

A surface example: Rancière notes that "the pseudo-European Constitution testifies to [hatred of democracy and egalitarianism] *a contrario*"; the absence of "the irreducible >power of the people<" is then constituted as ultra-elitist "expert management of monetary and population flows" (*Hatred* 95). In sum, democracy as freedom for individuals how to choose meaningful lives and pursue happiness is evacuated.

A middle-range glocal example: the global neoliberalist market imposes its "intelligibility grid" on all non-economical human affairs, so that whatever cannot be used as "human capital" and subjected to "cost-benefit" and "supply-demand" criteria (Foucault 249 and 252, cf. also 250–53 and 272) becomes simply non-intelligible – irrational and indeed inhuman – and is ruled out of court by power. Its perfect local complements are the carefully manipulated mini-nationalisms of globalisation that mean, most clearly in Africa and eastern Europe, "linguistic unhoming, the deaccession of archives [including their physical destruction, DS], the eradication of historical memory, internal colonization..." (Apter 195) – a creeping version of Newspeak.

A central depth example: the frantic interlocking planning, usually for a year if not less, of all capitalist bureaucracies – financial, political, military, corporative – with the goal of maximum profit is an absenting of a plebeian, workers' control system of flexible planning extending to long-duration coordination, where human welfare

Figure 1 In the Prison Library

overrides profit. To generalise: the ideal-type eutopia does not know the categories of profit or servitude, dystopia shows them as crazy and inhuman, antiutopia argues how to get more profit through servitude. Its mantra is There Is No Alternative; its biggest fear is freedom – while hypocritically invoking it in a castrated version: "like unto white[washe]d sepulchres, which indeed appear beautiful outward, but are within full of dead men's bones, and of all uncleanness" (Matthew 23: 27, *King James Version*). In sum, Marx's "profound hypocrisy and inherent barbarism of bourgeois civilisation," once nakedly visible only in colonies (*On Colonialism* 88), has now been globalised. Where he identified the reduction of the working day as the prerequisite for the realm of freedom, antiutopia is a whirling turbine of unceasingly frenzied activities on pain of instant failure: no wonder the German term for our age is turbocapitalism.

Finally, what about affects? I see around me in late capitalocene two opposed main ones: the officially required manic cheer on the road to success is always threatened by the much vaster reservoir of naked reactive <u>*fear*</u>, which when shunted off by the hegemony into the grey matter of subaltern brains becomes fear for naked survival. At the genetic and structural core of antiutopia, in my feeling, lies the rulers' fear of radical change that would mean plebeian self-empowerment (that is, revolution in and around production). Wegner noted that it is the passion for totality that accounts for the great fear of utopia which engendered the antiutopia.[11] Only the panic fear, rage, and loathing at the supposed Leninism – communism come to power – can explain the last 40-odd years of finally triumphant capitalism. Its allegorical emblem is the "terminator gene" introduced by mega-corporations into seeds to ensure they cannot be renewed, thus constituting the absence of thousands of years of human crop cultivation, of the utopian horizon of "bread for all" (cf. Matvejević). Fear, as Bloch repeatedly explained, was the negative affect we share with animals, to which hope, only present in humans, is opposed; furthermore, hope "allows for logical and concrete correction and sharpening," it is an "act of cognitive orientation (*Richtungsakt)*" (126 and 10, see also 83).

Today we are blithely returning to the mere animality in us. Centrally, the whole emancipatory panoply of capitalism's radical bourgeois beginnings – from humanist culture and Enlightenment through revolutions and Romanticism – is being ruthlessly and systematically scrapped, up to the shark-like liquidation of traces of welfare for (the) people. As Marx piercingly observed: when events force upon the bourgeoisie a democratic constitution, this helps the proletariat "and *threatens* the very foundations of bourgeois society" (*Class*). To give one weighty example: the abolition of torture, the favourite feudal and Church tool against rebelling lower classes, was the crown jewel of Enlightenment and bourgeois liberalism; it is now taken back (cf. Hobsbawm 143 and passim). Rewinding history *à rebours,* the revolutionary and liberatory *citoyen* (citizen) aspect is being thoroughly expunged. The result is the relentless deepening and broadening of the "zone of non-being" identified by Fanon for the racialised and colonialised subject (7). As Le Guin's protagonist in *The Dispossessed*, to my mind the best piece of utopian writing since Wells, if not More and Swift, tells the ambassador from a totally antiutopian Terra: "You would destroy us rather than admit out reality, rather than admit that there is hope!" (350)

Notes

* My warmest thanks for indispensable bibliographic guidance go to Lyman T. Sargent and Tom Moylan; for clarifying discussions and sending me their works to Fredric Jameson and the first two names, without whom Part 2 could not have been written; last not least, to Raffaella Baccolini, Antonis Balasopulos, John Clute, Zorica Đergović-Joksimović, Peter Fitting, Saša Hrnjez, Richard Ohmann, Patrick Parrinder, Tamara Prošić, Bülent Somay, Victor Strazzeri, Pavla Vesela, Darren Webb, and Phil Wegner.

I couldn't have done this without the kind and efficient help of the Clare College and Cambridge University Library staff, also of Jake Culank from Cambridge.

For the invitation to deliver the keynote speech at the Utopian Studies Society in Prato 2019 and much help on that occasion my thanks go to Andrew Milner.

To Part 1

1 I read culpably late Miéville's article, but entirely agree with most of it (except the final reflections what to do now). He rightly points out that "The very term 'Anthropocene', which gives with one hand, insisting on human drivers of ecological shift, misleads with its implied 'We'. After all, [what warranted] a new geochronological term [was] a shift in the political economy by which it and we are organised, an accelerating cycle of profit and accumulation.... Which means … standing directly against military power and violence. Three times as many land-rights and environmental activists were murdered in 2012 than a decade before..."; and he points to Jason W. Moore's 2017 coinage of the term "capitalocene" (see much more on this in chapter 24 of this book).

2 *Summary for Policymakers of the Global Assessment Report on Biodiversity and Ecosystem Services.* [subtitles] "Nature's Dangerous Decline 'Unprecedented' – Species Extinction Rates 'Accelerating'" – "Current global response insufficient; 'Transformative changes' needed to restore and protect nature. Opposition from vested interests can be overcome for public good." – "Most comprehensive assessment of its kind; 1,000,000 species threatened with extinction."

www.ipbes.net/news/Media-Release-Global-Assessment?utm_source=Tricontinental+subscribers +single+list&utm_campaign=44d16e48d7-EMAIL_CAMPAIGN_2019_05_15_06_55&utm_ medium=email&utm_term=0_bb06a786c7-44d16e48d7-190620865

I acknowledge the stimulus of the Tricontinental Institute for Social Research's Newsletter "We Are the Shadow-Ghosts…" (2019) that led me to these two reports, and from which I have appropriated, in my own way which differs from theirs, many formulations.

3 *Governance of economic transition: a scientific background document for the UN Global Sustainable Development Report 2019* [21.8.2018]. https://bios.fi/en/economic-transition-governance-a-scientific-background-document-to-the-un-global-sustainable-development-report-2019/?utm_source (see full url end in note 3).

4 I have been queried by the *Utopian Studies* editor, Professor Nicole Pohl, about the passage beginning "My example stems from a large exhibition called UTOPIA…." as to the correctness of the Jacoby quote, and asked why didn't I ask the curators of the exhibition, either Lyman T. Sargent and/or Gregory Claeys, "If this indeed was correct and the intention." She also contacted Professor Lyman Sargent, who responded to me in a longish e-mail from which I excerpt two central passages. First, he wrote "I find it hard to believe that anybody who actually saw the exhibit could say that either the kibbutz or National Socialism were presented as viable ideals. The name of the exhibit was *Utopia: The Search for the Ideal Society in the Western World*, and ALL the exhibits were about the search with no implication that any of them were viable…. Since we included photographs of Auschwitz, I simply can't believe that anyone actually at the exhibit could use the phrase viable utopia." Second, he clarified that "In NY both the kibbutz and National Socialism were in a room that also had listening posts so that people could hear King's I Have a Dream speech while view[ing] photographs and artifacts from the Civil Rights Movement."

My answer is that as a critic and scholar I am not at all interested in an author's – or a group of curators' – *intent* or personal belief; that is the business of their friends and relatives (or political friends and enemies). I am interested exclusively *in what is actually written or presented for others to see* – on the effect of any work on its consumers. To understand this, one must know what was being presented. From Professor Sargent's words above, I understand that the same room presented photographs, documents, audio-tapes, and other artifacts from the Israeli collective farms (kibbutzim), from Martin Luther King and the US Civil Rights Movement, and from Nazism – the latter included Nazi propaganda and it seems also a photograph of the Auschwitz "concentration" or more properly liquidation camp. No information pointing out that these were included as a contrary to utopia or utopianism seems to have been included.

How is one to understand that room in an exhibition called UTOPIA? True, this does leave it to the viewers to decide whether these were "viable" utopias or not. "Viable" is Jacoby's ambiguous term, to my mind conflating success of a project (could it have been accomplished?) with its right belonging to a category (was it right to call it utopia?) and I would not defend it too far. But I do share the main point of indignation with Jacoby: *Why put Nazism into a UTOPIA exhibition at all?* It strongly suggests that what any "identity group" chooses for its horizon and goes to search for can be called Utopia. This is to my mind plain wrong, and I discuss it in the main text on that basis.

Please remember that my paragraph begins by saying that it seems clear to me "there are no utopian studies without values." What is at stake here is first of all axiological: can scholarship be without values, which turns it into a pure affirmation of the status quo? Not to my mind – witness the telling "Western World" part of the exhibition title, which myopically refused the surely essential confrontation with what happened "East" of it, say in Russia and then China, Cuba, and so on… But secondly, it is also epistemological: how can we have a unified field of studies if it is unlimited, and anybody can put into it whatever he or she pleases? The answer is, I'm afraid, nohow – not a valid field of studies, anyway, in terms of categorical clarity and intellectual success.

Notes to Part 2

5 Cf. Moylan, *Demand* 1 and passim. Here I part company with the inclusiveness of the useful Sargisson title, from which I have learned a lot: for example, the Dubai architecture it discusses can be used as a typical component or indeed paragon of our existential antiutopia, akin to the Iron Heel's super-cities in Jack London, so that calling it utopia (in either eutopian and dystopian senses) means repeating Ernst Bloch's major mistake, the desire to equate utopia/nism and reality. I should add that to accept the use of "utopia" as a swearword – as in the massive anti-Obama campaign cited in Sargisson 22–24 – is the symmetrical obverse of accepting utopia as perfection.

6 Antiutopia was brilliantly diagnosed in Part 1 of Jameson's *Seeds* in the early 90s, and I shall use aspects of his argument, but those were still early days. Cf. also McAlear on how dystopia and antiutopia share the urgency of a *de facto* near-future story – whatever their ostensible spacetime – but remain incompatible because the former is to be understood as preventable, resistance is possible even if it fails in the plot, while the latter "seeks to shut down a discussion of alternatives" (30, and see 40 and passim; I should mention that he sees hope in the Newspeak segment of *1984*, where I do not).

The whole complex of differentiating antiutopia from dystopia and utopianism in general is insufficiently explored. Let me mention here only two further foci for testing: language and memory, and the relation of utopianism to death. A characteristic difference may well be the battle over language, memory, and expression that usually develops in dystopia (cf. Baccolini "Gender," also "Finding") vs. the monophonic refusal of intricate contradictions in favour of black-and-white adversariness in Ayn Rand or, for example, on all world media. Further, as I argue in "Using Negativities," utopia and death are akin as enemy brothers (*frères enemies*) that share "the point of view of the species upon human history," which denies atomic individuality in favour of "our species being, our insertion in the great chain of the generations, which we know as death." Therefore, personal death is if not easy then much easier to bear if there is a believable hope for such a linked humanity going on and even advancing. Where death *per se* affirms nothingness as rest, utopia affirms fullness of creative labour on the collective level. Antiutopia refuses to think about either, substituting as its supreme rule the Social Darwinist "survival of the fittest" – meaning the rich.

7 For the emblematic case of Wordsworth, see the richly argued Kantor, who finds "liberal ideology … a process by which we recover a way of seeing after we have been disabused of its utopian character" (517). The Immortality Ode registers the defeat of visionary revolution and opts for "incremental reform" (519): "Whither is fled the visionary gleam?/ Where is it now, the glory and the dream?/ --- /… relinquish[ing] delight/ To live beneath your habitual sway." Even in this early ancestor one finds essential characteristics of liberal abstract utopianism – order stemming out of disillusion and compensatory turn to timelessness (in Wordsworth: nature, childhood, and deism).

Another interesting ancestor to antiutopia, Jameson suggests in *Archaeologies* 144, would be Samuel Delany's *Trouble on Triton*, where the eponymous planetoid harbours a plethora of changing varieties of physical appearance, gender, and sexual orientation. It is unfortunately a much over-simplified and rather intolerant wish-dream of homosexual and cognate gender counterculture opposed to what he wrongly felt were Le Guin's totalising sociopolitical tendencies – and her foregrounding of heterosexuality – in the "critical utopia" of *The Dispossessed*. On the one hand *Triton* deals only with life-styles, and one can sympathise with its quest for freedom of experiment; on the other it presents a simple negation of however rainbow-like unity, and therefore of positive utopianism as such, in favour of enclave diversity within a magnified version of the 1960s New York and London yet without economics characteristically, even a mega-war is treated as peripheral. The undoubted verve and acuity of Delany is therefore sectarian and eminently cooptable, choosing ephemeral quasi-utopian enclaves – if sex and *jouissance* is your utopia – within the never shown "reigning dystopia of the system" (Jameson ibidem).

8 See to begin with Jameson *Archaeologies*, Sargent "Three" 7-10, and the titles by Baccolini and Moylan, most thoroughly in Moylan *Scraps*.

9 Autobiography: in 1964-65 I was a "special student" from a poor country at Yale. It was the exciting, ozone-laden age of anti-Vietnam-War and Black protests in the USA, full of great ideas sprouting at every corner; at the second US Conference of Socialist Scholars (yes!) I gave a paper on Brecht and had the speakers' privilege of breakfast with Herbert Marcuse... Though I was at the School of Drama, I fell in with some people interested in SF & utopia – Jacques Ehrmann in French studies, who died early, and my long-time friend Mike Holquist from Slavic studies, who then in the fatidic year of 1968 published the brilliant little piece on "How To Play Utopia." Their

central view was that utopia was a chronotopic equivalent of the conditional mode in grammar: not indicating but supposing and speculating.

A note on Cold War linguistics: I asked Mike how did a Minnesota Swede get into Slavic studies. He was drafted during the Korean war and told by the CIA he could go to the frontline or learn Russian in order to monitor army messages around that front; he chose the latter. On the other side, at the same time, Arkadiy Strugatsky was told by analogous entities to learn Japanese for the same purpose, and stationed in an anti-aircraft unit near Vladivostok. I myself was in the army for 11 months beginning Sept. 1, 1956, and offered my language knowledge to Belgrade, but the Yugoslav Army wasn't so sophisticated, so I served in an engineering unit at the Hungarian border, waiting for the Russian tanks to swing South from Budapest and finish off us too…

10 I came to the concept of constituted absence by being reminded of the role of the Baroque god in Pascal and Racine, whereof Lucien Goldmann speaks in *Le Dieu caché* – with thanks to Michael Löwy – or indeed of the Mbuya tribe's father god Ñamandu in Pierre Clastres (see Suvin "Power"). This absence was in history positively sublated by the appearance of a revolutionary wave of rich personalities like Denis Diderot, Jean-Jacques Rousseau or Tom Payne. Alas, the constitutive absence of value signalled by antiutopia is a repressed and anal-retentive obverse of the Baroque tragicalness. It flows out of triumphant counter-revolution and it is carried by impoverished *Übermenschen* like Ayn Rand and the Donalds, Rumsfeld and Trump. The return from *citoyen* democracy to a semi-masked (and often open) bourgeois tyranny adds to cynicism and it is also a confession of weakness: as Marx, cited here, often pointed out, true or plebeian democracy would work against capitalism.

11 See Wegner, "Jamesons" 199 and passim; I have been much stimulated by Jameson's chapter "Journey into Fear" and the general horizon of *Archaeologies*.

Works Cited

Part 1

All the URLs were accessed between April and June 2019.

Section 1.1

Bammer, Angelika. *Partial Visions: Feminism and Utopianism in the 1970s*, 2nd ed. P. Lang, 2015.

Chossudovsky, Michel. *The Globalization of Poverty and the New World Order*. Global Research, 2003.

Crick, Bernard. *George Orwell: A Life*. Penguin, 1982.

[Daly, Herman E.] *Ecological Economics and Sustainable Development, Selected Essays….* Ed. J. van den Bergh. Elgar, 2007.

[Daly, Herman E.] and Joshua Farley. *Ecological Economics*, 2nd ed. Island P, 2011, http://library.uniteddiversity. coop/Measuring_Progress_and_Eco_Footprinting/Ecological_Economics-Principles_and _Applications.pdf.

Foster, John Bellamy. *Naked Imperialism*. Monthly RP, 2006.

Foster, John Bellamy. "The New Imperialism of Globalized Monopoly-Finance Capital." *Monthly R*, monthlyreview.org/2015/07/01/the-new-imperialism-of-globalized-monopoly-finance-capital/.

Harvey, David. *The Enigma of Capital: And The Crises of Capitalism*. Profile Books, 2010.

Lenin, V.I. *The State and Revolution*. www.marxists.org/archive/lenin/works/1917/staterev/.

Luxemburg, Rosa. *The Accumulation of Capital*. Trans. A. Schwarzschild. www.marxists.org/archive/luxemburg/1913/accumulation-capital/index.htm.

Marcos, Subcomandante. *The Zapatistas' Dignified Rage*. Trans. H. Gales, ed. N. Henck. AK P, 2018.

Marx, Karl. *Grundrisse*. Trans. M. Nicolaus. www.marxists.org/archive/marx/works/1857/ grundrisse/.

Miéville, China. "Limits of Utopia". *Salvage* [2015], http://salvage.zone/mieville_all.html.

Nixon, Rob. *Slow Violence and the Environmentalism of the Poor*. Harvard UP, 2011.

Pogge, Thomas. *World Poverty and Human Rights*. Polity P, 2003.

Suvin, Darko. *Communism, Poetry: Communicating Vessels*. Political Animal, 2020.

Suvin, Darko. *In Leviathan's Belly: Essays for a Counter-Revolutionary Time*. Wildside P for Borgo P, 2012.

Wright, Eric Olin. *Taking the Social in Socialism Seriously*. U of Wisconsin, 2004, www.ssc.wisc.edu/~wright/Socialism.pdf.

Section 1.2

Jacoby, Russell. *Picture Imperfect*. Columbia UP, 2005.

Jameson, Fredric. *Archeologies of the Future*. Verso, 2005.

Strier, Richard. "Taking Utopia Seriously." *Moreana* 54.2 (2017): 141–8.

Suvin, Darko. "To Explain Fascism Today." *Critique* [Glasgow] 45.3 (2017): 259–302.

Webb, Darren. "Educational Studies and the Domestication of Utopia." *British J of Educational Studies* 64.4 (2016): 431–48.

Wegner, Phillip E. "Jameson's Modernisms; Or, the Desire Called Utopia." *Diacritics* 37.4 (2007): 3–20.

Part 2

Apter, Emily. "Untranslatability and the Geopolitics of Reading." *PMLA* 134.1 (2019): 194–200.

Baccolini, Raffaella. "Breaking the Boundaries: Gender, Genre, and Dystopia," in N. Minerva ed., *Per una definizione dell'utopia*. Longo, 1992, 137–46.

Baccolini, Raffaella. "Finding Utopia in Dystopia: Feminism, Memory, Nostalgia, and Hope," in Moylan and eadem eds. [below], 159–90.

Baccolini, Raffaella. "Gender and Genre in the Feminist Critical Dystopias of Katherine Burdekin, Margaret Atwood, and Octavia Butler," in M.S. Barr ed., *Future Females, The Next Generation*. Rowman & Littlefield, 2000, 13–34.

Baccolini, Raffaella, and Tom Moylan eds. *Dark Horizons: Science Fiction and the Dystopian Imagination*. Routledge, 2003.

Badiou, Alain. "The Idea of Communism," in C. Douzinas and S. Žižek eds., *The Idea of Communism*. Verso, 2010, 1–12.

Baggesen, Søren "Utopian and Dystopian Pessimism: Le Guin's *The Word for World is Forest* and Tiptree's "We Who Stole the Dream." *Science-Fiction Studies* 14.1 (1987): 34–43.
Barthes, Roland. *Sade – Fourier – Loyola*. Seuil, 1971.
Bauman, Zygmunt. *Socialism: The Active Utopia*. Holmes & Meier, 1976.
Bloch, Ernst. *Das Prinzip Hoffnung*, 2 vols. Suhrkamp, 1959.
Brown, Wendy. *Undoing the Demos*. MIT P, 2015.
Clute, John. "Fantasy," in idem and John Grant eds., *Encyclopedia of Fantasy*. 1997. http://sf-encyclopedia.uk/fe.php?nm=fantasy
Debord, Guy. *Society of the Spectacle*. www.marxists.org/reference/archive/debord/society.htm. Accessed Nov. 15, 2018.
Fanon, Frantz. *Black Skin, White Masks*. Trans. C. L. Markmann. Grove, 1967.
Foucault, Michel. *Naissance de la biopolitique*. Ed. M. Senellart. Gallimard, 2004.
[Freud, Sigmund]. "Dynamics of Transference," in *The Standard Edition of the Complete Psychological Works of Sigmund Freud*, vol. 12. https://chicagoanalysis.org/system/files/readings/Freud,%20S.%20%5B1912%5D%20-%20The%20Dynamics%20of%20Transference.pdf. Accessed Sep. 9, 2018.
Goldmann, Lucien. *Le Dieu caché*. Gallimard, 1956.
Hobsbawm, Eric. "Public Order in an Age of Violence," in his *Globalisation, Democracy and Terrorism*. Little, Brown, 2008, 138–54.
Jacoby, Russell. *Picture Imperfect*. Columbia UP, 2005.
Jameson, Fredric. *Archaeologies of the Future*. Verso, 2005.
Jameson, Fredric. *The Seeds of Time*. Columbia UP, 1994.
Jesi, Furio. *Il tempo della festa*. nottetempo, 2013.
Kantor, Jamison. "Immortality, Romanticism, and the Limit of Liberal Imagination." *PMLA* 133.3 (2018): 508–25.
King James Version, The Authorized: The New Testament. Winston & Pocket Books, 1944.
Le Guin, Ursula K. *The Dispossessed*. Harper Prism, 1994.
Lešaja, Ante. *Knjigocid: uništavanje knjiga u Hrvatskoj 1990tih [Destroying Books in Croatia in the 1990s]*. Profil & Srpsko nacionalno vijeće, 2012.
Levitas, Ruth A. "The Imaginary Reconstitution of Society," in Moylan and Baccolini eds., 47–68.
Marx, Karl. *Class Struggles in France, 1848 to 1850*. www.marxists.org/ archive/marx/works/1850/class-struggles-france/ch02.htm. Accessed Nov. 15, 2018.
Marx, Karl. *On Colonialism*. FLPH, n.d.
Marx, Karl. *Grundrisse*. Transl. M. Nicolaus. www.marxists.org/archive/marx/works/1857/grundrisse/. Accessed Nov. 11, 2018.
Matvejević, Predrag. *Pane nostro*. Garzanti, 2009.
McAlear, Rob. "The Value of Fear." *Interdisciplinary Humanities* 27.2 (2010): 24–42.
Moylan, Tom. *Demand the Impossible*. Methuen, 1986.
Moylan, Tom. "'Look into the dark': On Dystopia and the Novum," in P. Parrinder ed., *Learning from Other Worlds*. Duke UP, 2001, 51–71.
Moylan, Tom. *Scraps of the Untainted Sky: Science Fiction, Utopia, Dystopia*. Westview P, 2000.
Moylan, Tom. "Transgressive, Totalizing, Transformative: *Utopia*'s Utopian Surplus." *Utopian Studies* 29.3 (2018): 309–24.
Moylan, Tom, and Raffaella Baccolini eds. *Utopia Method Vision*. P. Lang, 2007.
Rancière, Jacques. *Hatred of Democracy*. Trans. S. Corcoran. Verso, 2014.

Sargent, Lyman Tower. "The Three Faces of Utopianism Revisited." *Utopian Studies* 5.1 (1994): 1–37.

Sargent, Lyman Tower. "Utopia – The Problem of Definition." *Extrapolation* 16.2 (1975): 137–45.

Sargent, Lyman Tower. *Utopianism: A Very Short Introduction*. Oxford UP, 2010.

Sargisson, Lucy. *Fool's Gold: Utopianism in the Twenty-First Century*. Palgrave Macmillan, 2012.

Suvin, Darko. "Brecht vs. Ibsen: Breaking Open the Individualist or Closed Dramaturgy," in his *To Brecht and Beyond*. Harvester P, and Barnes & Noble, 1984, 56–79.

Suvin, Darko. "To Explain Fascism Today." *Critique* [Glasgow] 45.3 (2017): 259–302.

Suvin, Darko. "Locus, Horizon and Orientation." *DBH*. P. Lang, 2010, 111–36.

Suvin, Darko. *Metamorphoses of Science Fiction*. Yale UP, 1979.

Suvin, Darko. "Parables and Uses of a Stumbling Stone." *Arcadia* 5.2 (2017): 271–300.

Suvin, Darko. "Power without Violence," in his *Communism, Poetry* [see below under "Using"], 135–46.

Suvin, Darko. "A Tractate on Dystopia 2001," *DBH*. P. Lang, 2010, 381–412.

Suvin, Darko. "Using Negativities: Brecht, Politics of Death," in his *Communism, Poetry: Communicating Vessels*. Political Animal, 2020, 227–43.

Wacquant, Loïc. *Punishing the Poor*. Duke UP, https://libcom.org/files/Lo%C3%AFc%20Wacquant%20-%20Punishing%20the%20Poor.pdf. Accessed Dec. 15, 2018.

Wegner, Phillip E. *Imaginary Communities*. U of California P, 2002.

Wegner, Phillip E. "Jameson's Modernisms; or, the Desire Called Utopia." *Diacritics* 37.4 (2007): 2–20.

Wegner, Phillip E. *Shockwaves of Possibility*. P. Lang, 2014.

24

Antiutopia in Coronisation Times: Capitalocene and Death (2020)*

Note Nov. 2020: This essay was written, exceptionally, in the midst of a developing mega-phenomenon I was attempting to understand, and substantially completed in the Summer 2020 lull between the two "coronisation" waves due to our incompetent and feral rulers. Any such cognition is not only incomplete but may also miss essential aspects visible at its end. The need outweighed the risk. The data gathering for this piece was not continued after Oct. 2020, and I leave them as found then. The essay has in part a function of noting how its final "here is what we should do" became mostly "here is what we should have done," and of helping to gauge how insufficient what we actually did was.

> *What keeps mankind alive? The fact that millions*
> *Are daily tortured, stifled, punished, silenced and oppressed*
> *Mankind can keep alive thanks to its brilliance*
> *At keeping its humanity repressed*
> *For once you must try not to shirk the facts:*
> *Mankind is kept alive by bestial acts.*
>
> Lyrics Bertolt Brecht, music Kurt Weill, transl. Tom Waits

> *Protests imply faith in the antagonist. This faith was misplaced and it must be restored to the creativity of the poor.... [T]his pandemic is a symptom of the greater plague which is the war on nature, on women, on the poor.... The expropriators of air, water, food, shelter, energy, and health — must be expropriated.*
>
> Quincy Saul

1. How to See the Pandemic Depth Events (January to August 2020)

1.1 The Ruling Antiutopianism and Its Mutating: Violence versus Care

Let me recall some conclusions in the final part of the preceding essay "Utopia or Bust," devoted to "Our Existential Antiutopia" and written in 2019. They identify the antiutopia we have lived in for 30 years now as *a global ruling-class counter-project* to the post-1917 Welfare-and-Warfare State, which first lost its welfare wing and was from the 1970s devolved to a Warfare-and-Bamboozlery State. Warfare was exported outside the State-system of the metropolitan (capitalist, patriarchal) North, and grew into a new norm in strict parallel to the dismantling of the attempts and achievements at solidarity and justice that had brought about and sustained the Welfare State in its Leninist as well as – reactively – in its Keynesian wing. Violence as war abroad also meant an increasing violence as repression within, needed to quell the rising despair over, and possibly protests against, the sabotage of decent incomes, public health, education, housing, and all other services for people and controls over savage capitalism without a human face, spearheaded by the rising exploitation of women and of immigrant workers without civic rights. Beside warfare, the new phase of capitalism is centrally developing through a depth *attack on life*. The pulsating heart of capitalism was always the unequal exchange of life (people's time and labour-power) for money: "Time Is Money." Now private property, having exhausted things, annexes also relationships – prominently including vital relations between things, to which people are reduced (reified) as equally strip-mined "human resources." A strategic link is private property on knowledge that exploded with the right to patent living matter – from genes to species – for profit, as of 1980. The true owners of life today are, besides the armed forces, the pharmaceutical companies, agrochemical monsters, and information profiteers, all connected through international mega-banks.

The unholy trinity of existential antiutopia – *hatred of plebeian creativity and roaming intelligence* (Denkverbot), *the State as repressive violence instead of as public power*, and *annihilating warfare instead of creative emulation* – grows into an imperious reality with the twin prongs of capitalist mass media shaping mass opinion so that radical differences become unthinkable, and militarised violence enforcing it when brainwashing fails. It entails a thoroughgoing abolition of free choice, on which any worthwhile life reposes. It is rooted in fear, a negative affect we share with animals, so that today we are blithely returning to the mere animality in us. Politically, the whole emancipatory panoply of capitalism's radical *citoyen* beginnings – from humanist culture and Enlightenment through revolutions and Romanticism – is being ruthlessly and systematically scrapped, up to the liquidation of traces of welfare for (the) people.

These considerations, developed before the outbreak of Covid-19 was dreamt of, can be confronted with the Covid-19 pandemic in its first seven months, counting from Feb. 1, 2020, as a test of their pertinence in an increasingly murderous practice. Why is the capitalocene veering toward suppressing freedom? First, because its system has for decades been in a deep crisis of capital accumulation stemming from the insane impoverishment imposed upon billions of working people that disrupts the circulation of goods. The proportion of people living in slums – that is, in totally unhealthy conditions – was in the world as a whole ca. 1/3 and in the 50+ poorest countries in Africa and Asia approaching 2/3 (see World Bank – no absolute numbers were to be found in this bureaucratic creation). Even in the officially wealthiest world country, the USA, a Federal Reserve study for 2018 found that 40% of US households cannot deal with unexpected expenses of around $400 and 74% live from paycheck to paycheck; in the European Union, 33% of households cannot bear similar unexpected expenses (see

Report, Martinchek, and Eurostat). Second, ecocide leads to global mass immiseration, obvious in the present pandemic, which favours measures amounting to a martial law.

In these straits, the chance development of a bit of dangerous quasi-living matter was an unexpected occasion for our ruling lords of zombiedom and dealers in death to profit from its destructive potentials, exploiting deep underground analogies to capitalist thriving from destruction in crises and regrouping. They need it, for the financial core of capitalism is in bad disarray or "secular stagnation" (Larry Summers, no less). Global debt is at ca. $250 trillion, with corporate debt already enormous. There are trillions of dollars swirling around stock markets and in tax havens, and a tsunami of bankruptcies is under way. Finding at hand an erupting pandemic that might infect over 3 billion people, with tens of millions of possible deaths (Christakis), antiutopia can wash its hands of the outworn neo-liberal past and patch up a different imaginary, though it would continue the deviation of public funds into hugely enriching capitalists. The waning of the reigning orthodoxy has recently been convincingly put by The Salvage Editorial Board:

> [N]eo-liberalism, which had persisted undead after the 2008 credit crunch, is finished. War economy, of which the current emergency era of global capitalism is an unusual variant, ... proves that it is possible to do without, even abolish, the price system. The calculus of "in-kind" prevails over pricing.... The economy becomes, not a spontaneous order, but a human organism requiring management and care. (Salvage 18–19)

The antiutopia and its "common sense of capitalist biopolitics" (idem 21) can therefore reach for a more oppressive dispensation. We are seeing strong signs of system mutation into a more maleficent sociopolitical formation that would employ both the State and intolerant nationalism up to racism to again save the profits and bamboozle the outraged people. The following is an attempt to gauge how supertechnological capitalocene accepted this deadly potentiality of pandemic death-in-life, hatred of plebeian roaming, and the State as repressive violence: it asks how could we understand its looming turn of the screw in order to counteract it. The central opposition is one between all human lives (plus its necessary environment of animals, plants, and minerals) as against the capitalocene's pivot on profit.[1] Our central choice is one between *violence and care* (and I shall return to self-defense against violence at the end).

It seems best to approach understanding this complex and powerful new threat by, first, specifying our orienting values, second, identifying a few notional foci for a clear opposing stance, and third, reaching for the only available causal explanation of the present pandemic. I do so in the next three subsections.

1.2. Situation: On Life and Liberty versus Capitalism and Its State

What is the main thing we may learn from the sociopolitical fallout of what is officially called Covid-19? It is *to put life (and liberty) before profit, and solidarity with working, suffering, and loving people before individualism or limited identity* – say national or gender identity, not to speak of the Nazi-type racism now being assiduously courted by most power-holders.

But it is also that all struggles with such a horizon – in this case, to minimise the effects of a global pandemic – can only have a chance of succeeding if some central preconditions are in place. They are of two kinds, *situational* and *epistemological*: the reality guiding and constricting people, the mental constructs attempting to grasp it (though the line separating them sometimes wears thin). I'll deal first with the situational preconditions.

First, that an intolerable situation of pandemic proportions, a mortal illness of the body politic, can be clearly identified, insisted, and focused on. Pertinent biopolitical plagues today are:

- old but no less virulent: the protracted duration and cynical insistence of our rulers upon both *global warming* (that brings huge profits) and global *warfare* (that both brings huge profits and politically ensures them);
- now: most strikingly and swiftly, this *huge mass disease* – which could be at any moment, because of climate disruption, followed by other, similarly but differently severe pandemics (cf. El-Sayed) or indeed recombined with another, say a flu, pandemic;
- and looming ahead: the huge complex of *climate deterioration* going from bad to worse, at the moment best visible in *water wars*, already well-known from Amazonia and Palestine/Israel, and now acute for the Nile, as well as mass dying from a combination of ill health and undernourishment (cf. much more in Prashad et al.), again easily resulting in wars.

All four are caused by capitalist interventions into the biome: first directly into our bodies, in reckless exploitation of living labour plus reckless indoctrination by the mass media; and second, into human bodies by way of reckless devastation of nature. I shall get in 1.4 to the causal explanation of the Covid-19 affair, which first created a latent threat and then boosted a manageable one into a lethal mass actuality.

Second, that a critical mass of people, even if initially a small minority, can influence and bend the political power nationally and internationally if it gains a wide access to public opinion.

Third, that from all evidence in the last 150 years our only possible lever for radical change is an operative nucleus of committed and competent people that can endure in time and space, a political and believing entity that acts following the best cognitive evidence available, historically tested, retested, and retestable at every step, and that it be internationally linked by solidarity with all working people and by central shared goals.

Fourth, that we reconsider the role of the States, both as concerns their absolutely indispensable intervention into and overall channelling of the national and international economies and as concerns their endangering personal freedoms, so that the State apparati are to be strictly monitored and where necessary opposed. Countries with strong State institutions – such as China or South Korea – have been able to handle the pandemic much more efficiently. The gigantic failure of "austerity" healthcare, leading to shoddy if any care for the mass of the people as opposed to excellent private medicine for the rich, is now clearly visible. The case that privatisation and mass immiseration are more efficient than State regulation, and where necessary its extraordinary intervention, has been definitively refuted by mass history: a system of multiple institutions for well-being of all people, underwritten by the whole national (and international) community is indispensable.

Yet life without the liberty of creative choice is only a repetitive, more or less animal cycle. We humans both are and are not animals: our bodies are subject to their needs of food and sex, also to decay and illness, but our personalities are different because we are shaped in and by social history. Closed cycles, however well they begin and however interesting they may be for the weary, soon turn inhuman. This holds for all the ages we know of, from Antique pharaohs to modern corporate bosses; the main innovation by capitalists is that they quite wrongly believe in an unending spiral of ever more profitable quantities that could transgress the entropy of a closed system – our planet Earth. Today we see how fake that "progress" was, for example in the grotesque mass spectacle of people in constant buzzing thrall of their communication (and brainwashing) devices – beginning with the clock, banned in Butler's *Erewhon* as in Rabelais's Abbey of Thélème. For in this way, and in many analogous ways, we are getting back to cyclical time, to Benjamin's mythical recurrence of the same (*das Immerwiedergleiche*) mendaciously disguised as fashionable novelty, which underlies all capitalism. The cycle of capitalism spurns all certainties except those of power and quantity in linear time: buy before the (stock) market closes or a competitor snatches the profitable prize from you! Back to zoology: Man is wolf to Man. At a time of great calamities to our bodies, such as a world war or the present pandemic, we can clearly see how Social Darwinism, that stupid and lying materialism of the rulers, leads straight to collective death. Capitalism is mass unnatural death, freedom is the life worth living. One excludes the other.

Therefore, successes of State centralisation, such as keeping a pandemic in bounds, should not lead to a plea for power either to monopoly capitalism or to the State. On the contrary, repressive States centered on brute force and false belief, have to be constantly guarded against. Today too, most existing political systems are, whatever they may claim, oligarchic – a small class block on the top rules. Not all systems are so overtly anti-democratic as the ruling castes of the EU and China. But in all cases, there is a huge absence of representing working people's interests, a veritable dictatorship of capitalist interest blocks (banks, mega-corporations, armed forces, bureaucracies) that has to be counteracted both by a true direct and associative democracy and a truly representative, mandated and recallable, parliament as its peak. Here, only a critical Left can serve as orientation, as in its perennial debates on the pros and cons of the State (in Russia by Kropotkin, Lenin, Serge, Bukharin, Rakovsky, and on): "Key to the politics of such demands as we must make of the State is never trusting the State of which we make them" (Salvage 32).

The huge perils of State intervention can be seen in the present discourse pivoting on – and limited by – scientism in its medical variant that progresses from the virus peril to the triumphant salvation by vaccine, and in between recurs to military discourse since it must necessarily (and for a while usefully) confine people. Such intervention tends to be manipulated by the ruling classes and their States, in places with the aid of well-financed Right-wing shock troops, into a state of siege for billions of people but not for the major sources of profit. It issues into an "ambiguous sanitary Leviathan" (Svampa), melding both beneficent and maleficent State intervention – such as Trump's financial aid package, clearest in its help to fracking industries – with hypersurveillance.

I shall dwell at length in 2.2 on our rulers' huge rush towards a complete surveillance State. The only answer to that is pressure from below, a strong plebeian democracy: for example, free access to mass media for citizen groups, and democratic vigilance including a major monitoring role by those vitally concerned in health services in properly funded associations of producers (here: medical staff plus the enabling producers of medicaments and equipment) and "consumers" (patients). As James Joyce put it: "My consumers are they not my producers?" To hyper-technological militarization, the working people must oppose the horizon of solidarity, plebeian power, and a red-green New Deal.[2]

1.3. Epistemology I: The Capitalocene Notion[3]

A second precondition for understanding is to ask: how can we identify any situation so that it might be understood and changed? Only if we *name it* in a way that situates it within a web of most probable, if complex, *causation*. My explanatory overarching category here is the capitalocene, and to introduce it I shall briefly mention some epistemological principles underlying any further useful debate – the semantic hygiene that is indispensable for any collective sociopolitical hygiene.

The Great Ancestor of this needful approach is to be found in the Confucian writings where these stress *zhengming* or "the rectification (proper use) of names," in order to make terms correspond to reality and make them function as the foundation of a just State and society (possibly that part is due to Mo-zi or Me-ti, Brecht's favourite Chinese philosopher). Names or terms establish publicly accessible standards and models of understanding, categories created in order to usefully intervene into practice: "names should be spoken appropriately, and what is spoken should be carried out appropriately" (*Analects* XIII.3, translation adjusted). Today it seems indispensable to add to this Mozian naming, traditionally used for obedience to rulers, elders, and males, much Hegel. If we call any object, property, event or relationship X, then – as was later argued by Wittgenstein – we never see X as a divinely given, fixed entity but always only X as A, and in Hegel any strategically important X is always a contradiction, both A and -A. In Marx this becomes materialist, ascending upwards from the human species' need to subsist, and historical, based upon a political economy consubstantial with class power. For an example we might take "work": Marx saw it both as *labour* (and then he rectified the term into *labour power*) that produces in interaction with nature all the *goods* the human species needs (A), and as bent by class power into *exploitation* and particularly as *alienated* by capitalism into *commodities* for the sake of *profit* (-A).

The term anthropocene was widely popularised from the beginning of the 21st Century by atmospheric scientists who proposed it as the name of our current geological epoch, beginning roughly with World War 2, because human impact on ecosystems and climate on land, air, and the seas had by then grown so huge that its results in decades were equivalent to geological changes that took tens or hundreds of millennia: for example, the human species has significantly halted the growth of biodiversity by accelerated species extinction. Of course the onset of human impact is spread out over time, but we need a readily popularisable date for handbooks. While good cases obtain for its roots in the European mastery over the world six centuries ago and the Industrial Revolution two centuries ago, I agree that the favourite is the first nuclear bombs in Summer 1945 – though I have a residual fondness for the onset of class society and the State thousands of years ago, which should perhaps be taken as the ancestral sparking point.

This use of anthropocene, still to be ratified by any international body, had the historically pioneering advantage of noticing that something quite major was afoot in the constitution of human habitat and that the responsibility lay with the humans. But here a huge problem surfaces: is an Indian slum-dweller or a Latin American landless *peon* or a lone intellectual in his working room equally responsible as the ruling classes and castes of our societies? Insofar as many humans profit from the anthropocene by multiplying and living longer, perhaps. But insofar as they might be decisive for the coming about of microplastics, heavy metals or the nuclear bombs, of genocides and ecocides, no. My solution is to say for the great majority of humans: we are not guilty, but we are probably responsible for not curbing or ditching capitalism.

The term capitalocene pinpoints more accurately the causal guilt for eco-destruction: for the cause is production, consumption, and circulation of commodities by profit-driven dirty technologies plus the power structures created by capitalism to bomb into the Stone Age any alternatives (for example, the unceasing war against Leninism that made possible its corruption). The attendant destruction of wide health services for the working people is not the cause of the corona virus but it is a secondary cause of the coronavirus pandemic. The virus of profit extraction from labour is more ancient and powerful but it can subsume secondary viruses. Therefore, *I propose to use capitalocene for the dominant of our times*. Capitalocene is the blind, violent, and often irreversible exploitation and degradation of nature all over the world by capital's economic and political power. It is the mark, the deep wound, that its unceasing profit-mania and speed-ups impose on all humans and on human metabolism with nature.

1.4. The Cause of the Covid-19 Pandemic: It's Agribusiness, Stupid![4]

Rob Wallace's important 2016 book *Big Farms Make Big Flu*, left unmentioned in the zillion blinkered articles I have read since February, provides the only causal theory I know of interaction between the industrial farming of agribusiness and viral epidemiology. Here is the causal linkage: the capitalocene is, among other expropriations of people and nature, "spearheading land grabs into the last of primary forest and smallholder-held farmland worldwide." The deforestation of huge tracts of land leads to previously boxed-in pathogens spilling over into local livestock and human communities. Therefore, capital centers such as London, New York, and Hong Kong should be considered our primary disease originators: "There are no capital-free pathogens at this point.... Ebola, Zika, the coronaviruses, yellow fever again, a variety of avian influenzas, and African swine fever ... are among the many pathogens making their way out of the most remote hinterlands into peri-urban loops, regional capitals" (Wallace C) – and ultimately onto the record-busting global commodity, migrational, and tourist networks.

The central institutions to be blamed here are the multinational agribusiness companies, their financiers, and their political – and where necessary military – protectors:

> Planet Earth is largely Planet Farm at this point, in both biomass and land used. Agribusiness is aiming to corner the food market. The near entirety of the neoliberal project is organized around supporting efforts by companies based in the [stronger] countries to steal the land and resources of weaker countries. As a result, many of those new pathogens previously held in check by long-evolved forest ecologies are being sprung free, threatening the whole world.... The capital-led agriculture that replaces more natural ecologies offers the exact means by which pathogens can evolve the most virulent and infectious phenotypes. You couldn't design a better system to breed deadly diseases. (Wallace C)

Thus capitalocene produces epidemics: "Plagues are very much the shadow [and harbinger] of capitalist industrialization" (chuang; the following two paragraphs paraphrase their argument, with occasional thefts); previously unknown and fast-evolving viruses are harvested from wild populations and distributed along global capital circuits, as in the current epidemic. The epidemics originated either at the core of agroeconomic production or in its hinterland; example: the so-called Spanish flu originated in the USA, probably via domesticated swine or poultry, to spread across the ocean as the first of capitalism's international plagues on urban working people. Livestock die-offs in the countryside were met in the densely packed cities of commercial capitalism by most unsanitary conditions for workers packed into capitalist factories or nearby proletarian settlements, providing an excellent basis for the spread of plagues. In the present case the major source for gestating and unleashing the deadly Covid-19 epidemic was the already largely subsumed fringe of the capitalocene system, dependent on the changed climate and sweeping urbanisation, and plugged into the global value chains.

As Wallace exhaustively shows, in all recent epidemics from the first SARS to (still ongoing) Ebola, reckless capitalist agribusiness disrupts local ecosystems, which introduces previously isolated or harmless viral strains into hyper-competitive environments that favour rapid viral lifecycles. The escalating selection provides the virus with a greater number of evolutionary pathways in a shorter time, enabling the most fit variants to outcompete the others, in particular to jump between carrier species and humans.

The way agribusiness deals with animals for food

> removes whatever immune firebreaks may be available to slow down transmission.... High throughput provides ... *the fuel for the evolution of virulence* [underline DS]. In other words, agribusiness ... companies can just externalize the costs of their epidemiologically dangerous operations on everyone else [– on animals, local environments, people near and far, and governments across jurisdictions.... I]f we were to return those costs onto company balance sheets, agribusiness as we know it would be ended forever. No company could support the costs of the damage it imposes. (Wallace C, cf. also Wallace B 56–57)

Thus, if the corner of Wholesale Sea Food Market in Wuhan where wild animals were held, appears to be the point at which the virus SARS-Cov-2 sprang over to humans, this misses the "events behind the events" in Brecht's sense. It was the causal mega-event of agribusiness's ceaseless expanding into primary or pristine forest that pressured wild food operators to dredge further into it, increasing the interface with, and spillover of, new pathogens – including the one eventually resulting in Covid-19. When these come into contact with numerous hosts of the same species – beginning with monogenetic cattle or birds packed together on industrial farms, which already have shortened lifecycles – increased virulence becomes an evolutionary advantage. This holds also for huge and dense human populations, as in the mega-city of Wuhan: only the most aggressive virus strains survive.

It follows that the politico-ideological problem hindering an effective fight against the pandemic is "the expedient refusal to grasp that each new [pandemic, like] Covid-19 is no isolated incident...." As long as every new outbreak is treated in isolation from "the structural causes that are driving multiple marginalized pathogens into sudden global celebrity, one after the other" (Wallace C), we are – to hark back to the deadliest non-viral infection of malaria – swatting at mosquitoes instead of draining the swamp.

The global unfolding of this capitalocene trauma is compounded by a largely mishandled pandemic in major States – first because of devastated public health facilities (see data on USA after 1975 in Suvin "How"), and second because of the lack of global coordination, to which is everywhere added government dawdling in order not to antagonise profit-makers. To vary and invert the *Communist Manifesto*: what are the slow building of the Great Chinese Wall, the Seven Wonders of Mediterranean Antiquity or the imperial States and Churches of five preceding millennia against the speed-of-light fake novums of the capitalocene? For these turn all the potentially wondrous novelties – aeroplane and electricity, medicine and physics, productivity and even the yearning for community! – to mass murders for profit and power.

We cannot meet this maleficent hegemony without hurrying to undo the worst ravages. But we should never forget the dialectics that this is being done so that we may, as William Morris put it, have humanity enter an Epoch of Rest. Which would have to include a stewardship rather than domination over nature.

2. On the Coronised Turn of the Capitalocene Screw

2.1. Epistemology II: The Coronisation Notion and Practice[5]

My second main term to be rectified is "Covid-19." I do not dispute that medically speaking this disease name is usable, for the hospitals and laboratories, as the proper brief designation for the pandemic. However, let us look at the scale and frequent irreversibility of what has been happening in and with this pandemic.

2.1.1. The Mass Medical Aspect: The Virus and the People

The *WHO Coronavirus* data dashboard on August 15, based on reports by member States, shows 21 million "confirmed cases" and 761,000 dead. The poorly ascertainable number of infected is not necessarily a key datum: the number of those admitted to hospital and especially of those dead of Covid-19 would be a better indicator, though our knowledge is there also woefully inaccurate. Covid-19's death rate (case fatality ratio or CFR) seems globally to be around 1%, though it spiked in spots to 5–7% among "pre-threatened" population groups such as US Blacks and very many of the poor and undernourished of the Earth – all groups for whom the capitalocene enforces low social determinants of health such as level of education, employment, ability to earn a living wage or, for example, the lack of parks and proliferation of fast-food restaurants instead of accessible supermarkets.

Although this CFR is much smaller than most previous pandemies from 1918 to Ebola (even if much larger than seasonal influenza's 0.1%), its "penetrance" of the global population is huge and unparalleled in modern times. This is in part due to the virus SARS-Cov-2 incubation period of say two weeks before it manifests itself, and in part to capitalist globalisation and its huge and rapid movements of goods and people, often ecologically most harmful yet profitable. With no specific medicines available for coronaviruses – specialists who clamoured for research in 2008 after the last Corona pandemic were denied funds by Big Pharma – and no coordination between countries, especially not with the poorer ones, <u>*an infection of almost three billion people is probable*</u> (40% of the 6.7 billion people on Earth, see Galloway and Christakis). This coincides perfectly with the number of super-exploited people in neocapitalism's class warfare from above, plus many middle-class elders and some unfortunates (see Foster in the previous). Thus 1% mortality would mean over 27 million dead, plus many survivors with long-range consequences. True, all our projections are inferences from insufficient knowledge, since infectivity, virulence or both may attenuate – but they also may grow. Furthermore, if another infection went pandemic, such as the yearly seasonal flu, unknown larger disasters could occur: "The emergence of multiple infections capable of going pandemic, attacking populations in combos, should be [our] front and center worry" (Wallace C).

The best expert guess at how many infected there may be in the USA is between 1/3 and 2/3 of the population, which translates into 110–220 million people. A general conclusion from this is that we need to disregard the much too low official statistics (see Dr Ribner's interview, and more in Suvin, "How"). The WHO estimate on August 15, 2020 of 21 million world Covid-19 "cases" – that is, people infected from the beginning up to now – is grotesquely wrong: I would speculate that we might have 200–230 million infected world cases already, ca. 9.5–11 times more. Thus retroactively, the official ¾ million dead, while by itself horrendous, may prudently have to be multiplied between 2 and 6 times (meaning 1.5 to 4.5 million). The WHO assumes that only 20% are obvious and only 5% require more intensive treatment, in many cases hospitalisation, so there might have so far globally been 10 million or more potential hospital "patients," most of them untreated. Neither should we forget the huge sufferings of those that died unable to breathe, and even of those saved through intensive care unless they were permanently under morphine. The toll on humanity approaches a major world war; if we apply the US calculations (see also 2.12 below), over 60% were preventable with proper warning, guidance, and care – this might be anywhere upward of 900,000 preventable deaths so far. All these numbers are speculative but indicate the proper qualitative scale.

In my focus on the USA in "How," I discussed at length how its emarginated poor majority is composed of those discriminated by gender, ethnicity, and "race," refugees and "internal migrant" labourers, the black and Latino US denizens, the elderly white people, and then both the "permanent" unemployed – the incarcerated and vagrants – plus the tens of millions of newly unemployed in the USA. This huge mass is caught in the capitalocene's public disinvestment from social welfare, it is subject to huge discrimination as well as to political traps of partial cooptation, too often resulting in either passivity or a turn to Rightist surfing on just resentments. Furthermore, all reports on coronisation show an increase in stress and violence against the poor both at work and at home. Clearly, mass groups like these are extremely propitious breeding grounds for mass dying from sheer hunger and exhaustion, least likely to get medical care, and sure hotbeds of potential epidemic resurgence – as are the camps where many of them are forcibly detained. Brutality against this legally invisible one third or more of humankind, forced to undergo either hunger or sickness or both (see Bouissou), is, as in the prisons, intertwined with the rulers' mindlessness.

Extra caution is due for such US statistics, deficient both ideologically – there are *NO* data by income group – and bureaucratically: you cannot see the wood among the profusion of trees (cf. Ribner). Nonetheless, we may conclude that we have to do in the USA, as well as in most other States, with *an enormous rainbow army – in fact, a majority in any State – of the poor and marginalised exposed to mass dying*. This is in good part due to previous unhealthy living, itself enforced by poverty, poor schooling, and misleading marketing, which result in obesity, diabetes, heart diseases, and similar, as well as to the deficient facilities of public mass health treatment, considered above: the shortage of primary care physicians in the majority Black American zip codes may be extended to all the world's immiserated groups, subsisting near or below the living wage. Statistics based on income have been systematically excluded by most press and internet media I managed to see, organised only by "age, sex, ethnicity," for they would reveal a *naked class warfare* tilted toward letting the poor die. One example: the "New York City" epidemic was more truthfully one of the poor boroughs, centered in the Bronx, and then parts of Queens and Staten Island. The average income of 1.4 million

Bronx inhabitants seems to be $21,000, and of 1.6 million in Manhattan $111,000; the ratio of Bronx dead per 100,000 of population was near to double that of Manhattan... The point was precisely put by a Bronx writer:

> [...] it's become the catchphrase and sentiment of our moment, a reminder that the coronavirus is a great equalizer, a symbol of our shared humanity: *We're all in this together.*
>
> Only we're not.
>
> The coronavirus has been [...] the great revealer, pulling the curtain back on the class divide, exposing how deeply unequal this country is and how deep the fissures are. Rather than trying to cover it all up with pithy sayings – rather than trying to sweep these divides under the rug with platitudes like "we're all in this together" – we should use this moment as an opportunity to take a hard look at the broken systems that perpetuate inequality: education, health coverage, distribution of opportunity and wealth, to name a few. (Guarnieri)

No vaccine can wave a magic wand here: elementary societal justice allowing every denizen to lead a healthy life is the needed vaccine.

2.1.2. The Mass Economic Aspect: Social Darwinism (Focus on the USA)

Accompanying the medical reports (which do not register sufferings) are huge economic consequences. The pandemic will result in economic destruction, as a rule welcomed by big capital as favouring both concentration and keeping the workers in straits, even though most of the dead were sacrificed to prevent it. Financial losses in the present crisis will be in trillions of dollars, nobody knows how many: five? more? It is extremely dubious that the world economy could return to pre-crisis levels by 2023: all bets are off.[6] As always, corporations will line up for bailouts, which we should NOT give to them but to the increasingly starving, sick, homeless, and dying working people. And since a third of the US workforce is "nonwhite" and half are women, guess who'll bear the main brunt?

Just one (by no means full) glimpse into the US upper class's profit from half a year of coronisation reveals that the wealth of US billionaires (without the hundreds of millionaires) "between 18 March 2020 and 4 June 2020, ... increased by $565 billion, reaching the level of $3.5 trillion in total, up 19% in the interval" (Brenner 19)! All such mega-plunder is merrily escalating.

In the first six months of the US pandemic, two other central parameters were: first, *<u>the economic cost of the federal government stimulus</u>* alone will probably surpass the costs of World War 2 (cf. Galloway). Second, the number of infected in the US is professionally estimated at ca. 42 million people (though I argued earlier this is highly optimistic), while *<u>the number of dead</u>*, officially "likely undercounted" (see for both Britt, "9 Things"), could be perhaps 200–220,000, and may by Nov. 1 reach between 250 and 300,000, unless other factors like the flu weigh in.

For all such reasons, I dispute the validity of calling Covid-19 *the overarching social (political, economical, psychological) use of the pandemic*, which has little to do with any virus as such but rather with how the hugest existing politico-economical forces deal with the pandemic and what is at stake in it. In particular, this use has to do with who – which societal groups and classes – will bear the cost in lives and the cost in expenses, or maybe even profit from it, *cui bono?* The domination of the compartmentalised and opaque term "Covid-19" suggests that people at large, dying of and/or paying for it, should not bother with nor intervene in the way these costs should be borne: leave that to our better informed ruling classes and State-sponsored apparati! The term is epistemologically fraught: it forecloses many directions of action. In an ethically dubious way, it enlists the authority of natural science to silence the overwhelming plebeian majority of the population. Therefore, I propose we use the term "*coronisation*." It may not be perfect, as all new terms it needs further explanation, but it is less opaque, for it suggests at least three semantemes: first, that it is not simply the domain of medical lingo, second, that it is somebody's activity ("-sation"), and third, that it is, in a happy pun, the crown of some foregoing state or stance. In the US fallout, a Columbia University study up to May 3 concluded that 36,000 out of 67,000 US deaths could have been prevented had social distancing policies been implemented one week sooner (Britt, "Covid-19's Other"). Since the proportion is surely higher after May 3 and the de-implementations, in my conservative opinion at least two thirds of the 167,000 US dead officially acknowledged by August 15 could have been prevented had Social Darwinism (on which see chapter 14 in this book) not been the reigning US ruling-class ideology. Coronisation could be called "a virus meets Social Darwinism": let us accept the clearly preventable 111,000 deaths of people (so far – possibly 200,000 by Nov. 1), as long as the NASDAQ has since February 20 risen by one-eighth, while the wealth of the billionaire class increased by 27.5% between April and July of 2020, with a record high at $10.2 trillion shared by just 2,189 billionaires (*Riding*)! So "this pandemic served as a mask off moment for the [USA…W]atching our politicians and corporations slowly begin to pressure us to … become sacrificial lambs for the stock market has been surreal and barbaric…" (Martinchek).

2.2. Our Rulers' Ongoing Torpedoing of Civil Liberties

2.2.1. The Surveillance Society (Means)

The illusions of the original liberals that free markets will lead to existential freedom is dead and buried in an age of unceasing imperialist wars, paupericide (genocide of the poor), and ecocide. The recourse to a strong dictatorial State in the face of dire threats was carried over from strict military dictatorship, organised in the capitalist World Wars of the last 110 years and whenever needed supplemented by more allegorical "wars" – against drugs or terrorism or the present pandemic. Governments everywhere react to the pandemic with authoritarian and punitive measures, such as a compulsory quarantine of entire areas: suspending the neo-liberal variant of capitalism even in peacetime is now a favorite option everywhere outside of the US and UK. As in the wars, so in the Police State: mass deaths are certain and the success for one's nation uncertain; no matter, if the capitalocene's relations of production can be salvaged in a new regime of accumulation, even at the price of a near-fascism.

No doubt, in cases of imminent danger to whole nations, drastic measures are justified. But two areas of deep democratic concern remain: during and after the pandemic peaks, in the tension between ruling-class violence and plebeian care for people and environments.

On the care pole, during any public health crisis,

> trust and compassion… are important epidemiological variables. Without either, jurisdictions lose their populations' support. A sense of solidarity and common respect is a critical part of eliciting the cooperation we need to survive such threats together. Self-quarantines with the proper support – check-ins by trained neighborhood groups, food supply trucks going door-to-door, work release, and unemployment insurance – can elicit that kind of cooperation. (Wallace C)

This must be accompanied by two major programs: "to work on developing the kind of public health resilience in which it doesn't matter who shows up with an infection, we have the means to treat and cure them. Of course, stop stealing people's land abroad and driving the poor people's exoduses in the first place, and we can keep the pathogens from emerging" (ibidem).

Further, all civic-minded people have to be very wary about the qualitative leaps abusing the pandemic's threat to life and the attendant economic collapse in order to dismantle hard-won legal and other measures of personal freedoms and ecological care. A few examples (there are many more in USA): in England, the ruling Conservatives – who have received £11 million from property developers in recent years – are proposing to shred planning laws that protect green spaces. In India, 40 new coalfields in the country's most ecologically sensitive forests are to be mined. In Brazil, a huge surge in executive acts is encouraging enormous devastations of forests and wildlife. Generally, are we witnessing a worldwide test for what our rulers see as the new normality of an ecocidal near future?

The central rung of the new fetters and greatest immediate danger is the perversion of internet's communitarian (and indeed communist) potentials and useful contacts into a planned police surveillance, as pioneered by the data-gathering "provider" companies such as Amazon or "social" media such as Facebook. Digital privacy has actually never fully existed, it was always largely porous and hypocritical, witness the mutual accusations about hacking by powerful States as well as the information extortion from users. But now, governments around the world, in cahoots with corporations that already hold vast stores of consumers' personal data, are enthusiastically jumping at the chance of using the coronisation pandemic by making permanent the extraordinary (and supposedly momentary) new surveillance powers. A double problem obtains here: first, most of what they want to write into granite would invade our privacy, deter our free speech, and disproportionately burden poorer and already marginalised groups of people, not to speak of dissenters tagged as being subversive. And second, at a deeper level, the capitalist production system could now strongly reduce the presence of human bodies – minds and hands working together – which always carries worrying elements of workers' solidarity and indispensability. Now such undue presence of gross humanity can be largely eliminated: the brains are in automatised programs and the hands are more and more robotic. A hypertechnological but much better hidden exploitation of people and nature can continue, less prone to strikes or other protest actions. How could these come about if public gatherings are forbidden (though there is no good medical reason for it, if masks and other "firewalls" are used) and the family apartments will be tantamount to do-it-yourself prisons? Was this what the technological horror SF was suggesting, from Richard Matheson or Philip K. Dick to *Tron* and *The Matrix*?

This dangerous turn can be easily grafted onto the national surveillance programs that were in the new century justified as "counter-terrorist" and persist two decades later, though terrorists have scarcely been a major threat to the imperial metropoles even after exporting warfare to West Asia and elsewhere augmented the pool of their potential adherents. The US Patriot Act gave its executive sweeping powers to spy on all people at home and in the whole world. Added in coronisation are "contact tracing" tools, which would with the attendant testing and interviews allow further surveillance measures to be applied to all, but uniquely impacting poor people, already subject to large amounts of data collection through "public benefits" and welfare programs. The next step would be to extend to them DNA sampling, as practiced for immigrants at the US border (cf. for all these Electronic Frontier).

The unholy alliance of capitalist internet mega-companies and governments is now undergoing a qualitative jump with the introduction and probable obligatoriness of new instruments (apps) running on all mobile internet devices for tracing people, beginning with the infected people but logically expanding to those potentially infected – that is, everybody. Even using only the lowly cellular phone, the instant, reliable, and universal tracing of one and all was approaching the wet dream of every tyranny and oligarchy. This model proved its worth in "ethnic Chinese" territories (PR China, Singapore, Taiwan) and its cultural neighbour, South Korea. It can be boosted to infinite chain links by new apps for contact tracing, which not only lead to much information but also to the horizon of personalised (but where necessary mass) lockdowns for all the undesirables the authorities want to isolate: today the coronised, tomorrow all the protesters, opponents, and dangerous scare-mongers that cannot be allowed to jeopardise "our" efforts (medical, military or whatever). Large US private companies and State agencies are racing to integrate useful telemedicine possibilities with apps that monitor and analyze geospatial, behavioural, and physiological data of large populations in real time. Do physicians have a role in regulating massive surveillance programs for public health? Do patients have an input? During a true or indeed a manufactured crisis, should some tools be opt-in, opt-out or mandatory? What are the criteria for a just monitoring, who defines them, and how do we balance the rights to personal privacy of the individual with the public good?

State apparati – notably US President Trump – as well as employers are licking their chops at the prospect of using such technology and the state of emergency for total capillary tyranny. Turning to corporate examples, not only are Amazon and Walmart planning to use contact tracing (that is whom do you meet) for employees, but many other employers in USA, that paradise of tyranny at work, have started using various "tattlewares." One of them downloads videos of employees' screens and takes a webcam picture of the employee every 10 minutes; an employee reported: "If you go to the bathroom or whatever, a pop-up will come up and it'll say, 'You have 60 seconds to start working again or we're going to pause your time'" (cut her pay). Another program for managers keeps a record of every task employees are doing on their computers, and points on the worker's "productivity score" are detracted for logging onto YouTube or Facebook. Some managers ask the at-home employees "to stay on video all day long so they can watch over them every minute of the day" (all quotes from Allyn).

If this meddling were to persist beyond the direct emergencies of pandemic infection, it would reduce the metropolitan North too to the condition of tyrannies from Indonesia to Hungary and Serbia. It would be reasonable to demand as a minimum three *initial safeguards*. First, that all legal and executive acts during the coronisation pandemic contain a "guillotine" clause specifying a measurable set of thresholds – say of newly infected people – below which they could no longer be used. Second, that the EU norms demanding individual consent for these apps be applied worldwide and bolstered by the financing of ombudsman civil groups to monitor them (apparently the apps need around 60% of adherents in a given population to work well). Third, that public financing be found for civic discussion as to who owns this data – physicians, governments, secret services, ad agencies? – and to what purposes can they be financially and politically exploited.

We should be particularly opposed to huge plans to develop contact tracing apps for systems that run on nearly every phone in the world, such as the Apple plus Google application programming interfaces (API) available to public health "authorities," with the government deciding who such "authorities" are. Indeed, in a second proposed phase of their plan, Apple and Google will bake this feature into their underlying platforms. In the usual high-handedly arrogant wont of all PC software developers from Microsoft on, there will then be no possibility for users to opt in or out.

2.2.2. Connected Grim Threats: Paupericide, Ecocide, Fascism… (Ends)

The insufficient lockdown and foolhardy reopening of most US places, now beginning in Europe too, puts most working people as well as small business owners in an impossible bind: risk death at work or risk death by destitution – financial ruin – at home (cf. Mull). Globally, I would estimate perhaps three-quarters if not more of the 2 billion "informal" workers and their suffering families have been made totally destitute by capitalocene's covidisation, most clearly in the millions (or is it tens of millions?) dismissed in India and USA. The pressure on politicians to reopen comes everywhere – most successfully in the USA, UK, Sweden, and Lombardy, and coupled with obviously dictatorial rule in Brasil and Russia – from the richest businessmen, themselves seemingly sheltered from the risk. This plutocracy should be hampered in the future, to begin with by strict election contribution laws, and then by more democracy from the bottom up – clearly lacking in Hubei too.

The wrong labelling characteristic of capitalism that I insisted on in 1.3 and 2.1 is a sign of evading and obfuscating reality: that all these (very real) emergencies are inner societal contradictions and have to be faced by enlightening and help, not murder. The practical fallout of the care vs. violence choice leads to alternative horizons: *either* some version of intelligent socialist/communist/anarchist human solidarity *or*, as in all capitalist crises, a massive aggrandisement of huge technological and power monopolies with the middle and small capitalists being pauperised alongside the huge majority; the latter solution historically favours Fascism 2.0, the legitimate child of overstressed dead-end capitalism. We are halfway there in much of Latin America, Asia, and eastern Europe, certainly moving towards it almost everywhere else, prominently including the USA: for, "[a] key feature of a fascist society is indifference to mass death. Which is precisely what America has felt towards 125,000 needlessly dead and counting" (haque, "America Is").

An awful warning may be the case of India. Rampant super-capitalism for the rich and its ruling class has a second pillar there in caste, still deeply intertwined with class: "social distancing" sounds especially weird when the government lockdown falls heavily on the lowest castes of India, the millions who do the vast sub-continent's work servicing the rich and middle classes. Many Indian constituent states "are extending the legal workday to 12 hours, and rolling back worker safety regulations, collective bargaining rights, and minimum wage protections won over a century of struggles" – a shining exception being communist-led Kerala. The words of an Indian worker abandoned in an industrial park with thousands of others: "It feels like we have been locked up in a jail" (quotes in this paragraph from Choudhury & Aga), may be an ominous pointer for the future of the world.

The conclusions of two rich articles I much learned from should be integrated here. Gabriel Winant notes how capital had created "a world of homelessness, hunger, debt, imprisonment, exploitation, addiction, racism, premature death, international strife, and rising temperatures before the pandemic struck," and that it has emphatically refused to secure food, shelter, schooling, and care for a population in the superadded lockdown. And Andrew Liu points out how, unlike an earthquake or famine, coronisation has resulted in perhaps the greatest ever accumulation of oil and steel (and we should add unused food being destroyed for want of capitalist circulation while millions hunger), while personal savings of the workers have been exhausted: "On trial is a whole global system of profiteering and its structural laws and incentives …."

The masters of our corrupt cognition and fake novelty will label the horizon propounded here, and shared I daresay by hundreds of millions of labouring people, as utopian. As usual, the masters don't know what they are saying. Since to their minds utopian simply means the impossible, a *Hirngespinst* (cobweb of the brain), I answer that all the proposals mooted here are not only materially or economically possible but also the only way to reduce the sweeping paupericide. If they would more properly realise that utopian means a non-existing (*ou*) yet radically better (*eu*) spacetime or common place (*topos*), they would still do all they could to obstruct it. Capitalocene's ends and organisation have as of the World Wars grown into a shackle on both science – such as medicine, perverted by Big Pharma entrepreneurs – and minimally acceptable life for billions.

Thus, we need a convergence of redistributive political reforms like a financial transactions tax with a new wave of working people militancy. If their convergence does not come about, the coronisation will become one of the largest capitalist restructuring depressions, on the scale of the 1929–33 one, "annihilating huge chunks of small and medium-sized business… [and] offering mega-monopoly the economy on a platter. All those 'distressed assets' – whether storefronts or, well, unemployed people? Mega-monopolies can now buy them up on the cheap" (haque "American"). These monopolies are in good part rentiers, subsisting by paying low or no taxes – as opposed to the reasonable taxation, rise of middle classes, and an almost full employment in the Welfare State, destroyed in its rollback by capitalism from the mid-1970s on.

This prospect is memorably summed up by haque's evoking

> [a complete] transformation of a once entrepreneurial economy … into a kind of caste economy of new poor and ultra-rich, without much in the middle. At the top, a tiny number of owners of capital – Bezos, Zuck, today's CEO of Goldman Sachs. Below them, a small 1% of their lieutenants. And then everyone else, trying to scrape together a living, whatever gig or low-wage service job comes their way today.
>
> […] In such an economy, education doesn't count much – see how today's PhDs already face mass unemployment. Neither does hard work, because there's nowhere to go, really. What counts is being a certain kind of person. Brutal, selfish, greedy, avaricious, thoughtless, ignorant, foolish. (both quotes from haque "American")

At a minimum, then, the state of siege will persist for years, and the political fallout of the resulting economic collapse will be, as suggested above, some form of Fascism 2.0 (I approached it far too briefly in "Explain"). At a maximum, the rotting supermonopoly and surveillance capitalism, updated with the newest AI and nanophysical surveillance and killing devices, will upgrade the real enough whip of hunger and misery for the "free contract" workers to overt shackles and bodily lesions – electronic, of course – for lower classes, in a huge misery and death toll, plus racist ideology against the poor. Eventually, such a rule over a tottering blend of oligopoly markets, feudal rent, and outright slavery must collapse for bio-ecological reasons. However, as I concluded in my April-May "Thoughts": the price would be many times lower if this happened through revolts by working people. We shall either organise or be ground down into a new slavery plus eco-catastrophe.

3. Radical Utopianism: The Only Chance to Fight Antiutopia

3.1. To Revolt (with Critical Utopianism) Is Healthy

What is then to be done?

I shall enter upon detailed proposals in Section 3.2. But there is a precondition for all of them: *a confluence of plebeian and utopian energies*. On the one hand, the working people, an overwhelming majority everywhere in the world, might begin to claim power for themselves. This is visible, say in the USA where it is best reported, so far in widespread defensive protests against racism and demands for the equipment and sanitary conditions the "essential" workers need to stay safe, walking off the job to resist endangerment by bosses, up to street protests; New York teachers and Philadelphia librarians forced their systems to shut down; Detroit bus drivers and riders won free fares and safety of the drivers. Auto workers have launched wildcat strikes to stop production completely while maintaining full wages; shopfloor action forced the Amazon Staten Island warehouse to accept social distancing; Verizon and McDonald's workers at some locations secured paid sick leave. Housing movement activists have won either moratoriums on evictions and/or utility shut-offs from New York City to San Francisco (compiled from Isser and Winant; see for Europe and North America Gall 218–20 and Salvage 33). In India, South Africa, and many Latin American countries, food riots are on the rise. Winant summarises some radical changes needed:

> This means an end to financialized hospitals and nursing homes stripped to the bone of staff and capacity, and the rapid emergence, instead, of full-capacity integrated care systems: behind the fully-staffed and expandable ICU, the hospital with pandemic-scale emergency capacity, there must be publicly available childcare, communal food delivery, and the provision of companionship and entertainment for isolated elders. It means safe food and stable housing for all – including the homeless…. It means putting money in the pockets of the millions of new unemployed and shielding them from the predations of landlords and bill collectors. It means freeing the prisoners, whether on the border or in the gulags operated by every city, state, and county – as well as by the federal government. It means building up international trust and cooperation, without which the global coordination necessary to fight the pandemic will be impossible…

However, the shopfloor and street protests occurring up to now are certainly insufficient: the total degradation of social-democratic parties and labour unions from Reagan and Thatcher on have accomplished what Fascism needed to bloodily enforce in the 1920s–30s: to leave the popular masses defenceless. To arm them we need to harness the energies of a properly understood critical utopianism as the best epistemological, and finally political, bet to counter existential antiutopia. We should begin with the realisation that capitalism can only exist by means of a ceaseless and pitiless "primordial accumulation," exemplarily broached in Marx's pages on "primitive accumulation" in 16th-century

England. As Rosa Luxemburg saw even before the World Wars (see her chapters 27–30), and other globalizations: "Violence [*Gewalt*] is the only solution open to capital: the accumulation of capital employs violence as a permanent weapon … down to the present day" (371); it was invariably accompanied by militarism, and by the eradication of rural industries in favour of a sharp rural-urban divide usually called industrialization.

This means today taking on board, for one example, Justin McBrien's insight that the capitalocene's drive toward world-ecological extinction is not confined to the huge and rising annihilation of biological species: within a large spectrum of disruptions caused by invasive capitalism, it boomerangs also into the extinguishing of cultures, languages, and of entire ethnic groups (genocide). He identifies violent "accumulation by extinction" as fundamental to capitalism from its beginning. In brief, capitalism is wedded to mass violent destruction, and the capitalocene is when this drive becomes a geological force and a "necrocene": an epoch of mass unnecessary death. The hugely productive capitalism now centrally produces destructive novums, it "undermin[es] the springs of all wealth: the earth and the worker" by practicing "systematic robbery of the preconditions for life..., of space, air, light..." (*Kapital* 449–50, transl. DS), and today we could add water, silence, and so on, culminating in the loss of air to breathe characteristic of both Covid-19 and of racist violence against people – such as the murdered Black American George Floyd. As Walter Benjamin memorably explained, death is the final horizon for a civilization of gambling, say on the stock-market, of worldwide unceasing wars, and of course of raping the planet by exploitation of working people and ecocide. Thus the ruling all-embracing antiutopia, which can be in terms of violent power called the capitalocene – and of which coronisation is a metonymy, an allegory, and one hopes the culmination but perhaps simply a decisive turn of the screw – threatens humanity as a species as well as a quality distinct from simple animality.

Now, the apparently powerless utopia shares with death – as all great political revolutions knew – an intervention into human history from the point of view of the species, what Feuerbach and the young Marx called our species being, our insertion in the great chain of the generations. Translating the utopian horizon of classless society into sociopolitical reality would bring about the needed confluence and synergy with plebeian power. Beside naming (on which see 1.3), the enabling device for deployment of utopian cognitive energies is map-making or spatialisation. Utopianism is a space-creating machine, coeval with early capitalism and its space-eating inventions of economic enclosure of lands and transoceanic ships, yet also a desperate attempt to use these huge weapons of domination for freedom (clearly seen in the first stirrings of air travel notions as liberatory and even beatific, from Wilkins and Cyrano to Restif). The omnipresent implied – or usually supplied – maps of eutopias, strategically aided by nomination, can become sense-making machines that attempt to turn the new spaces into purified and welcoming abodes of a better human living. They illustrate a Possible Island or other mini-world as a possibility of humanising power relationships, diametrically opposed to imperial colonies, killing grounds, and super-profit sources from enslaving the natives (one of the first and best formulations of such opposition is Montaigne's essay *Of Cannibals*). These eutopian horizons bet on the possibility and potentiality of power being divorced from violence, as in primitive communism (cf.

Suvin "Power"), and being used in different, entirely beneficent ways – in the best case, by full participation by a whole population. Eutopia's final horizon is therefore a just communist society, as adumbrated by the peak novels of Morus, Morris, Le Guin, Piercy, and Mitchison.

All such Possible Counter-Worlds are modelled upon our everyday Possible World as a totality, a however provisional and experimental *world*. Yet finally, many major utopian writings are in curious and ingenious ways *open-ended totalities*, from Morus's final wry sentence and Bacon's unfinished fragment to, say, the multiplicities of choice in K.S. Robinson's Mars trilogy (cf. Wegner, *Imaginary* 54). Utopian texts, and all utopianism, were born as political animals wedded to a possibility of freedom, to be negotiated between the individuals and various power currents in the collectivity. True, there were authoritarian utopias galore, most significantly the early ones by Bacon and Campanella, and even Morus oscillated between democracy and patriarchy. However, these were particular choices within and soundings of realistic possibilities within an epistemologically open horizon: if America exists, all is possible! – all kinds of freedom and even a new elite authoritarianism (there is a strong parallel to the early USSR here). I have been insisting now for almost half a century that though formally closed, significant utopia is thematically open: its pointings reflect back on the reader's "topia." Its pervasive and estranging dialectics is, as I cited Barthes, that the utopian *écriture* must mobilise at the same time an image and its contrary (*MOSF* 51).

3.2. A First (Improvable) Sketch of a Minimum and Maximum Program, Spring 2020

If coronisation is a sociopolitical matter of how to deal with the Covid-19 pandemic, then to counteract the worst blights of late capitalist trends revealed and hugely accelerated by it, and to oppose the most repressive and super-monopolistic outcomes in the offing, we need a minimum and immediate plus a maximum but not too distant program. Their division is strictly pragmatic, based on what is or will be possible: both programs are based on *care* as against *violence*. In all these planks violence against humanity and against our survival through knowledge flows from the central idol of capitalism, the *profit principle*, which must be first bridled and then extinguished. Let us press for the minimum to be adopted right now, while clamouring for the horizon of maximum! Yet the division might have its own wit: for the officially imaginable and sometimes partly practiced maximums are our "minimums."

A/ Minimum (bridling the profit principle)

- Suspend all work during the pandemic's climb and plateau, and including ca. 15–20 days of a falling curve, except essential medical and logistical personnel and those required to produce and distribute food and other basic goods. The State must assume the cost of the wages for those suspended, paid at 80–100% for the period of the quarantine. Production and circulation of basic goods such as food, medicines, and knowledge must go on, but we cannot allow profits to re-ignite the infection.

- Socialise de facto (*not* nationalise!) all hospitals and medical centres under the control of the national and international health authorities, of their staffs, and of the users' associations (to be fostered), also in view of the threatening future. Combine them (where not such) into a nation-wide health system, regardless of profit. Guarantee their income and work, also all patients' payments relating to life-threatening illness. Rush supplies to and increase the incomes of medical staff, teachers doing internet programmes, and other indispensable personnel.
- Put all big pharmaceutical companies under strict international control, authorise and enforce immediate international cooperation to find a vaccine and easier testing devices. If they sabotage this, expropriate them. Abolish intellectual property in the medical field beyond reasonable return of expenses and remuneration.
- Speed up production for sanitary materials for this crisis (testing kits, masks, respirators). Organise testing for the maximum possible amount of people.
- Just as for health, there is a basic need for food supply, clean water, and public safety. Emergency grain stocks and other staple food supplies must be immediately released for distribution. Preferences should go to the disproportionately stricken poor. A strong ombudsman or similar system should be established for monitoring possible "security" encroachments on basic human rights and existing legal safeguards, funded by the State but at arm's length from it (see 2.3).
- Suspend immediately all schools, from elementary to universities. Organise safe activities for students via] internet, supply free basic PCs to all concerned, bought wholesale by communities and PTAs at production price. Maintain teachers' pay, prolong for one or two years all part-time and limited contracts, all of them at a rate adjusted for extra work and extra expenses during the emergency. Assign authorial copyright for new internet "content" to their authors.
- Suspend immediately all rent and mortgage payments for those not working, also non-corporate debts and evictions. Demand the maximum extinction of all *debts and mortgages*, say when 150% of the initial sum has been paid.
- Break the stranglehold of financial capitalism on all the above, or none of them will happen. Begin with new legislation on banks (see below) and a financial transactions tax.
- End sanctions and economic blockades that prevent entire populations from importing necessary medical or other basic supplies (for example, against Cuba, Iran, Venezuela or North Korea).
- Finally: coronisation reveals clearly, first, nationalist chauvinism up to racism in the USA and Europe as well as in Asia (Chinese in Singapore, Burmese, Malaysian), denying even health help to other "races" or ethnic groups if these are immigrants, and second, that this quickly redounds on all denizens of an area, even when slave pens are reintroduced (now called temporary camps). It is indispensable that all States pass and enforce laws against "racial" or ethnic discrimination and, as in gender affairs, guarantee equal pay for equal work with strong penalties.

B/ Maximum (abolishing the profit principle)

B1. Introductory

The following planks are simply a first provisional proposal to implement fully the radical demands of peoples in all great revolutions (say the American, French, Russian and Chinese ones, as formulated in the terms of Jefferson, Robespierre with Saint-Just, and Lenin) for LIFE, LIBERTY, and a chance at the PURSUIT OF HAPPINESS. Some weak excuse for not implementing these demands for all might be found in the insufficient production forces before the Industrial Revolution. But as of then, there is absolutely none. Those who think that guarded gate communities or orbital weightless stations might save the rich and powerful, should learn from Covid-19 and all other "natural" disasters – rising oceans, spreading deserts, dying species, polluted air, water, and food – that humans are indeed members of one another, as well as of Terran ecosystems with all living beings. This fragile oasis of negentropy and life amid the merciless desert of the universe should be preserved!

The Jeffersonian trinity is really triune: we are talking here of mutually enhancing and indispensable aspects of FREEDOM. Freedom is like the air we breathe, or food and clear water, or light and knowledge: it is best noticed in its absence. Freedom without a guaranteed and enforced right to the material needs of life is fake and leads to mass murders happening now daily and globally.

The opposite of freedom is reduction of the quantity and quality of life through political subjection and economic exploitation. Patrick Henry's formulation is still our alternative: we shall have liberty or we shall have (speedier and much less dignified) death.

B2. Planks

Their gist is: *ban crimes against humanity* (the term was rightly used by the editor-in-chief of the prestigious UK medical periodical *The Lancet* for measures favouring the spread of the coronisation pandemic). The capitalist dilemma of saving lives OR saving livelihoods, its hold-up maxim of "your money or your life," is false and pernicious. Financial intervention of all levels of the social community, accompanied by speedy possibilities of democratic control from below, is needed to step out of this double bind. All such experiments must be defended from the compulsions of capitalist economics and the threat of State repression.

- Adopt *basic "defence of life" measures* in each country: for example, in US terms, $15 per hour minimum wage law, improved Medicare for All, Universal Basic Income (see third item below), cheap and in many cases free public transit, an end to fracking, oil drilling, and oil pipelines, no private prospecting in National Parks, and public works with the goal of achieving ecological conversion – a red-green New Deal (see Wallis). Food production has to be based on farmer autonomy and a strong public sector to curb environmental ratchets and runaway infections. As a first step, a stable economy can only be based on strong national (and then international) regulation of wages forcing capitalists to pay survival wages, at least as pegged to productivity growth and then more to offset past injustices. This may be done by way of government decision, say about the minimum wage, by law or by informal pressure on the companies.

- Charge the UN to reorganise so as to *enforce ending all warfare and reduce the huge armaments*. Drastically reduce all State armed forces in favour of immediate defense of a directly threatened population and universal civic service, extending the Swiss (and Fourierist and Jamesonian) model from armed to unarmed readiness to defend life. Insist on a *total* ban of and dismantlement of nuclear, bacteriological, and chemical weapons.
- Provide a *Universal Basic Income* as a human right in every country for all denizens that ensures food, also other survival needs such as basic access to clean air and water, electricity, heating or other climate control, and internet access; it should be accompanied by an obligation to communal work. The cost of providing these utilities can be covered by an at least 50% reduction of all world military budgets, plus increasing tax payments by major corporations (that as a rule pay nothing or very little), annuities from a national wealth fund benefitting from redistribution from richer nations, and royalty payments from tech companies like Amazon for mining our personal data.

  This can only work if paired with redrawing the *tax laws* in direction of the Welfare State: tax the rich on a sliding scale centered on 50% (I paid that much in Canada for 25 years, as all "middle classes" did, and did not begrudge it; the rich will, but must be curbed). If necessary, increase the percentage for the multimillionaires and higher. Abolish all offshore tax havens. Draw up strict laws for *banks*, mainly returning to the pre-1970 rules: the banks exist to facilitate producing more and better life, not billionaires and death.
- Agribusiness must be ended for good, as it endangers the entire humanity. Institute urgent price supports and consumer purchasing programs for the *agricultural producers* to increase the production of healthy food and supply it to the population at fair but accessible prices; abolish the stranglehold of middlemen distributors in favour of competition; use markets but monitor and where necessary control prices. Introduce varieties of stock and crops – and strategic rewilding – at both the farm and regional levels. Let food animals reproduce on-site to pass on tested immunities. Connect just production with just circulation.
- Organise widest possible civic debates, financed by territorial communities on all levels, to increase radically the financing of national *health services*, obligatory and available to all in feedback with the WHO which is to be supported by public rather than private financing, with the rich paying extra.
- Establish constitutional provisions for adequate – decent if modest – *housing* as a basic human right guaranteed to all denizens. Organise widest possible civic debates, financed by territorial communities on all levels, to establish provision of adequate housing as a basic human right and maximum extinction of debts and mortgages, say by the time the initial sum has been paid 150%. This means

eradicating the horrendous slums capitalism has multiplied ever since the Industrial Revolution.

- Establish constitutional provisions for increasing *teaching and research*, available to all working people and based on a legally fixed percentage of real national income, probably a two-digit one. Without direct contact between teachers and taught students, only trade schools and rote learning are possible, instead of true – that is, creatively unforeseeable – education in mutual feedback; furthermore, being a student, in the millenary European sense of persons in a youth collective learning life, may disappear (see Agamben). Organise the widest possible civic debates, financed by territorial communities on all levels, focused on how people's well-being should guide research. Organise strict monitoring against conflict of interest in research as well as in science.
- Resist and reverse the drift to omnipresent *surveillance* and the Leviathan State-cum-corporations. The State has no place in personal apartments, nor should we allow such surveillance in offices, on internet or on personal communication units; a camera on every street intersection is a sign of dire tyranny. Abolish all sale by Amazon, Google, and all other provider companies of personal preferences and usages. Enact safeguards against the surveillance State or Company (I propose some in 2.3 above) and finance independent civil society groups to participate in monitoring this.
- In particular, resist and reverse the huge push to "smart working" – a propaganda term for working tasks performed at one's private home and over the internet, usually badly paid. It not only unduly favours faceless relationships and renders impossible all performance art, including live music, and all true teaching as opposed to info dumps. It is also subject to most virulent neo-taylorism of time-and-motion control for everybody so "smart."
- Abolish private property over ideas and words. Turn Amazon, Google, Microsoft, Facebook, Apple, and TV emitters into public utilities overseen by combinations of local, regional, and international user groups; allow modest charges for internet and other communicational uses, depending on the income of the user and amount of usage (or, below a certain medium income, by a flat rate). Finance the main use of all such "social media" for social enlightenment, including learning and research, develop the electromagnetic infrastructure accessible to all. Open up societal development of computer programs and other software, with real respect for privacy (cf. Moglen).

3.3. Upshot: Self-Defence, TINA

Spiralling back to my beginning, I adumbrated there that the epochal collective alternative is between the rulers' violence and the plebeian care – which allows for *self-defence* as a basic human right. The careful approach to people, where mutual dealings avoid lesion, is the seed of all respect, delicacy, and tenderness in human culture as well as the presupposition for any love, such as the one Antigone says she was born for as opposed to the rulers' and warriors' hate. Yet we badly need also a discussion of violence, and in particular of ruling systemic violence, which I attempted in "Words." When facing a denial of personal psychophysical integrity that injures the body and human freedom, in stifling situations such as systematic armed repression by the ruling class and a reduction of legality to a suffocating minimum when not to zero, counter-violence is, alas, inescapable. It becomes a tool for personal and collective survival whenever it is truly necessary – that is, *when counter-violence is not so hurtful as the lack of it*. Such a right of self-defence should where possible be allied to nonviolent intervention, such as civil disobedience, withdrawal of services, forbidden marches, sit-ins, blockades, and occupations as well as the unauthorized release of electronic information (cf. also Marcuse and Moylan).

An understanding of when self-defence is right becomes thus the indispensable cognitive companion to a sober look at the new beast slouching towards Bethlehem. Provident care and provision will be especially necessary in the coming months (or years) of coronisation, beginning with Fall-Winter 2020 when most epidemiologists anticipate a second, possibly more serious wave of infections. Together with the larger proportion of people surviving serious Covid-19 infection and the milder visible symptoms, this means that "health services should prepare for long-term care, not just build pop-up, refrigerated morgues… [as well as] redouble their efforts to promote safety precautions" (Christakis).

I cannot put what this means today better than David Harvey:

> do we want to come out of this crisis by simply saying that there's 26 million people who need to get back to work, in some of those pretty awful jobs they may have been doing before? … Or do we want to ask: Is there some way to organise the production of basic goods and services so that everybody has something to eat, everybody has a decent place to live, and we can put a moratorium on evictions, and everybody can live rent free? Isn't this moment one where we could actually think seriously about the creation of an alternative society?

Or, as the chuang essay concluded, varying the young Marx, "this [pandemic] is a reminder that the only communism worth the name is one that includes the potential of a fully politicized naturalism."

True, dismantling structural capitalism may today look highly unrealistic. But what happens if and when we are faced by mass dying and a total surveillance State? Mass dying follows not only upon coronisation but also hunger and other diseases, and then the truly enormous climate-related upheavals to come – met only too often by callous pressures for "back to work" regardless of intensified exploitation and oppression; a total surveillance State comes as near to Fascism as no matter. It all depends on understanding and the will to associate in struggle. The underlying preconditions of a potential radical yearning as well as willingness can be found in many places, but I have seen them foregrounded only in a remarkable April study by YouGov in the UK for the Royal Society of the Arts. As Salvage noted, only 9% of those questioned wanted a return to the "normality" before the pandemic, while 85% would like to keep some of the changes of lockdown time: cleaner air, presence of more wildlife, less waste in preparing food, also more contact with family and friends and a growing sense of local community (40% for either of these – cf. Salvage 38 and www.thersa.org/about-us/media/2019/brits-see-cleaner-air-stronger-social-bonds-and-changing-food-habits-amid-lockdown).

We are now in the position of Aeschylus's Prometheus, bound with the eagle painfully picking at our innards. His is the first record we have of rectifying the dominant mythical celebration of Zeus's rule by stressing the immense degradation and suffering it is inflicting on humans, up to a planned full extermination, and audaciously naming it "an infamous spectacle" (v. 241). It is a stroke of genius that the play opens with Power (*Kratos*) and Force or better Violence (*Bia*) chaining him: power speaks but violence acts without speaking (parallels to today's USA are striking). So we must further say with the bitter but unbowed Titan: "…You are now in power and believe you can safely stay in the citadel. But I've seen two ruling systems fall from command, and I shall see your third one, now in saddle, fall very quickly and shamefully" (*Prometheus desmotes*, vv. 955–59, prosaic translation DS).

Therefore: I believe we should steal back Mrs. Thatcher's slogan (stolen from Marxists such as Lenin) and proclaim: There Is No Alternative!

Notes

* My warmest thanks go to the repeated help by encouragement, discussion, and correction of an earlier version in "How" to names mentioned there, to whom should be added Victor Wallis and Suren Moodliar; and in the redoing to Marina Ciccarini, Jodi Dean, Hugh O'Connell, Rada Iveković, Miklavž Komelj, Mladen Lazić, Tom Moylan, Michael Stöppler, Marc Silberman, Alberto Toscano, and some hints from Christoph Türcke. Special thanks also to Gerry Canavan for a comment in Feb. 2020 that was adapted in the final sentence of my <u>*Note 2020*</u>. All responsibility for formulations is mine.

1 I might have said that all lives matter, were this slogan not now in the US adopted by racist and neo-fascist groups (from whom it should be wrested), while the opposition between violent police and vigilantes on the one hand vs. working people on the other is pivoting on "Black lives matter." This should not exclude any other oppressed people, but all talk about freedom is meaningless unless Black lives matter as a first step.

2 I've devoted much attention to the key political mediation on the Left in previous works, such as *Splendour,* "Archeology," "Prescience," *Lessons,* and *Communism* (in particular its essay "What Is To Be Done" of 2015), where large bibliographies with many splendid works can be found. They should be updated for present pressing purposes.

3 I was under the illusion I had invented the term of capitalocene in 2018, but discovered this meant I had culpably not followed half a dozen years of discussion about it, now well summarised in the two titles by Jason Moore.

4 This sub-section is based on Wallace's book, his interview in March 2020, the long anonymous collective essay cited as chuang, and data and arguments from Suvin "How."

5 All sources and references to data in 2.1 may be found in Suvin "How."

6 Cf. https://peoplesdispatch.org/2020/03/22/the-cost-of-this-pandemic-must-not-bankrupt-the-people/?utm_source=Tricontinental. I acknowledge the stimulation of various recent newsletters sent by Vijay Prashad in the name of Tricontinental: Institute for Social Research, and in particular of their attempt at a program in points. I agree with their slogan "We Won't Go Back to Normal, Because Normal Was the Problem" (www.thetricontinental.org/newsletterissue/ newsletter-13-2020-new-world-order). I have re-checked and used some of their data, also cannibalised some formulations. I do not share their uncritical admiration of the Chinese State, efficacious as its ruthlessness against the local profit-making collusion and foot-dragging might have in this case been. A good antidote may be found in the detailed bleak picture at chuang.

Useful Works Mentioned

Agamben, Giorgio. "Requiem per gli studenti," in his *A che punto siamo? L'epidemia come politica*. Quodlibet, 2020, 99–101.

Allyn, Bobby. "Your Boss Is Watching You." www.npr.org/2020/05/13/854014403/your-boss-is-watching-you-work-from-home-boom-leads-to-more-surveillance?t=1589544415070. Accessed May 15, 2020.

Bouissou, Julien. "Dans les bidonvilles du monde entire...." *Le Monde* Apr. 6, 2020, www.lemonde.fr/international/article/2020/04/06/dans-les-bidonvilles-du-monde-entier-l-impossible-confinement_6035744_3210.html. Accessed April 30, 2020.

Brenner, Robert. "Escalating Plunder." *New Left Review* no. 123 (May–June 2020): 5–22.

Britt, Robert Roy. "Covid-19's Other Sobering Statistics." *Medium* May 28, 2020. https://medium.com/luminate/covid-19s-other-sobering-statistics-dfc828f5ccbc. Accessed June 5, 2020.

Britt, Robert Roy. "9 Things Experts Have Learned About Covid-19 So Far." *Your Coronavirus Update* July 29, 2020, newsletters@medium.com. Accessed July 29, 2020.

Choudhury, Chitrangada, and Aniket Aga. "India's Pandemic Response Is a Caste Atrocity." *NDTV* May 27, www.ndtv.com/opinion/india-s-pandemic-response-is-a-caste-atrocity-2236094?utm_source=FASPE_newslettersignup&utm_campaign=236db202f7-EMAIL_ CAMPAIGN2019_12_17_11_47_COPY_01&utm_medium=email&utm_term=0_15485411a8-236db202f7-68115585. Accessed June 30, 2020.

[Christakis, Nicholas A.] "Nicholas Christakis on Fighting Covid-19 by Truly Understanding the Virus." *The Economist* Aug. 10, 2020, www.economist.com/by-invitation/2020/08/10/ nicholas-christakis-on-fighting-covid-19-by-truly-understanding-the-virus?fsrc=newsletter &utm_campaign=the-economist-today&utm_medium=newsletter&utm_source=salesforce-marketing-cloud&utm_term=2020-08-12&utm_content=article-link-6. Accessed Aug. 13, 2020.

[chuang cn site]. "Social Contagion: Microbiological Class Warfare in China." http://chuangcn.org/2020/02/social-contagion/. Accessed Aug. 12, 2020.

Electronic Frontier Foundation, www.eff.org/

[El-Sayed, Abdul.] "Interview Dr Abdul El-Sayed on Covid-19." Current *Affairs* Apr. 7, 2020. www.currentaffairs.org/2020/04/interview-dr-abdul-el-sayed-on-covid-19

Emerson, Sarah. "Coronavirus Disproportionately Hurts Minorities. So Could Contact Tracing." *OneZero* Apr. 16, 2020. https://onezero.medium.com/coronavirus-disproportionately-hurts-minorities-so-could-contact-tracing-b0e6263bb47b. Accessed Apr. 21, 2020.

Gall, Gregor. "Striking in Striking Times." *Salvage* no. 8 (2020): 215–22.

Galloway, Scott. "Covid-19 Has Now Cost Us Nearly as Much as WWII." *MARKER Medium* Aug. 11, 2020.https://marker.medium.com/covid-19-has-now-cost-us-nearly-as-much-as-wwii-925bb98c9447. Accessed Aug. 12, 2020.

Guarnieri, Mya. "Stop Saying 'we're all in this together.' You have Money. It's not the Same." *The Washington Post* Apr. 18, 2020, www.washingtonpost.com/outlook/ 2020/04/18/coronavirus-retail-jobs-inequality/. Accessed Apr. 19, 2020.

haque, umair. "America is Losing the War Against Trump's Fascism." *Eudaimonia & Co.* June 28, https://eand.co/america-is-losing-the-war-against-trumps-fascism-edd42d0def28. Accessed June 30, 2020.

haque, umair. "The American Economy is Dying." *Eudaimonia & Co.* Apr. 29, 2020, https:// eand.co/the-american-economy-is-dying-f05a9f09af5a. Accessed May 1, 2020.

Harvey, David. "We Need a Collective Response to the Collective Dilemma of Coronavirus." *Jacobin* Apr. 24, 2020, www.jacobinmag.com/2020/04/david-harvey-coronavirus-pandemic-capital-economy. Accessed Apr. 27, 2020.

Isser, Mindy. "What Workers Have Already Won in the Face of Coronavirus." *In These Times* March 18, 2020, https://inthesetimes.com/working/entry/22392/workers-labor-coronavirus-concessions-rent-eviction-moratorium. Accessed March 29, 2020.

Jameson, Fredric. "An American Utopia," in S. Žižek ed., *An American Utopia*. Verso, 2016, 1–96.

Liu, Andrew. "'Chinese Virus,' World Market." *n+1 Magazine* Mar. 20, 2020, https://nplusonemag.com/online-only/online-only/chinese-virus-world-market/. Accessed March 23, 2020.

Luxemburg, Rosa. *The Accumulation of Capital*. Trans. A. Schwarzschild. Modern Reader, 1968.

Marcuse, Herbert. "The Problem of Violence and the Radical Opposition (1967)," in his *Five Lectures*. Trans. J.J. Shapiro and S.M. Weber. Beacon P, 1970, 83–108.

Martinchek, Lauren. "Coronavirus Didn't Kill the American Economy, It Just Sped Up the Dying Process." *Medium* May 14, https://medium.com/@xLauren_Mx/coronavirus-didnt-kill-the-american-economy-it-just-sped-up-the-dying-process-e9ef6e26524b. Accessed May 16, 2020.

Marx, Karl. *Das Kapital, Erster Band*. *Marx-Engels Werke*, Vol. 23. Dietz, 1993.

McBrien, Justin. "Accumulating Extinction: Planetary Catastrophism in the Necrocene," in J.W. Moore ed., *Anthropocene or Capitalocene?* [see under Moore], 116–37.

Moglen, Eben. "The Dotcommunist Manifesto." *Cabinet Magazine* no. 10 (Spring 2003), http://cabinetmagazine.org/issues/10/moglen.php. Accessed Sept. 15, 2011.

Moore, Jason W. *Capitalism in the Web of Life: Ecology and the Accumulation of Capital*. Verso, 2015.

Moore, Jason W. "Introduction," in idem ed., *Anthropocene or Capitalocene? Nature, History, and the Crisis of Capitalism*. PM P, 2016, 1–11.

Moylan, Tom. "'To live consciously is to sow the whirlwind': Reflections on the Utopian Standpoint of Nonviolence." *Utopian Studies* 26.1 (2015): 184–202.

Mull, Amanda. "Georgia's Experiment in Human Sacrifice." *The Atlantic* Apr. 29, 2020, https:// medium.com/the-atlantic/georgias-experiment-in-human-sacrifice-388029dee95e. Accessed May 1, 2020.

[Prashad, Vijay, et al.] "Hunger Gnaws at the Edges of the World." May 14, 2020, www.thetricontinental.org/newsletterissue/20-2020-famine/. Accessed May 16, 2020.

Report on the Economic Well-Being of U.S. Households in 2018, May 2019. www.federalreserve.gov/publications/2019-economic-well-being-of-us-households-in-2018-dealing-with-unexpected-expenses.htm?utm. Accessed Mar. 8, 2020.

[Ribner, Bruce]. Interview with A. Sifferlin, *Medium*, https://elemental.medium.com/coronavirus-advice-from-americas-foremost-ebola-doctor-8bdb98c07. Accessed Mar. 23, 2020.

Riding the Storm. www.ubs.com/content/dam/static/noindex/wealth-management/ubs-billionaires-report-2020-spread.pdf. Accessed Oct. 31, 2020.

Salvage Editorial Collective. "Comrades, This Is Madness." *Salvage* no. 8 (2020): 7–38.

Saul, Quincy. "April Theses with 2020 Vision." *Global Ecosocialist Network* Apr. 20, 2020, www.globalecosocialistnetwork.net/2020/04/20/april-theses-with-2020-vision/. Accessed May 4, 2020.

Suvin, Darko. "From the Archeology of Marxism and Communism." *Debatte* 21.2–3 (2013): 279–311.

Suvin, Darko. *Communism, Poetry: Communicating Vessels*. Political Animal, 2020.

Suvin, Darko. "To Explain Fascism Today." *Critique [Glasgow]* 45.3 (2017): 259–302.

Suvin, Darko. "How to Go On." *Socialism and Democracy* no. 83 (2020), www.tandfonline.com/doi/full/10.1080/08854300.2020.1821338?src=.

Suvin, Darko. *Lessons from the Russian Revolution and Its Fallout*. Rosa Luxemburg Foundation Southeast Europe, 2017.

Suvin, Darko. *Metamorphoses of Science Fiction*. Yale UP, 1979; rev. edn. ed. G. Canavan. P. Lang, 2016.

Suvin, Darko. "The Prescience of Lucio Magri." *Socialism and Democracy* 29.2 (2015): 91–98.

Suvin, Darko. "Power without Violence: A Lesson from Tribal Communism (2009–13)," in his *Communism, Poetry* [see above], 135–46.

Suvin, Darko. *Splendour, Misery, and Possibilities: An X-ray of Socialist Yugoslavia*. Brill, 2016, and Haymarket P, 2017.

Suvin, Darko. "Thoughts within the Coronising Siege." *Political Animal Magazine*, www.politicalanimalmagazine.com/2020/05/12/thoughts-within-the-coronising-siege.

Suvin, Darko. "Words and Lesions: Epistemological Reflections on Violence, the 1968 Moment, and Revolution…." *Critical Q* 62.1 (2020): 83–122.

Svampa, Maristella. "Reflexiones para un mundo post-coronavirus." *Nueva Sociedad* Apr. 2020, https://nuso.org/articulo/reflexiones-para-un-mundo-post-coronavirus/. Accessed May 30, 2020.

Wallace, Rob[ert G]. *Big Farms Make Big Flu*. Monthly RP and NYU P, 2016 [cited as Wallace B].

Wallace, Rob[ert G], and Yaak Pabst [for *Marx 21*]. "Capitalist Agriculture and Covid-19: A Deadly Combination." Mar. 11, 2020, https://climateandcapitalism.com/2020/03/11/capitalist-agriculture-and-covid-19-a-deadly-combination/?fbclid=IwAR2FWytHG3fwjhbIFY3s9TkHgVsZox5f E8 Bm4idsFugMLCa63DfQEmYNu1g [cited as Wallace C]. Accessed June 30.

Wallis, Victor. *Red-Green Revolution*. Political Animal, 2018.

Wegner, Phillip E. *Imaginary Communities: Utopia, the Nation, and the Spatial Histories of Modernity*. U of California P, 2002.

WHO Coronavirus Disease (COVID-19) Dashboard, Aug. 15, 2020. https://covid19.who.int/. Accessed Aug. 15, 2020.

Winant, Gabriel. "Coronavirus and Chronopolitics." *n+1 Magazine* Mar. 23, 2020, https://nplusonemag.com/authors/winant-gabriel/. Accessed Mar. 29, 2020.

World Bank. 2019, https://data.worldbank.org/indicator/EN.POP.SLUM.UR.ZS. Accessed May 15, 2020.

Appendix

D. Suvin: Publications after 2000 on SF and Utopia/nism

BOOKS

Naučna fantastika, spoznaja, sloboda [Science Fiction, Cognition, Freedom]. Ed. Dejan Ajdačić. Various translators. [Beograd] SlovoSlavia, 2009.

Metamorfoze znanstvene fantastike [Metamorphoses of SF]. Transl. M. Mrčela. [Zagreb] Profil, 2010. [Includes a new Preface for the Croatian reader, 19–31.]

Defined by a Hollow: Essays on Utopia, Science Fiction, and Political Epistemology. P. Lang, 2010.

Darko Suvin: A Life in Letters. Ed. Ph. E. Wegner. Paradoxa, 2011 [in part].

Ke Huan Xiao Shuo Bian Xing Ji [Metamorphoses of SF]. Transl. Ding Suping et al., ed. Shu Wei. Anhui Art and Literature P, 2011.

Ke Huan Xiao Shuo Mian Mian Guan [*Positions and Presuppositions in Science Fiction*, much expanded]. Trans. Hao Lin et al. Anhui Art and Literature P, 2011.

Preživjeti potop – Fantasy, po-robljenje i granična spoznaja [Surviving the Flood: Fantasy, Commodification, and Liminal Cognition]. Transl. A. Žiljak. [Zagreb] Mentor/UBIQ, 2012.

Metamorphoses of Science Fiction: On the Poetics and History of a Literary Genre [augmented edn.]. Ed. and with an Introduction by Gerry Canavan. P. Lang, 2016. [7 items added to 1979 version, 3 articles + 4 new prefaces of mine to the old text and the additions]

Brecht's Communist Manifesto Today. Foreword N. Malik and J. Malick. [Delhi] Aakar, 2020.

Parables of Freedom and Narrative Logics: Positions and Presuppositions in SF and Utopianism, 2 Vols. Ed. Eric Smith. Ralahine Studies. P. Lang, 2021.

IN VOLUMES EDITED BY DS

Co-editor (with G. Maniscalco Basile) of *Nuovissime mappe dell'inferno: Distopia oggi*. Monolite, 2004. [10 contributions, including a preface, postface, and an essay by me]

Guest editor of annual *Fictions* (Rome) no. 3, special issue on *US Science Fiction and War/ Militarism*. IEPI, 2005. [10 contributions, including 1 essay by me; see also below]

IN BOOKS BY VARIOUS HANDS (omitting numerous translations in ex-Yugoslavia)

"Theses on Dystopia 2001," in R. Baccolini and T. Moylan eds., *Dark Horizons: Science Fiction and the Dystopian Imagination*. Routledge, 2003, 187–201.

"Science Fiction Parables of Mutation and Cloning as/and Cognition," in D. Pastourmatzi ed. *Biotechnological and Medical Themes in Science Fiction*. [Thessaloniki] University Studio, 2002, 131–51; a portion as "Cloning: On Cognition in the Discourses of SF and Technoscience." *Femspec* 3.2 (2002): 67–74.

"Reflections on What Remains of Zamyatin's We after the Change of Leviathans: Must Collectivism Be Against People?" in *Envisioning the Future*. Ed. M. Barr. Wesleyan UP, 2003, 51–81; augmented rpt. *Contemporanea* no. 1 (2003): 71–89; German transl. 2004.

"Fantasy as Critique and Cognition," in C. Bordoni ed., *Linee d'ombra: letture del fantastico in onore di Romolo Runcini*. Pellegrini, 2004, 269–77.

"Trenta Tesi sulla Distopia" and "Narciso e Anteo: il collettivismo deve per forza essere contro la gente?" in G. Maniscalco Basile and D. Suvin eds., *Nuovissime mappe dell'inferno* [see above], 13–34 and 149–64.

"Darwinism, Left and Right: And Two S-F Probes." *Foundation* no. 109 (2010): 7–17; rpt.in Carlo Pagetti ed., *Darwin nel tempo*. Quaderni di Acme 127. Cisalpino, 2011, 251–64.

"Contradiction and Resistance," preface to the Classics edn. of DS, *Metamorphoses of SF* [see above], xxxvii–l.

Djergović-Joksimović, Zorica. "Intervju: Darko Suvin," in D. Igrošanac and M. Jakovljević eds., *Književna fantastika: Almanah 2016*, 157–66.

Spanish transl. of interview with Lomeña [see below] in Andres Lomeña Cantos ed., "Entrevista con Darko Suvin," *Ficcionología*. S.l.: Dado Ed., [2017?], 29–30.

"The Utopian Tradition of Russian SF," rpt. in A. Banerjee ed., *Russian Science Fiction Literature and Cinema: A Critical Reader*. Academic Studies P, 2018, 1–29.

ARTICLES (omitting numerous items in ex-Yugoslavia)

"Considering the Sense of 'Fantasy' or 'Fantastic Fiction.'" *Extrapolation* 41.3 (2000): 209–47; Italian trans. 2009; German transl. of a major part 2004.

"Answers to Questionnaire for New York Public Library Utopia Exhibition Website." http://utopia.nypl.org/I_meta_3.html [2000 on, no longer accessible]; augmented Greek trans. 2002.

(with questions by Van Ikin, Russell Blackford and Sylvia Kelso). "A Colloquium with Darko Suvin." *Science Fiction* [Perth] 16.1 (2001): 2–33; rpt. in D. Broderick and V. Ikin eds., *Warriors of the Tao*. Borgo P, 2011, 243–87.

"Goodbye and Hello: Differentiating within the Later P.K. Dick." *Extrapolation* 43.4 (2002): 368–97; Greek trans. 2003-04, Italian trans. 2006.

"The Horizons of Wells's Numerology." *Science Fiction Studies* 29.1 (2002): 148–9.

"Strugatski Remembrance." *Extrapolation* 44.2 (2003): 224–7.

"The Final Chapter of SF?: On Reading Brian Stableford." *SFRA R* no. 266 (2003): 5–9 and no. 267 (2004): 2–6; Italian trans. 2012.

"Intervista [di Carlo Bordoni] con Darko Suvin." *Robot* no. 42 (2003): 122–7.

"Sul concetto di utopia in epoca moderna." *Nuova secondaria* 5 (gennaio 2004): 105–11.

"Circumstances and Stances." *PMLA* 11.3 (2004): 535–8.

(with S. Proietti) "War and Militarism in Science Fiction: A Select Bibliography of Criticism in English," in D. Suvin ed. *Fictions* no. 3 (2005), 155–63 [see above].

"Of Starship Troopers and Refuseniks: War and Militarism in US Science Fiction, Part 2 (1975–2001: Post-Fordism, and Some Conclusions)," in D. Suvin ed. *Fictions* no. 3 (2005): 107–54 [see above]; rpt. of "Part 1 (1945-1974: Fordism)," in D.M. Hassler and C. Wilcox eds., *New Boundaries in Political Science Fiction*. Columbia SC: U of S. Carolina P, 2008, 115–44; "Part 2 (1975-2001: Post-Fordism, and Some Conclusions)." *Extrapolation* 48.1 (2007): 9–34.

"On U.K. Le Guin's 'Second Earthsea Trilogy' and Its Cognitions: A Commentary." *Extrapolation* 47.3 (Winter 2006): 488–504; Italian trans. *Anarres* 1.1 (2012).

"To Remember Stanisław Lem." *Studi slavistici* no. 3 (ott.-nov. 2006): electronic pp.; in part in *Extrapolation* 47.1 (2006): 30–4; German trans. 2006; Italian and Danish transl. 2007.

"Introduzione sui generi letterari e la Fantascienza." *Sincronie* [Roma] no. 20 (2007): 217–27.

"Cognition, Freedom, *The Dispossessed* as a Classic." *Paradoxa* no. 21 (2008): 23–49; rpt. in *Defined by a Hollow* [see above], 509–51.

"The Winter of the World." www.themontrealreview.com/2009/In-Leviathan-Belly.php [Introduction to my book *In Leviathan's Belly*].

"Logotekhnia, politike, outopia" [Literature, Politics, Utopia], interview with Maria Xilouri. *Aristera*! [Athens] March 20, 2009, Supplement 1–4.

"Stanley Weinbaum: We've Met the Aliens and They Are Us." *Extrapolation* 52.2 (2011): 227–45.

Ciccarelli, Roberto. "Gli esploratori del pianeta utopia [Interview with DS]." *Il Manifesto* May 29, 2011: 10; materialismostorico.blogspot.com/2011/05/darko-suvin-tra-fantasci enza-e.html.

"A Martial Epigram on Martians." *Socialism and Democracy* no. 42 (Apr. 2011), sdonline .org/42/preface-6/.

Interview with Andres Lomeña on *Metamorphoses of Science Fiction*. www.sociodicea.es /?p=79 or Archives -- March 2011; *Extrapolation* 53.2 (2012): 241–3.

"Postscript (2014)" [to reprint of "Estrangement and Cognition"]. //strangehorizons.com /2014/20141124/1suvin-a.shtml.

"A Note on Ursula K. Le Guin and Her Declaration of the Arts' Independence from Capitalism" [intro to her speech at Nat. Book Awards 2014]. *Kamen'* no. 28 (2016): 99–102; Italian transl. E. Stacchiotti Binni ibidem 103–7.

"On the Poetics of the Science Fiction Genre," rpt. in Rob Latham ed., *Science Fiction Criticism: An Anthology of Essential Writings*. Bloomsbury Academic, 2017, 116–27.

"On Communism, Science Fiction, and Utopia: The Blagoevgrad Theses." *Mediations* 32.2 (2019), www.mediationsjournal.org/articles/communism-science-fiction-utopia.

"Keynote speech to meeting of Society of Utopian Studies (Europe)." July 3, 2019, *Utopia or Bust: Capitalocene, Method, Antiutopia*, www.youtube.com/watch?v=VCCANxcL_vw.

Interview with Tamara Prošić, Prato July 2, 2019, https://youtu.be/V8pobS1AlGM.

"Orwell and *Nineteen Eighty-Four* Today: Genius and Tunnel Vision." *Historical Materialism* (Fall 2020): 1–29.

Index of Names

Only proper names of non-imaginary persons have been retained; excluded are names mentioned only in passing, such as editors of works by other authors and translators. References to a pair or to a work by two authors are given under the name of the first person mentioned. The titles are mentioned in parenthesis after the name when they stood as metonymies for an author, or used in italics if anonymous.

www.ingramcontent.com/pod-product-compliance
Lightning Source LLC
Chambersburg PA
CBHW060319100726
47907CB00002B/456

* 9 7 8 1 5 0 1 3 8 4 7 7 6 *